XML f

XML for Data Management

Peter Aiken
David Allen

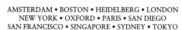

AMSTERDAM • BOSTON • HEIDELBERG • LONDON
NEW YORK • OXFORD • PARIS • SAN DIEGO
SAN FRANCISCO • SINGAPORE • SYDNEY • TOKYO

Morgan Kaufmann Publishers is an imprint of Elsevier

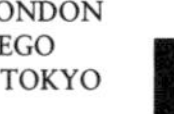

MORGAN KAUFMANN PUBLISHERS

Acquisitions Editor	Lothlórien Homet
Acquisitions Editor	Rick Adams
Publishing Services Manager	André Cuello
Project Manager	Justin R. Palmeiro
Marketing Manager	Brent Dela Cruz
Editorial Assistant	Corina Derman
Cover Design	Frances Baca
Composition	Kolam, Inc.
Full Service Provider	Kolam USA
Copyeditor	Kolam USA
Proofreader	Kolam USA
Indexer	Kolam USA

Morgan Kaufmann Publishers is an imprint of Elsevier.
500 Sansome Street, Suite 400, San Francisco, CA 94111

This book is printed on acid-free paper.

Library of Congress Cataloging-in-Publication Data
Application submitted.

ISBN: 0-12-045599-4

For information on all Morgan Kaufmann publications, visit our website at *www.mkp.com.*

Printed in the United States of America
04 05 06 07 08 5 4 3 2 1

Preface

"Hey, you got peanut butter on my chocolate bar!"
"No way, you got chocolate in my peanut butter!"

If you consider data management (DM) as peanut butter and XML as chocolate—and you like the combination—then you will easily understand what we are attempting to explain in this book. If you don't like the combination of peanut butter and chocolate, then pick your own favorite flavor combination. We like the yin and yang analogy, but you should go for some combination that works together. These analogies have helped the literally thousands who we have assisted or have seen us present on XML and DM topics over the past few years.

You may be confused by XML hype but nevertheless you are intrigued as to what it—XML, that is—is all about. You understand the basics of what XML can do, but you can't seem to find any guide as to how best to make use of it. Well look no further! You won't be coding much XML yourself, but as a director/strategic thinker/manager, you must understand your organizational requirements and conceive of how best to use XML to support the organization. You need to gain an understanding quickly of how to use XML to architect solutions to specific data-engineering challenges. The material we present is based on dozens of person-years of effort, creating and implementing the advanced DM concepts that we describe.

Your technical background also permits you to understand the importance of good DM practices to the organization. It has been a constant source of frustration that you have been unable to improve support of the organizational DM function; many have not managed to put together an effective approach given the current economic climate. The question is also, What should be done right now? What DM tools and techniques can you apply effectively in today's environment? Our extensive experience in these and related areas allows us to describe the new XML-enabled DM direction.

One question remains—how to decide what to read among the vast array of titles on the subject. There are (for example) at least four other titles that might be competing for your attention:

- *XML for Data Architects*
- *XML: A Manager's Guide*
- *XML Data Management*
- *Professional XML Meta Data*

These texts are either very technical or more narrowly focused on specific subjects. This book was necessary to describe how XML will make your job easier, give you increased DM capabilities, or save your organization resources.

Well, as a result of the happy mixing of XML and data management, by reading this book you will discover that significant synergies exist between XML and DM. XML and DM go together like yin and yang! Between the two of us authors, we have more than a decade of XML experience and—working on various Data Blueprint (http://datablueprint.com) projects—more than a half century of combined DM experience. XML, while not a silver bullet, does offer significant support to DM functions—support that will dramatically alter the level of investment required to produce positive return on investment. In short, XML will significantly lower DM implementation costs in a way that has not yet been imagined except by a very few organizations. This book will permit yours to be one of them.

Thank you for reading. Please enjoy your learning experience and do get back to us with any suggestions or corrections.

Peter Aiken and David Allen
Richmond, VA, April 2004
peter@datablueprint.com
mda@datablueprint.com

Contents

1

XML and DM Basics

Introduction

XML equips organizations with the tools to develop programmatic solutions to manage their data interchange environments using the same economies of scale associated with their DM environments. XML complements existing DM efforts nicely and enables the development of new and innovative DM techniques. Rather than looking at data management as a set of many problems, each consisting of a method of transporting, transforming, or otherwise evolving data from one point to alternate forms, practitioners can now look at the big picture of DM—the complete set of systems working together, and how data moves amongst them. This is jumping up one conceptual level—moving from thinking of the challenge in terms of its individual instances to thinking of it in terms of a class of similar challenges. It is an architectural pattern that is seen frequently as systems evolve. First, a solution is created for a specific problem. Next, a slightly different problem arises that requires another specific solution. As more and more conceptually similar problems arise that differ only in the details, eventually it makes sense from an architectural standpoint to develop a general solution that deals with an entire class of similar problems by focusing on their commonalities rather than their differences.

This first chapter begins by describing a present-day DM challenge. We then present the definitions of DATA and METADATA used throughout the book. The next section presents a brief overview of DM. This is followed by a justification for investing in metadata/DM. We acknowledge the challenge of XML's hype, but we will provide a brief introduction and two short examples. These lead to an overview of the intersection of DM and XML. The chapter closes with a few XML caveats. We are presenting this information in order to help you make the case that investing in metadata is not only a good idea, but also necessary in order to realize the full benefit of XML and related IT investments.

The DM Challenge

An organization that we worked with once presented us with our most vexing DM challenge. When working with them to resolve a structural data quality situation, our team discovered it would be helpful to have access to a certain master list that was maintained on another machine located physically elsewhere in the organization. Better access to the master list would have sped up validation efforts we were performing as part of the corrective data quality engineering. In order to obtain a more timely copy—ours was a 1-year-old extract refreshed annually—we requested access through the proper channels, crossing many desks without action. As the situation was elevated, one individual decided to address the problem by informally creating a means of accessing the master list data. Volunteering to take on the effort, the individual neglected to mention the effort to our team, and consequently never understood the team's access requirements. Ten months after the initial request, the individual approached us with a solution created over two weeks. The solution allowed us to retrieve up to twelve records of master data at a time with a web browser, and access incorporated a substantial lag time.

After realizing that this solution was inadequate, our team managed to get the attention of developers who worked with the master list directly. They in turn offered their own solution—a utility that they described as capable of handling large volumes of data. This solution also proved inadequate. After one year, our requirements had not changed. We needed approximately four million records weekly to ensure that we were working with the most current data. These extracts were necessary since transactional access to live data was not available.

This was a reasonable and remarkably unchallenging technical request. The sticking point that made both of the offered solutions inappropriate was the way they were built. Because of the way the system was constructed, queries on particular items had to be done one at a time, and could not be done in bulk. This meant that when tools were built for us to access "large volumes of data," those tools simply automated the process of issuing tens of thousands of individual requests. Not surprisingly, extracting the volumes of data that we needed would have put an untenable burden on the system.

While this organization had many technically brilliant individuals, they only used the tools that they knew. As a result, we were unable to gain access to the data that we required. Many aspects of this situation might have been helped by the judicious application of XML to their DM practices.

Over the coming pages, we will describe many of the lessons we have learned with respect to how XML can help data managers. Organizations have resources in the knowledge that resides in the heads of their workers as well as in their systems. The way systems are built can either take advantage of that knowledge, or render it impotent.

Whether you are a database manager, administrator, or an application developer, XML will profoundly impact the way in which you think about and practice data management. Understanding how to correctly manage and apply XML-based metadata will be the key to advancements in the field. XML represents a large and varied body of metadata-related technologies, each of which has individual applications and strengths. Understanding the XML conceptual architecture is central to understanding the applications and strengths of XML, which are presented later in this chapter.

Why are you reading this book? Chances are that you opened the cover because XML is impacting your organization already, or will be very shortly. If you are interested in this material, our experience shows us that one or more of the following is probably true:

- You are leading a group that is working with XML.
- Your new application will benefit from the ability to speak a common language with other platforms.
- You are a technical analyst and need higher-level information on the XML component architecture.
- You are in a business group tasked with ensuring return on existing or potential technology investment.
- You are in IT planning and you need to understand how XML will impact various technology investment decisions.

- You are a CIO and you want to ensure that the organization is able to take advantage of modern XML-based DM technologies.

As a group, you are busy professionals who share a concern for effective architecture-driven development practices. You are as likely to be a manager tasked with leading XML development, as you are to be a technical XML specialist. If you are the latter, you already know that the best and most up-to-date XML documentation is of course on the web precisely because of the web's superior ability to publish and republish information from a central location. Because of the proliferation of excellent documentation on the technical aspects of XML, we will be focusing on the strategic implications for a variety of different roles within the organization.

Definitions

This section presents the definitions that we will use when referring to data and metadata.

Data and Information

Before defining DM, it is necessary to formally define data and metadata. These definitions may be understood with the assistance of Figure 1.1.

Figure 1.1

Deriving information from its two predecessors—facts and data. (Original description from Appleton, 1983.)

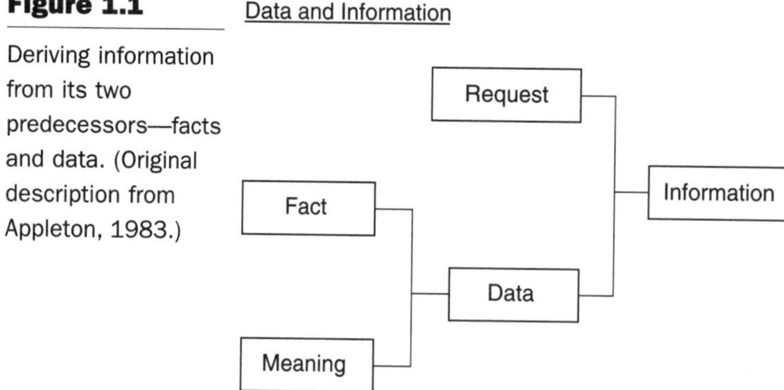

1. Each *fact* combines with one or more *meanings*. For example, the fact "$5.99" combines with the meaning "price."
2. Each specific *fact* and *meaning* combination is referred to as a *datum*. For example, the fact "$5.99" is combined with the meaning "price" to form an understandable sentence: The item has a price of USD $5.99.
3. *Information* is one or more pieces of *data* that are returned in response to a specific *request* such as, How much does that used CD cost? The answer, or returned data, is USD $5.99. This request could be a simple acquisition of the data. But whether the data is pulled from a system or pushed to a user, a dataset is used to answer a specific question. This request or acquisition of the data is essentially the question being asked.

There are numerous other possible definitions and organizations of these terms relative to one another, usually specific to certain information disciplines, like applications development. The reason for using this set of definitions is that it acknowledges the need to pair context with an information system's raw response. The fact "123 Pine Street" means nothing without the paired meaning "address." A particular dataset is only useful within the context of a request. For example, what looks like a random assortment of house-for-sale listings becomes meaningful when we know that it was the result of a query requesting all houses within a particular price range in a particular area of town. This contextual model of data and information is important when we consider that one of the most common problems in information systems is that organizations have huge quantities of data that cannot be accessed properly or put into context. Facts without meanings are of limited value. The way facts are paired with meanings touches on the next term we will define—*metadata*.

Metadata

The concept of metadata is central to understanding the usefulness of XML. If an organization is to invest in XML and metadata, it is important to understand what it is, so that those investments can be exploited to their fullest potential.

Many people incorrectly believe that metadata is a special type or class of data that they already have. While organizations have it whether they have looked at it or not, *metadata actually represents a use of existing facts* rather than a type of data itself. What does it mean to say that it is a use of facts? Metadata has to do with the structure and meaning of facts. In other words, metadata describes the use of those facts. Looking back at Figure 1.1, metadata acts as the meaning paired with the facts used to create data.

Take for example a standard hammer. This object can be looked at in two ways. On one hand, it is just an ordinary object, like an automobile, or even a highway bridge. While it is possible to look at it as an object just like any other, what makes the hammer powerful is the understanding of its use. A hammer is something that drives nails—that is how we understand the hammer! Metadata is the same. Rather than understanding it just as data (as some might claim that the hammer is just an object), we understand it in terms of its use—metadata is a categorization and explanation of facts. The implications of the actual meaning of metadata must be understood. In the coming discussion, we will outline why understanding of metadata is critical.

When metadata is treated like data, the benefits are no more or less than just having more data in an existing system. This is because looking at it simply as data causes it to be treated like any other data. When metadata is viewed as a *use* of data, it gains additional properties. For example, data sources can be conceptually "indexed" using the metadata, allowing anyone to determine which data is being captured by which system. Wouldn't it be useful to know all of the places throughout a system where integer data was used within the context of uniquely identifying a customer? The benefits of data transparency throughout the organization are numerous—the application of metadata to create this transparency is one of the topics that we will address.

To explain why the understanding of a concept is important in the way it is used, let's take another example. When the first personal computers were coming onto the market for households, most people thought of them as curious toys that were useful for things such as playing games, writing rudimentary programs, and possibly even keeping track of personal information. The evolution of personal computers is marked primarily by shifts in the way people think about them, leading to computers branching into new areas. Today, many people think of personal computers mainly as platforms to enable connectivity to the Internet, and subsequently as communication devices even though their conceptual operation has not changed since their earliest days. While the speed of computers may have increased by leaps and bounds, their underlying architecture, based on the original Von Neumann computer architecture,* has not

*http://www.csupomona.edu/~hnriley/www/VonN.html

changed. The critical aspect that allowed computers to radically expand their utility to home users was a shift in the way people thought about them. Similarly, as practitioners shift their understanding of metadata toward looking at it as an application of data, so too can the benefits derived increase substantially.

Traditional Views of Metadata

The basic definition of the term "metadata" has been limited, and as a result, metadata has been underutilized both in research and in practice. Widely used "poor" metadata definitions and practices lead to higher systems costs. Most savings that compound from proper recognition of metadata are simply not articulated in practice. Incorporating the correct definition of metadata into our collective understanding will lead to more efficient systems development practices and more effective information technology investments. In short, widening the way that we think about metadata will inevitably widen its applicability and value.

Let us take a quick look at metadata's most popular definitions, which are examples of definitions of *types* of data:

- **Popularly:** "data about data"[*]
- **Newly:** data resource data—"data that is useful to understand how data can be used as a resource" (Bracket, 2002)
- **Formally:** the international standard, ISO 11179. The data that makes datasets more useable by users.[†]
- **Intellectual Property:** At one point in time, attempting to make the term proprietary, one organization/person copyrighted/patented the term as intellectual property.[‡]

The main point to take away from this discussion of metadata is that how a concept is understood greatly impacts how useful it is in practice. The distinction presented between the two possible ways of understanding

---

[*]ISO 11179

[†]http://www.iso.org/iso/en/CatalogueDetailPage.CatalogueDetail?CSNUMBER=31367&ICS1=35&ICS2=40&ICS3=.

[‡]The metadata company did this as a trademark: http://www.metadata.com/word.htm.

metadata may seem like a small point, but as we will see with examples throughout the book, its impact is profound. Next, we will present an overview of DM.

DM Overview

Between 1994 and 1995, research at the MITRE Corporation near Washington, DC, formalized a definition of DM as the interrelated coordination of six functions (Figure 1.2) in a way that has become a de facto standard. Each DM function will be described in the sections below. (The DM framework, figure, and definitions that follow are all derived from Parker [1995] and Aiken [In press].) The first three functions of DM provide direction to the latter three—responsible for implementation of a process designed with the specific aim of producing business value. Please note that we specifically differentiate this definition from the previous, narrower DM practices. The figure illustrates the effect of business direction–based input to DM, providing guidance to individual functions. Several functions also exchange specific feedback of the process information and these have also been noted on the figure—the feedback permits process fine-tuning. These functions provide the next level of granularity at which we have asked organizations to rate their DM maturity.

Data Program Coordination is the definition, coordination, sourcing, implementation, and monitoring of enterprise DM vision, goals, organization, processes, policies, plans, standards, metrics, audits, and schedules for enterprise DM activities as a coherent set of activities.

Data Program Coordination

The focus of the data program coordination function (Figure 1.3) is the management of data program data (or meta-meta-metadata). These are descriptive propositions or observations needed to establish, document, sustain, control, and improve enterprise data-oriented activities (e.g., vision, goals, policies, processes, standards, plans, budgets, metrics, training, feedback, and repositories and their contents). Every organization that creates and manipulates collections of data has a data program coordination function, whether it is called that or not. The effectiveness of the data program depends on whether or not it is actively managed, with well-understood responsibilities, procedures, processes, metrics, and two-way lines of communication, and has the ability to improve its

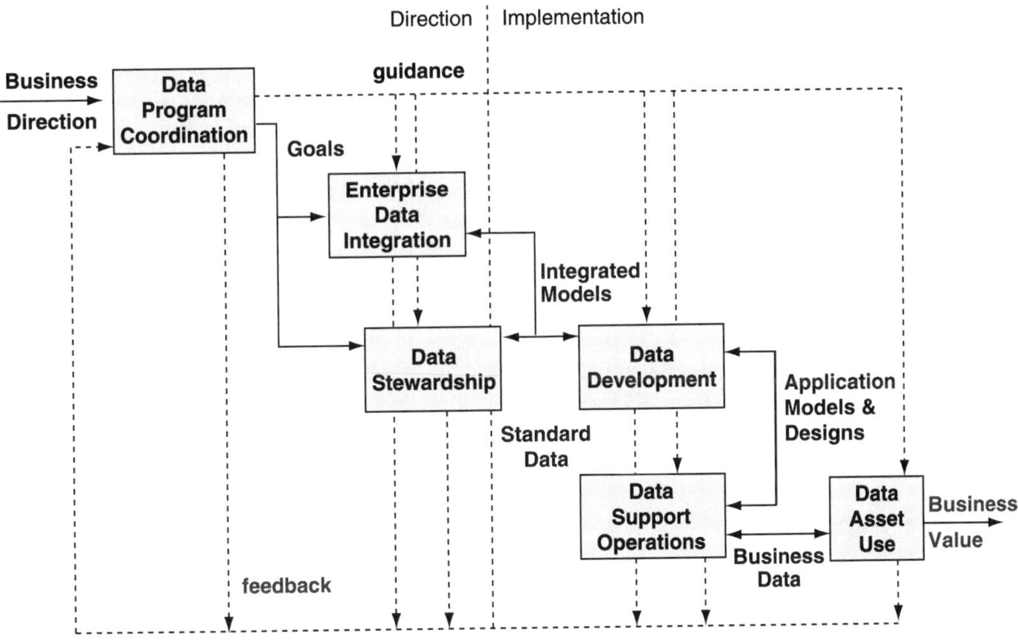

Function Name	Description	Concerned With	Function Focus
Data Program Coordination	*Provide appropriate DM process and technological infrastructure*	*Data Program Data*	*Direction*
Enterprise Data Integration	*Achieve enterprise data sharing of appropriate data*	*Data Development Data*	
Data Stewardship	*Achieve business-entity subject area data integration*	*Data Stewardship Data*	
Data Development	*Achieve sharing of data within a business area*	*Business Data*	*Implementation*
Data Support Operations	*Provide reliable access to data*		
Data Asset Use	*Leverage data in business activities*		

Figure 1.2

Enterprise DM functions and their interrelationships.

Requirements Management..	Process for tracing data requirements from identification and documentation, through implementation and use
Project Oversight	Management tracking of data aspects of application projects to permit early corrective actions and schedule adjustment
Project Planning....................	Proper incorporation of DM processes and data assets in application project plans
Quality Assurance.................	Management oversight process of the quality of enterprise DM processes and data assets
Contract Management	DM support to enterprise contracting activities, including data or DM process outsourcing
Configuration Management...	Manage changes in all DM processes and assets (configuration item identification, baseline management, change control, configuration audit)

Figure 1.3

Data program coordination—Definition and key process area definitions.

practices based on feedback gathered proactively from business users, administrators, programmers, analysts, designers, data stewards, integrators, and coordinators. A mature data program is further characterized by its use of a system to plan for, allocate resources for, and track and manage data program-related activities in an accurate, repeatable fashion. Results from historical activities captured by the system are used to optimize data program management practices. Data program management characteristics include vision, goals, policies, organization, processes, plans, standards, measures, audits, guidance, and schedules.

Enterprise Data Integration

The focus of the Enterprise Data Integration function (Figure 1.4) is the management of data-development data or meta-metadata. These are descriptive facts, propositions, or observations used to develop and document the structures and interrelationships of data (e.g., data models, database designs, specifications, and data registries and their contents).

Enterprise Data Integration is the identification, modeling, coordination, organization, distribution, and architecting of data shared across business areas or the enterprise.

Enterprise Data Integration measures assess the extent to which an organization understands and manages collections of data and data architectures across functional boundaries and is a measure of the degree to which the data of an enterprise can be considered to be integrated. Maturity in this arena is measured in terms of proactive versus reactive management. Mature enterprise data inte-

Asset Development/Maintenance	Appropriate processes, methods, and tools in use for development and maintenance of all data assets
Product Review	Process for peer reviews of all data assets to identify problems, improve quality, and track corrective actions
Process Focus	Assigned organizational responsibilities for DM processes and the management of their improvement
Process Definition	Standardized enterprise-wide DM processes, and associated methods and products
Training Management	Process to identify and fulfill training needs of personnel accomplishing DM processes
Group Coordination	Process to coordinate among data-engineering groups and other IM groups to better accommodate business objectives and user needs

Figure 1.4

Enterprise data integration—Definition and key process area definitions.

gration practices include the proactive observation and study of data integration patterns, managed by an enterprise-wide entity consisting of IT personnel and business users, utilizing tools with Computer-Aided Software Engineering (CASE)-like functionality. This entity constantly anticipates and reevaluates the organization's data integration needs, and manages their fulfillment. Enterprise data integration sub-functions include identification, definition, specification, sourcing, standardization, planning, measures, cost leverage, productivity, enterprise data engineering commitment, budgeting, developing metrics, guidance, policies, and standards.

Data Stewardship

The focus of the enterprise data integration function (Figure 1.5) is the management of data-stewardship data or metadata. These are descriptive facts about data, documenting their semantics and syntax, e.g., name, definition, format, length, and data dictionaries and their contents. Data stewardship's primary objective is the management of the enterprise data assets in order to improve their accessibility, reusability, and quality. A data stewardship entity's responsibilities include the capture, documentation, and dissemination of data naming standards, entity, and attribute definitions; business rules; and data retention criteria, data change management procedures, and data quality analysis. The data stewardship function is most effective, and therefore most mature, if managed at an enterprise level, with well-understood responsibilities and procedures, and

Integrated Management......	Established enterprise DM program to integrate all enterprise standard DM processes and synchronize them with other enterprise information-management activities
Quality Management...........	Established quality objectives for DM processes and assets and provide the process and resources to achieve them
Quantitative Management...	Established quantitative goals and metrics in monitoring and analyzing DM processes and assets, and recommend improvements

Figure 1.5

Data stewardship—Definition and key process area definitions.

Data Stewardship is the identification, definition, specification, sourcing, and standardization of all business data across all business areas within a specific business subject area consisting of some set of entity types, e.g., customers.

the ability to improve its practices over time. Data stewardship sub-functions are more narrowly focused on identification definition, specification, sourcing, and standardization.

Data Development

The focus of the data program coordination function (Figure 1.6) is the management of business. These are business facts and their constructs used to accomplish enterprise business activities, e.g., data elements, records, files, databases, data warehouses, reports, displays, and their contents. As new data collections are created to satisfy a new line of business, or the needs or practices of an existing line of business necessitate change, at what organizational level are the challenges of database design managed? Enterprises with more mature data development practices are characterized by their ability to estimate the resources necessary for a given data development activity, their proactive discovery and correction of data

Process Change Management.....	Established process to continually review and evaluate DM processes; and identify and implement improvements in a controlled and systematic way
Technology Management.............	Established process to maintain awareness of the state-of-practice and innovations in DM-related software, methods, and tools; and manage their introduction to minimize disruptions and achieve effective migrations
Defect Prevention Management...	Established process to identify the sources of data-asset errors and issues, and take action to fix the processes producing the problematic data assets

Figure 1.6

Data development—Definition and key process area definitions.

quality problems, and by their use of tools with CASE-like functionality at an organization-wide level.

Data Development is requirements analysis, modeling, design, organization, implementation, distribution, and architecting of business data needed for a business area's activities.

Data Support Operations

Data support operations are also focused on business data. Organizations with mature data support operations have established standards and procedures at the enterprise level for managing and optimizing the performance of their databases, managing changes to their data catalog, and managing the physical aspects of their data assets, including data backup and recovery, and disaster recovery.

Data Support Operations are the initialization, operation, tuning, maintenance, backup/recovery, and archiving or disposal of business data in support of business activities.

Data Asset Use

The data use function is also focused on business data and how it is used—however, this is its sole function.

This concludes the description of the six DM functions. In the next section, we will explain why it is important to invest in metadata/DM.

Data Asset Use is the execution of business operations and planning, analysis, and decision making using business data.

Investing in Metadata/Data Management

Organizations that understand the true power of metadata and XML stand to gain competitive advantages in two areas. First, a significant reduction in the amount of resources spent transforming data from one format to another, both inside and outside the organization, is one of the benefits of XML as it is frequently used today. Second, using XML-based metadata allows for the development of more flexible systems architectures.

Fundamentally, having architectural components exist as metadata permits them to be programmatically manipulated and reused by existing technologies. If you are still having trouble convincing your management to invest in XML, try the following argument: Ask them which version of the following two sets of data they would find easier to comprehend. In

Figure 1.7, the context and semantics of the data are unspecified and subject to misinterpretation.

In the second version, shown in Figure 1.8, XML tags have been added describing the structure and the definition of the concepts "shopping list," and "flight status." The XML version with its embedded metadata structure makes the data easier to understand—not only at the high level of "shopping list" or "flight status," but also at lower levels, giving meaning to individual data points ("product price") within the context of a larger data structure. This is critical to understanding the ability of organizations to use this powerful simplicity. XML labels should be designed to be human understandable, as opposed to labels defined for the convenience of computer processing—the implications resulting from the human ability to understand metadata structures at multiple levels are substantial. In Figure 1.8, we see another case of how metadata is a use of data. In the shopping list, we see the product "lettuce." The word "lettuce" all by itself is simply a string, but the metadata "product" in this case shows the user of the document how that string variable is being used, not as a non sequitur or as a request for something on a burger, but as a string variable to identify a product within the context of a shopping list.

Typical Systems Evolution

To appreciate the situation that most organizations are in today with respect to their DM practices, it is important to understand how they evolved over time. It helps to have a solid idea of where organizations are coming from in order to understand the challenges of the present.

Figure 1.7

Two sample documents containing only facts without context or meaning.

XML Example Document #1	XML Example Document #2
Edwards	NorthWest
Britta	449
April 17, 1998	Cancelled
Cucumber	640
5	0100
1.25	Delayed
Lettuce	TWA
2	1010
.98	17
	Gold

Figure 1.8

Two example XML documents containing both facts and meanings.

XML Example Document #1

```
<?XML version="1.0"?>
<DOCUMENT>
<CUSTOMER>
<NAME>
<LASTNAME>Edwards</LASTNAME>
<FIRSTNAME>Britta</FIRSTNAME>
</NAME>
<DATE>April 17, 1998</DATE>
<ORDERS>
<ITEM>
<PRODUCT>Cucumber</PRODUCT>
<NUMBER>5</NUMBER>
<PRICE>1.25</PRICE>
</ITEM>
<ITEM>
<PRODUCT>Lettuce</PRODUCT>
<NUMBER>2</NUMBER>
<PRICE>.98</PRICE>
</ITEM>
</ORDERS>
</CUSTOMER>
</DOCUMENT>
```

XML Example Document #2

```
<?XML version="1.0"?>
<SCHEDULE>
<AIRLINE>NorthWest</AIRLINE>
<FLIGHT>
<NUMBER>449</NUMBER>
<STATUS>Cancelled</STATUS>
</FLIGHT>
<FLIGHT>
<NUMBER>640</NUMBER>
<STATUS
    depart="0100">Delayed</STATUS>
</FLIGHT>
<AIRLINE>TWA</AIRLINE>
<FLIGHT>
<NUMBER>1010</NUMBER>
<STATUS gate="17 Gold">On
    Time</STATUS>
</FLIGHT>
</SCHEDULE>
```

Historically, large organizations have had a number of individual systems run by various groups, each of which deals with a particular portion of the enterprise. For example, many organizations have systems that hold marketing data related to finding new business, manufacturing data related to production and potentially forecasting, research and development data, payroll data for employees, personnel data within human resources, and a number of other systems as illustrated in Figure 1.9.

At first, these systems were not connected because of the fact that they evolved in different ways at different paces. As organizations have learned of the numerous benefits of connecting these systems, the need to build interfaces between systems has grown quickly. For example, it is often very useful for the marketing department working with marketing data to have some type of access to manufacturing data, to ensure that customer promises are in line with manufacturing capacity. It is also critical to join payroll and personnel data so that if employees move or change names and notify human resources, their paychecks can be sent to the appropriate names and addresses.

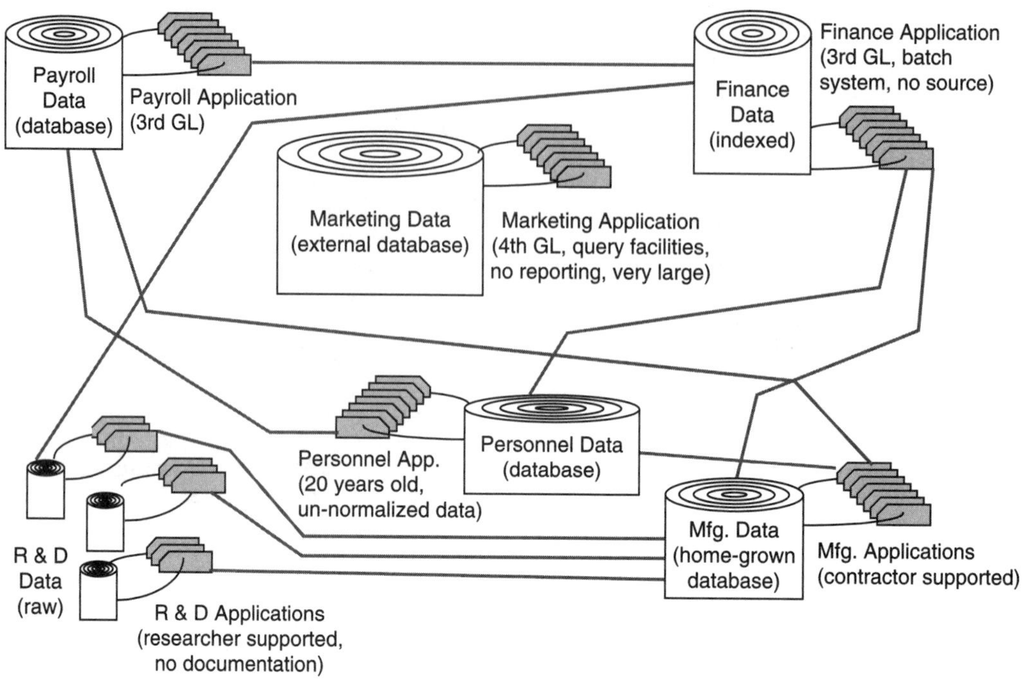

Figure 1.9

Gordion knot of legacy application interconnections.

XML Integration

The solution to the issue of integrating many disparate data systems was frequently to develop one-time solutions to data interchange. The costs related to maintaining custom electronic data interchange (EDI) solutions were often underestimated, and organizations to this day are frequently plagued by inflexible, brittle software meant to perform these tasks. The essential problem with these systems as they have traditionally been designed is that the thinking that went into their architecture was essentially point to point. Developers of a link from System A to System B developed what was requested, but may not have taken into account the way the individual systems interacted with other systems that perhaps were not within the immediate scope of their data interchange project.

Today, many organizations have grown their data systems to quite an amazing size and level of complexity. This level has long since exceeded the level of complexity where it made sense to think of the relationships between systems in terms of point-to-point connections. While the point-to-point connections were initially cheaper to implement than considering "the big picture" of intercommunication between systems, they are now major barriers to future development. Not only are they typically limited in functionality, they also tend to require quite astounding ongoing investments in the way of routine maintenance, updating the software as the system evolves underneath it, and working around its architectural limitations. XML's ability to increase the number of programmatic solutions that organizations are able to develop can only help this situation.

Data Integration/Exchange Challenges

The same word or term may have many different meanings depending on whom you ask. Take as an example the word "customer"—what does it mean? If a person from the accounting department is asked for a definition of customer, he or she might respond that a customer is an organization or individual that buys products or services. If a person in the service department was asked, the individual might respond that a customer is a client in the general public who bought a product and needs service on that product. Asking a third person in the sales department yields a third answer. In the sales department, a customer is a potential retailer of a product line.

Definition confusion doesn't stop at simple terms, but extends to phrases and concepts that would otherwise seem clear. For example, our colleague Burt Parker has made the following illustration numerous times (Table 1.1).

Table 1.1 An example of confusion in how different entities understand a simple request

Within the Department of Defense "lines of business," the phrase "secure the building" can elicit very different responses. For example:	
Army	Post guards at all entrances and ensure no unauthorized access.
Navy	Turn out all of the lights, lock all of the doors, and leave.
Marines	Send in a company to clear the building room-by-room, and form a perimeter defense around the building.
Air Force	Obtain a three-year lease with an option to buy the building.

Every organization of any size will find a multitude of its own examples of phrases that have different meanings to different branches internally. Often it seems that the most solid concepts are the ones that most frequently cause problems of interpretation. The concept of "unique identifier" seems quite solid, but in fact the data that comprise a unique identifier even for the same concept may differ across various data systems.

What is needed is information that explains and details what is stored in a particular data store and what its actual meaning is. As we've just found out, it may not be enough to know that a particular data item contains information on a particular "customer." Since the concept of customer can differ based on context, more information is needed about the surrounding data and business context in order to decipher seemingly simple terms.

Managing Joan Smith's Metadata

Another challenge frequently encountered is that of data duplication, and the issue of data in some systems being "out of sync" with what should be complementary data in another system. To illustrate this point, the example of Joan Smith is provided. Joan Smith is a loyal and frequent customer of a particular organization. The organization would like to know more about Joan Smith in order to better serve her, but efforts at pulling together the information about her contained in different data stores have encountered a number of thorny problems. As illustrated in the SAS Institute's articulation of a somewhat typical data engineering challenge, this company's problem was that they did not have a good idea who its customers were. This translated directly into a lack of understanding of the company's organizational DM practices and its metadata.

As an example, consider how a single customer, Ms. Joan E. Smith, appears multiple times in data stores for a number of reasons. As it turns out, "Joan Smith" is not really "Joan Smith" but a number of different individual data items whose metadata must be reconciled. In the customer database, Joan Smith is known as "Joan E. Smith." The next instance occurred when the call center operator misheard or mistyped Ms. Smith's name during a customer contact. The call center database only has record of calls placed to "Joanie Smitt." The third instance occurred because Ms. Smith's browser reported her identify as "J E Smith" when she visited the web site. The fourth identity was created because of data from a vendor list of prospective customers. The process to acquire this list did not require that

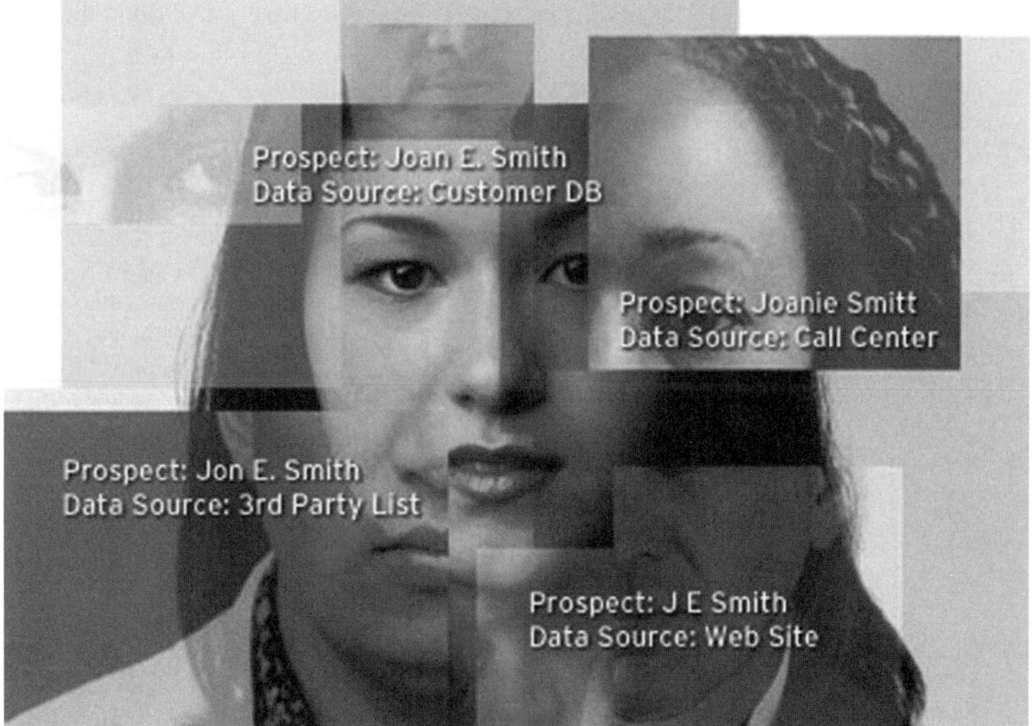

Figure 1.10

A very nice articulation of a common type of data-quality problem—not having a good idea who your customers really are. (Advertisement courtesy of SAS Industries, www.sas.com. Copyright © 2004 SAS Institute Inc. Cary, NC, USA. All rights reserved.)

existing customers be removed. It is reasonable to ask whether the goal of obtaining the most accurate and complete information is possible, given the poor quality of the data. Ms. Smith might even acquire a fourth identify as "Jon E. Smith" through some other system or business process. The authors of this book often even fill in forms with name variations in order to track who is selling information to whom. These problems of multiple records for a single individual lead to excessive maintenance costs if they are addressed at all, and create an inability to provide reliable information.

In this example, the DM challenge is rooted in the metadata as the organization has no idea from where it gets its data. Understanding how XML has developed in the minds of management and even its core users is an important part of knowing what perceptions already surround XML and how the hype can be tempered with fact. This is presented in the next subsection.

XML Hype: Management by Magazine

Managers have been told a number of different things about XML and its impacts. It has been promised to us as the "silver bullet." DM technology adoption is high and still rising, but our experience indicates that most organizations have not yet developed sufficient maturity to use XML-based DM successfully. Unfortunately, some organizations have brought XML-related technologies in-house so that they can be seen as applying a new technology—not in response to a particular challenge to which XML is well suited. Organizations are being driven by magazine article pressure to "adopt XML." Most organizations "adopt XML" by wrapping a few data items up in unstructured XML tags, most of which likely don't fall into a larger architecture or pattern. Some organizations actually structure their XML elements into larger architectural components, and gains the advantages associated with utilizing those architectural components, as opposed to using individual data items.

This section closes with a set of descriptions of hype-related statistics surrounding XML adoption. The first points out that more than half of organizations do not use metadata cataloging tools, which strongly suggests that they may not be using or valuing their metadata as appropriate. Since metadata is such a crucial component of work with XML and just about any other data technology, it makes sense that those organizations that are not making investments in their metadata may not see the maximum benefit possible from those investments.

Figure 1.11

Less than half of organizations manage their metadata using repository technologies.

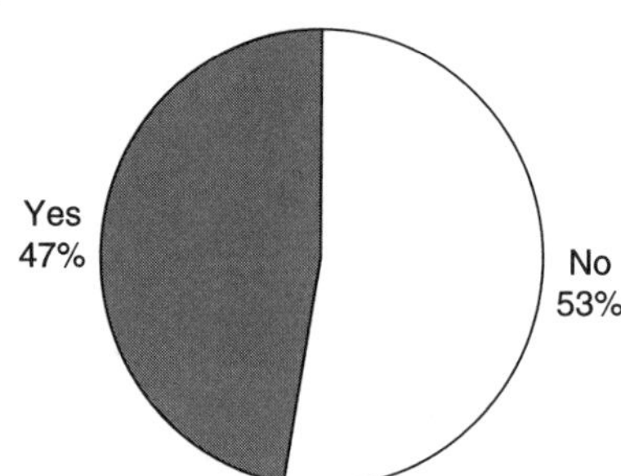

Figure 1.12

Just over half of repository builders use a structured approach to repository development.

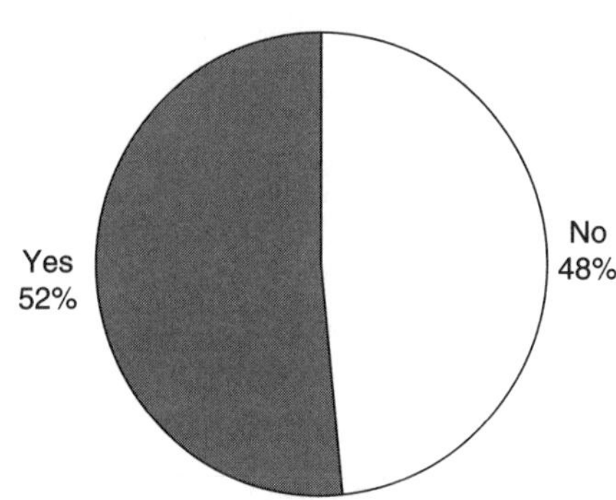

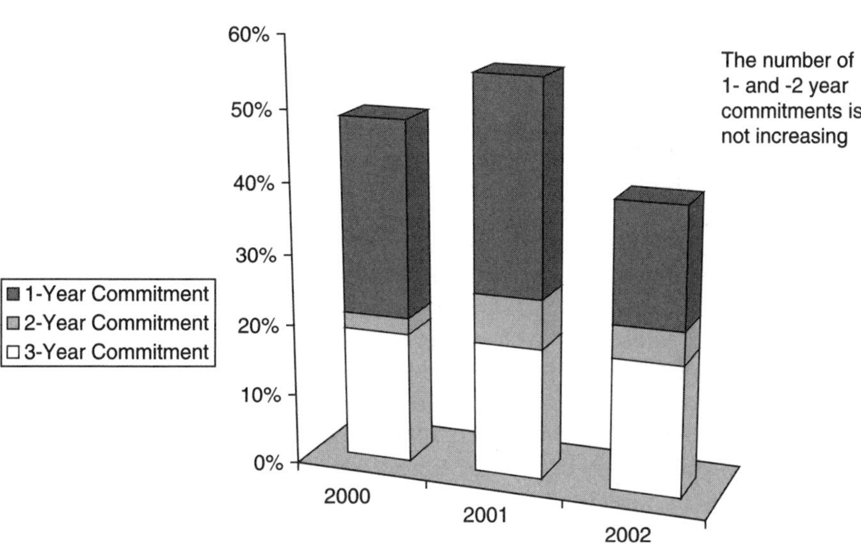

Figure 1.13

Less than half plan to adopt repository technology.

Repositories are often used within organizations to store metadata and other derived data assets. These repositories keep track of metadata so that it can be reused in other projects elsewhere in the organization—they help enable information reuse. In Figures 1.12 and 1.13, we see that

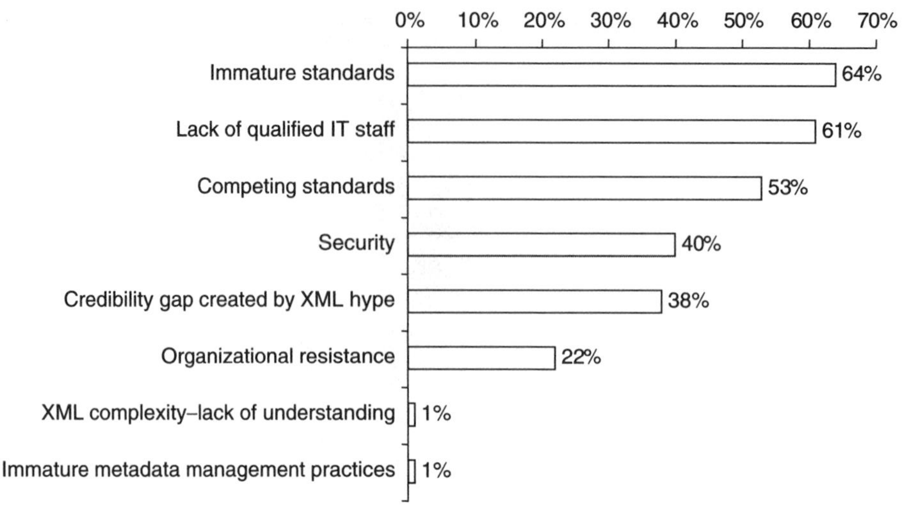

Figure 1.14

XML adoption challenges.

barely more than 50% of repository builders take a structured approach to the development of their repository, and less than half plan to adopt repository technology in the future. Organizations have long known that an unstructured approach to other projects such as applications development can be costly, and repository development is no different.

Figure 1.14 lists perceived XML adoption challenges. A commonly held perception has been that immature XML standards have been a barrier to its adoption. In truth, these days there are numerous mature and solid standards to work with, and while some standards are still being developed, the majority of what is needed for most organizations is ready for implementation and has been for some time. Toward the bottom of the figure, we see that organizations do not view the complexity of XML as a barrier to adoption. Later, we will see that this perception is correct and that XML does have an elegant simplicity to it that eases adoption. Finally, immature metadata management practices are not seen as a barrier to XML adoption. There are two sides to that issue. While it is true that an organization need not have mature metadata management capabilities to adopt XML, we would argue that these capabilities are crucial to getting the most out of any XML investment.

This section has dealt with what managers and users have been told about XML. But what is it that you really need to know about XML? Let us take a look at a few things that are important to keep in mind, from the perspective of those who developed XML and what they think is important to know about it.

Two Examples of XML in Context

XML is architected to be architected. Most of the XML technologies and standards that exist today are built on top of "lower layers" of XML—it is possible to stack XML on top of itself, building more robust structures by applying existing engineering principles. In this way, newly developed XML technologies can take advantage of the already existing technologies. This can be thought of like floors in a building—the foundation supports each layer of the building. If the foundation is built correctly, an architect can even build a skyscraper on top of it.

In this section, we will discuss two specific applications of XML within context. These are examples of building an application on top of the foundation that XML provides, and the benefits that come along with doing this. The purpose of these examples is to give you a taste for some of the possibilities that come with using XML-based data and metadata.

Internet Congestion and Application Efficiency

Internet congestion can be reduced using XML-based delivery architectures. This is accomplished by reducing the number of transfers required to complete a business transaction on the Internet. The current approach requires a given server—for example, a travel savings server—to respond to each inquiry with an entire web page. In typical scenarios, refining travel options often requires six or more queries for each trip. This allows the passenger to find the right seats, times, and flights for the trip. In many cases, extra server requests are generated by simple rearrangements of data that the client already has. For example, sometimes it may be preferable to sort flights by total price when budget is the concern, while other times the customer may want to see them sorted by departure times when scheduling is the greater concern. In this situation, another request is generated even though the data being returned will be identical, only ordered differently.

Large savings are possible if the efficiency of the server could be increased. The necessary task is to eliminate redundant work done by the server—the process of sending documents with identical data differing only in the order of the records. Using XML-based data management, an organization would serve up a copy of the most likely used data, wrapped in XML and accompanied by an XML-aware Java applet or equivalent. This approach permits the Java program to manipulate the XML on the client side. The idea can further be expanded with the use of related XML technologies that aid other aspects of the process, such as data presentation. Rather than sending the same redundant presentation data over and over to the client, the XML document the client receives may refer to another resource that describes how the data is to be presented. The result is that presentation data is fetched once, rather than each time any modification to the displayed data is requested. While the savings created from reducing the load from an average of six to two queries might not seem significant, its effect is amplified when there are 6,000 transactions per minute, effectively reducing the overall number of requests for that resource by two-thirds.

Some people might accurately point out that XML also has the potential to increase total traffic on the Internet. Once organizations find out the types of services and capabilities that are possible with XML, they may begin to consume these services more and more. In this sense, traffic may increase not because of a technical problem with XML, but because of increased overall demand for the services provided by XML and related technologies. This is strangely similar to situations that manufacturers find themselves in all the time—by reducing the individual price of an item (which can be equated with increasing the ease of use and power of an existing application reworked to take advantage of XML) the total demand for the item increases dramatically. In this sense, increased network traffic should be seen as a sign that the use of XML is succeeding—it should not be viewed simply as an increased cost.

Information Location

One of the most immediately promising aspects of using XML is exploiting its self-describing nature to aid in information location problems. Many organizational information tasks can be broken down into two systems communicating with one another. The key to this communication is in the answers to two questions—What does the system on the other end of the line actually store, and what does the data being stored mean? XML-based metadata is the answer to these questions that allows the communication to take place.

One common solution to the problem of locating data is to create a system in which metadata is published by various other systems. This metadata clearinghouse then acts as a central location that the larger community of applications can consult. Such a metadata repository can answer common systems questions such as, "Which systems store information on customers?" and "What are the acceptable values for this particular code?" This central XML repository eliminates the old point-to-point thinking along with the way data interchange is often done, and introduces a new concept of dialog between networks of related systems. Such systems exist today, and their users are already reaping the benefits. The architecture of most systems will eventually change from the semi-chaotic legacy base of today, teeming with individually maintained connections between systems, to one that values metadata. This will enable huge savings as both low-level devices and high-level systems become capable of information location and analysis as a direct result of their access to metadata.

Let us take an example that is often seen in many corporate environments. Due to new requirements, a new system must be built that generates reports and statistics from many different data sources. At a high level, the business wants to see reports that logically span several different information storage areas, for example, linking customers to shipping records, and so on. The old way of developing this type of system would have involved setting up links between the new reporting application and the many different data sources from which it pulled. That in turn would involve first figuring out which data was stored where, how it might be accessed, and how the data would be formatted once the application received it. Using XML's information location abilities, if the systems from which the data were to be pulled would publish XML metadata descriptions of what the systems contain, things could be simplified. The new application would simply consult this "metadata catalog," quickly discovering which data items were located in which systems. Again using an XML-based messaging method, it could connect directly to these systems and fetch the necessary information. Given that the data would be formatted in XML and the metadata would already be understood, the new application would not even have to put as much effort into reformatting data from whatever arcane format the other system's platform dictated.

The change from the existing legacy systems to metadata-consuming systems has started slowly, but will likely accelerate. One major area of competition between companies is the level of efficiency at which they can operate with respect to their goods, services, and management of data. As many companies begin to adopt new practices, the benefits derived from these practices will be reaped in terms of efficiency, creating more competition and impetus for others to follow. Effective and efficient management of data is already a best business practice as well as a critical success factor for most organizations. Some organizations may choose better DM for its benefits. Others in the future will choose it because they are forced to—keeping up with the competition may require it! XML-based metadata management simply extends existing ideas about organizational data and metadata management by attempting to extend the gains already seen within this area.

The architectural aspects of XML have important and wide-ranging implications for how it is used as a component of DM approaches. The next section deals with how these core features of XML translate into changes in the role of data management.

XML & DM Interaction Overview

DM is the practice of organizing and using data resources to the maximal benefit of the organization. DM is understood in several different contexts, from a high-level strategic discipline to a very low-level technical practice. DM often encompasses efforts at standardizing naming and usage conventions for data, profiling and analyzing data in search of trends, storing and formatting it for use in numerous different contexts, and evaluating data quality. In short, one might say that DM is tasked with making sure the right people have the right data at the right time, and that it is factually correct, useful, relevant, and accessible.

XML is more than just a way to represent data. Just as we noted about metadata toward the beginning of the chapter, the way XML is understood will impact how it is used and what benefit is derived from it. One of the specific profound impacts of XML that is appearing is its effect on data management. XML will change DM in three major ways:

1. XML will allow the management of data that was previously unstructured. This will expand the definition of DM to include data sources that previously were not addressed by existing DM capabilities.
2. XML will expand data management's role in applications development. As applications are increasingly developed in ways that

focus primarily on the data and how it is used in the application, XML and its connection to DM will grow in influence.

3. XML's capabilities will influence the increasingly frequent DM task of preparing data for interchange, along with associated data quality issues.

As XML changes DM overall, organizations must be sure that their DM practices are mature so that they can take advantage of the benefits. Organizations have typically shown low- or entry-level metadata management practices both across time and industry. A number of different attempts have been made to effectively measure the status of DM within organizations—most recently, the authors have researched the maturity of organizational DM practices. Given the correct surveying tool, it is possible to assess how mature the practices of a particular organization are. When comparing this data against data of other companies within the same industry, an organization can gain knowledge about its relative strengths and weaknesses. This information is crucial for organizations to discover where they are lacking or where they might yet find additional efficiencies relative to their competition.

Aside from information concerning outside competition, a DM assessment can indicate which benefits of XML can be immediately realized. For organizations with mature DM practices, it is likely that some of the advantages XML brings to the table will be like a breath of fresh air, prompting data managers to exclaim, "I always wished there was something that could do that!" For organizations with less mature practices, some of XML's advantages may not be within immediate reach.

Let's take a look at the three XML and DM interactions previously stated and address them individually.

Management of Unstructured Data

Organizational data can be divided into two categories, structured and unstructured. Structured data is what most people think of when they think of organizational data to be managed. Unstructured data, on the other hand, is data stored in formats that is not as easily accessible or searchable as data one might find in a relational database. Examples of unstructured data would include Word documents, PowerPoint presentations, e-mails, memos, notes, and basically just about anything that would be found on the average worker's PC as opposed to in a centralized "data store." Another way of describing unstructured data is that it is usually intended for human consumption, where the read mechanism is a pair of eyes, and the write mechanism is a keyboard. Structured information, conversely, is usually intended for consumption by computer systems and intermediaries before it reaches humans. Some people prefer to describe structured and unstructured data as tabular and non-tabular data—tabular data could be viewed as data that would fit into a table, or a rectangular array, while non-tabular data tends to represent more complicated and less atomic information that has to be put in a different form in order to be utilized. This definition generally captures the right idea, but is slightly inaccurate since structured information need not necessarily be tabular.

When asked, most managers would initially respond that the bulk of their important data is stored in structured formats where it is most easily accessible. In fact, research into the overall quantity and location of data (Finkelstein, 1998) within organizations tends to point in quite the opposite direction—80% of data is stored in unstructured formats, while only 20% is stored in structured formats. This large skew is due in part to the massive amount of valuable information transmitted as unstructured e-mails between workers. The effect, though, is that organizations are applying DM ideas to only 20% of their data! Large quantities of data that are critical to everyday operation are floating around in a number of different formats on desktop PCs. Many people have experienced problems in the past with multiple versions of a document floating around, not being able to locate the right document in a timely manner, and problems surrounding possession and versioning control of documents that are collaborative efforts. Furthermore, when a worker leaves an organization, the information in his or her head is lost.

The concept of XML-based metadata brings a number of new possibilities to the arena of managing this unstructured information. Part of the problem with today's unstructured information is that the amount of metadata related to the documents is insufficient, and because of this the search facilities that exist to locate documents tend to be somewhat lacking. For example, it is very difficult to query documents with questions like, "Show me all documents that contain annotations by Joan Smith between November 1 and November 20." Similar queries inside of structured datasets are much more straightforward. When structure can be given to previously unstructured information and metadata associated with particular data items within documents, the number of ways that the documents can be used and reused increases dramatically.

Expanded DM Roles

Some of data management's roles related to applications development will be expanded with the use of XML. For example,

- Greatly expanded volumes of data will require a fundamentally different approach than has been practiced in the past.
- DM can play a greater role in areas that have previously been off-limits, such as capacity management.
- As an integration technology, DM permits more effective use of technologies focusing on the management of both data and metadata.

The amount of data being managed today far exceeds the amounts managed even a few years ago. As organizations start new data initiatives, including correlation of their data with external datasets, data mining, and business intelligence, the variety and quantity that must be managed have grown rapidly. DM technology itself must then change with the evolving requirements of the data itself if the organization is to keep pace and not lose ground by increasing its overall management burden.

People normally do not think of data managers as individuals who can help in more technical areas such as capacity management. But keeping in mind our earlier example dealing with the airline reservation system and the potential to reduce the total number of queries against the system, we see that data managers can make quite a splash. The way that data is delivered determines how much capacity will be needed in order to accomplish delivery. The way the data is structured and managed in turn determines the way in which it is delivered. In other words, by creating effective data structures at the outset, benefits can be obtained further "down the pipeline," minimizing the resources necessary to disseminate the data to the appropriate parties. The structure of data is important. Shipping companies have long known how to stack boxes and crates of all sizes and shapes to maximize space efficiency inside trucks. DM may play a similar role to get the most out of existing technical capacity.

Technologies within the overall architectural family of XML bring a number of new methods to the table in terms of the way we think about data. Take for example a subsystem that consists of three distinct processes, each of which is intended to perform a particular transformation upon the inputted data. In order to get the data from one format to another, it has to first go through a three-step pipeline on the way to its destination. One of the core concepts of good architecture has always been simplicity; wherever there are three components that can be replaced by one component, it is frequently wise to do so. The trick is to have enough information so that you can determine which configuration is most appropriate for any given situation.

In the case of this collaborative data transformation system described, had the data at the first stage been expressed in terms of an XML structure, another XML technology known as XSLT (Extensible Stylesheet Language Transformations) could have been applied to transform the structure from its original form into its final form in one simple step. XSLT, a component that will be addressed in more detail in the component architecture chapter, essentially allows one form of XML document to be transformed into another. In the case of our example, eliminating the intermediate steps obviates the need to maintain three legacy systems and the associated code. It also simplifies the overall process, which makes it easier to document, understand, and manage. Finally, the XSLT transformations we allude to are also XML documents, and are subject to all of the advantages of any other XML document. This means that you can use XSLT to transform XML documents, or other XSLT structures, replacing volumes of spaghetti code and if/then statements with well-defined data structures that can perform common data manipulation tasks. These structures in turn can be applied to thousands of documents as easily as they are applied to one document.

Let us take a look at a solid example of how XSLT and other XML technologies can reduce the burden related to data transformation. Imagine a system that contains 15,000 XML documents, each of which relates to a particular employee within the organization. This data must be moved into another system for subsequent processing, but unfortunately the foreign system requires that the <employee> XML element be transcribed as <associate>. Using previous DM approaches, this potentially could have required modification of thousands of lines of legacy code (written by programmers who are no longer on staff) at an enormous cost of both time and money. Since XML is designed to operate on itself and to be "reflexive," XSLT allows the trained analyst to quickly design a service that will do simple and even complex tag modifications. In other words, since XSLT allows data transformations to be expressed in terms of already well-understood XML documents, the transformation processes themselves can be managed the same as any other data. How many legacy systems out there allow data transformation business rules to be stored, modified, and managed like any other data structure? The answer is not many.

Preparation of Organizational Data for E-Business

Another way in which XML will greatly impact DM is that data will require better preparation. Anyone can put arbitrary XML tags around existing data, but in order to take advantage of the benefits of XML, the data has to be properly prepared so that it makes sense within its new XML "context." Again we see the theme of XML requiring a shift in the way managers think about their data. It is worth mentioning that this particular impact of XML on DM is something that requires some work in order to be of benefit. Effective XML usage requires addressing data at a structural level as well as at the "tag" level. Most data management groups within organizations have not advanced past wrapping individual data items up in tags, and have not yet taken a serious look at the overall structure and how it fits into a larger organizational DM challenge.

Most of the chapter up until this point has been talking about the positive aspects of XML, and what it is good for. To avoid the pitfall of misapplication or over-application of technology that seems so common in information technology, it is important to temper enthusiasm with a bit of reality by discussing what XML is not, and where it should not be used.

What XML Is Not: XML Drawbacks and Limitations

Frequently, XML is sold as the "silver bullet" technology, when in fact it is not. While it is a vital addition to the tool chest of just about any organization, it is ultimately the judicious and appropriate application of the technology that solves problems rather than any "magic" that is attributed to the mere existence of it.

As with any data technology, effective use of XML requires forethought and planning. Architectural decisions that are made before the technology component of a project comes into play often determine the benefit that the organization will derive from the use of XML-based technologies. Early adopters of XML, who were driven by the "management by magazine" phenomenon described earlier in the chapter, sometimes feel that the benefits of XML are limited. In these situations, the benefits of XML *are* in fact somewhat limited. In order to reap the full benefit of XML, metadata must be understood in terms of its proper definition—an application of data—and strategy must be put in place accordingly. When XML is used simply as a new data format and nothing else, it is not surprising that the gains associated with it are accordingly limited.

One of the concepts that will be addressed repeatedly throughout this book is that the abilities of XML should be used in conjunction with solid DM and engineering principles. Just as steel beams can be used to craft magnificent skyscrapers in the hands of a skilled architect, XML can do wonderful things when handled skillfully. If the architect does not spend sufficient time fleshing out the plans, however, nothing about the steel beam itself will prevent the building from falling.

There is more on what XML is and is not in Chapter 3. Please also see numerous entries under the CONTENT section at Fabian Pascal's site at http://www.dbdebunk.com/.

Chapter Summary

The purpose of this chapter has basically been just to warm up for what is coming in the rest of the book. The basic definitions have been laid out, along with a discussion of what XML is, and what it is not. The points in this chapter are good to keep in mind throughout the rest of the book. The next chapter examines XML technologies as a way of building on the understanding gained in this chapter.

References

Aiken, P., Mattia, A., et al. (in press). Measuring data management's maturity: An industry's self-assessment. *IEEE IT Computer*.

Appleton, D. (1983). Law of the data jungle. *Datamation*. **29:** 225-230.

Brackett, M. H. (2002). *Data resource design and remodeling*. Olympia, WA.

Finkelstein, C., and Aiken, P. H. (1998). *Building corporate portals using XML*. New York: McGraw-Hill.

Parker, B., Chambless, L., et al. (1995). *Data management capability maturity model*. McLean, VA: MITRE.

2

XML from the Builder's Perspective: Using XML to Support DM

Chapter Overview

We use this chapter to present an overview of how XML works and how it has been used to support DM from the system builder's perspective. We also want to introduce some concepts that are specific to XML, and are used repeatedly in XML-based solutions. We will start by introducing XML terminology and the structural characteristics of XML. We will then outline the basic XML "ground rules" about how the documents are structured. We will not spend much time on the actual structure and syntax of XML documents since that is a topic very capably handled by a number of other texts.* We will, however, provide a set of basic characteristics of XML documents, and point out how they relate to data management and what they say about XML as a language. Toward the end of the chapter, we will cover a number of different uses of XML, from its use as an integration language, to performing data translation, and a host of other examples, along with discussions of their business benefits. By the

*For example see Bean (2003); Dick (2000); Chaudhri, A., Rashid, A., et al. (2003); Ahmed, K., Ayers, D., et al. (2001). Also just google the term "XML" and you will gain access to much good technical content.

end of the chapter, you should have a firm idea not only of what XML is and how it works, but where it has been successfully used in the past to solve specific problems.

XML Builder's Overview

Before jumping into the terms, it will be useful to note that we expect users to already be aware of the wealth of information, shareware, and standards upon which to build. There already exist metadata markets, XML databases, stacks of standards, lots of free software, interoperability testing, etc. In this section, our discussion begins with a number of XML-related terms and definitions, along with descriptions of how the concepts behind them benefit data management. Understanding these concepts is important in grasping the "hows" and the "whys" of XML's impact on data management.

XML Terms

Embedded Tagging

When people refer to "embedded tagging," they are talking about the powerful ability to add structure to data elements—grouping them in various ways to provide support for organizational objectives. Knowledge workers are familiar with relational and tabular data storage using the Relational Database Management System, or RDBMS. While XML is fully capable of representing these types of data, most XML documents are stored hierarchically. An XML document is simply a text document that contains at least one XML element (pair of tags). Embedded tagging is the process of including sub-elements to the primary data element in a document. This means that any data element in an XML document can have subordinate data elements underneath it, which inherit the higher-level "container" element properties. As an example, consider a communications framework expressed in XML. The communications system uses the framework to keep track of who communicated with whom, and when the communication took place. All of this is metadata and it should be maintained using modern data management technologies. The actual content of the communication (in this case, a quick note) is stored in a separate location and is often the only portion of the system to use any sort of

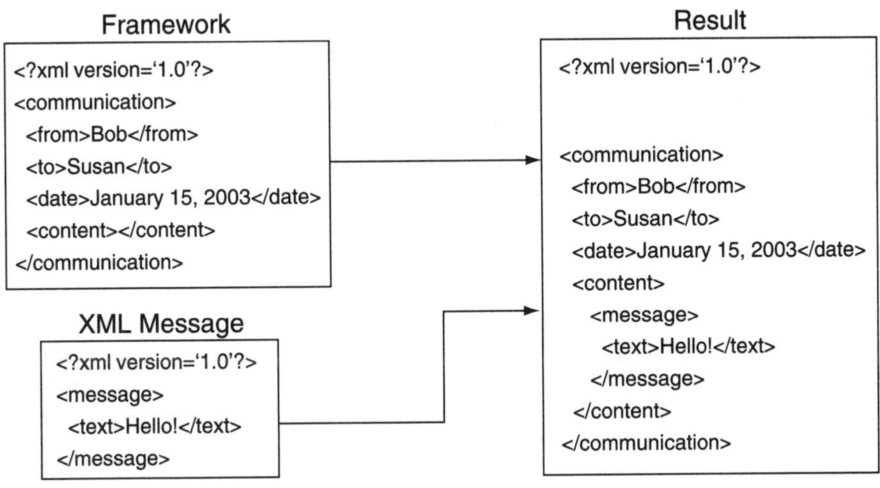

Figure 2.1

Combining two different XML documents into a single, unified document.

database at all. Figure 2.1 shows how the data and the metadata can be integrated and structured into a result.

As the need arises to have a more complete picture of a particular communication that has taken place, it would be helpful to combine the two pieces of data into a unified document. Figure 2.1 shows how the XML message is combined with the framework to produce a resulting document that contains all of the data of both. While this should be considered a reasonably advanced use of XML, it really isn't that complex. The XML message is "embedded" inside the <content> element of the framework document. In this way, XML documents are quite like Russian nesting dolls; inside of one XML element is another, which itself contains another, and so on. With nesting dolls, there is a limit based on how small or large a doll you can actually pick up and hold, but with XML, there is no predefined limit.

Tag embedding in general simply allows XML documents to be mixed and matched, combined, taken apart, and reassembled. Just as we inserted one document into another in this example, we might also have extracted one document from another. The business value that arises from this is that no direct one-to-one mapping from an XML document to a data source or system is necessary. One document may represent several sources, or several XML documents may be combined to represent one source. The impact to data management is that data can be structured according to how it will be understood and used, rather than according to artificial platform or representational constraints.

Meta-Language

A meta-language is a language that describes another language. XML is a meta-language that has several important capabilities:

- **Referenceability:** Data in one XML document can refer to the element names in a different XML document.
- **Structurability:** The ability to nest itself. As described in the section on embedded tagging, XML documents can be packaged up and included in larger documents.
- **Layerability:** The ability to layer itself. The core XML language is quite small and compact. Other technologies in the XML "family" are all built on the features of base XML. With each additional layer of technology, the toolset becomes more powerful and flexible.

Data managers understand that XML provides two specific opportunities. Organizations can develop languages for very specific tasks, tailoring their language to the requirements at hand, and they can also develop "bridge languages" to permit communication in ways that are less cumbersome than strict application of standards.

XML Parser/XML Processor

The term "XML parser" is frequently heard in discussions of XML. Another term frequently heard in its place is "XML processor." An XML parser is simply a piece of software that is designed to take the raw text of an XML document and convert it into a data structure that can be used by just about any tool that is capable of dealing with XML. Parsers are used to get data out of a document for actual use. There are generally two different types of parsers—SAX parsers, and DOM parsers.

SAX parsers tend to present the data to the application that is using the parser as a sequence of individual events. Those events might be a particular element in the document, or data within an element. DOM parsers read the entire XML document and represent it as a hierarchical tree internally. Basically, SAX parsers allow for very selective, sequential access to XML documents, while DOM parsers allow for global random access to documents. Broadly speaking, SAX parsers tend to be faster and more memory efficient, while DOM parsers provide more options for accessing data in documents. It is important to note that a parser acts as the intermediary between an XML document and the software that uses the document for some purpose. This piece of software is the "magic" that happens between XML that is stored somewhere and data from the document that an application is using. In other words, the parser makes the data in the document available in terms that the application understands.

For data managers, the parser is the most basic piece of XML software necessary to make XML documents useful. Fortunately, most XML toolkits and just about any application that knows how to deal with XML either comes with its own built-in parser, or uses one that may already be distributed with the platform being used.

Vocabularies

The vocabulary of an XML document often refers to the concepts, elements, and attributes that are present in the document. Since XML elements and attributes are just text names, it is possible to label each item of data in a document with a name that best represents the data's meaning or applicability. The vocabulary of a document is then the collection of all of the elements that are found in a document, along with their meanings. XML as a whole has a way to formalize and express these vocabularies—this is usually done in the form of a DTD (Document Type Definition) or an XML Schema, although these two are only the most recognized among many options.

Vocabularies are important because they are intricately tied to the meaning of the XML document. When converting from one form of XML document to another, it is crucial to understand the vocabulary of both documents in order to make sure that the document comparison and conversion is apples-to-apples, and not apples-to-oranges. This problem arises when similar terms mean different things in different contexts, as described in Chapter 1's example of "secure the building." Data managers are often justifiably interested in these vocabulary reconciliation issues, since they are crucial to ironing out issues of semantics in data.

XML-Wrapped

The term "XML-wrapped" is often used as a buzzword, but at its core, it just means that the data in question has XML elements surrounding key data items, and that the document has been given some sort of XML structure. It is important to keep in mind that just because data is "XML-wrapped" does not mean that it is useful or easy to work with, just that the data is represented as XML.

Many data managers have seen quite a bit of data that is coming "XML-wrapped," and will see even more of it as time goes on. Data managers can understand "XML-wrapped" to mean that someone along the line is attempting to pair meaning with his or her data.

HTML Drawbacks

Many people have pointed out that visually, XML looks quite similar to HTML, so they wonder why XML was even needed. Why couldn't they just stick with HTML?

> *"What's odd about HTML is that while it does a perfectly good job of describing how a web page will look and function and what words it will contain, HTML has no idea at all what any of those words actually mean. The page could be a baby food ad, or plans to build an atomic bomb. While HTML knows a great deal about words, it knows nothing at all about information."—Robert X. Cringely*

When representing data in computers, there are essentially two bases to cover—the structure and the semantics. The structure of the data is physically how it is put together, and it includes what format particular data items are in, and where they occur. Facts paired with context and meaning produce data. The semantics of the data are what the data actually mean—is the isolated piece of data "1.86" a person's height expressed in meters? Is it the price of a pound of fruit? Is it a particular company's yearly revenue, in billions of dollars? The semantics represent the rhyme and reason of the data. The problem with HTML is that it does not cover semantics at all. And as for structure, HTML only knows how to represent the visual structure of the data and nothing else.

In summary, the drawbacks of HTML include the following:

- There is no effective way to identify the content of a page. HTML tags describe the visual layout of a page. Web browsers use the tags for presentation purposes, but the actual text content has no meaning associated with it. To a browser, text is only a series of words to be presented visually.

- HTML creates problems locating content with search engines. Because there is no semantic data, there is no automatic way that search engines can determine meaning, except by indexing relevant words. Search engines have improved tremendously over the past few years, but clever search algorithms still occasionally fail, and are no substitute for representing data properly.
- Many capabilities require special extensions to HTML. In order to perform more complex functions such as dynamic content, special extensions are needed that don't necessarily have much in common with HTML. For example, ask your local web developer, and you may find that he or she is familiar with a number of different computer languages, all of which have different syntaxes that must be cobbled together to produce the desired effect. Examples of this are DHTML, JavaScript, CSS, and others.
- HTML has encouraged "bad habits." In the early days of HTML, browsers and other software that interpreted HTML came with a variety of different exceptions and special cases to correctly interpret badly written HTML that didn't conform to the standard. As users got accustomed to this, taking shortcuts in HTML became the norm, to the point that the standard has warped slightly. Allowing bad habits in HTML has had the strange side effect of making the task of parsing what was originally a very simple markup language into an incredibly complex task.

XML "Rules"

Before diving into a discussion of the rules associated with XML documents, let us first take a look at the technological foundations of XML. The Extensible Markup Language can be considered a descendant of an earlier markup language, SGML (Standard Generalized Markup Language). Developed in 1974 by Charles F. Goldfarb and a host of others, SGML was meant to create a single basis for any type of markup language. In 1986 it became an international standard (ISO), and was in use in numerous organizations for many years. XML can be thought of as a subset of SGML. The two are similar in some ways, but SGML is a more complicated language. As a structure, SGML provides the ability to *create* arbitrary markup languages, while XML is a particular markup language. SGML acted as the foundation for the development of HTML and later XML, but is not widely used today. Most SGML documents seen today are either legacy documents, or deal with the typesetting of printed documents in different ways. SGML didn't ever achieve the penetration into the realm of representation of organizational data that XML has.

At its core, XML is a very simple language. One could say that the two main architectural goals of XML were simplicity and power. Simplicity is important because the simpler a language is, the easier it is to learn and use, and the less likely that it will contain errors, problems, or internal contradictions that make the language inconsistent. To maximize the power of a language, it must be created in such a way that it can be applied to a range of different problems efficiently, not designed to serve a few niche cases. XML accomplished these two goals admirably. It is built in a very simple way, and its similarity to other existing markup languages such as HTML means that the learning curve is about as good as it could possibly be. In this section, we will discuss the core set of "rules" that dictate how XML documents are structured and interpreted. The designers of XML attempted to minimize the number of rules that users must know in order to use the language. This simplicity has led to many of the advantages for which XML is known; namely, the fewer rules a language has, the easier it is to learn, and the easier it is to build software to work with the language.

Tags Must Come in Pairs

In the XML vernacular, a tag or an element is the marker that is put around a piece of data. It effectively acts like parentheses in writing, showing the reader where some comment or piece of information starts, and where it ends. Figure 2.2 shows how XML doesn't have a tabular or field structure like other data representation formats. In other formats, where the data begins and ends is largely a function of where it falls in a grid-like structure. Because there is no strictly enforced grid-like structure in XML, data must be delimited clearly. There are no exceptions to this rule, although in some XML documents you may see what are called "singleton" tags—these appear as XML tags that contain a slash ("/") character after their name. This is XML short hand for an opening and a closing tag; it just means that the implied content within the tag is empty. Singleton

Figure 2.2

An example of XML tag pairing.

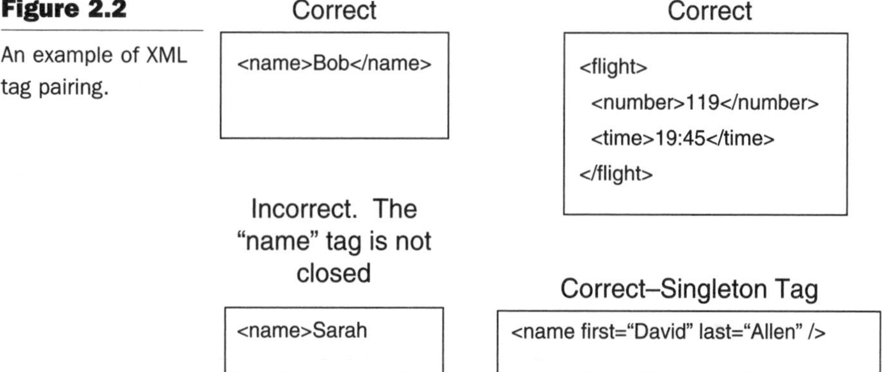
Correct
<name>Bob</name>
Correct
<flight>
<number>119</number>
<time>19:45</time>
</flight>
Incorrect. The "name" tag is not closed
<name>Sarah
Correct–Singleton Tag
<name first="David" last="Allen" />

tags are not exceptions to the rule that all tags must come in pairs; they are simply a shortcut in the case where the tag contains no content. In the example provided here, the singleton tag for "name" is used—note the slash before the end of the tag. This is the same as expressing the "name" tag as <name first="David" last="Allen"></name>.

Tag Pairs Can Be Nested Inside One Another at Multiple Levels

The first rule, that tags always come in pairs, essentially acts to identify the XML concept of a piece of data. The second rule, that tags can be nested within one another, is what provides XML documents with their real structure. If one tag is nested within another, we can say that there is a "parent" tag (the outer tag) and a "child" tag (the inner tag). When this principle is applied to complex data structures, the result is an XML tree. The very first element in an XML document can be seen as the root of the tree, with various branches corresponding to the child tags of the first element. Those sub-tags may in turn have their own child tags, each of which represents further branching of the tree.

There are several reasons why this hierarchical structure is used. When documents are structured in this way, it allows software to treat the entire document (or subsections of it) as a tree internally. Trees are data structures that are extremely well understood in computer science terms—there are already a multitude of algorithms in existence that can effectively process trees in a variety of ways. This allows a large body of previous research on trees to be applied to XML documents. But that is a low-level technical reason. At the user level, it permits easy representation of common parent-child relationships in data. It also allows related data items to be "grouped" together under a common parent tag for semantic reasons. In the relational model, this logical grouping of related pieces of data is often done at the record level, with one record holding a number of different data points that logically hang together. Figure 2.3 illustrates a conversion between tabular data and XML-wrapped data. In XML documents, that might translate into an XML structure where each record of data is captured as a "chunk" of XML with an enclosing tag, such as the "flight" tag seen in this example.

One interesting point about the hierarchical nature of XML that rarely gets mentioned is this: While there are established methods of converting tabular and relational data structures into hierarchical structures, the opposite is not true. Converting hierarchical structures into relational or tabular data can be extremely difficult, not because the hierarchical structure is somehow more powerful than the relational form of data storage, but simply because of differences between the two models. Converting from one model to the other is a challenge often faced when organizations want to store XML data in relational databases. In later chapters, we will discuss XML databases and how their storage model may be better in certain cases.

XML Is Unicode Based

Unicode is a relatively new form of encoding characters in computers. The need for Unicode resulted from the recognition that the primary standard for representing characters (known as ASCII) was extremely limited and basically only allowed representation of characters from Latin alphabets. As computers crossed more international boundaries and came to be used in almost every human language on the planet, it became desirable to have a single way of representing characters that could cover languages that do

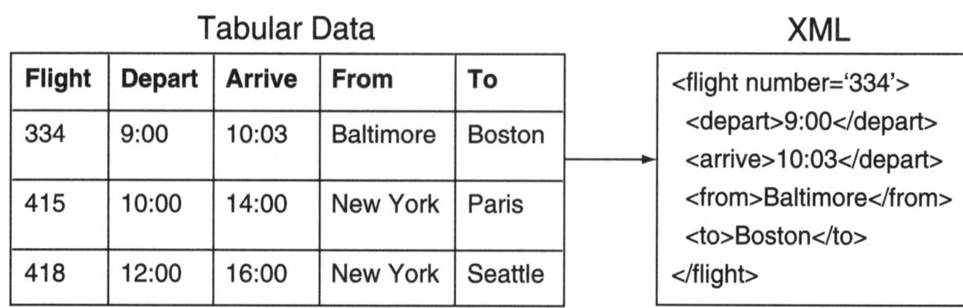
Tabular Data
XML
<flight number='334'>
<depart>9:00</depart>
<arrive>10:03</depart>
<from>Baltimore</from>
<to>Boston</to>
</flight>

Flight	Depart	Arrive	From	To
334	9:00	10:03	Baltimore	Boston
415	10:00	14:00	New York	Paris
418	12:00	16:00	New York	Seattle

Figure 2.3

Comparing tabular and XML representations of data.

not necessarily use a Latin alphabet. In short, Unicode provides a unique number for every character, no matter what the platform, no matter what the program, no matter what the language.*

XML uses UTF as the default character encoding for all documents. UTF in turn is a way of representing the numbers and characters from Unicode as bytes that can be stored. This basic feature of XML makes a lot of sense when examined together with XML's other features. It certainly wouldn't do to create a generalized data representation markup language that was unable to express characters from different languages. XML's use of Unicode makes it easy to exchange documents over national and cultural boundaries, and does not require the romanization of foreign words. XML element names, attribute values, and document data can be specified in a way that is easiest for the author and is still interoperable, making XML truly an international format.

Designing Your Own Language

XML allows element names to be whatever the author prefers. Data publishers are free to refer to pieces of data in their own terms. But with this capability comes some responsibility. In order for a defined language to make sense, it too must conform to several rules that help give the language meaning for other computers and software packages. It wouldn't do to have everyone choose their own unique set of 20 different elements, mixing them freely and in any order. The confusion that would result from this would be analogous to people randomly ordering the words in their sentences, perhaps occasionally mixing in words from other languages. The results might sometimes be humorous, but would not often be of much use. So the definition of any language within XML should include the following three pieces of information that form the rules of the language.

1. The list of allowed tags must be defined.
2. The nesting structure of the defined tags must be laid out.
3. There should be descriptions of how to process the tags.

These rules are not strictly required. It is possible to use XML documents without following any of these rules, but it is rarely a good idea. If XML

*http://www.unicode.org/

documents could be thought of as cities, with individual data items as citizens, then these rules are like a sheriff and a court system. While it's technically possible to do without them, nobody will like the resulting anarchy.

Figure 2.4 illustrates how creating a list of allowed tags in the document is similar to writing a dictionary for the language. It lays out which terms can be used. Words that are in this dictionary make sense in the language, just like the words in an English dictionary are understandable to speakers of English. The nesting structure of the defined tags must also be defined, to give some meaning to the collection of "words" in the language. This is similar to grammar rules in the English language. Speakers of English cannot simply order words in any way they want, since result it would sentences in garbled!

In this example, we see two documents that contain identical data, with different nesting conventions. On the left of the figure is a standard representation with a "route" tag clearly specifying that the flight goes from Washington to New York City. The right side contains the same data, but it is rearranged, so it has a different meaning. Without solid and enforced nesting rules, this second document might be interpreted as a flight with no departure time that goes from one place named "559" to another place named "9:30"!

As an illustration of how XML itself is a "meta-language," consider how most of the time when new XML languages are created, the tags that are allowed in the document and the nesting rules that must be in place are themselves expressed in the XML document. The two major XML architectural components used to accomplish this are referred to as DTDs and XML Schemas. Later, we will go into more depth about these particular

Figure 2.4

Why nesting rules matter.

This Makes Sense...

```
<flight>
  <number>559</number>
  <depart>9:30</depart>
  <arrive>10:21</arrive>
  <route>
    <from>Washington</from>
    <to>New York</to>
  </route>
</flight>
```

But What Does This Mean?

```
<flight>
  <arrive>10:21</arrive>
  <from>Washington</from>
  <to>New York</to>
  <route>
    <number>559</number>
    <depart>9:30</depart>
  </route>
</flight>
```

components and how they fit into the overall XML component architectural model.

The last part of defining any created XML language is specifying how the tags should be processed. At times, it may be important to deal with certain data items before others, or even to skip processing some items depending on the values of others. The need for formalized rules about how the tags are processed varies with the complexity of the language that is created. The more optional tags and special cases that exist in the language to represent particular data structures, the wiser it is to lay out a set of rules that describe how the language is processed, and what that processing means in terms of the phenomenon the data represent.

XML is to data what Java is to programming languages. The excitement over Java was that you could "Write it once. Play it back anywhere!" With XML capabilities you can "Wrap your data once in XML and utilize it anywhere!" XML represents what Mike Hammer terms a disruptive technology—that is, a technology that has the potential to impact-related processes (Hammer & Champy, 1993). XML has the potential to simplify our data management operations in much the same way that EDI simplified data communications exchange.

HTML versus XML

With regard to the way the rules of the two markup languages work, there are a number of differences between HTML and XML. In HTML, there is a fixed set of tags that are allowed to be included in HTML documents, while all other tags are ignored. In XML documents, on the other hand, tag formatting can be specified for any application—there is no fixed set of tags that are acceptable in base XML. While tag limitations can be put in place on XML documents for particular applications, as discussed earlier, there are no inherent limitations on XML itself as there are in HTML. Another difference between the two concerns how browsers interpret the data. HTML documents are interpreted in terms of a visual layout, whereas XML documents can be interpreted in a number of different ways according to what data is actually in the document. XML technologies exist that allow browsers to display data documents in a visually pleasing way just as HTML would have done, while at the same time preserving the metadata and semantic context of the data.

In an excellent article, two of XML's creators describe two of the motivations that led them to develop XML (Bosak & Bray, 1999). The first was Internet congestion. Using HTML required updating a quality field by accessing a server and reloading the page. With XML, more work can be accomplished on the client side. The second motivation was to address information location difficulties. With HTML, you cannot search for anything marked as "price" on the web beyond searching for the string "price." XML-based data is "self describing," which means that devices will be more capable of local analysis of information. As we shall see, the goals of XML's creators directly complement several data management objectives.

Now that we have taken a look at some of the important terms to understand with XML and what rules of the road need to be followed, it's time to take a look at examples of how XML is actually used in practice.

XML Usage in Support of DM: Builder's Perspective

We begin this section by showing how understanding the way a browser works can be an important tool for learning XML. We next present a number of increasingly detailed examples of how XML has been used to support DM. The examples are presented from the perspective of someone responsible for developing and implementing these types of solutions.

Integration at the Browser

XML has been making its way to the browser—support for rudimentary XML structures existed in the Microsoft Internet Explorer (IE) browser in version 5 and in Netscape V6. In spite of frustration with popup windows, viruses, and tracking software, the majority of knowledge workers today are running version Microsoft Internet Explorer 6, which includes support for a number of XML technologies. Browser designers as a group have wisely decided that as the browser moves toward being a standard application deployment platform, XML will not only be a nice feature, it will be pivotal. The reason it's safe to bet on XML is that the core of the technology is stable and will not change. The "layered" aspect of the related standards also allows implementers to put into place a core functionality that allows subsequent higher layers to be easily added.

Currently, XML integration at the browser is not being used to its full potential. Part of the reason for this is the worry that different browsers implement some of the XML technologies in slightly different ways, so the proliferation of different browsers makes effective use more difficult. In fact, XML within the browser is more frequently used in situations where the browser population is largely known, such as for internal applications rather than those distributed over the wider Internet to the general public. Open up an XML document with Internet Explorer 5 or higher and you will see some XML features illustrated. Figure 2.5 shows that Internet Explorer correctly laid out the hierarchical structure of XML—for example, notice how the "<head>" and "</head>" tags align. Because browsers

```
<?xml version="1.0" ?>
- <xsl:stylesheet xmlns:xsl="http://www.w3.org/TR/WD-xsl">
  - <xsl:template match="/">
    - <html>
      - <head>
          <title>FLIGHT OPTIONS FROM RICHMOND TO LONDON</title>
        </head>
      - <body>
          <h1 align="center">FLIGHT OPTIONS FROM RICHMOND TO LONDON</h1>
          <br />
        - <xsl:for-each select="trip">
          - <xsl:for-each select="option">
            - <h2>
                <b>Option:</b>
              </h2>
            - <h3>
              - <xsl:for-each select="carrier">
                  <i>Carrier:</i>
                  <xsl:value-of />
                </xsl:for-each>
              </h3>
            - <h3>
              - <xsl:for-each select="price">
                  <i>Price:</i>
                  <xsl:value-of />
                </xsl:for-each>
              </h3>
            - <xsl:for-each select="passenger-list">
              - <h3>
                  <i>Passengers List:</i>
                </h3>
              - <xsl:for-each select="person">
                - <h3>
                    <xsl:value-of select="@fname" />
                    <xsl:value-of select="@lname" />
```

Figure 2.5

Opening an XML document (in this case an XML style sheet—XSLT) with IE 5.5 for Mac.

Figure 2.6

Browser-based XML integration is useful for prototyping and debugging XML solutions.

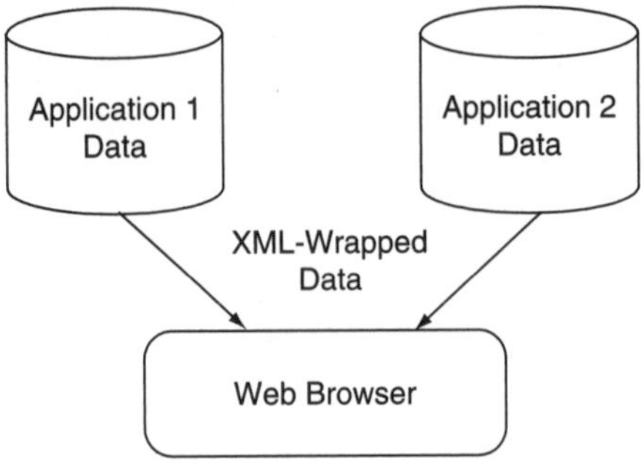

understand the structure of XML, they can be used to illustrate how XML can be used to integrate disparate data items.

Figure 2.6 illustrates how browsers can be used to achieve integration on a small scale if both sources of data (in this case from applications 1 and 2) are "wrapped" in the appropriate XML. This is not to say that you should depend on your browser to manage your data integration, but a browser can be a valuable means of prototyping and debugging XML solutions.

Integration via Hub and Spoke

We can extend the model of this example to further illustrate the power of XML. Figure 2.7 shows how the addition of an XML parser or processor can be used to ensure that application 3 can "understand" the data of any application wrapped in the appropriate XML.

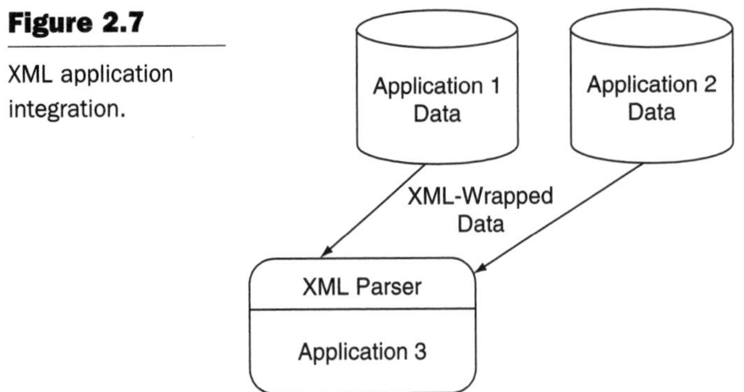

Figure 2.7

XML application integration.

Extending the previous example leads to one of the most important XML architectural devices—the hub and spoke integration model. XML and the transformation powers permit organizations to take advantage of interconnectivity. While realizing that not every application is connected to every other application, it is useful to realize the ranges that are of concern here.

Figure 2.8 shows that the possible number of interconnections that an organization would be required to maintain is given by the following formula:

$$(N*(N-1))/1$$

where N is the number of interfaces and we get a total of 15 interfaces that might be required to completely interconnect 6 applications. When the number of applications that might need interconnecting reaches 60, then N becomes 1,770. (Some would argue for higher numbers because interfaces are typically developed to work in one direction only.) That the same interconnection could be resolved using just 60 interfaces illustrates the efficacy of the adoption of a hub and spoke solution to this problem, since the XML hub approach requires N connections for N applications. The XML hub approach requires a number of connections that grows proportionately to the number of applications present. This shift in thinking about the way systems are connected has actually been around for quite some time. What XML really brings to the table here is the ability to use freely available software components to facilitate the connection to the

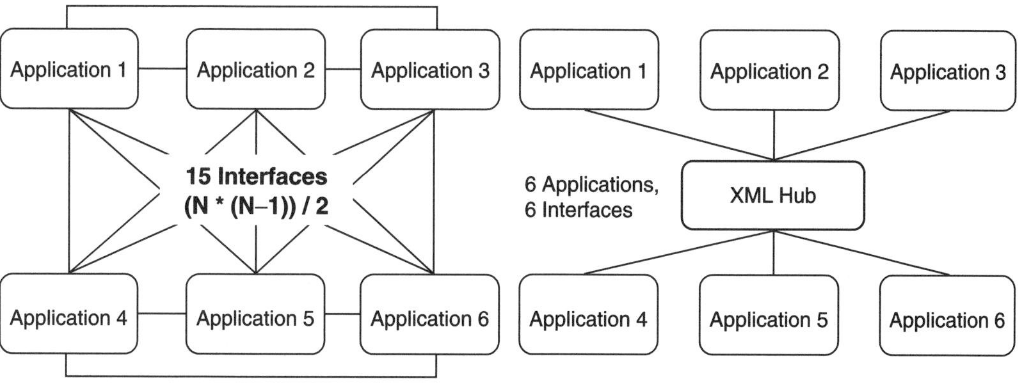

Figure 2.8

Interconnections between applications using point-to-point organization versus an XML hub.

hub, and the tremendous benefits that come from the "ripple effect" as all systems start to use this interface.

A virtual hub and spoke implementation is illustrated in Figure 2.9. As each application becomes aware of XML, it is able to "understand" and translate the mapping between the internally required data formats and the XML-wrapped data from each application. This is not an intuitive understanding of concepts like humans have, but rather a structural understanding of the pairing of metadata with data in XML. In Figure 2.9, just the finance data is wrapped initially. Once at least one other application (for example, the Mfg. data) can understand the XML-wrapped finance data, the business value from the use of XML becomes apparent. This is because data engineers can correctly specify the transformations required to make data from one application useful to other applications.

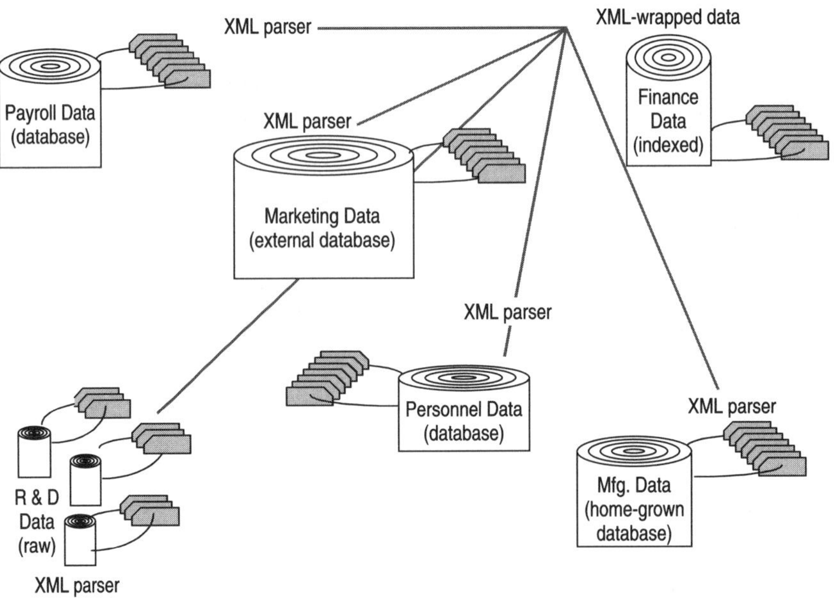

Figure 2.9

Virtual hub and spoke implementation.

There are two main ways to expand the way that organizations deal with XML.

- One way is to increase the number of applications that can understand the XML-wrapped finance data. The parser itself does not understand the data, but allows the application to understand it by using the metadata.
- The other way of expanding XML capabilities is to increase the number of tags that each application is able to "understand." Adding new sets of tags might be as simple as replacing a table. Technically, all that is happening is that you are expanding the rules that each application understands and trying to maintain them so each application might implement the same rules using different technologies. Adding "understanding" of XML-wrapped data from new applications is done using a single source of entry and maintenance.

Figure 2.9 depicts a situation that can be described in terms of three different organizational levels. First, consider the situation as presented—multiple applications working in concert to support attainment of objectives. We will refer to this as the 100% view. The smaller view (say 25%) is that instead of applications, the code components are subroutines that need to communicate with each other. XML in this view facilitates the interconnectivity between application subsystems. There is also an interorganizational view (say 500%) where instead of cooperating systems within an organization, the applications are cooperating business partners and the interfaces are connected to external entities. In each instance, the XML hub and spoke architectural model supports the business objectives, decreasing the effort spent in dealing with data interchange and transformation.

B2B Example

While the term B2B (business to business) may not seem as useful now that we are on the bust side of the .COM boom, the next example will show how XML was used to solve a problem at a major airline by implementing the hub that we just described.

World Wide Airlines needed to solve the data integration problem described in Figure 2.10. World Wide (WW) needed to get large amounts of data into its Mileage Accounting and Reporting System (MARS).

The data was provided by many different business partners, each sending in data using its own format. Transforming the data from each business partner was originally done using standard "conversion programs" consisting of spaghetti code implementing countless transformation rules.

Replacing the transformation portion of the system required separating the conversion rules from the remainder of the code. The business value added by the program was now focused on

- Reward rates (within and across partners)
- Distinguishing different status program participants
- Integrating rotating promotional offers
- Integrating with airline booking systems
- Integrating with affiliated airline web sites
- Printing accurate and timely statement packages

World Wide simply asked that each affiliate wrap the data using XML before sending it to MARS. This enabled them to decode the tags used, clarify any confusion, and encode the XML into a big parsing engine that focused on putting the data into the correct format required by MARS. There were two main benefits to this approach—not only were the savings substantial since there was much less manual data analysis of problematic

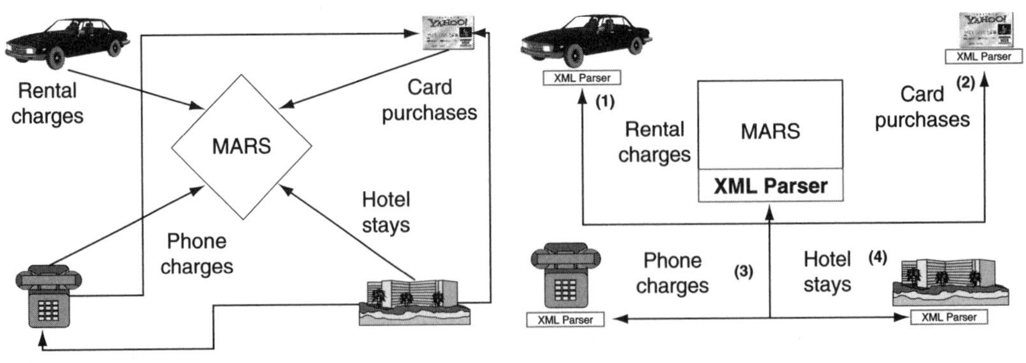

Figure 2.10

Before and after XML implementation supporting MARS data importation.

input, but call center volumes decreased as well, as fewer customers had problems with what did go through.

For other data managers, let us abstract this to something more generally useful. Many organizations must deal with the flow of various forms of data—a credit card company that pulls credit reports from many different bureaus; an insurance carrier that electronically resells and purchases policies; or a pharmaceutical company that receives data related to studies on its upcoming products. In any case, we know that this data is often difficult to deal with because the producers usually send it whichever way is most convenient for them. The MARS example points out that it is possible to agree on a central format—XML—that both parties can deal with. That format in turn is specified in terms of the vital metadata involved in the process. XML as a format is a compromise, and a good one. The vendor is not imposing its own pet data format on the consumer of data, and the consumer is not imposing its format on the vendor. Both are able to get what is needed from the transaction by compromising, with the crucial metadata at the center of that compromise.

Legacy Application Conversion

In this next example, the hub is replaced by an XML message bus that is used to manage the flow of XML-wrapped data between system components.

XML played a key role in selling a legacy application conversion to management and technically performing it. This effort has been partially described elsewhere (see Swafford et al., 2000). The core legacy system was more than 16 million lines of COBOL. The overall plan of the project was broken down into three steps:

1. Split the system into smaller chunks. Enable better understanding of it using the "divide and conquer" approach.
2. Allow communication between areas of the system using an XML message bus. By using this bus, components could talk to one another in the way seen in Figure 2.8.
3. Reengineer the components simultaneously using modern methods and technologies. By breaking down the system into parts, different groups could work on each part individually, speeding progress.

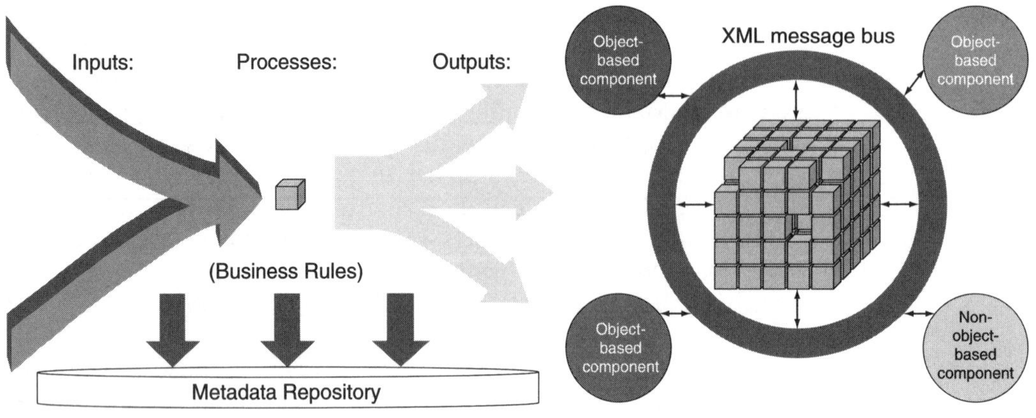

Figure 2.11

Overview of legacy architecture conversion project—changing the tires on the bus as it is rolling down the road—replace existing, understood components with more maintainable/better-performing components.

This approach was ultimately successful (see Krantz, 2003). Figure 2.11 illustrates how each individual component was added to the XML-based repository. The value of this repository lies in its ability to store XML descriptions of the components that the system was broken down into. These components were used to develop improved functionality using object- and non-object-oriented technologies. By storing the components individually and examining their descriptions, it was also possible to see where effort was being duplicated. Components could then be altered to work together more efficiently. When a project is undertaken that breaks a system up into components and changes them while the system is still functioning, we refer to this as "changing the tires on the bus while it rolls down the road."

The value of this example is that data managers do not have to pull the plug on a system and tear it down to the ground in order to make substantial improvements. These systems can be broken down into logical components that are examined individually. By understanding the relationships between them, individual components can be changed and plugged back into the system.

XML relates to this approach in two ways. First, it can facilitate communication between components when there is an "XML hub" through which the components can send information. Second, it provides a method for actually representing the components, so that their metadata and interaction with the rest of the system can be better understood. The information that goes into an XML representation of the components is typically taken from the subject matter experts who work with the system. The process of representing this in XML is situation specific and non trivial, but when it is accomplished, it provides a level of architectural freedom that can be used to take old, groaning systems and make them do things one might not have thought possible.

XML Conversion

Next are two longer examples illustrating the importance of understanding XML architecture when using it to solve an organizational data interchange problem.

Since the move to XML will inevitably involve a substantial amount of work converting existing data to XML, it is appropriate to take a look at an example of such an effort, as well as to point out the potential pitfalls and benefits. This particular example involved two companies—one will be referred to as MedCorp, a large multinational health company, and the other is the actual firm Data Blueprint, our university spin-off company that develops and delivers data and metadata solutions.

The Challenge

MedCorp approached Data Blueprint about converting about 15,000 legacy HTML documents that contained internal documentation into an XML format. MedCorp actually stored their documents in a number of different formats, but most often referred to the HTML edition. One problem they were experiencing was that the format used to create the print edition of their documentation was not the HTML edition, so that when corrections were made to the HTML edition, they often didn't find their way back to the original. With several different formats floating around the organization, change management was rapidly becoming a nightmare with the growing need for resources to keep all editions in sync enough for them to be useable.

Display of the documents was also an issue. Ideally, MedCorp wanted to be able to deploy these documents to other platforms as well, such as wireless phones or PDAs for salesmen in the field, but they weren't about to try to manage yet another edition of the documentation, given all the problems they were already having. What was really needed was a way to store the documents centrally in one place, where all modifications would be made. The actual presentation of the documents could then be regenerated automatically from the source documents by pressing a button as the need arose. Enter XML. One of its most basic strengths is *write it once and read it everywhere* (see Figure 2.12).

The Process

The project consisted of different parts, which would in the end yield a master set of documentation for MedCorp that could be easily managed, edited, and repurposed. The steps of the conversion process included

1. Requirements Gathering and Planning—Before even starting the project, it is critical to have a solid idea of exactly what is desired as a result of the project. This allows efforts to be focused on critical goals, and non-value-added work may be avoided.
2. Construction of the Data Model—A solid representation of the data in the documents was needed. The data model must not only accurately reflect the current contents of the documents, it must also take into account relationships within and between documents, as well as potential future enhancements and modifications.
3. Creation of an Automated XML Conversion Process—In this step, a toolset had to be developed that would extract the data out of the source documents and populate a new XML document.
4. Quality Assurance—In order to assure that documents are converted properly, random samples must be taken and inspected to ensure that all of the source data has been transitioned.
5. Presentation—A presentation framework must be created to allow for rapid repurposing of the resulting XML documents. This phase involves the distribution of the data in a number of different formats on different platforms.

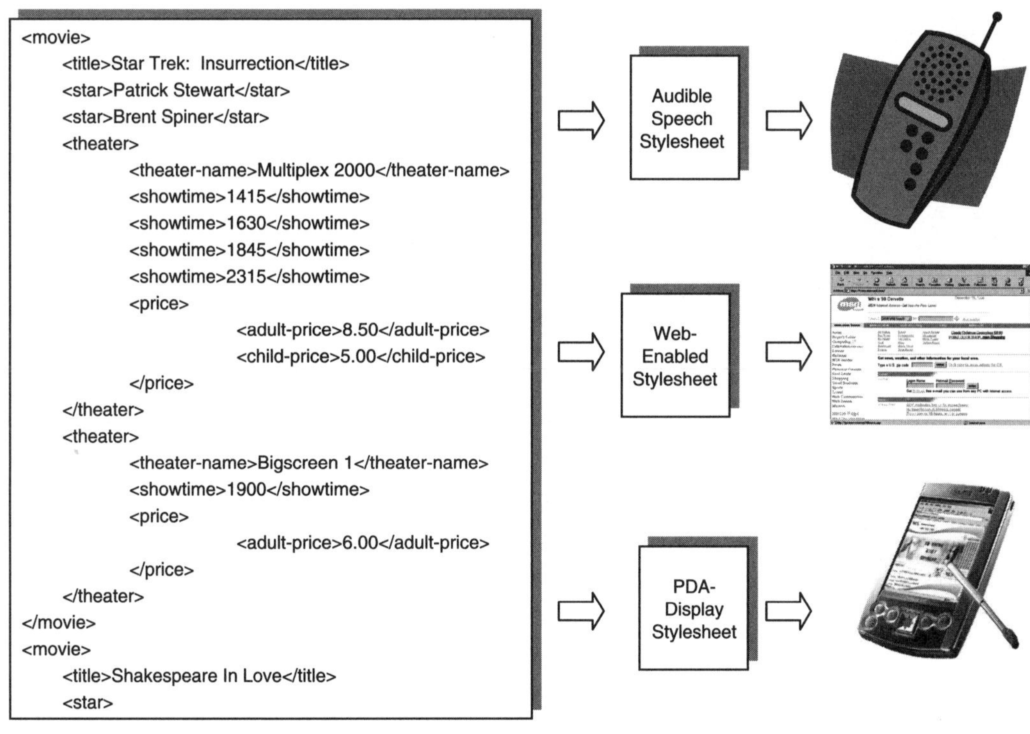
<movie>
<title>Star Trek: Insurrection</title>
<star>Patrick Stewart</star>
<star>Brent Spiner</star>
<theater>
<theater-name>Multiplex 2000</theater-name>
<showtime>1415</showtime>
<showtime>1630</showtime>
<showtime>1845</showtime>
<showtime>2315</showtime>
<price>
<adult-price>8.50</adult-price>
<child-price>5.00</child-price>
</price>
</theater>
<theater>
<theater-name>Bigscreen 1</theater-name>
<showtime>1900</showtime>
<price>
<adult-price>6.00</adult-price>
</price>
</theater>
</movie>
<movie>
<title>Shakespeare In Love</title>
<star>
Audible Speech Stylesheet
Web-Enabled Stylesheet
PDA-Display Stylesheet

Figure 2.12

Write it once and read it everywhere! (Source unknown.)

Important Outcomes and Insights

There were several important project outcomes:

- The material was completely converted to XML, delivered on time and under budget.
- Data siphoning was developed as a new semi-automated technology for wrapping XML—capturing the content of some object in order to be able to subsequently manage the content in XML form. This often requires content re-architecting (see Figure 2.13).

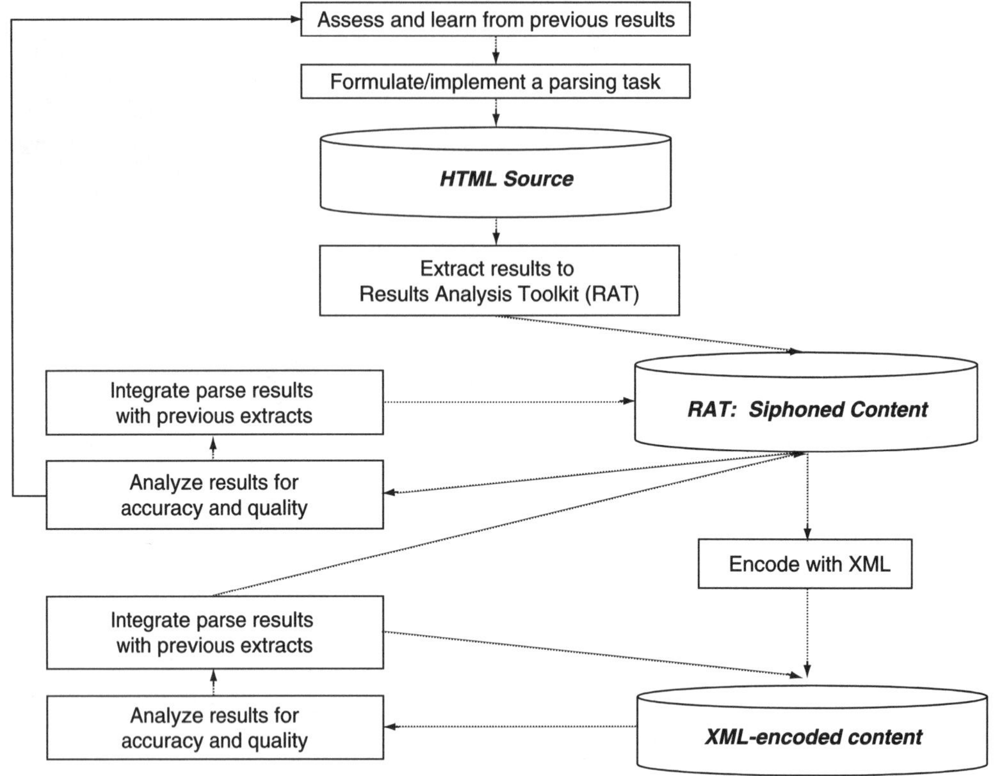

Figure 2.13

XML siphoning technique.

- Conversion facilities were slowly developed and made available to the business team participants who had initial problems "viewing" the conversion results. These conversions in turn were built on other XML components.
- Indexing and other restructuring decisions dictated use of "conversion freezes" and limited subsequent architectural options.

The last one is hardly typical but bears repeating. Earlier recognition of unanticipated business requirements would have made it possible to increase efficiency. Instead, many business requirements surfaced after conversion freezes—other business requirements were assumed; for example, the need to create new materials, new linking and navigation structures within XML, and code retention from the original HTML through to the XML.

Given this last bullet point, the real lesson was that it is important to identify all architectural decisions before the process begins, to prevent the substantial amount of work that it takes to change those decisions and assumptions midstream. When organizations underestimate the value of the baseline architecture, they are more likely to neglect proper planning in the initial stages, and later in the project they may want to change some of their earlier faulty assumptions. One prominent example that required a work-around was the determination of the actual physical XML file sizes. Selection of a physical size below a certain "object size" required the development of a programmatic work-around. The difference forced by the rework is illustrated in Figure 2.14.

To wrap up this example, we offer a few important points on the process of converting data from its original format to XML:

- The process can and has been successfully accomplished by many organizations.
- It is important to identify the use of the data that is being converted—its metadata—along with the architectural requirements of how the resulting XML will be used. It can make the difference between a project that runs smoothly, and a much more costly engagement.

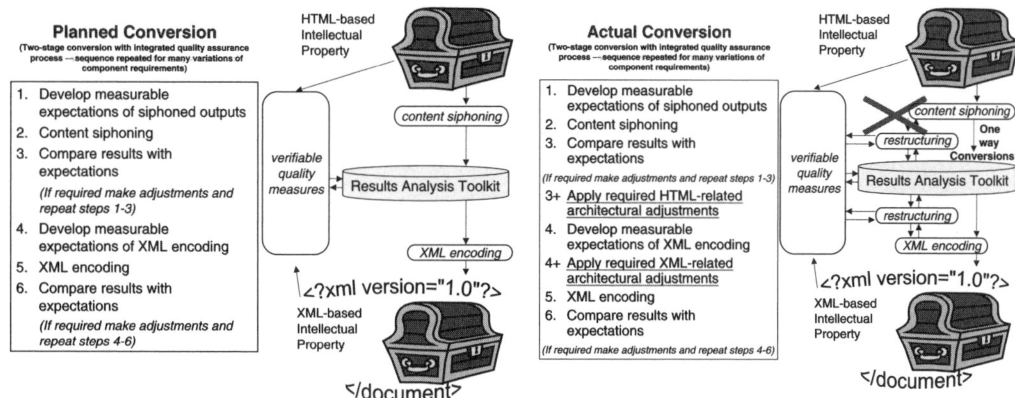

Figure 2.14

Planned and actual XML conversions due to incomplete architectural requirements.

- If the process is performed correctly, the resulting XML data will be more valuable than the source was, in part because of the work put into the metadata and architectural aspects of that data.

Metadata Management Example

We close the chapter with an example of how the role of XML was made visible by one organization who used it to make some of their legacy metadata more useable.

The preceding example makes obvious the reasons for carefully integrating your XML and your DM operations. The next example describes a more practical introductory approach to organization XML learning where we have taken some rather cumbersome legacy documentation and made it more accessible by evolving it into XML.

Imagine a typical legacy system that an organization is trying to eliminate before moving to a newer system that will provide more flexibility. As a major component of the migration process, the data and processes from the legacy system must be thoroughly understood, extracted, and cleaned before they can be moved over to the new system. Typical for most systems, the data ideally should have been online yesterday. The primary documentation for the functions and processes of the legacy system is a 700-page Word document that describes the functional decomposition of the system (see Figure 2.15). The legacy system itself is composed of a total of 1,887 units, of which 35 are high-level functions and 1,852 are processes. New programmers were given copies of this document in MS-Word format to help them understand the functionality.

Metadata Identification and Extraction

The gigantic document itself is fairly well structured, laying out the hierarchy of functions and processes and how they relate to each other. Still, there is no way to effectively take advantage of this structure since searching through the documents for particular strings is slow, and often returns "false positives" of a particular term used in a context other than what was meant. (For example, searching for a particular function might first find it in the context of being a subordinate of some other function, rather than finding its actual definition.) Ideally, the document would be extensively

Figure 2.15

MMS functional decomposition.

Activity Definition

Model : MMS FINAL

06 Apr. 2003

Name:	AMS_ASSET_MANAGEMENT
	DESC: This function includes requisitioning, inventory control, as well as maintaining master files, reference files and generation of reports.
	The requisition-processing systems edit and validate requisitions, referrals, passing orders, and requisition-related documents. The inventory-control systems maintains physical inventories, accomplishes-location reconciliation, support Depot Balance Transaction Register, control item/balance freezes, and reviews on-hand assets.
Type:	Function
Subordinate of:	MMS_MANAGEMENT
Subordinates:	AMS_PROCESS_REQSN_RELTD_TYPE_DOC AMS_PROCESS_RECEIPTS AMS_PERFORM_LOGISTIC_REASSESSMENT AMS_MANAGE_DISCREPANCIES AMS_MAINTAIN_INVENTORY_CONTROL AMS_DETERMINE_STOCK_POSITIONING AMS_CONTROL_GFM
Name:	AMS_CONTROL_GFM
Description:	ORIGIN: MMS
	DESC: Geneva Furnished Material (GFM) Control. The Geneva Furnished Material (GFM) subsystem involves the establishment and maintenance of an accountable system for tracking Geneva Furnished Material (GFM), Geneva Loaned Property (GLP), and Geneva Furnished Equipment (GFE) in the hands of End Item contractors. This function includes Provide GFM Control and Management Control Activity (MCA) Control. The GFM Control provides a complete audit trail of all issues, receipts, returns, and adjustments relating to each End Item contract. The MCA Control ensures that only authorized GFN, GFE, and GLP are issued to authorized End Item Contractors.
	LEGACY: None.
Type:	Function
Subordinate of:	AMS_ASSET_MANAGEMENT

cross-referenced, allowing the reader to jump back and forth from any point to any other point according to what was relevant at the time. Since the functions and processes are arranged hierarchically, it would be useful to be able to move up the tree and down it, but also across it, enabling the analyst to take a look at the sibling nodes in the tree for any particular item.

What is needed here is effective management and application of the metadata, since that is really all the document is. XML in and of itself does not automatically do this, but what it does provide is a solid framework in which the concepts of interest can be articulated and exploited. The first step is to take the original document and use its inherent structure to build a corresponding XML document that marks each element of data in the document appropriately. The purpose of this stage is to attach names and meanings to individual pieces of data, rather than having them float around in amorphous blocks of text. The second stage then is to exploit this newly created structure to make the document more readable and searchable, so that the analysts can better understand the legacy system they are working with and spend more of their time solving problems, and less of it working around the annoyances of the original manual's inadequate data representation.

Figure 2.16 shows a conversion example. It is it clear that the text of the document implies a certain structure to the data without actually specifying that structure. Converting the information into XML allows particular data items to be explicitly referred to according to their metadata. For example, when searching the original Word document for the term "Function_5," many dozens of matches might have been found—one where Function_5 was defined, one where it was listed as a child of another function, yet another where it was listed as a reference from some other process. By wrapping the data in XML, the analyst can essentially "ask" the document more specific questions using the metadata—"Show me the item that refers to Function_5 as a child," instead of "Show me everything about Function_5."

Presentation

Once the data has been extracted from its original semi-structured format, some way of presenting it to users must be devised. The original Word document itself was in something of a presentation format in that the document was page oriented, and had the concept of particular fonts and sizes attached to portions of text. Even though the original document was meant for presentation, now that the data has been moved to an XML for-

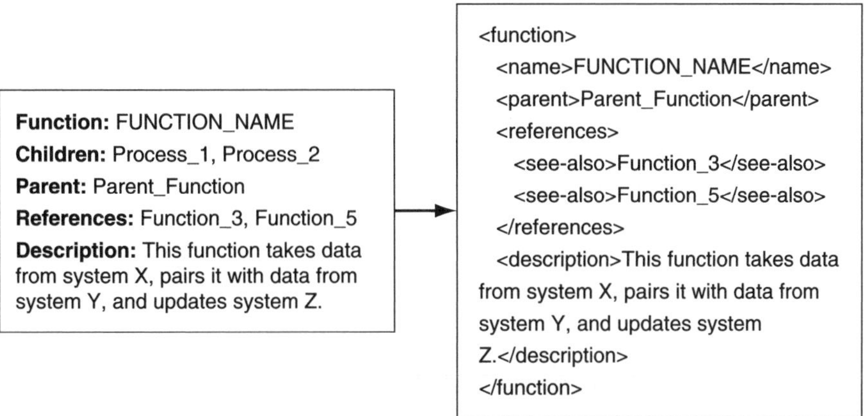

Function: FUNCTION_NAME
Children: Process_1, Process_2
Parent: Parent_Function
References: Function_3, Function_5
Description: This function takes data from system X, pairs it with data from system Y, and updates system Z.
<function>
<name>FUNCTION_NAME</name>
<parent>Parent_Function</parent>
<references>
<see-also>Function_3</see-also>
<see-also>Function_5</see-also>
</references>
<description>This function takes data from system X, pairs it with data from system Y, and updates system Z.</description>
</function>

Figure 2.16

Converting a structured Word document into XML.

mat, a number of additional presentation options are available. Normally in Word or HTML format, the presentation would have been hard-wired and would not be modifiable without a serious reworking of the document. Putting the data into an XML format helps us focus on the data of the document, and to see the presentation as arising as a consequence of the relationships inside of the data, instead of seeing presentation as a unique way to simply throw the data up onto the screen.

Access to the metadata that is clearly marked in the XML document opens up new presentation possibilities. The original Word document contained a seemingly endless procession of blocks of text, each describing a particular function or process. With the addition of contextual data in the XML document comes the ability to have the presentation layer take advantage of it. In this case, the presentation of the document was completely reengineered to take advantage of the data about the relationships between the data items. Instead of presenting "chunks" of information about each process, the data was rearranged into a family tree, and navigation became possible up, down, and across the tree. The processes and functions in the document were no longer thought of as blocks of text, but as valuable links between other processes and functions.

Further, since the complete list of what constitutes a function or a process was available, it became possible to have an "index" into the document at any time. From within a browser, the user could view all of the data about a particular function or process, while also having links to related information, and an index on the left-hand side of the screen showing all other data items that were in the same family. The goal of presentation should be to provide a number of different ways of looking at the data wherever possible, since the more options the information consumers have in terms of drilling into the data, the more likely they are to find what they need quickly. The only way these different options can be provided is by understanding the relationships inherent in the data, and how everything fits together. Understanding the relationships in the data and formalizing that understanding is the process of identifying and documenting the metadata.

Converting Documents to XML

For structured documents like the one in this example, the process of converting the data from its original form to XML is relatively straightforward. Particular items in predetermined places in the source data correspond to well-known data items. There are a number of up-and-coming technologies that allow unstructured data in a number of different formats to be converted into XML documents. Generally, there are few problems with converting tabular and relational data into XML; most of the work in that case deals with finding the appropriate tags and nesting rules that form an overall coherent data model. However, in the case of unstructured information, the source data can be quite a bit more unruly. Take for example most current HTML pages, which describe how the page looks, but nothing at all about what is actually in the page. The analyst can either choose to use one of several widely available software packages to parse the data out of the unstructured format and wrap it in XML, or develop a small custom program to extract particular pieces of information out of documents. Typically, the amount of effort that is required to convert documents is directly related to how structured the document already was. For highly structured documents, less effort will be needed, while for very unstructured documents, the process is far more challenging.

In the context of extracting data, we sometimes refer to the idea of "metadata markers," or particular "flags" seen in unstructured data that would normally signify to humans that a particular type of data is coming. In the above example, the word "Function" followed by a colon might act as a metadata marker for the function data. Converting unstructured information to XML is largely an exercise of locating the appropriate metadata markers, extracting the data that it is marking, and wrapping the result in a more appropriate XML tag. The XML tags in a document are themselves basically metadata markers. The advantage to using them over unstructured formats is that they were designed expressly for that purpose, while unstructured formats generally have ad hoc metadata markers that are frequently misleading or incomplete. Figures 2.17 and 2.18 illustrate the conversion outcome.

Overall, this example touches on several different issues. For data managers, it illustrates how XML can be useful for presenting, storing, and manipulating metadata about systems. It also provides another example of how document conversion can be accomplished, and how this conversion is not always done from source data, but sometimes from semi-structured information that represents system documentation. XML is a valuable tool for data managers in many different phases of system migration projects. In this example, we refer to the metadata of the system being migrated; in other cases, XML may be involved with the actual data being migrated, it might be used as a method of communication between the new system and other systems, or in any number of other areas.

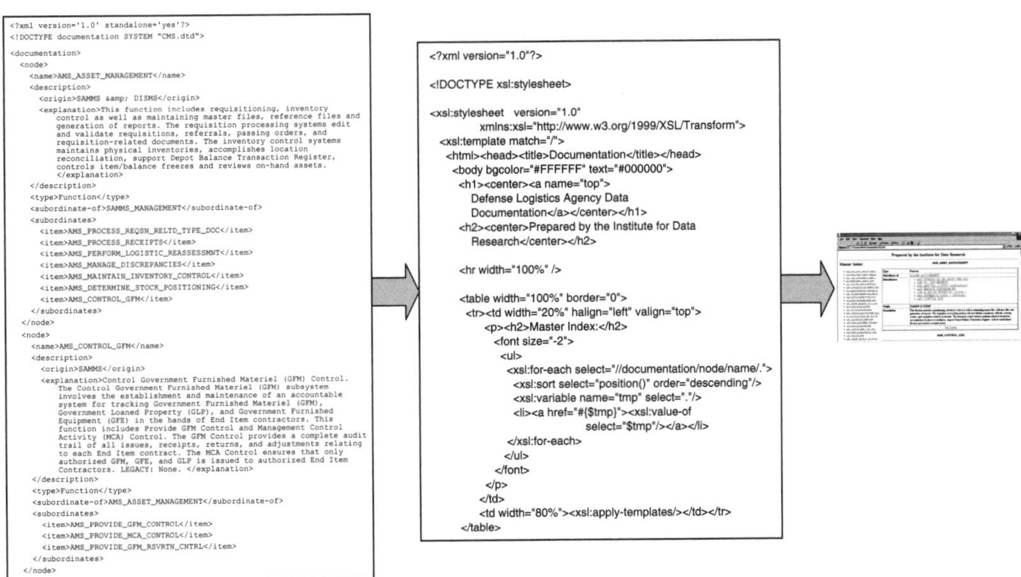

```
<?xml version='1.0' standalone='yes'?>
<!DOCTYPE documentation SYSTEM "CMS.dtd">

<documentation>
  <node>
    <name>AMS_ASSET_MANAGEMENT</name>
    <description>
      <origin>SAMMS &amp; DISMS</origin>
      <explanation>This function includes requisitioning, inventory
         control as well as maintaining master files, reference files and
         generation of reports. The requisition processing systems edit
         and validate requisitions, referrals, passing orders, and
         requisition-related documents. The inventory control systems
         maintains physical inventories, accomplishes location
         reconciliation, support Depot Balance Transaction Register,
         controls item/balance freezes and reviews on-hand assets.
         </explanation>
    </description>
    <type>Function</type>
    <subordinate-of>SAMMS_MANAGEMENT</subordinate-of>
    <subordinates>
      <item>AMS_PROCESS_REQSN_RELTD_TYPE_DOC</item>
      <item>AMS_PROCESS_RECEIPTS</item>
      <item>AMS_PERFORM_LOGISTIC_REASSESSMNT</item>
      <item>AMS_MANAGE_DISCREPANCIES</item>
      <item>AMS_MAINTAIN_INVENTORY_CONTROL</item>
      <item>AMS_DETERMINE_STOCK_POSITIONING</item>
      <item>AMS_CONTROL_GFM</item>
    </subordinates>
  </node>
  <node>
    <name>AMS_CONTROL_GFM</name>
    <description>
      <origin>SAMMS</origin>
      <explanation>Control Government Furnished Materiel (GFM) Control.
         The Control Government Furnished Materiel (GFM) subsystem
         involves the establishment and maintenance of an accountable
         system for tracking Government Furnished Materiel (GFM),
         Government Loaned Property (GLP), and Government Furnished
         Equipment (GFE) in the hands of End Item contractors. This
         function includes Provide GFM Control and Management Control
         Activity (MCA) Control. The GFM Control provides a complete audit
         trail of all issues, receipts, returns, and adjustments relating
         to each End Item contract. The MCA Control ensures that only
         authorized GFM, GFE, and GLP is issued to authorized End Item
         Contractors. LEGACY: None. </explanation>
    </description>
    <type>Function</type>
    <subordinate-of>AMS_ASSET_MANAGEMENT</subordinate-of>
    <subordinates>
      <item>AMS_PROVIDE_GFM_CONTROL</item>
      <item>AMS_PROVIDE_MCA_CONTROL</item>
      <item>AMS_PROVIDE_GFM_RSVRTN_CNTRL</item>
    </subordinates>
  </node>
```

```
<?xml version="1.0"?>

<!DOCTYPE xsl:stylesheet>

<xsl:stylesheet version="1.0"
        xmlns:xsl="http://www.w3.org/1999/XSL/Transform">
  <xsl:template match="/">
   <html><head><title>Documentation</title></head>
    <body bgcolor="#FFFFFF" text="#000000">
     <h1><center><a name="top">
       Defense Logistics Agency Data
       Documentation</a></center></h1>
     <h2><center>Prepared by the Institute for Data
       Research</center></h2>

     <hr width="100%" />

     <table width="100%" border="0">
      <tr><td width="20%" halign="left" valign="top">
        <p><h2>Master Index:</h2>
         <font size="-2">
          <ul>
           <xsl:for-each select="//documentation/node/name/.">
            <xsl:sort select="position()" order="descending"/>
            <xsl:variable name="tmp" select="."/>
            <li><a href="#{$tmp}"><xsl:value-of
                             select="$tmp"/></a></li>
           </xsl:for-each>
          </ul>
         </font>
        </p>
       </td>
       <td width="80%"><xsl:apply-templates/></td></tr>
     </table>
```

Figure 2.17

After conversion to XML, the contents are created as HTML by passing it through an XSLT transformation.

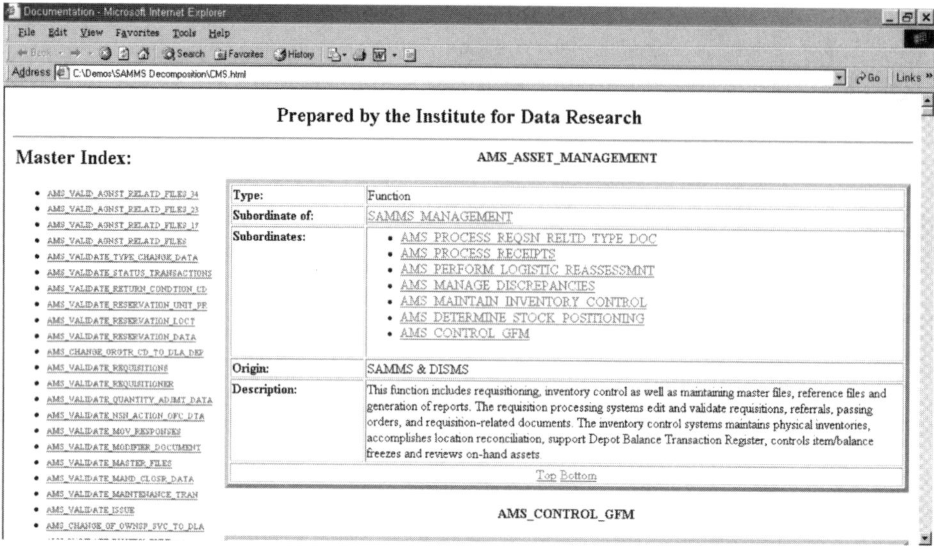

Figure 2.18

Conversion from a structured document to an immediately useful XML utility.

Chapter Summary

This concludes a chapter that has attempted to provide you with a good overview of how XML works and how it is used in practice. It has covered basic XML rules and format, how XML differs from other technologies such as HTML, and a number of examples of the XML's architectural concepts at work. When data managers embark on systems work, the work usually falls into one or more of several categories:

- Building a new system
- Modifying an existing system
- Simply understanding how something that is already in place operates
- Converting data for use in a system
- Facilitating communication between systems

In all of these situations, there is a potential application for XML. For the data manager, it is more important that he or she understands how XML fits into the architectural "big picture" than it is to know the nuances of XML syntax. This chapter has provided a number of examples of how XML fits into systems work. With this basic understanding, we can now build on it to take a look at the different technology components of XML, and how these can be applied to build higher-level solutions. Many other usages of XML are described in other upcoming chapters, particularly in these two areas, which have entire chapters devoted to them:

- Toolkits and XML frameworks (RosettaNet, BizTalk, ebXML, etc.). Companies build toolkits based on XML, creating further "layering" of standards to provide particular services.
- XML-based portal implementation

These examples present a number of ways that XML has been applied in support of DM functions. While there isn't enough room here to catalog the specific benefits accruing to the developing organization, we believe you will see how you as a system builder can consider XML as a new tool in your builder's toolkit.

References

Ahmed, K., Ayers, D., et al. (2001). *Professional XML meta data*. Birmingham, AL: Wrox Press.

Aiken, P. (2001). *XML conversion observations*. Proceedings of the XML and Meta-Data Management & Technical Conference, Dallas, TX, Wiltshire Conferences.

Bean, J. (2003). *XML for data architects*. New York: Morgan Kaufmann/Elsevier.

Bosak, J., & Bray, T. (1999). XML and the second-generation Web: The combination of hypertext and a global Internet started a revolution. A new ingredient, XML, is poised to finish the job. *Scientific American*.

Chaudhri, A., Rashid, A., et al. (2003). *XML data management: Native XML and XML-enabled data systems*. Boston: Addison-Wesley.

Dick, K. (2000). *XML: A manager's guide*. Boston: Addison-Wesley.

Hammer, M., & Champy, J. (1993). *Reengineering the corporation*. New York: Harper Business Press.

Krantz, G. (2003). *Architecting your data center with XML*. TechTarget Network. SearchTechTarget.com; search390.com; techtarget.com. Hall of Fame.

Swafford, D., Elman, D., et al. (2000). Experiences reverse engineering manually. *CSMR 2000*. Zurich, Switzerland: IEEE Publishing.

3

XML Component Architecture (as it relates to DM)

Introduction

When people discuss XML, it is sometimes unclear exactly what they are referring to. XML consists of a growing number of architectural components that we will describe in this chapter. We start off with a description of the design goals, and how these goals influenced XML's development. Understanding these design goals gives data managers insight into how XML is different, and how it has avoided some of the drawbacks associated with other technologies. Next, in a section called "What XML Is Not," we further explore the most common issue that have caused confusion about XML. The next section describes the overall organization of the components, and how they evolved. The rest of the chapter is devoted to individual descriptions of the various components. Covered in this chapter are DTD, XML Schema, DOM, XPath, XLink, XPointer, XSL, XSLT, RDF, SOAP, WSDL, UDDI, and ADML—a veritable alphabet soup of XML acronyms. At the end of the chapter, you will have a more complete picture of the constellation of components, and you will understand what is meant when "XML" is referred to in various contexts, along with a solid list of capabilities it brings to the table.

Like many other technologies, XML tends to build on itself—the syntax acts as the foundation of the component architecture, which is built up through multiple levels, each addressing an area of functional need. Nearly all the various XML components are either built on the core XML syntax, or with it in mind. This is a very important point that will be illuminated throughout the chapter. Building these new component technologies on top of an XML language-based foundation has a number of advantages:

1. Since XML is an open standard, new developments have something stable, open, and accepted to use as a foundation.
2. Since XML is a powerful data representation language, new technologies have ready-made facilities for expressing business rules, programming code structures, data structures, and for that matter any type of information that can be represented digitally.
3. The wide availability of XML-processing software means that if new technologies are constructed using XML, existing software such as parsers and processors may be of use in working with the newly created XML-based technologies.
4. XML tools and technologies that are created using XML will retain the advantages of XML as well as its stability and flexibility.
5. Vendors are discouraged from creating proprietary versions of XML because tools and technologies built on top of XML will not work. This will effectively prevent XML from suffering the fate of Java.

Since XML is widely used and still growing, the component list presented here does not cover every component that currently exists, but concentrates on the most important items as they relate to data management technologies. New development in the future will likely be centered on two distinct areas—refining existing components to better address evolving requirements, and creating components in areas where new needs are being discovered. In order to better understand where XML is coming from and how it avoids some of the pitfalls of other systems, it is a good idea to explore the design goals and how they affect the overall component architecture.

XML Design Considerations

XML Design Goals

When the core XML standard was created, mindful of the Java controversies, the creators began with a number of important design goals.* These design goals describe something akin to an "XML philosophy," and help explain why XML was designed to permit developers a more stable basis on which to plan their development. The following are some of the ideas that went into the development of XML from a very early stage that have greatly affected how XML is used and the advantages it provides. XML's design goals include the following:

- XML shall be straightforwardly usable over the Internet.
- It shall be easy to write programs that process XML documents.
- The number of optional features in XML is to be kept to the absolute minimum, ideally zero.
- XML documents should be human legible and reasonably clear.
- The XML design should be prepared quickly.
- The design of XML shall be formal and concise.
- XML documents shall be easy to create.
- Terseness in XML markup is of minimal importance.

Each of these goals is explained in the sections below.

XML shall be straightforwardly usable over the Internet

XML was designed in the era of the Internet, and its designers wisely decided that one way to maximize its usefulness was to make sure it was easily usable over the Internet. That meant taking steps to minimize the

---

*For more information on XML design goals, please see Bosak and Bray's *Scientific American* feature article: XML and the Second Generation Web: May 1999 http://www.sciam.com/1999/0599issue/0599bosak.html

changes that would be required for server-side software to serve up XML. Today's web servers require very little work in terms of additional configuration to serve up XML documents. The impact of this design principle on data managers is twofold. First, existing web-based data delivery systems will also require few or no architectural changes—unless they were badly architected in the first place. Second, unimplemented XML-based data delivery systems will find that today's servers are likely already equipped with tools and technologies that will greatly facilitate delivery of XML-based data structures.

Additionally, XML documents use a number of conventions that are already widespread in web-based information delivery. A good example of this is the use of URIs (Uniform Resource Identifiers). Rather than inventing a new way of referring to hosts on the Internet and to particular resources found on those hosts, as well as referring to which protocols allow access to the resources, the designers avoided reinventing the wheel by aiding Internet compatibility using existing tools, techniques and constructs. In many XML documents today, indicators that look much like World Wide Web URLs can be found. This means that XML can be implemented in existing delivery architectures without significant re-architecting or recoding.

It shall be easy to write programs that process XML documents

In order for a language to gain widespread adoption, it must be as easy as possible to implement in just about any type of computing device. Much of the early experimental XML software was originally written in the Java programming language, but today, libraries or toolkits exist for XML processing and manipulation for just about every programming language in existence. Developers aggressively reuse these (often freely) available toolkits. As a result it is now very easy to "XML-enable" applications by simply reusing software that does most of the heavy lifting for the developer automatically.

Figure 3.1 illustrates the role of the parser. "Parsers" may also be called XML "processors," which can be confusing. To help clarify, we will describe two types of parsers. The first is typically used for low-level technical purposes, by taking XML-wrapped data and converting it into some internal data structure that can then be dealt with by a programmer. Generally, though, when we use the term parser, we are referring to a slightly higher abstraction of software—a software component that can be put on top of an existing system and that acts as something of an "XML

Figure 3.1

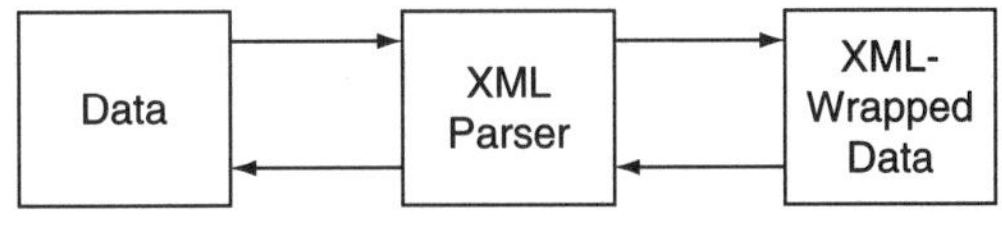

Data flowing in and out of an XML parser.

gateway." In this figure, we see that a parser might take data and wrap it in XML (as the case would be if the user were trying to export a volume of data for interoperability). The parser might also take existing XML documents that are intended for the system, and convert them into individual data items that would then be inserted at a lower level. For now it is sufficient to say that XML parsers permit data structures from an existing application to be wrapped in XML so that it can be reused by other applications that understand the XML structures. The implications of these capabilities for data managers are truly profound. This parsing technology forms the basis for enterprise application integration (EAI), and a number of other fundamental technologies. Still, it is important to keep in mind that the strength of the parser will be directly related to the strengths of the data structures with which it works.

XML has succeeded admirably with this design goal—software that processes it is proliferating rapidly. Software built around XML is currently running on supercomputers, desktop PCs, and even embedded devices such as mobile phones and PDAs. The easier it is to write software for a language, the more compact the software tends to be, which makes it possible to deploy the software on just about any platform, from embedded devices with limited memory, to huge parallel machines. This proliferation of XML-enabled software means that the reach of data managers now extends to virtually any machine that can understand XML.

What constitutes a language that is easy to process? In the case of XML, it has several features that give it this property. First, XML is simply plain text represented in Unicode. Unlike some binary data formats that require reference books to indicate byte offsets and code numbering interpretations, since XML is plain text, users already have a text editor they can use to create sample documents for testing. Second, the grammar or organizing constructs of XML, or the elements that are considered legal in the language, are very simple. This makes it easy to create compact and easy-to-maintain software programs that parse and manipulate XML. This item is intimately related to another design goal, that XML should have as few optional features as possible, which will be discussed next.

The number of optional features in XML is to be kept to the absolute minimum, ideally zero.

This particular design goal came predominantly from XML's heritage as the successor of SGML. Standard Generalized Markup Language had a reputation for containing many optional features, which tended to complicate the use of the language. The more optional features a language contains, the more difficult it is to create a working software implementation to deal with that language. While it's true that optional features may provide multiple ways of doing the same or similar things, programmers and people who are interested in computer languages often refer to these options as "syntactic sugar"—they are sweet, and may be convenient to work with for a while, but they eventually rot teeth.

The similarities between XML and SGML prompt many people to comment that the base XML specification is essentially SGML relabeled with a new acronym and without many of the arcane features of the original. XML is a subset of SGML that is less complex to use. SGML processing has been around for a long time, so there is a wealth of experience and information from which to draw—ranging from programmers to the processing systems themselves. The inherent simplicity of XML creates opportunities for implementing uncomplicated, well-structured XML applications. It also encourages the XML itself to be processed in a straightforward manner.

When using XML, there is only one way to express an attribute name and value within a particular element. The author of the document has ultimate control over which elements and attributes appear in the document, but attributes and elements have to be specified in a particular way. When there is only one way to do something, it tends to be clear and unambiguous—the software does not have to choose between many different possibilities for representing the same structure. The learning curve is also important; the fewer optional structures a language has, the easier it is to learn. When a new structure or concept is learned, it can be reused in many different contexts. The one notable exception to this is the XML singleton tag, or empty tag. If an XML tag contains no child elements, it can be written either as "<tagname></tagname>" or as "<tagname/>"—both have the same meaning. This simplicity is a welcome development for data managers who can easily transfer what they know of data and information representation concepts to XML. They are then free to concentrate on getting the semantics correct—often the more difficult task.

XML documents should be human legible and reasonably clear

Documents encoded in XML have the unique and curious property of being understandable both to humans and machines. Since the documents are just plain text files, humans can usually open them using a variety of different software packages and read their contents quite easily. Furthermore, since the element names typically correspond to words in human language that hold meaning for human readers, it is usually quite easy for a human to read and understand an XML document, even if he or she is not previously familiar with the tagging structure. While there are some exceptions to this rule, such as when the author of an XML document uses a less common character encoding, many documents can be read using the simplest of tools.

As a design goal, the results of this are that XML documents are easy to create, test, and interpret for humans. Clarity of formatting also makes it easy for newcomers to quickly pick up the technology and start work instead of spending large amounts of time with reference books, documentation, and obscure examples. This design goal is critical for the adoption of XML—one of the reasons that HTML spread as quickly as it did was because it had this same readability and ease of use. Even people who would not necessarily consider themselves very computer savvy could quickly pick up HTML and start creating their own web pages. In the same way, users can quickly pick up and begin using XML for their own tasks.

There are two considerations of this design goal that are important for data managers. First, it will enable you to get the business users to finally agree on data names. Just tell them you cannot make their application use XML unless they first give you a name for the XML tags required. As an important related issue, data managers should adopt a proactive approach to XML adoption in organizations. In situations where they have not done this, it often happens that multiple groups implement XML differently, adding to an already confusing mess. None of the above addresses another obvious advantage—that XML tagged structures are much easier to read than structures that are not delivered with their own metadata.

One final item on XML readability—there is a lot of current hype about a subject called "XML security." Certainly if an organization sends its data, and the meaning of that data, unencrypted over a variety of transmission devices, it will be much easier for industrial spies to "see" what is going on internally. But this is not an XML security problem—it is a bad system design. Many security concerns can be addressed with the judicious application of existing security measures. Because security is such an important topic, though, it should be pointed out that not everyone would agree with the authors on this point. There are many possible scenarios where XML security could be important; for example, what if most of a document was fine for everyone to see, but there were a few crucial elements that should remain protected? For these and other situations, a host of new security-related XML standards are being worked on to provide data managers with the necessary tools. Security is part of a process, rather than something that is attached to a final product. That process might include where the data comes from, where it is going, and how it is used, which are topics outside the scope of those who are simply interested in presenting data in XML. More than anything, security should be considered its own topic that needs to be addressed in depth, both within the context of XML representation and independent of XML.

The XML design should be prepared quickly

The XML standard is an evolving technology. The base components that are most frequently used have been stable since 2000. The W3C web site* maintains a list of various XML standards and their status for those who need specific information about a particular technology. The technology is far from stagnant; it is growing rapidly. One of the original design goals was that the design should be prepared quickly, since the need for the technology was immediate. The developers of XML have done an astounding job at putting together a number of world-class technologies in record time. That they were able to put it together quickly while still producing a high-quality product is a testament to the wisdom of the architectural and design decisions that went into the front end of the development process. And as the adoption rates of XML increase, the growth and development rate increases as well. Best of all, the XML design process complements everything that data managers already know about good data design.

The design of XML shall be formal and concise

The official syntax guidelines for XML are simple and easy to understand. While some languages are specified in terms of examples, counterexamples, and "how things should look," the XML definition is formalized, that is, it is written out in terms of a scientific grammar (or the formal definition of the syntactic structure of a language). The grammar specifies exactly what

*http://www.w3c.org/

is allowed and what is not in every context, so there is never any question about how XML operates. With some languages, when everything is not made explicit, the people who implement the software are left with some wiggle room to determine how the software should behave in certain circumstances. If a particular type of error is not thoroughly described and there is no specific method for handling it, some software writers will choose to handle it in one way, while others will do it in another way that happens to be more convenient for them. This results in odd differences of behavior between software programs dealing with the same input data. Users should never be in a situation where a particular document will work with one XML parser, but generate many warnings or errors when using another. It is because of this undesirable behavior that XML specified a grammar along with the description of the language, to eliminate ambiguity from the start.

To take another example specific to XML, we can look at the way elements are encoded in documents. The language dictates exactly which characters are allowed to be part of an element name, along with rules about how they must occur. Attribute specification is laid out exactly, along with how white space in documents is processed, and so on. The XML grammar does everything it can to ensure that software using it will be reliable, predictable, and robust. Leaving no loopholes in the language, no "what-if" questions unanswered, is the way XML accomplishes this.

For data managers, this formality and conciseness complements existing data designs, especially *good* data designs. In XML, language formality is akin to the rules of normalization for relational structures, and is equally important. One small difference is that XML directly supports hierarchical data structures, while it is somewhat more difficult to express the same structures in a relational context. That is not to say that XML cannot work with the relational world; it can. But since more than half of all organizational data is still stored directly in hierarchical databases, this is not as much of a problem as you might think.

XML documents shall be easy to create

It certainly would not do to develop a new data format that had to be created using a particular expensive software package, since that would defeat one of the purposes of an open standard. The ease of creating XML documents is largely related to the fact that it is done using plain text. As a result, every computer user that has a program capable of editing text already possesses the ability to create XML documents. Since the language is simple and software for processing it is ubiquitous, developers can also easily create XML documents inside of programs.

Ensuring that XML documents are easy to create is yet another aspect of a common theme running through XML's design goals—that it should have a minimal learning and application curve. XML developers want users to spend their time solving problems with the technology rather than tearing their hair out over learning it.

XML documents should be thought of by data managers as datasets containing metadata. Now instead of sending obscure bits and bytes of data over a line or on a bus, data managers can send the data and its meaning to applications that will be able to interpret it. While the true implications of this simultaneous transmission of data and metadata are not covered in detail until later in this book, experienced data managers should begin to see the possibilities.

Terseness in XML markup is of minimal importance

If the decision has to be made between having a language that is clear, and a language that is very terse and occupies the minimum number of bytes on a computer, it is often wise to choose clarity over size. This is one of the areas where XML has traditionally been criticized. When dealing with very large XML documents, users see long element names repeated thousands of times, and notice that the XML document is quite a bit larger than the same data represented in some other way. While it is true that XML documents are generally larger than other representations, a number of points are important to keep in mind:

- The size difference is a trade-off, not a penalty. When inflating the size of documents, users see a number of benefits. First, data can be expressed in a way that is clear and that leaves no doubt as to what the document means. Second, XML allows metadata to be encoded along with the source data. So even though XML tends to be larger, users are gaining extra benefits in exchange.
- Document sizes are still bounded. XML documents tend to be larger than other representations by some multiple of the original size, often a small multiple. The implications of this are that if a 5000-character document is represented in XML with twice as many characters, a 40,000-character document will also be represented in twice as many characters, not 5 times or 100 times as many characters. The size of the resulting XML document is relative to the size of the source data, and typically does not get out of hand with respect to the original document's size.

- Computer storage is cheap; human intelligence is not. This argument is frequently used in situations where technologies viewed as less efficient are being defended, but it is true. Extra disk space to store XML documents can be very cheaply acquired, if it is needed at all. But the human time and effort necessary to cope with poorly represented and unclear data are often hugely expensive. The real question about the difference in size between XML and other formats is whether or not the added benefits of the larger format are worth the difference. In the case of XML, the answer is clearly yes.
- Finally, judicious use of data compression techniques can help to offset larger file sizes. We have worked with an organization that felt it was worthwhile to encode a single character of data in a 255-character tag. This represented a large multiple in file size but was for all practical purposes eliminated when the file was compressed from 5 megabytes to 70 kilobytes!

From an operational perspective, elimination of strange abbreviations, acronyms, and other technological quirks that serve to obfuscate the data from users typically pays off in greater user comprehension, faster system diagnostics, and user affinity with their data.

Design Goal Summary

In short, the XML design goals serve to complement and even reinforce good data management practices and perhaps more importantly, they also become useful when transforming data from an existing use to a new use.

Looking at the ideas that went into the creation of XML is like looking from the inside to the outside of the technology, from the perspective of the designers. Now, let us take a look from the outside into XML, namely, some of the confusions that have arisen about it, where they came from, and in some cases the kernel of truth that lies at their core.

What XML Should Not Be Used For

Since its inception, XML has received a huge amount of hype as the next big thing that will solve all problems for all people. While some of XML's hype is well deserved, like with any other technology, hype is one part fiction and one part fact. No technology will solve all problems for all people, but XML is built on a solid foundation with substantial architectural thought that went into it from the ground up, which makes us confident in saying that it can in fact help solve many problems for many people. There are a number of common misconceptions about what it is, and what it is not, which we will cover here. The discussion that follows owes a debt to both Robert Cringely and Fabian Pascal.

The purpose of this section is to make an attempt at separating the wheat from the chaff in terms of what is claimed about XML. Effective application of XML for data managers requires a thorough understanding of what it is and is not. This knowledge allows savvy users to call vendors on the carpet when they make questionable claims, and to understand the situations in which the use of XML might be akin to pounding a square peg into a round hole. Given the amount of interest, press, and discussion that the technology has generated, this section clearly could not hope to present the total picture of inaccurate claims about XML, but the most frequently overheard will be addressed.

XML Is Not a Type of Database

The common misconception that XML is a type of database is based on a misunderstanding of what XML is, along with a somewhat inaccurate definition of what a database is. XML is not a relational database like Oracle or DB2. At its core, an XML document is simply a text document, and should not be considered any more of a database than a regular email message, which is also a text document.

Still, this area can get fairly fuzzy. First, many relational database engines are starting to incorporate XML components that allow for quick loading and dumping of data to and from XML formats. This does not make XML a database, but it becomes easier to see where the confusion stems from. In the past few years, a number of software packages have also come into the market that call themselves "XML databases," which further adds to the confusion. In fact, these "XML databases" are excellent at storing XML documents, fragments of documents, and even individual elements. Many even employ a storage and retrieval method that is modeled after the structure of an XML document. XML databases are real database packages that work with XML, but a distinction must be made between the XML language, and the external technologies that arise around the core language, which are intended to be used in conjunction with the actual XML language.

XML Is Not a Replacement for Data Modeling

XML is a powerful way of representing data, which has led many people to confuse it for a tool that helps with data modeling. In many cases, the critical aspects of data modeling involve making the decisions about which pieces of data should be stored in which places, how they should be stored, and the justification for those decisions—basically, the "where," the "how," and the "why." However, this inevitably involves application of at least one person's intelligence—people often find that completely computer-generated data models are woefully inadequate in many situations. XML does not automate the process of data modeling. Rather, one could think of XML as a giant container with infinite racks and shelves that can be configured in whichever way suits the user. The container provides a staggering number of possibilities in terms of how the data might be stored within, but of course it is still possible to choose an inefficient way to store that data that makes it hard to find and access at a later date.

Data modeling is best done by a smart human who knows his or her trade, the data, and the business for which the data is being stored—inside and out. Not only does XML not do one's data modeling automatically, even if it could, one probably would not want it to. XML descriptions of the data modeling process might be generated as a way of documenting the "wheres," "hows," and "whys" of the modeling effort, but the thoughts must be entered by a person. Once the data modeling effort is completed, of course, XML can be brought back into the picture as a representational language that allows documentation, archiving, and publishing of the knowledge that was created as a result of the effort.

XML Is Not Something with which You Should Replace Your Web Site

In discussions of technology, particularly at a sales level, one of the most common confusions arises when a technology that aids with a particular process is subsequently claimed to replace the *need* for the process, or make that process obsolete. This is unique to technology—after all, no one would confuse the help that a hammer lends in the construction of a house with the actual house itself. From the earliest days of the development of XML, it has been used on web sites in a number of different forms, to aid in the process of delivering the right documents to the right people. But just as a hammer is not a house, nor can a house be built of nothing but hammers, XML is not a web site, nor can web sites be built of nothing but XML. A web site is a large and complicated operation, frequently involving aspects of data, display, networking, hardware, and software.

XML helps substantially with issues of data storage and display, through some of the various components discussed later in the chapter. What it does *not* help with, however, is the software that actually delivers the documents to users, or coordination of the entire effort. The use of XML on web sites is growing substantially with time, from organizations that store most of their web documents in a content management system that uses XML internally, to plain XML documents converted to a display format using eXtensible Stylesheet Language Transformations (XSLT) discussed in the next section, to special formats of XML that allow web site operators to syndicate their content to other sites. This is an exciting and promising area where many efficiencies and benefits can be realized, but it is important to keep the component concepts that go into the entirety of a "web site" separate.

XML Is Not a Replacement for Electronic Data Interchange

This confusion is somewhat related to the confusion about web sites being replaced with XML. A number of electronic data interchange (EDI) applications and systems rely heavily on XML in order to do their work. The key is to identify the business reasons for replacing EDI transactions with XML; in many instances, XML can reduce the per-transaction expense typically incurred by EDI users.

Within some EDI systems, XML acts as the format in which the data is represented. It still requires additional software in order to get from place to place, however—in some ways it is easy to see how EDI confusion has arisen around XML. Thinking of XML as EDI or as a replacement for EDI is like confusing a hammer with the act of using a hammer to drive a nail. XML is like the hammer—it is a tool, but it requires action and usage in order to accomplish a task, just as a hammer does not drive nails by itself.

There are two tasks typically involved in the design of any EDI system—determining exactly how transactions should proceed, and how that information should be encoded. Quite a bit of good work has been done in the area of designing how the transactions operate. This means that using XML as the encoding portion of the EDI system allows its authors to really leverage all of their hard work in the transaction design phase and express their design decisions in terms of XML.

Since we have taken a look at a number of different confusions surrounding XML, the next step would be an attempt to trace these confusions to the misunderstanding that they arise from. Tying these confusions together by their common threads allows users to separate the legitimate claims from the baseless hype.

Confusion Conclusion

There is a pattern in the types of confusion that arise when discussing XML. This pattern is by no means specific to XML, but applies to most other technologies that benefit from heavy "buzz" for any period of time. Understanding and recognizing these confusions can help with the effective evaluation of applications of XML, as well as that of other technologies. If users were to replace the word "XML" with another technology in each of these confusions, would they recognize familiar claims about the other technology?

1. **Confusing XML with a process, when XML merely aids the process**—XML aids the process of delivering web content by providing methods of representing data and presentation, but XML is not a web site or web server.
2. **Claims that XML does something "automatically"**—Software can perform tasks automatically, and many software applications provide support and extensive use of XML, but it is important to distinguish between something being accomplished by application of the language, and something that is accomplished by application of some software package that *uses* the XML language. Nothing inherent in XML eliminates the need for solid data design skills, and failure to incorporate data design principles can result in a situation in which XML can make an existing mess worse.
3. **Claims that XML replaces something outside of its target domain**—These confusions are sometimes tricky to recognize. In some situations, it is appropriate and correct to claim that XML can replace another technology, for example, other binary-only data representation formats. But to say that XML replaces data modeling or that it accomplishes data modeling by itself is a bit too optimistic. If a particular field or practice such as data modeling is not referred to or even alluded to in the design goals of a technology, it is unlikely that the field can be replaced by the technology in question. Again, it is important to distinguish between the technology itself and applications that utilize it.

XML Component Architecture *(Parts & Pieces)*

The XML Community

Sometimes reference is made to the XML community when discussing the development of various standards and new technologies. One of the drivers of the community is the W3C (The World Wide Web Consortium), an organization founded by Tim Berners-Lee, the technical inventor of the web. The W3C has over 400 organizational members, and strives for vendor neutrality in the way that it is organized. The group is consensus driven, and before decisions are made there is typically a period of public comment on various proposals. Given the eclectic membership, the technical community considers the W3C to be an organization that is extremely comprehensive in background and expertise, and fairly representative of whose who use W3C-created technologies.

Many of the XML standards and technologies that will be discussed in this chapter were originally drafted, written, and published by the W3C. One key difference that the W3C brings to the table is a standard process that is faster than traditional processes used by other organizations. But other professional and trade organizations also exist that come together and publish their own standards, so the XML community is even broader than just the W3C. Early in the development of the language, individual hobbyist contributors played an important part in the creation of the technology foundations; they created many of the first available XML software packages.

Next, we will take a look at the way the various components fit together; their logical categories, relationships, and the real meat: what they are good for.

XML Component Organization

As a family of components, XML is extraordinarily rich and diverse. Many individuals and organizations have seized the open technology that was given them and begun to build a number of different components, most of which are related to the core XML language. These components extend XML to provide additional functionality and representational power. To have a complete picture of XML, it is a good idea to take a brief look at the parties that originally created it, and how they mesh together.

Examining the organization of the community is often the factor that convinces people that XML is a solid standard that is here to stay, rather than a temporary fad that is bound to fade.

With many different organizations and individuals creating their own XML-based technologies, it might come as a surprise to some that there has not been much duplication of effort in the XML community. Typically, the standards that have been developed are comprehensive and robust not only for the target area of the original developers, but for other areas as well—this is a theme that will be seen again and again in the review of the various components.

We put forward a method of organizing the various XML components that we will discuss in this chapter, grouped by each component's function and purpose. Some of these technologies are rather low-level standards that often are being used whether the end user knows it or not—for example, DOM and SAX. Others are much higher-level standards that are intended to facilitate complex processes, such as ADML (Architectural Definition Markup Language). Still others fall somewhere in the middle and are geared toward solving a specific problem, such as the presentation of data encoded in XML (XSL and XSLT).

Our first version of this articulation is pictured in Figure 3.2. This version had the advantage of being easy to PowerPoint audiences with. We also developed a second iteration of the XML component architecture in an attempt to simplify the message. This is shown in Figure 3.3.

Figure 3.3 shows one possible organization of a number of different XML components, grouped by purpose and relationship. As indicated by lines connecting different components, some technologies are actually descendants or extensions of other components, such as the relationship between XSL and XSLT. Not all relationships between components are diagrammed here—the interconnections between and reuse of various technologies are extensive. For example, the schema and DTD components could realistically be linked to most of the other technologies. Rather than display the almost endless numbers of connections, we will provide a thorough description of each component from which most of the connections can be inferred.

The groupings in Figure 3.3 correspond to the way users typically apply various XML technologies. If the overall XML component architecture is likened to all of the hand tools that are available at your local hardware store, certainly there will be subgroups of carpentry tools, plumbing tools, landscaping tools, and so on. Similarly, users who are interested in XML for aiding presentation and formatting tend to look to XSL and XSLT, while people who are interested in providing

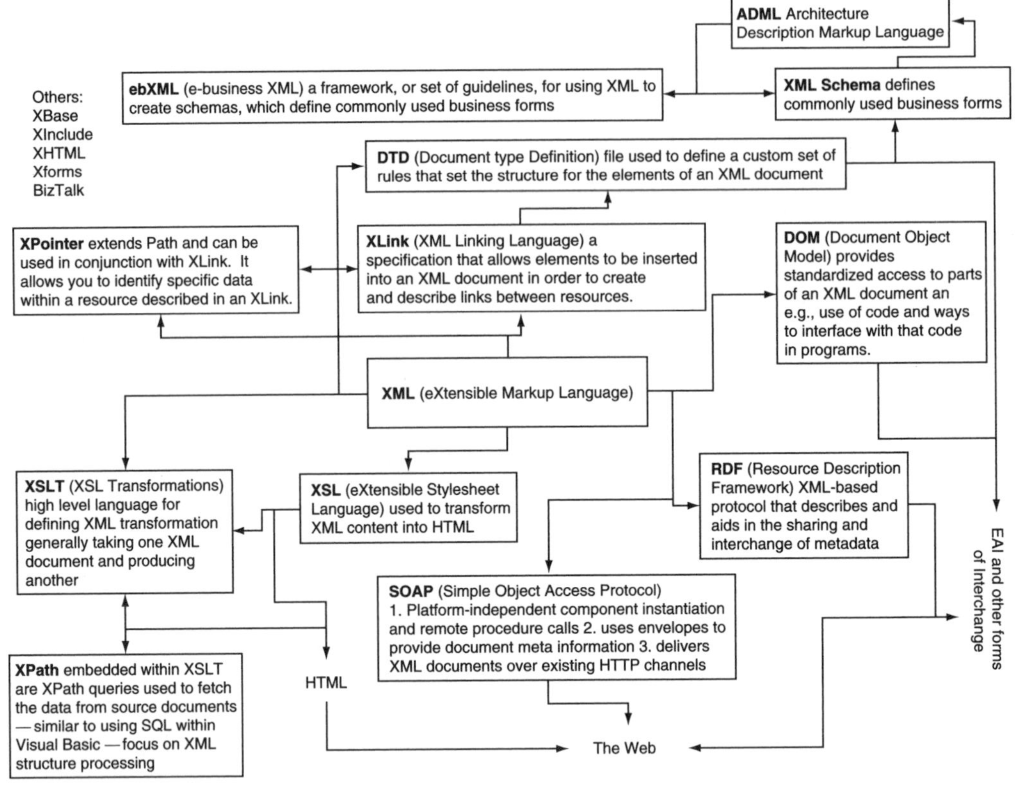

Figure 3.2

XML component architecture articulation, Version 1.

automated services through networks tend to look to WSDL, UDDI, and SOAP.

Now it is time to describe each component listed in Figure 3.3, generally moving from components closest to the core near the top of the diagram, toward the most advanced components furthest from the core, shown at the bottom of the diagram. The first one we will look at is XML Namespaces, one of the components that aids in the structuring of complex documents.

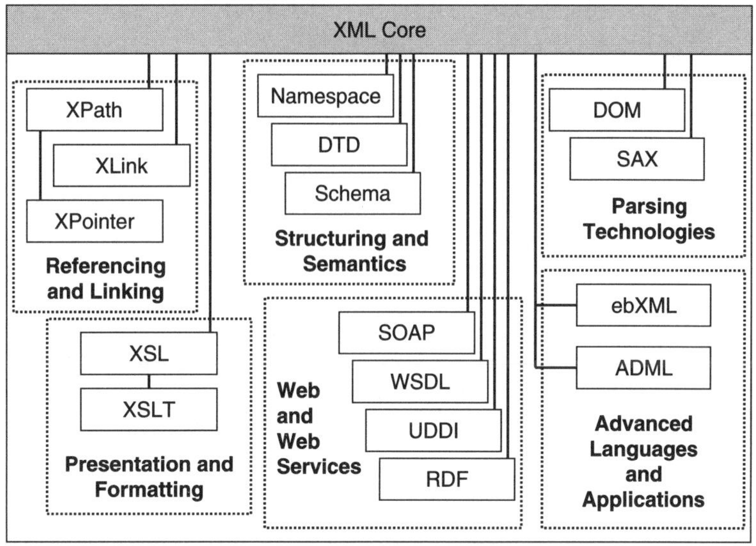

Figure 3.3

A small part of the overall XML component heirarchy.

XML Namespaces

XML documents do not exist in a vacuum, but are often part of more complicated systems where multiple systems are being used. One interesting consequence of this is seen in the way systems handle elements that have identical names, but different definitions. For example, if the "name" element is defined in two different ways, how is the system to tell which definition of "name" applies to a particular instance? In light of the earlier discussion of how the same terms might have different meanings in different locations within the same organization, this issue can come up quite frequently.

XML namespaces provide a way of associating element and attribute names with a particular URI. Users can choose a prefix along with a particular URI to disambiguate elements from one another. If the accounting and manufacturing departments have a different concept of the same element name "customerID," then a prefix can be used for each to make them clear. For example, if the prefix for the accounting department was defined to be "acct," and "mfg" was used for manufacturing, then the "customerID" element would be written as either "acct:customerID" or "mfg:customerID" depending on which was meant in a particular context. This allows XML processors and systems to tell the difference between elements, even when using two different sets of overlapping definitions of elements and attributes.

As more XML "languages" begin to proliferate, XML namespaces are being used more and more. At first, they were not strictly necessary since multiple document types were seldom used together. The number of types of XML documents is growing rapidly though, and many common words have been used in several different places for element names, so the use of XML namespaces has become more important to ensure that the correct element is being referred to.

From a data management perspective, the use of namespaces permits organizations a means of controlling the scope of various data-standardization efforts within the organization and among cooperating organizational partners. By incorporating namespaces in the rollout of various element "vocabularies," data managers can easily disambiguate individual vocabularies. XML namespaces allow users to separate those different groups of terms—the next component, DTDs, describes how XML users can actually define those groups of terms.

DTD: Document Type Definition

The DTD is frequently the first XML-related technology with which users of XML come into contact. Earlier, we stated that when organizations and individuals create their own tags, it is very important to have some type of idea about the order in which those tags should appear, and the meaning associated with the tags. The Document Type Definition was the first attempt at creating a technology that allowed users to express these ideas about their XML documents.

When discussing XML documents, people say that a document is either well formed, valid, or both. A well-formed document is one that conforms to all of the syntactic rules of XML, all elements have a corresponding closing tag, attributes are properly specified, and so on. Valid documents, on the other hand, are those that have a set of associated rules that specify which elements are valid, which are not valid, and what the appropriate tag nesting structure should be. Since the job of the DTD is essentially to specify those rules, an XML document must generally be associated with a particular DTD in order to be valid. Document Type Definitions are not the only way to specify legal elements and nesting structures; an XML schema, which is discussed in the next section, is one of many options that can also perform this job.

Basically, a DTD is a series of definitions. Users are able to define four types of items that appear in XML documents that give them structure and meaning; these correspond to existing data management concepts already practiced by most organizations. The first and most important type of item that is defined in the DTD is the element.

Element Names

Which elements occur in the document, and what are their names? Elements form the core vocabulary of a document and should be relatively descriptive of the data that is contained inside them. Optionally, documentation about particular elements can be placed near the element's definition to allow for easy reference to what the element should mean. Element names frequently contain the context of a particular piece of data that makes it meaningful. Without context, the number "102.5" does not mean much. With an appropriate element name-wrapped around it such as "radio frequency" or "temperature," the small piece of data takes on context and meaning, transforming it into information. Elements are also frequently referred to as "tags," although there is a subtle difference. The element is the name that occurs *within* a tag. In other words, given the example "<XMLTag />," the element is "XMLTag," while the tag is "<XMLTag />."

When defining elements, not only the name must be defined, but also a list of valid attributes for the element, as well as potential sub-elements. When taken together, this gives a more complete picture of the element's meaning and place within larger data structures. Elements go hand in hand with attributes, which is why the next function of a DTD is also critical: defining the attribute names and values.

Attribute Names

Optionally, some elements may have attribute names along with values for those attributes. Which attributes are allowed inside of which elements? A DTD allows users to specify not only which attributes are allowed, but also which ones are optional, potential default values for attributes if they are not specified, and which attributes are required. In many cases, it makes sense to require attributes. Consider an example using a travel industry vocabulary, if an element called "flight" was used, it would be useful to require an attribute called "number" to be present, and hold the value of the flight number of the particular flight in question. On the other hand, in an ordering system it might be a good idea to make the “quantity” attribute of a particular ordered item optional. If the quantity is not specified, then a quantity of 1 is assumed.

Attributes frequently represent aspects of metadata around a particular data item. Given a “temperature” element, an associated attribute might contain information such as “measurement=‘Fahrenheit’ ” to allow the user to understand more about the information being presented. Depending on the way the data is modeled, attributes can function as metadata, or almost as the data equivalent of a parenthetical comment.

Still, attributes and elements by themselves are not enough. For any real level of complexity or power to be achieved in XML documents, we need entire groups, families, and hierarchies of elements and attributes—data structures, not just single lonely elements. Toward this end, the DTD defines the way the elements and attributes relate to one another—the nesting rules.

Nesting Rules

From a structural perspective, the most critical responsibility of the DTD is to describe which elements are allowed to occur inside of which other elements. While it makes sense for a human to see a price element inside of another element that makes clear that the price refers to a particular product, the same price element might not make any sense in a different context without being associated with a product. A properly written DTD allows the author to make sure that valid documents will only contain a price element underneath a product element, and nowhere else.

The nesting rules of a DTD are the order brought to the otherwise soupy chaos of large numbers of interacting elements and attributes. Together with elements and attributes, the nesting rules almost complete the picture of what can occur in an XML document. One last small piece is missing though—the XML entity.

Entities

An entity is a particular symbol or glyph that appears in an XML document, and acts as a stand-in for something else. It might also be a full text string, or even a full DTD. As an example, take the angle brackets. Since the characters “<” and “>” are frequently used inside of XML documents to represent the beginning of an element, some special way of expressing the “<” character must be used when it is intended literally rather than as the beginning of an element. For these two characters, the most frequently used entity names are “>” for the “>” character, and “<” for the “<” character, where “gt” stands for “greater than” and “lt” for “less than.”

When looking at the specific element for the ">" sign, "gt" is referred to as the entity name, while ">" is called an entity reference. In fact, since the ampersand character "&" itself is used as a special character for entity referencing, it too must be defined as entity in order to be used literally. In most situations, it is referenced as "&".

Entity names and values are declared as part of the DTD. XML users are not restricted to particular names or values for XML entities, but the facility is there to allow any type of entity to be declared. In practice, though, many DTDs contain a very similar set of entities since the same types of characters and entities are frequently needed. The entity conventions that are seen in XML documents borrow heavily from XML's SGML and HTML precursors, providing a bit of continuity for those already familiar with the other languages.

Now that we have had a look at all of the facilities of the DTD, there are a few places where the DTD is somewhat lacking. The limitations of DTDs themselves are quite interesting.

Limitations

While using DTDs to describe XML document structure is quite sufficient for many users, DTDs do have a number of drawbacks. First and foremost, they are something of an oddity with regard to other XML technologies since DTDs are not written using standard element and attribute syntax – that is, DTDs are not written in XML and cannot be processed as XML documents themselves. There is nothing wrong with this per se, but they are different from regular XML entities. Another limitation of DTDs is that they are good only for defining attributes, entities, elements, and nesting order. They do not provide support for data typing, or allow the user to restrict the values of data that can be contained in certain elements.

When using XML documents as a method of modeling and expressing data, this is a serious drawback. It is obvious to human users that the "price" attribute of a particular element should contain numeric data, and should not ever contain somebody's name, or just plain character data. But a DTD has no way of expressing which types of data are allowed in particular places, and as a result, a document can be considered valid even if it contains data that is clearly incorrect. To a DTD, the concept of document validity ends when the document has met the DTD's constraints in terms of elements, attributes, entities, and nesting order.

What is needed is something more powerful that will let us accomplish the same things that a DTD can do, but with more features and flexibility.

These facilities are provided by the successor to the DTD, the XML schema.

XML Schema

As the limitations of DTDs began to show, the need for a replacement grew. The facilities provided by DTDs are very useful, but fall somewhat short of ideal. In addition, the fact that DTDs were not written using XML elements made them a bit more difficult to learn than necessary, and made extensibility of the format somewhat limited. One of the overarching design goals of XML, embodied in its name, is that of extensibility. Wherever possible, it is usually a good idea to make the facilities of XML extensible. This is because no one has the ability to foresee which features will be indispensable in the future. The best the designers of any technology can do is to design it in such a way as to make it as flexible as possible, so that when the technology inevitably has to change and adapt, it can do so without the feeling that the new features were crudely "tacked on."

The XML schema standard (implemented as a recommendation in May 2001) has a number of advantages that rightfully make it the best choice for modeling data structures in XML.

XML Schemas Are Written Using XML Elements and Attributes

In contrast to DTDs, XML schemas are written using actual XML elements and attributes. This comes with all of the attendant benefits of XML. Users do not have to learn a new language—schemas can be incorporated as parts of other documents, and they can be manipulated by just about any XML-capable program or technology. Most importantly, like the core XML language itself, XML schemas are extensible. A number of new features have been added to XML schemas that were not present in DTDs, but since schemas themselves are written in XML, future releases of the schema specification will be able to add new features as needed, rather than requiring a different specification altogether, as was required in the DTD-to-schema process.

XML Schemas Support Data Types

The major new feature that was the most lacking from DTDs was the ability to model data types within elements. By specifying a data constraint on a particular element, XML users can further narrow down the definition of what a "valid" document really means. Specifying and enforcing data types is also the most rudimentary step in attempting to ensure data quality. Without knowing the general form of acceptable data, it is difficult to quickly tell whether a particular piece of data is useful or not.

The data type specification that XML schemas allow falls into two categories. First, the schema author can specify an actual data type, and second, the author can define an acceptable range of values, or a domain. XML schemas by default recognize a number of different common data types, such as strings, integers, boolean, URIs, and so on. In addition, facilities are provided to allow users to define their own data types. For example, authors can define a special integer data type called "score," which ranges exactly from 0 to 100. That data type can then be associated with a particular element, so that the data in the element can only be an integer value in that range. If the data is anything else, the document will not be considered valid. Aside from simple numeric ranges, actual domains can also be specified. For example, data inside of an element that expresses a product name might be limited to a list of products that a company actually produces.

When constraints like this are put on the data, and valid documents are required, data managers can be sure that orders are not being placed for nonexistent items, and that scores represented in documents will be within the valid range. This reduces the amount of complexity that must be present in the system that actually does the processing of the data on the other end. Invalid documents will be rejected, and valid documents can allow the system to focus on processing the data in a meaningful way rather than spending excessive effort doing data validation.

XML Schemas Support Namespaces

Standard DTD definitions did not readily allow authors to use namespaces as part of their elements. XML schemas have fixed this situation by including support for namespaces. In fact, namespaces are so common in schemas that most examples that are used include the prefix "xsi" for all elements within the schema language itself. Of course, this naturally allows authors of XML schemas to reuse even the names of schema elements in their own documents. In fact, the XML schema language itself has a corresponding schema.

After the schema standard had been developed, users rapidly saw that it represented an advance, and wanted to use it. The next question was, "How do we get all of our old DTDs moved to schemas?"

Transitioning From DTDs to XML Schemas

While schemas are meant as the replacement for DTDs, the number of DTDs already in existence is large enough that they will be around for quite some time. The ability to use DTDs with existing XML documents is not going to disappear, but users are encouraged to move toward XML schemas for future use. Where possible, it may be desirable to transition DTDs toward XML schemas, but it is not strictly necessary.

A number of applications and tools are already available that provide mechanisms for automatically converting old DTDs into newer XML schemas. This is a straightforward task to perform since both languages specify much of the same information. It is particularly easy to convert from a DTD to a schema because schemas provide more information about elements and entities than DTDs do. It is important to note, however, that when translating DTDs to schemas, the only information that will be included is what was in the original DTD. Without further modification, the schema will not provide any extra benefit that the DTD did not.

Looking at the situation from the other direction, converting XML schemas to DTDs is a potentially difficult task, since converting the information in a schema to a DTD requires an application to drop information about data types and constraints from the resulting DTD. This is not desirable, and should be avoided unless absolutely necessary. Fortunately, conversion of XML schemas to DTDs is not much of an issue since almost all XML-capable software now supports schemas.

At this point, we have covered several different components that describe the structure and semantics of a document. Now we will move into a description of how programs actually get access to data within XML documents, starting with a discussion of the Document Object Model.

DOM: Document Object Model

The Document Object Model (DOM) is a way of thinking about and addressing XML documents. At its core, the DOM represents an entire XML document as a tree in a computer's memory. The advantage of tree representation is that it makes any piece of information in an XML document accessible at any point, and allows for navigation through the document along paths of parent/child elemental relationships. Documents can be formally searched like hierarchical data structures, and just about any algorithm that deals with tree data structures can be applied to XML documents represented in the document object model.

Unlike some of the other items discussed in this chapter, the DOM is not a technology that is written using the XML language, but rather it is a way of dealing with and thinking about XML documents.

In Figure 3.4, we see on the left-hand side a simple XML document, and on the right-hand side a picture of how the data might be organized inside of a computer, in a tree structure. Notice that lines moving from particular nodes in the tree on the right-hand side correspond directly to the nesting depth seen on the left-hand side. For the sake of simplicity, the actual data inside the XML elements is represented in the tree form inside parentheses. This figure illustrates two points about the DOM; first, it organizes an XML document in memory as a tree, and second, it provides access to the actual data items inside XML elements.

The DOM represents the entire document as a tree. But what if the document is very large, or if we are only interested in a very small subset of the elements in the document? The next component, XPath, addresses this requirement and provides a facility for arbitrary selectivity of data in documents.

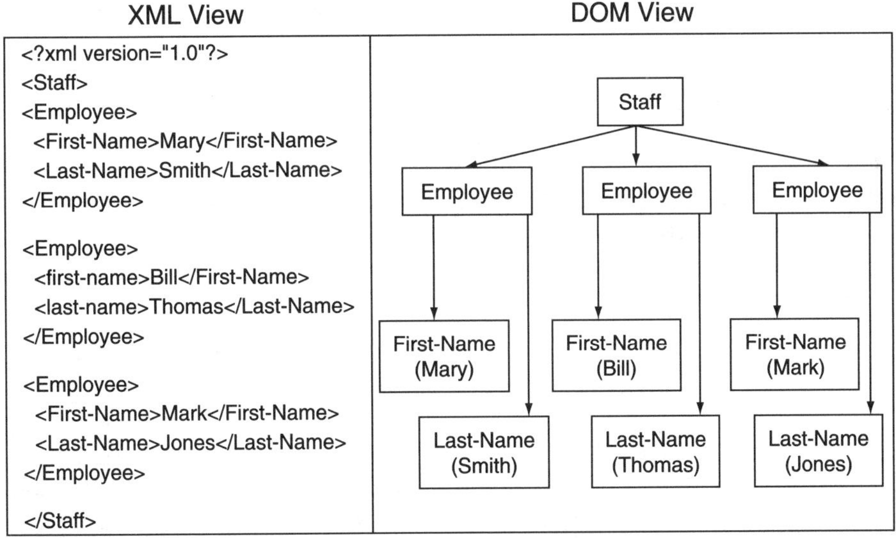

Figure 3.4

A demonstration of an XML document in text form, and represented by the DOM.

XPath

The XPath component of XML is a simple language that allows for an arbitrary group of elements and attributes to be selected from a document. When dealing with very complex or large XML documents, it is often useful to be able to refer to a very specific set of elements and attributes. Maybe the set in question is the "first name" element underneath every single "employee" element in the document. Maybe the set in question is the value of every "age" attribute in the "employee" elements. Frequently the set is simply one element, for example, the "employee" element that surrounds Bill Richard's XML record.

Often, when the set being referred to is just one single element, users choose to think of an XPath expression as identifying a pathway through an XML document down to the element in question. Frequently this is how XPath is used—for example, in many situations, users who are writing XSLT style sheets will use an XPath expression to refer to and extract data from a particular element in the document.

In Figure 3.5, we illustrate the same XML document, represented in its visual DOM form as a tree, and illustrate the two different ways of thinking of XPath expressions and how they relate to XML documents. In the first instance, the interesting element is the "last name" element associated with the employee Mary Smith. In this XML document, there is a way to refer to that element and *only* that element. This comes in handy when the data from that particular element is needed for some external processing, or when the element is being used as a reference point for some other data. In the second situation, XPath allows the user to select a set of nodes, in this case, every single "first name" element in the document. This is accomplished by effectively crafting an XPath expression that refers to the "first name" element underneath the "employee" element. Since there is more than one, the result of the XPath expression is a set of nodes in the tree.

XPath allows users to develop quite powerful expressions for referring to data within an XML document. The syntax of XPath is put together in a way that is sufficiently flexible for just about any referencing that would need to be done. XPath is something of an anomaly compared to other pieces of the XML component architecture, because in its most common form, it is not a set of attributes or elements as other components are, but simple text strings. While the learning curve is quite good for those new to XPath, it cannot be learned solely through the addition of new elements and attributes to an existing XML document. But it is used often enough

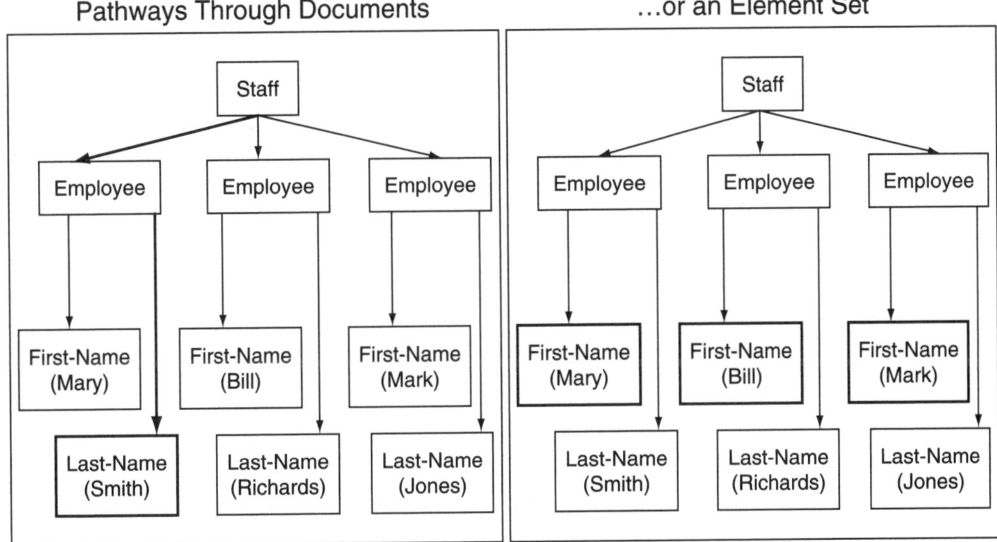

Figure 3.5

Two different ways of conceptualizing XPath expressions.

to make the time it takes to learn and apply the component worthwhile in light of its utility.

The DOM and XPath allow users to access various items within XML documents. What about cases where we are more interested in referencing other data items, but not actively finding out the value? The next section discusses how references can be made between documents via a component called XLink.

XLink: XML Linking

Links are the data concepts that really created the web. Without hyperlinking between documents, the web would not be anything more than an extremely large collection of standalone documents. The ability to instantaneously jump from one resource to another on the web is one of its "killer features" that made such tremendous growth and interest possible. Given how indispensable the linking feature is, the designers of XML wanted to provide a flexible framework for the same feature in XML documents.

Hyperlinks as they exist on the web have a number of problems though. They still work quite well for what they actually do, but all you need to do to investigate the weaknesses of regular HTML hyperlinks is to ask the maintainer of a large HTML-based web site what he or she thinks about the challenges involved with maintaining such monstrous "link farms." Ever since HTML-based sites reached a fairly large size, the problems with the original concept of the hyperlink were fairly apparent. Since XML itself is rather new, the designers fortunately had the accumulated experience and knowledge to begin the creation of a new linking facility that would not encounter the problems experienced with traditional hyperlinking.

Specifically, here are a few of the drawbacks associated with HTML links:

1. Hyperlinks may only have one target. A link goes from one page to another page, or to another location within the same page. If the destination page is mirrored on any one of 10 different systems, 10 links are needed even though the document being pointed at is the same on all of the systems.
2. Linking requires a special element. It is not possible to put a link inside a different element—the link must be an element unto itself.
3. No link-traversal strategy is provided. There are many potential ways that links could be processed and followed, but since no additional information comes with the link, there really is only one way to follow it.
4. No metadata about the link is provided. Metadata could be very useful; for example, who created the link, and when was it created? If the resource has an expiration date on it, perhaps the link should point elsewhere or cease to exist after a certain date.

The XLink XML architectural component was a result of an analysis of these issues, and the desire to fix them. Like other XML components, it was designed from the start to be human readable, and to represent all relevant data for the link in a way that conformed to the rules of base XML—that is, XML links can be added to existing well-formed XML documents, and the documents will still be well formed.

A link that is specified with XLink can support multiple destinations, define link endpoints and traversal rules, and even allow the author to have some control over the direction of travel involved with a particular link. Finally, given the huge amount of HTML that is already out there, one vital feature of XML linking is that it is compatible with HTML-linking structures.

The construction of an XML link actually has three distinct parts. Separating the concept out from a link into three constituent pieces that interact allows users to avoid the limitations of the overly simplistic HTML link. The three pieces are the participating resources, the actual link definition, and the arcs.

Participating Resources

The participating resources of a link are simply the document or documents that are on either end of a link. Given the original linking structure in HTML, there was no need for a concept like this because the participating resources were either implied or explicit—the document being pointed at was explicitly labeled in the link, and the document that was linked from was obviously the document in which the link occurred. The problem with this strategy is that it forces users into a situation where links can only represent one-to-one relationships. Why not provide a mechanism for producing links that can represent one-to-many or many-to-many linking relationships? XLink is in fact a very useful capability, but in order to be used, it must be clear which resources are on either side of the link. Specifying the participating resources of a link does just that.

As described earlier, these links provide the capability for having more than one target for a given link. With HTML, in order to connect three resources, three links are needed, each of which has its own element in its own location. Using XLink, it is possible to create a single link that "forks" to three different resources. This forking is simply a result of using more than one participating resource on the destination end of a link (as shown in Figure 3.6).

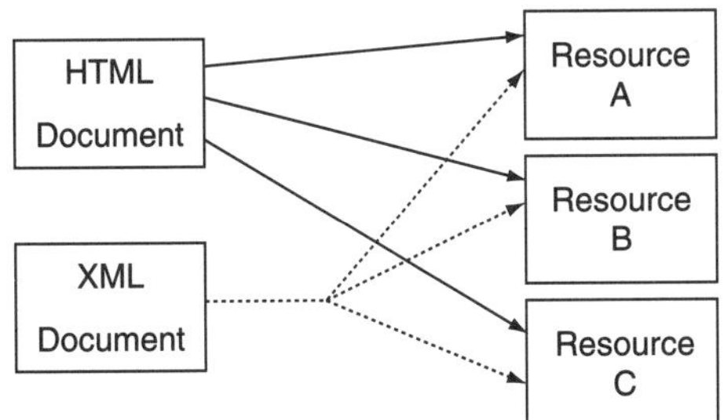

Figure 3.6

Referencing multiple destinations with a single XML link.

Link Definition

As part of a link, additional information might be included that helps users of the link understand its relevance. It is often useful to have a title for links, authors associated with them, or a brief description of the resource on the other end of the link. Automated programs that are processing XML documents can use this type of information, or people inspecting some presented form of the document might use it. There are ways of accomplishing this type of thing in HTML, but they tend to be very limited, clunky, unreliable, and non-standard. XLink took the approach of assuming from the start that extra definition information about the link would be useful, and built it in from the beginning so that the data looks as if it belongs there, rather than shoehorned in after the fact.

Link definitions also allow link "locators" to be defined. In many situations, the actual address of a particular resource might be long and cumbersome. In addition, if a particular resource is referred to many times, it is useful to be able to label that resource with some name, and then use that name whenever the resource is being referred to. This allows the actual resource address to be changed only in one place and for all of the references to that resource to change accordingly. Link definitions found in XLink constructs provide just this capability.

Arcs

Arcs specify the direction of travel of the link in question. They are also occasionally referred to as traversal rules, and there are three basic types, shown in Figure 3.7. Outbound arcs mean that the link in question goes from a local resource to some other non-local resource. Inbound arcs are links that go from a non-local resource to a local resource. Finally, third-party arcs are present in links that connect two non-local resources. These three possibilities effectively cover every situation in which links might be needed, by categorizing the resources in terms of whether or not they are local.

One of the interesting consequences of being able to describe links in these three different ways is that the user does not have to be capable of writing a document in order to produce a link with that document as the source. Using old HTML links, the user must have the ability to actually modify the file in question if he or she wishes to create a link from that document to some other document. Using XLink, the source of the link is as flexible as the destination. Another interesting point is that the concept

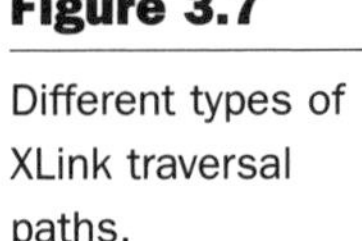

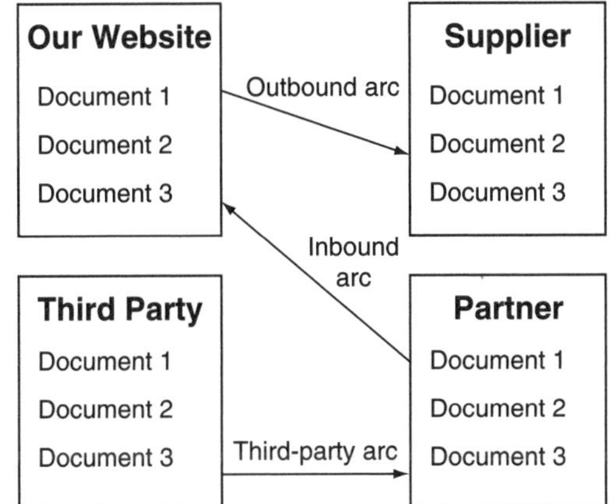

Figure 3.7

Different types of XLink traversal paths.

of the inbound link means that documents can be aware (possess self-knowledge) of who is creating links with the document in question as an endpoint.

XLink is a good starting point for creating references to other resources, but it is not the end of the story. Just as DOM and XPath both exist to satisfy different needs for access to data according to the level of granularity needed, XPath dovetails with the next component, XPointer, to provide two different levels of granularity for linking.

XPointer

XLink provides a very useful mechanism for pointing to particular resources, but it does not allow users to link to particular snippets of data. XPointer, on the other hand, does allow XML documents and elements to point to specific snippets of data within other resources, along with any potential contextual information that might be needed. Given the fact that essentially XPointer is pointing at other XML data, it does have one limitation; the data being pointed to must be XML.

Based on this description, it might sound as if XPointer is similar to XPath, since XPath allows users to refer to particular elements and attributes within a document. In fact, XPointer is very similar to XPath, and was based on XPath. This again illustrates the architectural trend in XML to build on existing technologies and to extend them with new capabilities rather than creating a completely different technology for a slightly different purpose. XPointer extends many of the concepts in XPath and adds a few new tricks to the bag. From the start, XPointer was intended as a solution that should be able to point at any user selectable region of a document, by encoding the selection criteria into the XPointer expression. As with XPath, powerful expressions can be built that make reference to human concepts, such as "the second section of the fifth chapter" or "all elements that contain the text 'Mary Smith,'" rather than referring to elements specifically by name, or worse, by some arcane unique identifier. Conversely, if elements are tagged with unique identifiers, XPointer provides a mechanism for referring to them as well.

These descriptions mean that the data is not even required to be in the place where the user might expect it. The actual XPointer expression provides a bit of "context" around the data—the element or attribute in question must be surrounded by a certain structure in order to satisfy the XPointer statement. As long as the context around the data remains the same, the actual document being referred to may freely change.

When combined with XLink, XPointer further extends the ability of users to connect multiple documents in interesting and powerful ways. The original hyperlink concept in HTML was astonishing for many people, due to the huge range of possibilities it provided with regard to connecting different types of information. Imagine then the possibilities provided by combining XLink and XPointer to provide linking without limits.

While facilities for linking are indispensable, it would not be terribly useful to have a beautiful set of interlinked documents that no one could read. Given this issue, what follows is a discussion of components related to document formatting and presentation. This allows us to transform documents for other purposes, or to bring them entirely out of the database and onto paper.

XSL and XSLT

The two components described in this section are the Extensible Stylesheet Language (XSL) and XSL Transformations (XSLT). From an architectural perspective, these are actually two different components, but they will both be dealt with together since, correctly or not, the terms are often used interchangeably.

One of the things many users take away from our seminars on XML-based data management is that "XML is to data what Java was supposed to be to programming languages." Using XML, organizations can manage their data in XML form and then "pour" that data into a variety of other forms. XML stylesheets and stylesheet-based transformation are used to repurpose the information—these transformations can then be managed using existing technologies just like other XML documents.

The purpose of both of these components is to create a flexible system for presentation of XML documents. Up until now, all of the XML components discussed have focused on data representation, access, interchange, and other aspects of the actual data that is in XML documents. XSL and XSLT provide methods of taking XML documents as input, and outputting something different—XSL is used for paginated output, while XSLT allows for transformation from one XML dialect to another (which may include presentation in XHTML form on the web).

Like many other XML components, the brainstorming and creation of this particular component was partially a result of looking out at the landscape of current styling technologies in use, and attempting to find ways to improve on their good spots while avoiding their bad spots. The most frequently used styling language is probably CSS, which stands for Cascading Style Sheets, and is used in conjunction with HTML documents. In many situations, the user only needs to write a short CSS description of how each HTML element should be presented, and the rest is left to the browser. For example, the author of a page might want to make sure that all text within a paragraph tag was rendered as 12-point Arial. CSS makes this easy, but even goes a step further and allows users to define their own classes of tags by inserting special attributes into their HTML elements, and then using the specific class of a tag as a basis for how it should be marked up.

While these same features can be used in XSL, it is a much more general mechanism for displaying data. In HTML, the number of elements is restricted, and their meaning is well understood. On the other hand, in XML, users can define their own elements, so even the most basic display properties of elements are unknown to browsers and other software. XSL is the method by which users can define exactly how each of the elements should work. But that is only part of it. There are two primary differences between CSS and XSL. First, XSL can actually use XSLT to reorganize the document tree completely, which CSS is unable to do. In addition, while XSL provides the concept of pagination and physical page layout, CSS does not. Those who only display documents on the web often do not need the pagination feature, so some elect to use XSLT and CSS together.

XSL has three main subcomponents that it uses, depending on what type of transformation is being accomplished:

- **XPath.** Described earlier, this component aids in referencing particular portions of documents for presentation.

- **XSL Formatting Objects.** This component allows far more fine-grained control over presentation than CSS, including top-to-bottom and right-to-left text formatting, headers and footers, and page numbers.
- **XSLT.** This component allows XML documents of one form to be transformed into a different form of XML.

Of these three components, XPath and XSLT are the most frequently used. XSL Formatting Objects is an extremely powerful component that can accomplish fine-tuning of presentation in ways that are not possible using the other two. But for most presentation tasks, formatting objects are not needed. Use of XSL formatting objects are most frequently encountered in places where more control over presentation is a requirement, such as when XML documents must be transformed into PDF files. Since PDF files and certain other formats require more advanced information about spacing and layout of documents, which is not needed in an (X)HTML document, XSL formatting objects are often used in those situations (see Figure 3.8).

XSLT

When most people think of display of XML documents, they normally think of XSLT, since it is the primary tool used when transforming XML documents into HTML and XHTML for display on the web. In actuality, it is a subcomponent of XSL, and works in concert with XSL much like other components such as XPath and XSL formatting objects. The core mission of XSLT is quite simple—it transforms documents from one form of XML to some other form. The new form could be HTML, XML, or

Figure 3.8

Using XSL to transform XML to other formats.

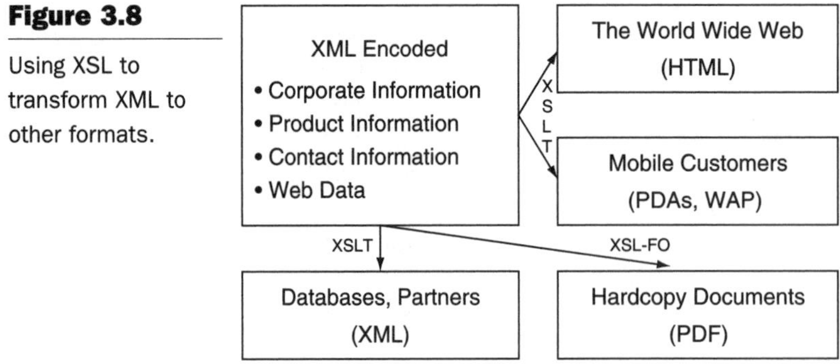

even comma-delimited text. The way it accomplishes this is by taking a set of user-defined rules and applying them to a given XML document to produce a resulting document that must also be well-formed XML. Given the DOM view of XML documents, sometimes XSLT is spoken of as having an input tree and a result tree.

XSLT is rule driven. This means that when users want to translate documents from one form of XML to another, rules are specified as to what should be done with each element in the document. This can range from quite simple, to quite complex. For example, if the only difference between two forms of XML is that one uses an "employee" element, while the other uses "emp" for the same purpose, an XSLT program can quickly be developed that converts from one to the other. On the other hand, XSLT also contains sophisticated functions and capabilities that allow users to insert extra elements, transform only some of the source document's elements, perform limited mathematical operations on data, string manipulation, and much more. While it should not be used as a full-featured programming language, XSLT does contain quite a few features that are normally found in professional programming languages. The difference between XSLT and a generic programming language is that XSLT is extremely well suited to its particular problem domain, and its syntax is something users are already familiar with—straight XML.

XSLT and the fact that it is written entirely in XML creates a number of benefits. Up until now, XML has been discussed as a data-representation language, but with the addition of XSLT, it now has the ability to model business rules, transformation processes, and to a limited extent, programming code. Although XSLT is often used to transform entire documents into new documents, it can also work with small subsections of a document (as shown in Figure 3.9). The implications of this are quite interesting. In programming terms, one of the reasons that

Figure 3.9

An XML object, including data and the operations on that data.

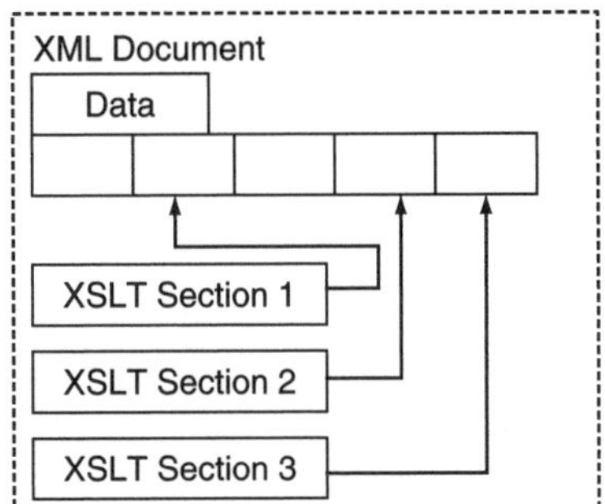

object-oriented programming is so powerful is that it provides methods of operating on the data together with the data itself, bundled into a useful package referred to as an object. XSLT allows users to construct their own "XML objects," which can then be used in much the same way as objects in a programming language. This rests on three important capabilities:

1. XSLT programs are XML documents, and as such they can be embedded inside other XML documents.
2. XSLT programs can operate on a portion of the tree if they choose—it need not always be a straight document-to-document conversion process.
3. XML provides an ideal way to represent the information that comes along with objects.

As of this writing, there does not appear to be a widely available or used implementation of this "XML object" concept—it is intended to serve as an example of what is possible when combining the capabilities of several XML components with architectural thinking.

What is of particular interest to data managers is the fact that stylesheet transformations allow data transformation without requiring application code, and are managed using modern data management technologies. By storing transformations written in XML inside of databases, the transformation process is easier to manage, because the transformations can be managed properly as the data that they are, instead of managing lines of programming code (which is traditionally very difficult and expensive). Furthermore, as these transformations become better understood, data managers have unique opportunities to eliminate other code applications and replace them with XML-based transformations. After all, what do applications do but transform data from one form to another? The potential to reduce the organizational application code base to one-fifth of its original size will be explored in more detail in later chapters on the more advanced applications of XML technologies.

XSLT Browser and Web Integration

As XML has caught on, a number of different ways to use XSL and XSLT have come along. At this point, most recent browsers support XSLT for transforming XML documents into XHTML. This is quite convenient since it means that essentially all the content publisher has to do is insert a reference to the relevant XSLT program inside of an XML file, and serve the XML file directly to the browser. A simple example of this can be seen in Figure 3.10, which shows an XML file describing flights from Richmond, Virginia, to London displayed in a Mac browser window. The browser will recognize that an external stylesheet is needed in order to present the document, and will download it and apply it before the user sees the page in question. This is much the same model that HTML uses—many HTML pages make reference to an external file containing CSS instructions for the presentation of an HTML page.

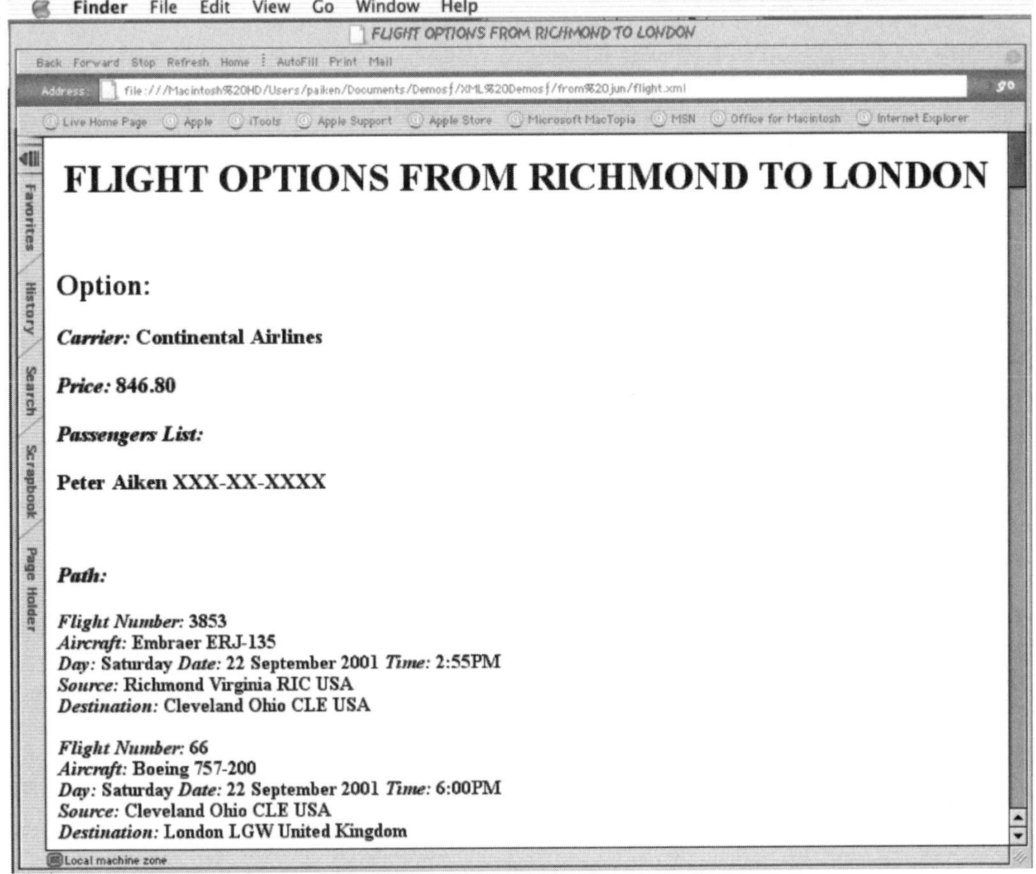

Figure 3.10

An XML file rendered as XHTML in a browser.

Still, these implementations are not yet perfect. There are some differences between software packages as to what type of reference they require for the XSLT program, and how the resulting interpreted XML comes out. Because of these differences, some content providers who wish to control as much of the presentation as possible will occasionally choose to apply the XSLT to the XML on the server side, and serve only the resulting document to the client. In this way, the content provider can be sure that all browsers will see the same result, and that small differences in XSLT implementation between browsers will not cause unexpected presentation. This approach is likely to be used for a while to come. Mixed approaches are also often employed; for example, using XSLT on the server side, and CSS on the client side to handle other presentation issues.

We have talked a bit about how the presentation technology fits into the web, but that is not the end of XML's applicability to the web. In the next sections, we will discuss other XML components and their relationship to the web, starting with a facility to help us overcome the information overload—The Resource Description Framework.

RDF: Resource Description Framework

As the web has grown, the need to be able to summarize the contents of entire sites has grown as well. There are a number of different Internet portals out there that attempt to bring together the best resources from a number of different sites into one place where they can all be perused and potentially used. Individual documents often have metadata about them that is used to summarize the resource (author, title, publishing date, key words, etc.) and entire sites or collections of documents can as well. The way these sites and collections are summarized and categorized is through the use of the Resource Description Framework (RDF).

The most common application of RDF is the concept of site syndication. Many Internet sites allow users to add to their gateway page a summary of the headlines on other sites. For example, a user who has a gateway page with one of the more popular portals might be able to see at a glance the leading headlines with four different news carriers, sports results, and links to local entertainment listings all in one place. Generally, the way this is actually implemented is by using RDF.

These days, most large sites regularly create and publish an RDF description of the data that is available on their site. News sites keep a running list of the top stories, software sites keep lists of the latest downloads, and so on. All that the Internet portal has to do is to regularly update their copy of the RDF document for a number of different sites. This provides the portal with the ability to deliver the latest headlines and links directly to the user.

RDF actually started life as a generic framework for metadata. Its creator's goal was to provide a system that could allow automated sharing of semantic information by programs over the web. It allows resource discovery, cataloging, and content aggregation. Resource discovery is the process of finding resources on a particular topic, through whatever means; cataloging is simply storing many RDF descriptions for later searching based on the metadata; and content aggregation is taking several information resources in different places and documents and combining them into a new composite document to meet a specific need. As a more specific example of content aggregation, RDF makes it possible to build software that can automatically create a composite document that contains all news reports from that day in which a particular organization is mentioned. By using RDF, the software knows where the documents are, which topics the documents deal with, and when they were published. This is yet another example of the powerful possibilities of effectively using metadata (in this case, article locations, topic descriptions, and publishing dates).

Many people make reference to the fact that XML will help improve Internet searching. The idea is that as more data comes tagged along with metadata describing its content, search engines will have more specific information to tailor search results. Currently, if a user searches for the name of a particular popular author, the user might potentially see thousands of results. On the other hand, if it were possible to search for a particular name only in situations where the name occurred as the author of a resource, the results would be limited to articles and books that the author had actually written. At the moment, RDF is the XML architectural component that best provides these facilities.

As with other XML technologies, efforts were made to make RDF general enough that it would be applicable in many situations, not just syndication of web content. So RDF also contains the ability to use different existing ontologies, and other ways of hierarchically categorizing information according to its essential qualities. This feature is what allows RDF to live up to its original goal—to be a method of publishing and searching machine processable information to allow as much information on the Internet as possible to be machine processable.

Currently, RDF is being used is primarily in the area of traditional web sites. However, web services is a new topic area in which XML figures in heavily. SOAP, the next component that we will discuss, is at the very center of the relationship between XML and web services.

SOAP: Simple Object Access Protocol

SOAP is one of the XML components that had had the most buzz surrounding it for the past few years, mostly due to the fact that it is a cornerstone technology of the new push toward web services. At its core, SOAP is an XML-encoded method by which programs or services on two completely different systems can communicate. This type of technology has quite a history—a number of technologies have been created to allow this type of facility, but not all of them caught on very well. Because SOAP is XML-based, it is the ideal candidate for this type of technology, because it provides an easy method of understanding what is being sent down the wire. Since there are readily available XML toolkits for just about every programming language in use, almost any language can speak SOAP and communicate with other technologies elsewhere. In this case, the base XML language can be thought of as the platform, while SOAP is something of an application running on that platform. Since a large number of technologies already are capable of processing XML, using SOAP to open up lines of communication between technologies is not that much of a leap.

SOAP is also often associated with the HTTP network protocol, which is best known for its role in serving up the web pages of the world. By piggybacking SOAP on top of HTTP, the designers took advantage of a number of benefits:

1. HTTP is already widely deployed, quite stable, and mature. Rather than setting out to design networking and data interchange technologies, the SOAP designers were able to stick to the important parts and let the issue of networking, which had already been solved by HTTP, be handled by a protocol that had already proven itself capable.
2. HTTP is well understood. Again in the spirit of the XML developers striving to reuse existing open technologies rather than reinventing the wheel, HTTP was used because many people, from web designers to programmers, are already comfortable with HTTP, reducing the learning curve.
3. The protocol, which was originally used for the web, tends to easily permeate firewalls and existing technology within organizations. This is an important point, since almost all organizations have their own unique security patterns, blocking some traffic and allowing other traffic. Almost all sites let

web traffic through, so piggybacking SOAP on top of HTTP maximizes the chances that it will be useful in as many places as possible.

From a technology perspective, SOAP provides a way of encoding a particular request to a service somewhere on the network, and sending information along with that request. For example, take a particular manufacturing company that provides an electronic catalog of all of its materials through a web service to its customers. Customers can connect to the company's server and send SOAP messages indicating a price query on a particular part. The server will then respond with the item name, description, price, and ordering information. All of this is done automatically—customers can even place orders through a SOAP interface automatically. Figure 3.11 shows how each of the statements made is understood by the other party, along with the parameters that come with them This is what SOAP enables programs to do.

SOAP documents that are sent back and forth contain what is called the SOAP "envelope." The envelope in turn is composed of two parts, the header and the body. The header, which is optional, can contain metadata about the request, or instructions for various intermediate programs that might process the data in the document. The body, on the other hand, which is mandatory, contains the content of the request that is intended for the last program that will process the request. In some situations, SOAP documents may be passed through multiple systems and/or services before they reach their destination.

To take a concrete example, if a customer were querying a supplier's site about product prices, the header of the SOAP document might contain a bit of metadata, and a statement that requires the server to

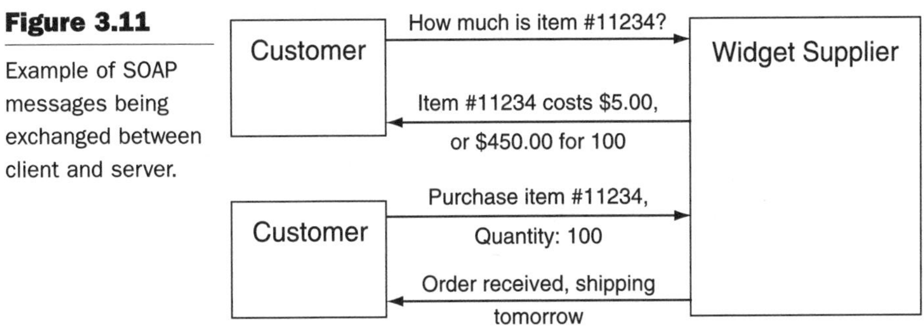

Figure 3.11

Example of SOAP messages being exchanged between client and server.

understand a particular version of the SOAP protocol in order to process the request and ensure compatibility. The body would contain just a few simple elements whose meaning would amount to a price query on a particular item number. The item number would be contained within the body of the SOAP request. When encoding the information in this way, it is crystal clear to the supplier exactly what the customer is looking for. On the other end, the server looks up the price for that particular item, adds extra information about availability, purchasing, and whatever else is needed, wraps the entire chunk of information up into a SOAP envelope, and sends it back to the customer.

SOAP services are wonderful to use, if people know how to use them. The issue of figuring out how to use someone else's web service is addressed using WSDL, the next component we will discuss.

WSDL: Web Services Definition Language

The WSDL specification often goes hand in hand with SOAP. When describing SOAP, we mentioned that systems can communicate with one another by exchanging SOAP documents with particular elements that describe the request being made, along with any parameter information that might be necessary to complete the request, such as the item number of an item whose price is being requested. What we did not discuss in the SOAP section is how exactly the client system is supposed to know what format the server expects the request to be sent in. The client cannot simply make up its own elements and hope that the server will understand—it must send the server the request according to how the server expects it. The Web Services Definition Language (WSDL) fills this need. The main purpose of this XML component is to let clients know how to communicate with a particular web service. Ideally, each unique web service that provides a set of capabilities will have its own dedicated WSDL document that is publicly available and details to the client how to actually use the SOAP-based service.

WSDL definitions generally contain a number of different pieces of information about the web service, all of which are needed in order to use it effectively. First, the actual address or URL of the service is provided. Next, a description of what protocol is needed to communicate with the service is given. Many web services communicate over HTTP as described in the section on SOAP, but HTTP is not the only way to exchange SOAP messages; FTP (File Transfer Protocol) and SHTTP (Secure HTTP) may also be used. If another protocol is needed, that can be noted in the WSDL description.

Next, the semantics of the service are described. There are three types of transactions—request only, request and response, and response only, each of which has its own use. Request only might be useful when the client only wants to send data to the server, and no response is needed. The utility of request and response is fairly clear—in many web services situations, the client asks for something, and the server responds with an answer, such as in the price inquiry example given earlier. The response-only transaction may also be useful if no input parameters are needed. For example, if a web service provides the temperature in Richmond, Virginia, then no request is actually needed. The fact that the client connected is the request.

Finally, the WSDL document contains a description of the messages that can be passed between machines. In this case, it has to actually lay out which elements are expected and what order they might occur in. Given the patterns of reuse that we have seen in the XML architecture, it is no surprise that schemas are used for this purpose, and are actually embedded in the WSDL document.

WSDL descriptions are frequently exchanged between partners in various businesses, or individuals who want to use services. But given that the web is so huge, invariably users would be missing out on many opportunities if they were to stick to the services they already know about. More importantly, WSDL allows an interface to be broken down into the "what" of the interface and the "how." Sometimes, applications may need to accomplish a particular "what," but might not care about the "how," in which case a different but equivalent web service is used depending on what is most convenient and available.

But how does an organization find out about new web services and how to interact with them? The next component allows users to discover new services to fit specific needs.

UDDI: Universal Description, Discovery, and Integration

UDDI is another important component in the overall area of XML-enabled data and metadata interchange. The most commonly used metaphor to describe UDDI is that it acts as the virtual yellow pages of organizations and the services that they offer. It can be thought of as a catalog of web services along with where the corresponding WSDL documents can be found for each web service. One of the larger goals that XML technologies have been working toward is making machine navigation of semantic content on the Internet as easy and understandable as possible. Perhaps after a number of years, people will say that standardized XML components did for data interchange and systems communication what the set of networking protocols (i.e., TCP/IP) did for the Internet in its early years. We have taken a look at SOAP and WSDL, which focus on how machines actually carry out conversations (SOAP), and how they know which language to use when communicating with one another (WSDL), but we have not discussed a technology that helps these machines find each other in the first place. That gap is filled by UDDI.

UDDI is most often used inside a repository. This repository is the actual electronic yellow pages, and contains a number of XML documents that can describe various services that are available. The services need not be strictly tied to SOAP and web services, although in practical implementations they often are. This is another example of how the various XML components were architected for generic rather than specific situations. WSDL provides the ability to describe more services than what are strictly thought of when SOAP/HTTP is mentioned. The approach was to create a generic technology that could describe a wide range of possibilities, and then to specialize the technology for current implementations. UDDI functions in the same way, in that the services described in a UDDI registry do not have to be "normal" web services—UDDI merely contains the representational power to refer to web services quite conveniently.

Universal Description, Discovery, and Integration repositories can be public, meaning that the entries in the repository are available to the wider Internet, or private, meaning available on a more limited basis according to the desires of the publishers. Each type of registry contains four types of data about services in the registry:

1. **The Organization.** This comprises information about the organization—its name, where it might be located on a map, and even contact information. UDDI also has the ability to categorize this information for specific searching, so that when users use a repository, they can choose to look at organizations by name, location, etc.

2. **The Service.** In this section, a brief description of the service is given, along with technical information about the service, such as a category, or a business process that the service is associated with. Again, providing this extra metadata about the ser-

vice provides UDDI publishers the flexibility to allow advanced searches for various services in the repository.

3. **The Template.** This section contains information that is intended for applications that need to use the service, rather than the other pieces of data mentioned earlier, which tend to be more useful to humans. Included in this section is the actual location of the service on the Internet, as well as load-balancing and/or routing information.
4. **The Model.** This area holds rather advanced information about what model the given service may conform to. For example, since each service would potentially want clients to speak a different type of XML, it would be useful to be able to categorize various services and put them in a taxonomy according to what type of structure they use for communication. If a program knows that using certain formatted XML messages are required to communicate with one service, it is often helpful to know what other services might be used with the same format.

Model information stored in the repository is particularly interesting, since it begins the process of aggregating disparate services into larger categories based on what types of formats are required to communicate with them. Further aggregation is inherently possible based on other metadata fields in the registry. For example, aggregation of services by company, by business process, or by specific information output could be very useful, depending on the situation.

Given all of the information in the repository, generally three types of searches are possible—white pages searches, yellow pages searches, and green pages searches. White pages searches allow services to be located based on a specific piece of information that the user already knows, much like in a telephone book. If the name or unique identifier of a business is known, that business can be rapidly located. Yellow pages searches work just like searches in the standard yellow pages—rather than aggregating entries by name, they are aggregated according to various taxonomies, such as by industry. If a service is needed within a particular industry without specific knowledge of the name of the service or an organization that provides it, yellow pages searches are often best. Finally, green pages searches allow the location of services based on technical information about the services, such as specifications for interfaces, and so on.

Now let us take a look at the way the SOAP, WSDL, and UDDI XML components can be combined. In Figure 3.12, we see the process that a client might go through to accomplish a particular task. First, the client needs to locate a particular service that can provide some information or facility to the client. In order to do this, the client connects to a UDDI repository, issues a search, and successfully locates a particular service that will provide pricing information for bulk purchasing of widgets. Next, using the information from the UDDI repository, the client connects to another server, which returns a WSDL description of how exactly the client should interact with the particular service. After consulting the WSDL description, the client has all the information that it needs to connect to the actual service, issue legal requests, and collect the information that comes back.

In some ways, this is an extreme example. It does seem rather complicated that a client would have to do this many steps just to fetch pricing information. It is worth keeping in mind that this is a special case where the client had no previous knowledge of any service that would fill its needs. For all subsequent uses of the service, of course, there would be no need to reconnect to the UDDI repository, or even to re-fetch the WSDL description—the client could simply connect to the service and conduct its business. The point of this diagram and discussion is to illustrate that the XML components discussed here not only provide a flexible method for data and metadata encoding, but also provide the building blocks for very useful facilities. The main problem with the Internet today is that it contains too much information that is understandable only by humans. Automated programs have no intelligence, and need their own way to

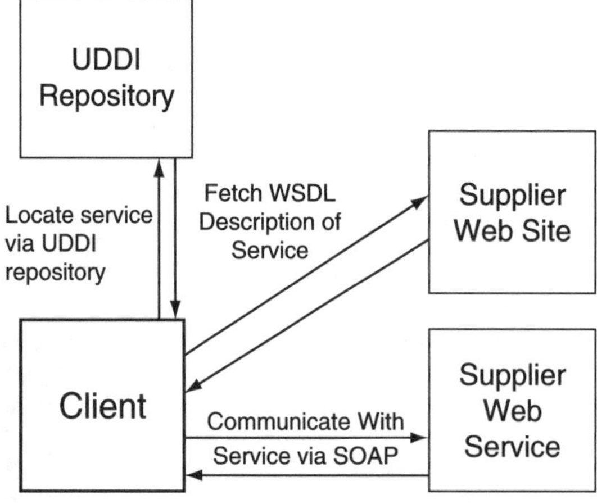

Figure 3.12

Web services communication architecture.

make sense of the information they are getting, as well as a method of getting around on the Internet on their own. The combination of WSDL, SOAP, and UDDI provides just that.

Using SOAP, UDDI, and web services, organizational data managers can re-architect some legacy applications into smaller, more compact, easier to maintain services that cost less, perform better, and are far easier to integrate than was previously thought possible. This is partly due to the fact that many components of this architecture are already freely available to be used, but also because the architecture forces the designer to think of the overall structure in terms of the form of the data and how it is supplied to users of the data, rather than focusing on platform-specific details.

SOAP, WSDL, and UDDI comprise a higher level system on top of the core XML language. Rather than simply representing data, they are meant to describe activities—the use of a particular service, or invocation of another process. The next component, ADML, goes to an even higher level, attempting to use XML's structure to represent a second level of structure—that used in the architectural process.

ADML: Architecture Description Markup Language

Given the architectural possibilities that XML has, and the work that has gone into architecting the XML components themselves, it was pretty much inevitable that someone would use XML to describe those and other architectural activities. That is indeed what the Architecture Description Markup Language has done. The function of this component is exactly what one might guess from its name—it allows the description of architectural concepts in XML. This type of XML format is often not used directly by a person, but its benefit is derived from tool support. In the past, many organizations have been locked into a particular set of design tools because they were not able to transition the data out of those tools into something else. Tools that are able to encode information in an ADML format will be more easily integrated into open systems.

Rather than storing architectural information in arcane binary-only files, or in stacks of paper documentation, it makes sense to encode this information and start using it in other ways. Making architectural documents available and highly usable via their XML format will likely allow other system designers to understand more about the architectural context that their new system must fit into, including existing interconnections and standard ways of accomplishing particular tasks. In order to effectively apply an enterprise-wide architecture, it must be formalized and able to be communicated. XML again fits the bill as a format everyone can understand (even if they only have a lowly text editor) and promotes use of and reference to the information in the document. From an architectural perspective, many concepts are necessarily reused in the architectural process to give the entire architecture a uniformity that lessens the learning curve and eases maintenance. Encoding architectural information in ADML allows chunks to be reused in the right places, as necessary.

One traditional confusion about ADML deals with its relationship to UML, or the Unified Modeling Language. While UML is meant as a systems design language that allows the user to specify aspects of the way one particular system will be constructed, ADML focuses on the way multiple systems interact, and therefore could be said to be one conceptual level higher than UML. Sometimes, though, the line between architecture and design is not always perfectly clear, and there are some concepts that carry over between the two.

Conclusion

The XML Component Architecture contains a number of components to accomplish a variety of tasks. Of the components that are described in this chapter, the related tasks can be broken down into the following categories:

- **Structuring and Semantics**. The Namespace, DTD, and Schema components described handle the ways that document assembly and meaning is conveyed to users and to other computer systems.
- **Parsing Technologies**. DOM and SAX are two different methods of parsing XML documents and gaining access to the underlying data that they represent.
- **Referencing and Linking**. XLink and XPath provide mechanisms for creating links between and across XML documents to help tie resources together and minimize duplication of data in different places.
- **Presentation and Formatting**. XSL, XSLT, and XSL-FOP handle the transformation of XML documents into both visually

oriented final products meant for humans, and different forms of XML for subsequent processing.

- **Web and Web Services**. RDF, SOAP, UDDI, and WSDL allow users to invoke foreign applications directly, and exchange metadata descriptions of information.
- **Advanced Languages and Applications**. ADML and ebXML (which will be covered more thoroughly in the XML Frameworks chapter) are two examples of higher-level systems and languages built on top of the core XML standard for specific functionality.

Effective use of XML requires that the user know about the various options that XML presents, so that the right tool can be used for the right job. Almost all of these components are based on the core XML standard, and frequently one finds relationships between various components. The number of XML components is likely to expand with the needs of the user community, as well as the number of organizations that use it on all manner of critical tasks.

4

XML and Data Engineering

Introduction

This chapter describes the intersection between XML and data engineering, pictured in Figure 4.1. We believe that the area of overlap is large, and this permits speculation about leveraging investments. The short lesson to take away from this chapter is that organizations must simultaneously consider reengineering their data structures as they prepare their data for use in an XML environment. Before embarking on XML-related initiatives, organizations should ensure that the maturity of their DM practices is sufficient to implement the concepts described in this chapter. XML holds a lot of promise, but when it is used in the wrong context, or used in conjunction with data structures and architectures that are already lacking, most people find that it does not live up to its reputation. The structure and thought that surround the use of XML must be coherent and reasonable in order for XML to achieve the desired results. Given a poor architecture or design for a building, the strongest building materials will fail. This is not the fault of the building materials, but the structure into which they were put.

The chapter begins with a discussion of where not to stop with your initial XML implementation. We next describe data engineering as it relates to participant roles, followed by system migration. We continue, describing various data engineering tasks as well as data structure difficulties. These concepts are illustrated with a case study that shows the

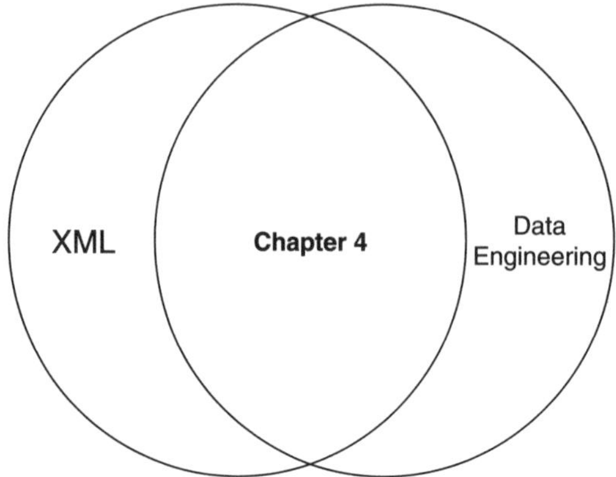

Figure 4.1

The intersection between XML and data engineering.

value XML can have when performing something as seemingly routine as the implementation of a large Enterprise Resource Planning (ERP) application. XML-related data security engineering issues are briefly described in the next section. As with quality, security (and particularly data security) cannot be engineered into finished products after the fact of production. Instead, it must be an integrated portion of the development process. The latter third of this chapter is devoted to a discussion of the fundamentals when it comes to engineering an organizational data architecture. After reading this chapter, the relationship between data engineering and the effective use of XML will be clear, enabling data managers to apply XML where it is most appropriate.

As many data managers have experienced in their careers, projects can live or die based on what data is available and how it is structured. Well-structured data that is understandable is not a blue-sky wishlist item for organizations—it is a necessity. Those who do not address poor structure typically get bitten by it until they do. But in many situations, management is not willing to invest in an enterprise-wide evaluation of data structures. In most cases, this is wise on their part, since the task can be unmanageably large. The challenge is to find a way to break down a daunting problem into chunks that can be dealt with.

Another theme that runs throughout this chapter is that work done on day-to-day systems projects affects information architecture. Data managers have the opportunity to build metadata components from the systems work that they do, and reuse these components in other ways. Some of the techniques in this chapter describe how to break things down so that the resulting components are reusable, and how to structure those components so that they can be reassembled into a larger organization goal in the future. Before we do this, though, we need to briefly discuss the way organizations typically adopt XML in the early stages, and to see how those first steps look from a data engineering perspective. (Note: Portions of this chapter were co-authored by Elizabeth R. White.)

Typical XML First Steps

The most typical approach to XML seen in organizations is to start using XML documents as "wrappers" on existing data—a one-to-one mapping between the attributes and data items in the existing system is established with XML elements, and documents are created that reflect the system in every architectural detail, the only difference being that the syntax used to express the data happens to be XML. In these situations, is should be expected that the XML documents created in such a way will have the same set of advantages and disadvantages as the original system. In such cases, there may be an incremental gain in functionality based on some of the characteristics and related technologies that the use of XML brings to the table, but the important point to note is that the system as a whole is still constrained by its original design.

There is an alternative to this, however. Motivated by the desire to get the most out of XML, we hope that organizations might address the larger issue of their data architecture and the structures that are contained within that architecture. Some might view this as a distraction from the core goal of getting XML implemented, but it is one of the most important steps. People are attracted to XML partly based on what they have seen and have been told is possible with XML. Unfortunately, the underlying structure that allowed the judicious application of XML technology to shine through and deliver all of those benefits has not been discussed outside of this book. The main idea to take from this chapter is this: Architecture and structure matter, and if there is any area of a system that needs to be right, this is it. With a well-designed structure, benefits are only limited by the creativity of those working with it. With poorly designed structures, it takes all of one's creativity just to work around the system to make it do what it was supposed to do. Next, we will take a look at what data engineering really is, and what types of talents and capabilities are necessary to make it work.

Engineering XML-Based Data Structures as Part of an Organizational Data Architecture

Data engineering is fundamentally concerned with the design and manufacture of complex data products using calculated manipulation or direction.* Controlling data evolution, moving data between systems, and ensuring the structural soundness and appropriate transformation of data are typical tasks that we associate with the definition of data engineering for the purposes of this chapter. In many places, the concept of data engineering is somewhat new. Consider for example the typical evolution of data systems within organizations. Traditionally, as a small organization starts out, individual systems are developed according to what is needed. As the organization segments into many different areas based on function, new systems are built. At some point, all of the different systems must be integrated (for example, integrating a sales system that takes orders with a manufacturing system that schedules production), but in many places there has not been a calculated, well-planned effort at putting together a system that is coherent overall. Working in the right directions requires getting the right people in the right roles to bring their talents to bear on the project.

If Software Companies Made Bridges

Let us look at an example of what is possible with real world engineering of solid objects, such as a bridge over a river. Just like an information system, a bridge is built with certain requirements in terms of how much load it must be able to bear, how frequently, where it should be located, and what function it should perform. Bridges are built of concrete, steel, and bolts, just as information systems are built of data structures, people, and processes.

In real world engineering, problems often arise with structures that must be dealt with based on the understanding of how the structure was engineered in the first place. For example, take a train bridge over a river. In the case of this particular bridge, when the river floods and comes close to covering the entire structure, the response from the engineers is to pull a train full of coal onto the bridge. The weight of the fully loaded train provides the extra weight to the bridge that prevents it from being overcome by the horizontal pressure and weight of the water flowing down the river.

**Merriam Webster's Unabridged Dictionary.* (2003).

The engineers knew how heavy the train could be, and that the bridge could accommodate the train. They also were able to figure out how much pressure the water would bring to bear, so they could come up with the solution. The point here is that the engineers were not thinking of the nuts and bolts in the bridge coming when devising a solution, but of the overall structure. In other words, even though a bridge is a complex structure, the construction and architecture of the bridge as a whole could be assessed, rather than its individual components. The engineers' design of the bridge structure is complex enough to serve its purpose, and simple enough to be understandable. The important thing to note is that only by understanding the properties of the structure as a whole was it possible to come up with a solution to this particular problem.

In information systems, the focus is too frequently on low-level aspects of the system, with an incomplete understanding of how they combine to form the whole. Inevitably, the solutions that are often employed end up being brittle and somewhat lacking.

Part of this problem is due to the fact that civil engineers have advantages over data engineers. They receive more intensive training specific to their field, and they have a long history of knowing what works and what does not. Their industry also does not change as quickly or drastically as the data industry. Civil engineers have quantifiable requirements for their projects—a bridge should be able to carry so many tons, etc.—while it takes special skills in the data world just to elicit all of the critical requirements from users. All of this together means that data engineers already have the deck stacked against them. They need a greater-than-average amount of skill to accomplish something that is merely usable. This perspective makes it a bit clearer why assigning teams of end users, business analysts, or even database administrators yields structures that are so often suboptimal.

The process of building specific data structures really should not be that different from building a bridge. For example, there should be a clear and solid plan for accomplishing the task, and there should be a clear definition of what roles and people are needed for the project. Most people would not want a house architect building a large data structure, just as they would not want to drive across a bridge that was designed by a software engineer.

So now let's look at the results of a project where there was not a clear plan to begin with. The Winchester House* in San Jose, California, was built by the wealthy heiress to the Winchester fortune, earned from the sales of the world's first repeating rifle. The house started with a reasonable base, but was under continuous construction for a period of more

*Example from Spewack (1993). http:www.winchestermysteryhouse.com

than 30 years. Subsequent construction was somewhat haphazard, with new additions made according to whim and available space. The result is a unique house of 160 rooms that contains such puzzling features as staircases that lead nowhere and two incomplete ballrooms. There isn't even an overall set of blueprints that describe the current structure of the house.

The experience of a person wandering around in this house is similar to that of a software developer wandering around through ad hoc data structures. In both cases, the path that must be taken is often not the intuitive one, and there is a feeling of needing to work *around* the system rather than *with* it to get something accomplished. As time goes on, just as the Winchester house had strange features added, information systems have been modified in strange ways, including tacking new fields onto existing structures, and repurposing existing fields for new (and unrelated) data. Over time, these modifications add up and mutate the original system into a monstrosity whose primary purpose seems to be to provide job security for the few that fully understand it. Systems that are built and evolved without a plan end up feeling like cranky co-workers that make even the simplest tasks more complicated than they should be.

One of the reactions to system organization of this type was a framework for building enterprise architecture that is directed and purposeful—the Zachman Framework (Zachman, 1987). This framework is of interest to data managers working with XML because it represents a method of structuring systems and information that avoids the "Winchester House" syndrome described above. Data management planning and strategy must be going on simultaneously with XML work—an XML project should not be used as a surrogate for that planning. The Zachman framework provides a skeletal structure for how information components can be arranged within an organization to get the most benefit out of systems investments. It is therefore worthy of serious consideration for data managers working with XML who want to understand how their efforts should fit into the overall picture of the organization.

While much has been written of John Zachman's framework, it is always good to read the original article, and so we advise data managers to get a copy of the paper and read it. It has been reproduced in numerous books and collections—searching for it on the web will yield a number of sources, including the Zachman Institute for Framework Advancement at http://www.zifa.com/.

In his article, Zachman articulates the case for large and complex technology systems to be developed using frameworks similar to those used to build airplanes and buildings. There is a well-defined process for huge physical engineering projects, and in some ways the goal of the Zachman framework is to learn from those processes in order to get better results in the data world. Large, complex system development is articulated using a series of plans representing different metadata, categorized according to the six primary questions and five levels of abstraction for large complex projects (see Figure 4.2). The intersections in the grid refer to areas that must be systematically understood rather than approached in an ad hoc way.

While we will address repository technologies and strategies later in the book, it is sufficient at this point to know two facts. Fact 1: Data managers cannot expect to find the features in a product that will enable a multi-year investment, so they should set their repository aspirations lower and build up their capabilities. Fact 2: XML-based metadata is so flexible that data managers can create a formal metadata evolution strategy, making it easy to transform XML-based metadata to meet changing requirements.

So data managers can begin to build up their "repository capabilities" by creating small implementations such as maintaining their XML in a small online database. Some organizations are able to begin implementing repositories using just operating system file naming conventions. As these become more sophisticated, the actual metadata can be migrated and evolved with increasingly sophisticated repository management techniques. To achieve this, the XML-based metadata is stored as XML documents. These documents can be modified using XSLT technologies. The changes to the metadata and aspects of metadata implementation strategy can then be implemented using database management technologies.

	Interrogatives					
Perspectives	What	How	Where	Who	When	Why
Planner						
Owner						
Designer						
Builder						
Sub-contractor						

Figure 4.2

Zachman framework organization.

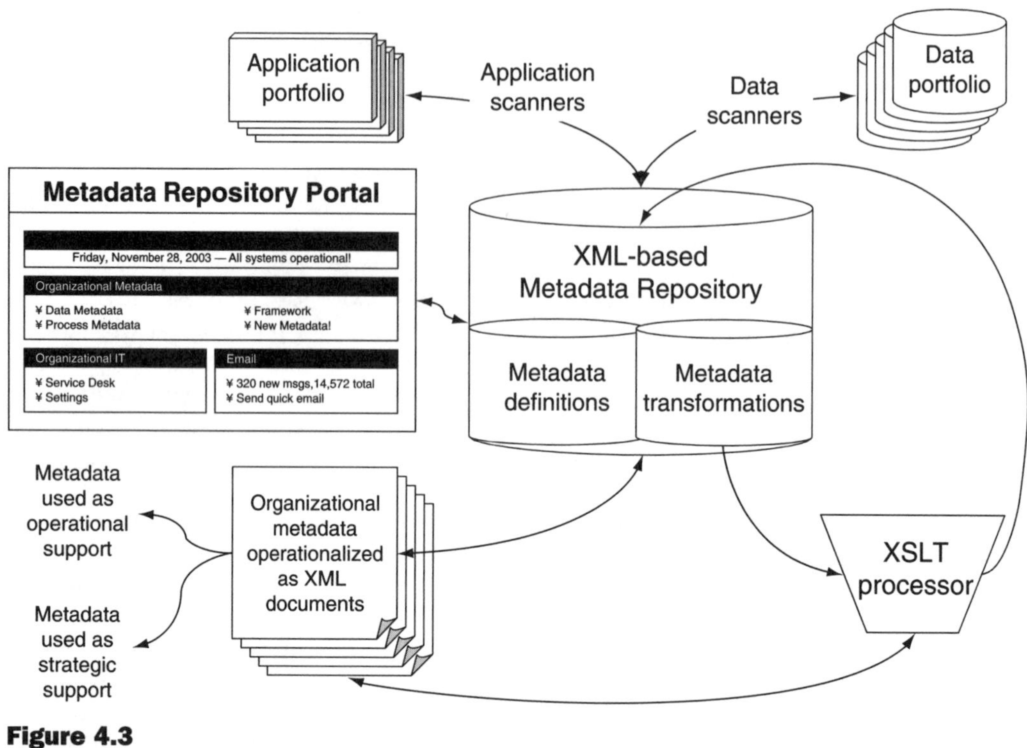

Figure 4.3

XML-based metadata repository architecture.

Figure 4.3 shows how XML-based metadata is stored as XML documents, permitting them to be incorporated into an XSLT environment in order to evolve the metadata.

What is kept in these frameworks and how is it organized? A combination of rough categorization of the *row* (perspective)/*column* (interrogative) and XML-based metadata itself argues strongly for maintaining the metadata as XML and creating what we refer to as framework hosted, XML-based metadata, or XM. From the planning perspective, the "what" question corresponds to a list of the business "items" that are of most interest to the organization. For a credit card company, this might be a cardholder, or a statement. These items are maintained as an XML list, along with the associated metadata, making the list useful to different applications. Aside from other applications, this list could be published on the organization's intranet for perusal by key staff. The XML document

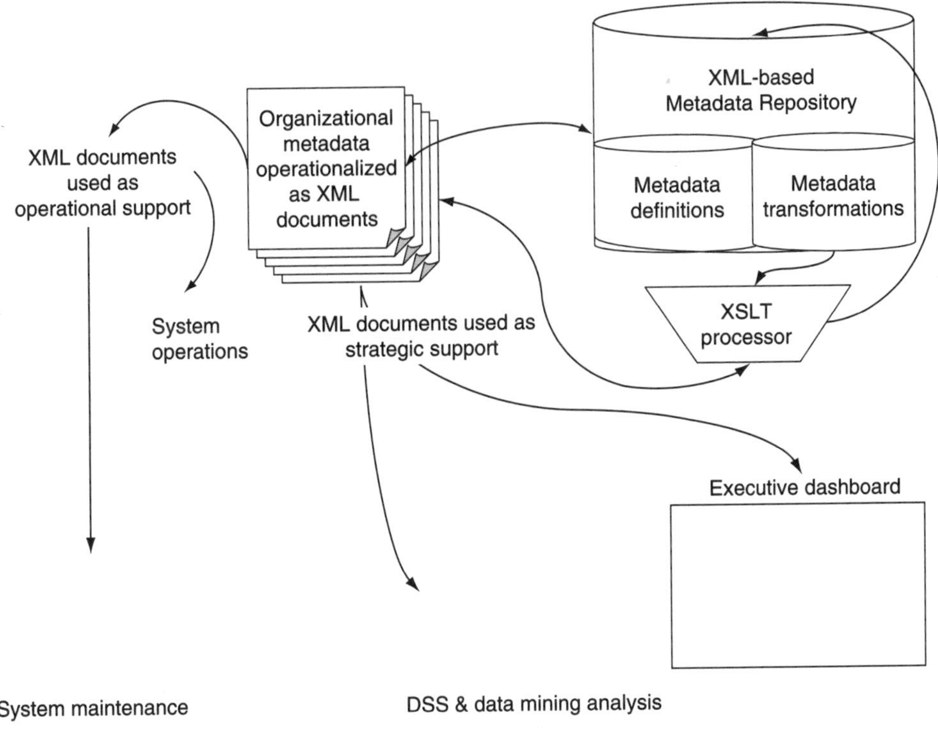

Figure 4.4

Metadata as operational and strategic support.

containing the "whats" from the owner's perspective could be repeatedly accessed. Framework-based XML documents containing XML metadata are stored, published on the data management group's intranet, and printed for strategic planning guidance. These documents are also available to other business executives via their electronic dashboards (Figure 4.4).

The purpose of populating the framework is to acquire information about the overall enterprise architecture. Gone are the days when organizations will permit data managers the luxury of a five-year data management plan. Textbooks indicate that the proper means of developing enterprise architecture is to develop the high-level enterprise model and various tactical-level models. Figure 4.5 shows framework-based XML documents containing XML-based metadata. Reasonable estimates indicate this approach has increased from a 5- to a 10-year project, and organizations generally will not invest in such long-term projects.

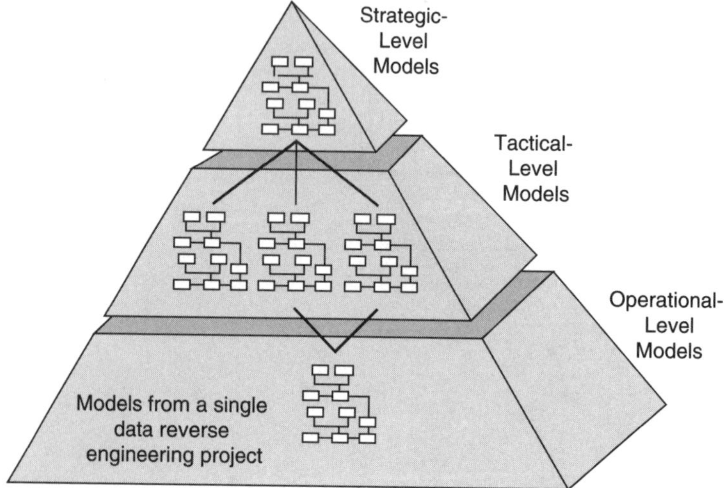

Figure 4.5

Information engineering via the original version.

What must happen now is the discovery of the enterprise architecture as a byproduct of other data engineering activities. Since data managers clearly cannot stop what they are doing and go work on enterprise architecture for a few years, it is important that some effort be made to derive enterprise architecture components from necessary work that is being performed anyway. As metadata is developed as part of other projects, it is added to the "repository" and classified according to the framework cell or cells that it occupies. It is necessary to develop enough critical mass in the components to permit users to discover combinations of components where one plus one is equal to three. For example, in order to have the list of business processes that interact with data items, an organization must first have both the list of data items and of business processes. By combining those two pieces of information, the whole is greater than the sum of the parts.

There is a reason that the architecture must be developed from the bottom up. While large complex structures such as the National Cathedral in Washington, DC, were developed top down, guided by detailed blueprints for more than 80 years and 4 generations of craftsmen, our legacy environment has not been maintained as well as we would have liked. Those detailed blueprints that cathedral builders have are nowhere to be found for many complex systems. Simply put, "plans and documentation . . . are poor or non-existent, and the original designers and craftsmen are no longer available. The result is increasing maintenance costs and decreasing programmer productivity—a situation that is inefficient, wasteful and costly to our businesses" (Spewak, 1993).

Architecture-based understanding is important because only from an architectural perspective can we consider a combination as more than the sum of its parts. Enterprise architecture is the combination of the data, process, and technology architectures. Data managers need to know that what they do has potential strategic implications beyond simply supporting the business with an information system. Just as engineers must be aware of the various strengths and weaknesses of raw materials used to create the architectural components, so too must data engineers understand the various strengths and weaknesses of their system's architectural components.

Let us go back to the bridge discussion for another example of what most organizations have done with respect to development of their data structures. The approach that some have taken is analogous to an attempt to build a bridge across a body of water that is strong enough to support a continuous line of fully-loaded, 100-ton coal cars passing each other, by throwing lots of pebbles into the river, knowing that enough pebbles will eventually create a bridge of sorts that will allow passage of trains over the river. It is probably possible to do this so that the requirements of the train weight will be met, but even under the best conditions it will be slow, costly, prone to shifting, and may have unexpected side effects for the organization (in this case, the river would be dammed).

The introduction of XML permits the organization to perform what has perhaps been viewed as of questionable value to the organization—data standardization. But it cannot be directly referred to as "data standardization." Business owners will pay for the development of XML data structure tags but not for data standardization because they perceive that it does not contribute to the achievement of organizational goals. The difference in an XML-based data management environment is that you need analyze only bite-sized chunks, permitting the smaller and better-defined projects to be executed within a budget cycle, with the results made visible to the remainder of the organization.

So each time any development work is done in the business or technical environment, it will be well worth it to spend the extra 5% and formally extract, analyze, understand, and improve the organizational metadata that informs and is produced by the development work. Figure 4.6 illustrates how development activities, input, maintenance, improvement, and new development activities and produce more useful metadata that is captured in a repository. The tasks are easier to conceive and manage if the development activities are prepared and treated as metadata engineering analyses.

The next section will discuss several specific data engineering challenges.

- Metadata engineering analysis magnitude
- XML and data quality engineering
- XML and metadata modeling
- Data structure difficulties
- Data engineering roles
- Measuring data engineering tasks

Metadata Engineering Analyses

Metadata engineering analyses can be defined using Figure 4.6 as focused analyses developed specifically to obtain a "chunk" of metadata that will inform a larger IT or business-development task. For example, data incor-

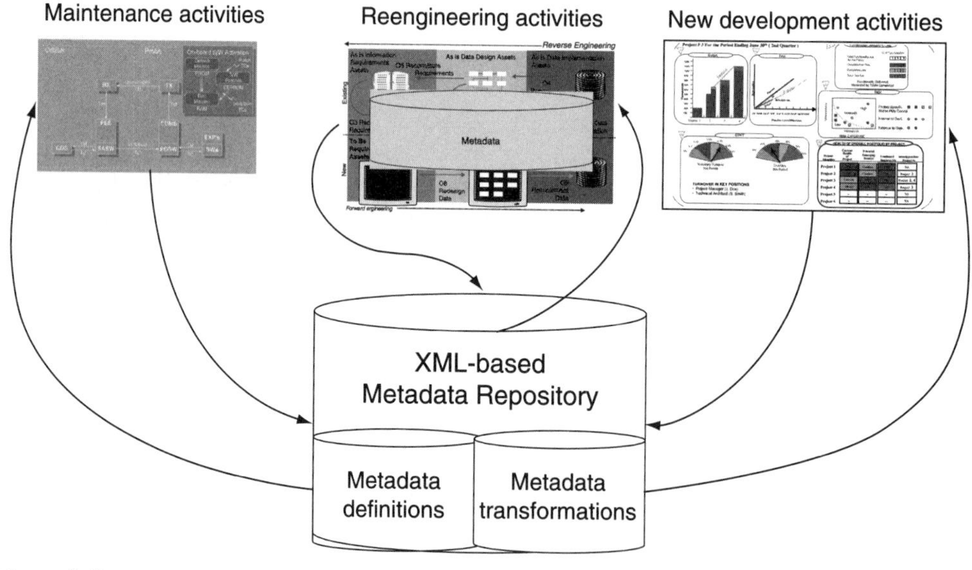

Figure 4.6

Virtually all engineering activities produce metadata for the XML-based repository.

porating the owner's descriptions of the major business items can be used as input to a metadata engineering task specifying the next layer down—the designer perspective. To justify the extra 5% investment in the metadata engineering analyses, the organization must first come to view data as an asset. XML-based metadata itself has several characteristics that are good to keep in mind while working with it—using a resource effectively always entails understanding its properties and taking advantage of them. The most important characteristics of data that are often overlooked include the following:

- Data cannot be used up. In this, data is unique—it is the only organizational resource that cannot be exhausted, no matter how it is applied. Unlike the time, skills, and patience of good workers, or even budget dollars, data does not disappear after it has been used.
- Data tends to be self-perpetuating. The more data organizations have, the more they use and tend to want. This can in some cases become a problem in which organizations capture more data than they can realistically manage and use.
- It contains more information than expected. Individual pieces of data are nice, but combining a number of different data sources often yields new insights. The field of data mining shows us that volumes of data often contain information about hidden trends. Synthesis of disparate data sources also frequently yields more information. In the data world, the whole is often more than the sum of its parts.

Each metadata engineering project should use a combination of framework specific and metadata engineering specific vocabularies. All of this information is maintained as Repository-based, XML Metadata Documents (RXMD).

The metadata engineering diagram is presented in Figure 4.7. This form of XML-Based Metadata Engineering (XBME) reinforces the point that reengineering can only be done when the forward engineering is based on coordinated metadata engineering. It illustrates the required coordination among various metadata engineering activities. When reengineering, the basic procedure is to begin with the as-is implemented assets and reverse engineer them into the logical as-is assets. Only when the logical business-data requirements and related metadata are understood can any reengineering hope to avoid problems with the existing

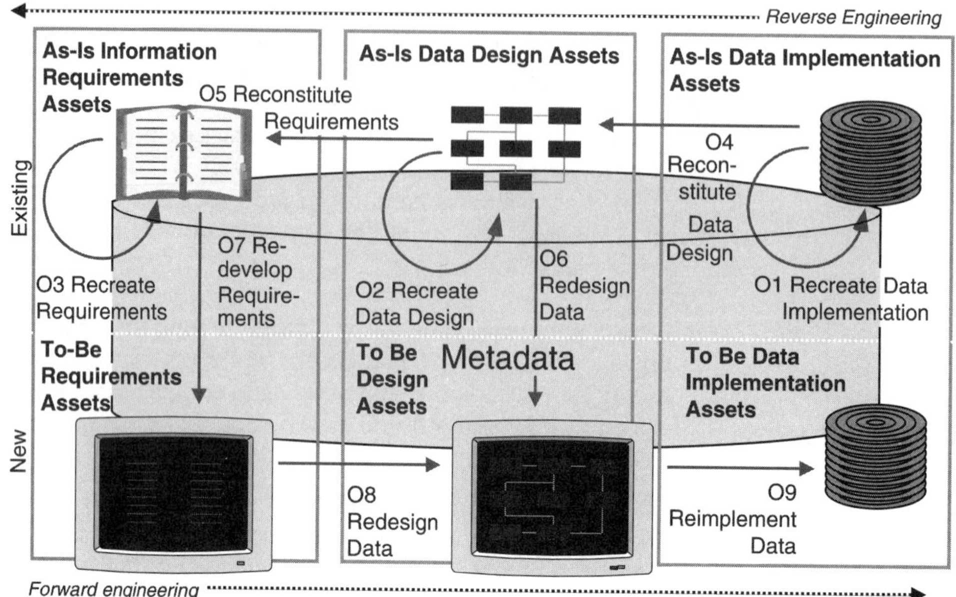

Figure 4.7

XBME activity specification framework.

data implementation. An example of a repository-based XML metadata project would be expressed as "a target analysis to take the as-is implemented data pertaining to the customer data and reverse engineer it from the *Subcontractor/What* cell into the *Builder/What* cell."

Consider another example, focusing this time on the billing information from an existing system. At first observation, the system's organization by queuing the A–F requests on a single machine is puzzling. On deeper analysis, it turns out that the hard disk drives could only maintain a 20-MB file system. Recreating that structure would not necessarily provide the best support of organizational strategy. The previous discussion of how bad ideas from past systems can creep into new systems still applies here. New systems should start off as a clean slate. Of course, good features from the previous system can be intentionally brought forward. Which features or aspects of the legacy system worked well? The important distinction to make is that some features should be brought forward because they were good and they worked, not simply because they were there. During XML-based metadata reengineering, data gets wrapped into

XML structures and is available for reuse immediately. This is the point at which quality must be engineered into both data and the metadata of the repository functions.

XML and Data Quality

Data quality is an important topic when discussing the effectiveness of XML or any other data technology, because ultimately XML documents can only be as useful as the data that is contained within them. Important decisions get made based on the contents of data stores, and if the source information that the decisions are based on is wrong, there is not much reason to put faith in the decision that was made in the first place.

XML increases the importance of the quality of the metadata layer. One important point is that there is a one-to-many relationship between the architect and the user. This means that there is more information closer to the user end and less toward the architect. Programmatic correction fixes multiple individual problems, and if fixes are made upstream, they will truly trickle down and not only save money but prevent future problems.

XML and Metadata Modeling

When you have prepared the data quality engineering aspects of your metadata engineering analysis, you can begin the process of extracting metadata. Use the Common Metadata Model (CM2) described below as the basis for organizing your information within each framework cell. If you do not implement the right or perfect format for the data structure, you can have XML transformations developed to correct and improve your existing metadata. The CM2 forms the basis for developing the XML-based data structures according to three specific model decompositions. In this section, we present an overview of the metamodel framework (see Figure 4.8). More on the common metadata model, including business rule translations, can be found in Chapter 9 of Finkelstein and Aiken (1998).

The same figure also illustrates the required metadata structure to support basic repository access requirements. There are two key success factors to each XML-based metadata reengineering analysis. First, the analysis chunks should be sized in a way that makes results easy to show. Second, the analysts should be rather choosy about which framework and

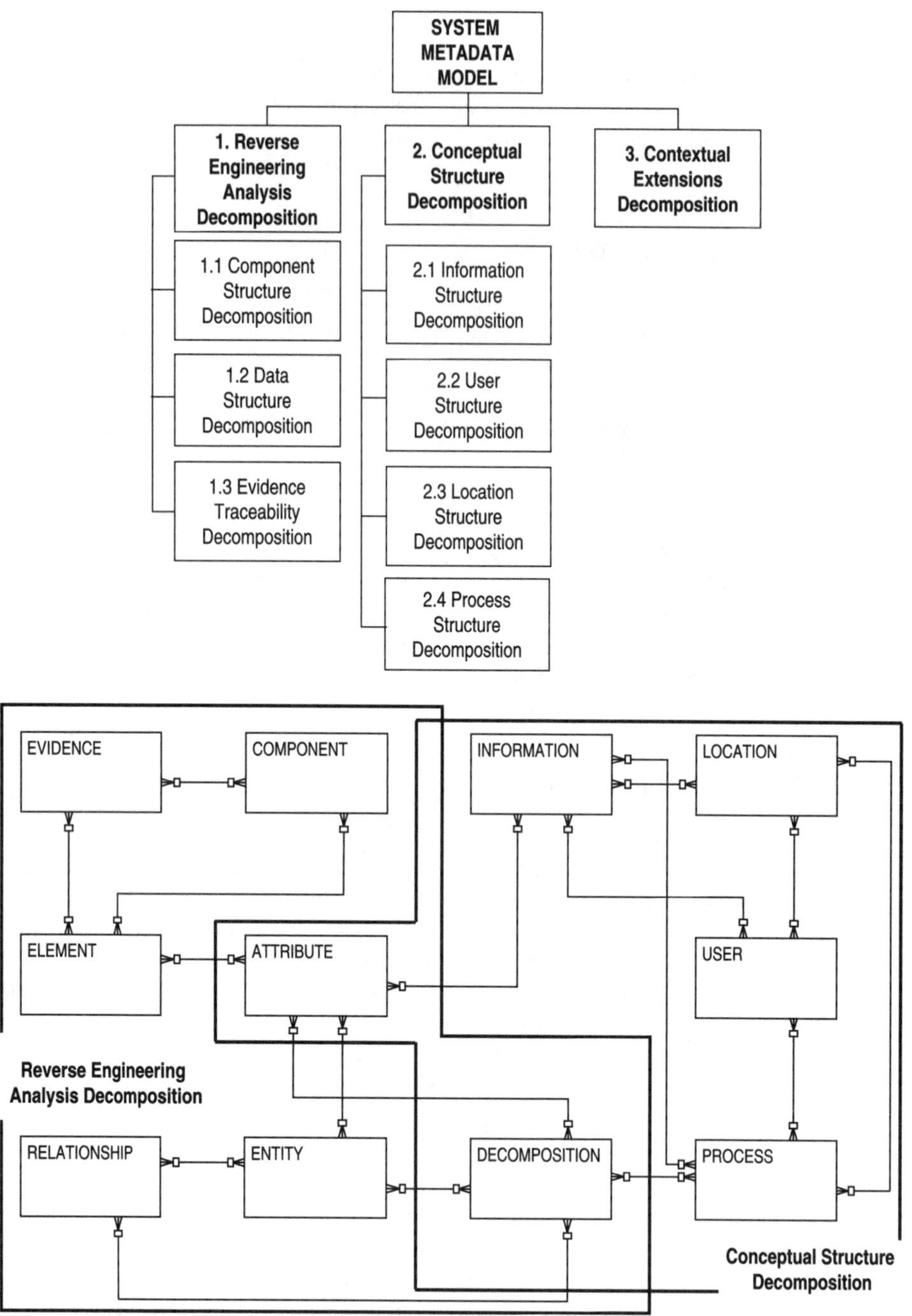

Figure 4.8

Three primary and seven second level model view decompositions used to organize the system metadata. This comprises the required reverse engineering analysis and conceptual structure decompositions.

common metadata model components get the most focus. Smaller, more focused projects make it easier to demonstrate results.

The set of optional, contextual extensions can also be managed in a separate decomposition. Some of these metadata items may be easily gathered during the process and should be gathered if they are relevant to the analysis. Contextual extensions might include:

- Data usage type—operational or decision support
- Data residency—functional, subject, geographic, etc.
- Data archival type—continuous, event-discrete, periodic-discrete
- Data granularity type—defining the smallest unit of addressable data as an attribute, an entity, or some other unit of measure
- Data access frequency—measured by accesses per measurement period
- Data access probability—probability that an individual logical data attribute will be accessed during a processing period
- Data update probability—probability that a logical data attribute will be updated during a processing period
- Data integration requirements—the number and possible classes of integration points
- Data subject types—the number and possible subject area breakdowns
- Data location types—the number and availability of possible node locations
- Data stewardship—the business unit charged with maintaining the logical data attribute
- Data attribute system component of record—the system component responsible for maintaining the logical data attribute

Data Structure Problem Difficulties

Getting the right data structures in the XML that you use with your systems is important because the cost associated with doing it with poor data structures at an individual attribute level is very high. When the amounts of data that have to be considered get so large, it makes sense for the data engineer to shift focus from spending all of his or her time thinking at the attribute level to concentrating on the data structure level. After all, every attribute should be just that—an attribute of a higher-level data structure, whether that is the relational concept of the entity, or anything else. An attribute is an aspect of a phenomenon or item that an organization wants to capture data about. When viewed in isolation, an attribute is not very useful. For example, what good is the information "123 Pine Lane" when there is no customer with whom to associate this address information? The thinking process should not be focused on addresses or capturing the date on which a customer placed an order—the level of granularity is too low.

Taking the initiative to implement XML in an organization should be an introduction into the process of learning about and improving existing data structures. To use XML as a stopgap solution, substitute for real analysis work, or way of avoiding the real issue of data engineering is to exacerbate the problem in the long run. In the next sections, we will take a look at why this approach has been used so frequently, and how the cycle might be broken.

With all of the benefits of sound architecture articulated, it is still often difficult for organizations to understand the importance of data structures. One of the arguments is typically that if data have been managed in the traditional way the entire time, and the organization has gotten along, why not continue to follow this route? In fact, while continuing along the same path may or may not be a feasible option, the efficiency gain resulting from appropriate data management can never be realized without some effort on the front end. What are other reasons that organizations have had a hard time understanding the importance of data structures?

The design of data structures is a discipline that does not have many metrics or judgment guidelines associated with it. It is difficult to take two examples of a particular data model and compare them, since there may be dozens of bases on which they could be compared, each of which may be hard to quantify. Many experienced data managers can gauge the quality of a design based on ethereal concepts such as elegance or beauty, but it is extremely difficult to assess exactly what characteristics of a design within a particular context indicate that it is elegant or beautiful. The reasons why one particular data structure would work and why another would not work also tend to be subtle. How much programming code is going to be needed to support the data structure and data flow? How many people are going to be required to maintain the system? How much flexibility does the structure provide for future expansion? Even given a set of answers to all of these and a host of other questions, along with weightings for the relative importance of the answers, it is difficult to judge a "best" solution.

This is a primary reason why organizations have had difficulty understanding the importance of data structures—because they have difficulty judging which is better or best. From the perspective of the enterprise, data structures either work or they do not work, for a very complicated set of reasons, and the analysis often does not go much deeper than that.

Data structures tend to be complicated, and many of those in common use are built on foundations whose soundness is questionable. This is usually the case when a legacy system has gone through many revisions and updates, stretching its functionality well beyond its originally intended limits. The more complex a structure is, the more brittle it tends to be, which can also necessitate huge changes in code to accommodate small data changes, along with many other unintended implications. When things get complicated in this way, workers tend to approach the problem by decomposing the system into smaller and smaller pieces until the problem is manageable. This is a completely reasonable approach, but if the system is complicated enough, this approach can yield to the "can't see the forest for the trees" type of problem. Attempting to understand a massive system in terms of individual attributes is an example of understanding a system at too low a level.

This illustrates another reason for the difficulty in understanding data structures. In many cases, organizations simply are not paying attention to them. Mired down in the details of managing complexity, thoughts of changing entire structures are unthinkable since it would require code changes, reporting changes, and perhaps even process changes. It is indeed difficult to perform brain surgery on an existing legacy system by removing brittle components and replacing them with more robust ones. This underscores the importance of getting the data structures right from the start, rather than assuming that reform sometime in the future will be an option. Examining the way that physical structures are built in a little more depth will shed some light on what lessons can be learned from an engineering practice that is already much more advanced than that of data engineering.

Engineering Roles

Systems built in the past have frequently been constructed in a very ad hoc way. This approach is fine for small systems whose mission is simple and whose volume is low. Scaling these systems up as the organization grows and evolves, though, can be enormously difficult. New systems sometimes get implemented simply because the old system has been stretched to the absolute limit of scalability, and other times because the old system contained too many brittle assumptions about the organization that simply do not apply anymore. Regardless of whether one is building a new system, or attempting to update an older system, the work involved typically falls into one of three categories—"physical data work," "logical data work," and "architectural data work," and are characterized by the types of questions about the data and the systems that are asked by people in these respective roles, as illustrated in Figure 4.9.

Systems are complicated, and building comprehensive, flexible systems is something that takes many people with many different types of expertise. To come back to our earlier analogy, most people understand that it would take more than one skill set to design and build something like a bridge over a river—it takes a group of professionals who all specialize in different areas. The same is true of large data systems. The high-level goal of the system might be very simple, for example, to provide human resources information to an organization, just like the high-level goal of a bridge is very simple—perhaps to get a train over a river safely. But that high-level goal has many smaller requirements. In the case of the

Figure 4.9

Different layers of data work.

Architectural	• How does this system fit in with others? • How does data flow through the system? • How is the system evolving?
Logical	• How do I join entities X and Y together? • Which constraints exist between entities? • How do I convert this data to information?
Physical	• What is the name of the database? • What platform does it run on? • Are the various attributes indexed?

bridge, it has to be able to withstand a particular amount of weight, the horizontal force of the water in the river, the effect of the climate and weather on the materials, and so on.

One of the reasons that many traditional systems have been inadequate in the eyes of those who work with them is that they have not been properly engineered. Inside your organization, is there a clear delineation between the physical, logical, and architectural roles? In many cases, the worker in charge of running the physical platform is creating the entity-relationship description of the system; the business analyst, who is ultimately an end user of the system and a data consumer, is trying to map out the flow of data through the system; and there may or may not be anyone assigned to the architectural role. It is not that these people cannot perform the necessary duties—they can. But there is a qualitative difference between the result of an effort by someone trained in that area, and an effort by someone who must learn the area and get moving by necessity. If these assignments, levels of expertise, and role confusions were the state of events in the engineering of bridges, people might be wise to think twice about crossing rivers.

Still other considerations must be taken into account. Unlike many new physical structures that are built from scratch, earlier systems influence subsequent systems heavily, because ultimately the data must be evolved from the old system to the new.

Measuring Data Engineering Tasks

We have discussed that the best case scenario might be one attribute per minute in terms of data mapping. From anecdotal information in the industry, however, it appears that a more realistic estimate would be 3–5 hours per attribute on average. Clearly, some attributes will take more time than others, as some data structures are more heavily modified in new systems. When estimating the amount of time that it will take to work with one attribute, a number of things must be taken into consideration:

- What type of data is in the attribute, and how does that data change in the new system?
- Which coding standards are in use, and do they change? For example, in many systems, a 1-character code might have an alphabet of possibilities, each of which has a different

high-level meaning for the way that record is dealt with or understood within the context of the system.

- How does this attribute match other attributes in other structures? From a relational perspective, is this attribute a primary or foreign key? If so, how does that change the requirements of what can be allowed in the attribute? Does the attribute have the same restrictions in the legacy system, and if not, how does one reconcile those differences?
- Given profiling information about the attribute (the number of distinct occurrences, total number of records, and so on), does that information change as the attribute is migrated? If so, how does that affect performance, normalization, and how it interacts with other attributes?

All of these factors and a host of others go into estimates of the actual amount of time it would take to migrate a particular attribute. As the complexity of both the legacy and target systems increase, the number of attributes tends to grow, and the implications of these issues also tend to increase.

It becomes easier to see why the average is closer to 3–5 hours per attribute, rather than 1 minute per attribute. The effects of the new estimate on the overall length of the project are profound. If data managers retain but temper their optimism, and estimate that for a particular systems migration project, each attribute will take 1 hour, the estimate grows to approximately 1 decade of person work. That might be doable in 1 year of work for 10 people, but likely could not be accomplished by 120 people in 1 month, even if there was not the massive burden of training and coordinating so many people.*

With these estimates in mind, it becomes quite clear why getting these efforts right the first time becomes critical. If the mapping is done incorrectly, or a portion of the data cannot be migrated due to an error in understanding of the attributes that were mapped, there is a good chance that substantial extra cost and effort will have to be undertaken to repair the damage. Typically, the consequences of putting the wrong roles on the project are significant budget and time overruns, paired with less than expected functionality. Keeping these ideas in mind allows us to make the most out of XML efforts related to these projects.

*For more information on this issue of "too many cooks in the kitchen," see Fred Brooks's work, *The Mythical Man-Month* (1995).

XML, Security, and Data Engineering

Of all of the various aspects of data management, security is one of the areas that XML did not thoroughly address until recently. In this section, we will briefly discuss what XML has to offer in the way of security, and what data managers might expect.

In many organizations, security is not really thought of as a core mission of data management. Still, it is something that most who work in the field will tell you should be part of the overall process, and not something that is tacked onto an existing system. Security should be integrated into the process from the start. When people talk about security, there are many topics they refer to that are worth considering, such as data authenticity, confidentiality, integrity, and availability. In addition, some refer to the security topic of nonrepudiation, which deals with auditing to determine who performed which action at which time, and to minimize deniability of actions.

When people refer to XML and security, there are two large areas that they speak about. The first deals with security in situations where queries are executed against XML documents, such as when a user wishes to pull a certain set of elements out of an XML document. The second deals with the security of the structure of the data themselves as they are in transit over a network. This can be loosely thought of as security *within* a document, versus the security of the *overall* document.

As of the writing of this book, there were several standards and approaches to security in querying XML data sources, but they were not particularly advanced or widely implemented. While those standards are developing and will be used in the near future, for this discussion we will focus on protecting documents in transit.

Figure 4.10 illustrates how XML security is actually considered another "layer" of security on top of several that already exist. The widely accepted OSI model of networking breaks up the functions of networking into several layers, such as the transport, protocol, and application layers. Security concepts have been developed at each layer, which is why some might suggest that XML security can be done using other technologies that already exist. Those technologies include IP Security (IPSec) at the Internet-protocol level, Transport Layer Security (TLS) for the transport-control protocol (TCP) at the transport level, and Secure Socket Layer (SSL) at the protocol layer. When people refer to XML security standards that protect documents in transit, they are usually referring to those that would logically fall into the very top row of Figure 4.10. When XML documents travel over networks, the process of communication involves all of the different layers, even if the specific technologies in those layers may differ.

Figure 4.10

XML security and the OSI model of layered standards.

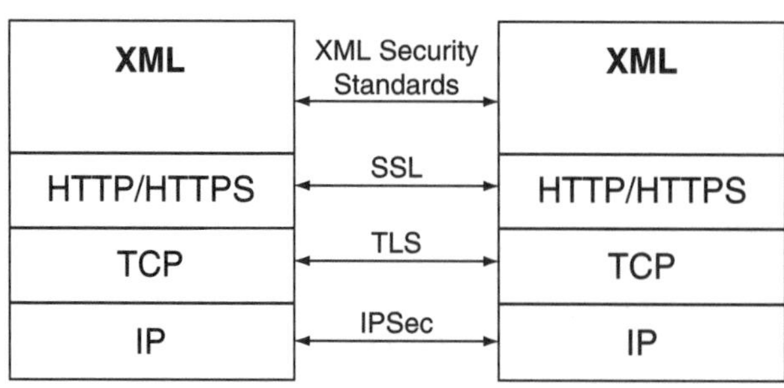

There are three main security standards that data managers should be aware of for working with XML. These standards are already mature and can be implemented by data managers in existing systems, or as part of new development to secure XML documents. They are SAML, XML Signatures, and XKMS, described below.

SAML—Security Assertions Markup Language

The Security Assertions Markup Language (SAML) has been ratified by OASIS as a standard, and provides a public key infrastructure (PKI) interface for XML. The standard gives XML a framework for exchanging authentication and authorization information, but it does not provide a facility for actually checking or revoking credentials. In other words, SAML offers the XML structure needed to request and understand authentication information, but it does not actually check the information. This might sound like a drawback, but actually, it is an advantage; SAML provides a generic mechanism for gathering the data that can then be verified according to what is right for the application. In some cases, that may be a username and password, in others a cryptographic key, or in others just a pass phrase.

There are three kinds of SAML statements in the assertions schema:

1. Authentication, stating who the requester is
2. Authorization decision, stating whether or not the request was granted
3. Attribute, stating what is actually being requested

Through combinations of these statements, SAML allows application designers to determine how authorization information should be exchanged, and when that transaction should happen. SAML is a good example of an XML meta-language for security.

XML Signatures

XML Signatures is a standard that enables the recipient to be sure that the message was not tampered with, and to verify the identity of the sender. This is actually an extension to XML of a very common security mechanism—the signature. If documents have to pass through several hands or many different networks before they reach their final destination, it is crucial to have a signature attached that lets the recipient be confident of the information being received. If an XML signature is verified, the recipient knows that the document is in the same form in which the sender sent it, and if the signature fails to verify, the recipient would be wise to ignore the document and contact the sender. The two security concepts that are most relevant to data signatures are data integrity and nonrepudiation.

The one important thing to keep in mind about signatures is that they are only as good as the signing party. If someone or some organization that you know and trust created the XML signature, then it may be useful. But if a signature was created by an identity that you are not familiar with, then the signature is only as trustworthy as the identity behind it. For this reason, when people create signatures they usually use standard identities that can be checked and verified using the public key infrastructure (PKI). The concepts behind PKI and encryption are covered at length in other texts, which describe in more detail the important aspects of trust, how it is cultivated and revoked in digital environments. Before working with XML signatures, it would be wise to familiarize yourself with this information.

XKMS—The XML Key Management Services/System

XKMS provides a facility for performing PKI operations as XML requests and replies. PKI, the public key infrastructure, is the basic trust mechanism behind encryption and digital signatures. Normally, individuals and organizations have standard identities that they publish and maintain. Those identities are published on central servers where they can be requested and updated. When information is needed about a particular identity, XKMS is an XML-based way to ask for the information and receive a response.

This might be used in conjunction with XML signatures as part of a larger security solution. When documents come in with particular XML signatures, the application might utilize XKMS to fetch the identity that corresponds to the signature in the document. That identity could then be checked against a list of known identities to determine whether or not the data in the document was trustworthy.

Overall, XML security standards, like other components of the XML architecture, are meant to handle a piece of a problem, and to be combined to solve larger problems. There is no one single XML technology that addresses all security concerns, nor is there likely to be. But by surveying the landscape of available XML security technologies, data managers already have the tools necessary to ensure the confidentiality and integrity of critical information transmitted in XML form.

Data Mapping Case Study

Let us take a look at the issue of migrating from a legacy system to a new system, and how XML-based architecture engineering plays into it. This example is essential in the next chapter. Often, the process of migrating data from a legacy system to a new system consists of an analyst trying to come up with a set of mappings between two systems, old and new or "as is" and "to be." Given a particular attribute, a number of questions immediately arise about how this attribute might be migrated.

- Does this attribute map to the new system?
- Does it map to just one element or data item in the new system, or more than one?
- Do multiple attributes in the old system have to be combined for insertion into the new system (as is often the case with ill-advised "smart keys")?
- Does this attribute remain associated with the same entity or a different one? What is the implication for the data values and normalization?

When analysis is approached in this way, it tends to remain unfocused and much too granular. In such a case, the form of the data in the legacy system has an inappropriately large impact on the way the data is thought of and moved over to the new system. One of the reasons that we implement new systems is to free ourselves from the mistakes and shortcuts of the past that caused organizational pain—and to think of the new solution and/or data in terms of the old system is to invite some of those old, ill-advised practices to crop up in the new system, albeit perhaps under a different guise.

Attempting to migrate individual attributes focuses on the wrong level of the problem and results in solving individual many to many individual mappings. This is shown as the top half of Figure 4.11. Rather than looking at attributes, or even individual entities, what really should be considered is the overall data structure. What information is being captured, and why? Migration efforts must take into account the thinking that went into the architecture of both the old and the new systems. For example, the old legacy system stored address information at the customer "household" level (a common approach for certain types of businesses such as catalog marketers, etc.), with each household potentially containing many customers. The new system, however, stores address information at the individual customer level. If this migration is attempted at the attribute level, the complexity is profound, since the total number of records for address will likely increase substantially; the attribute has to be moved into a different entity, the ability to aggregate customer records into households changes, and so on. Considering the

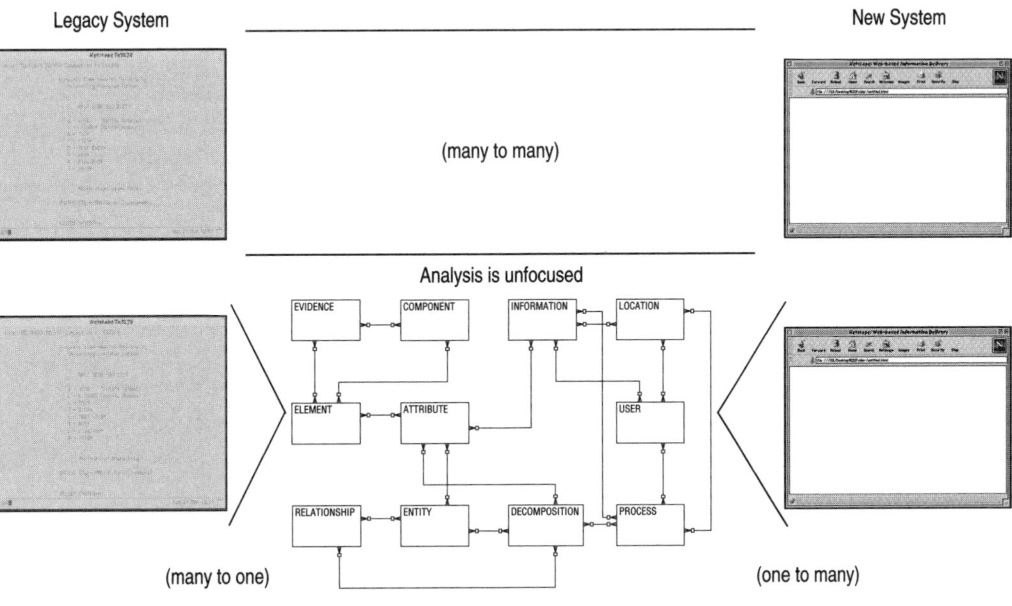

Figure 4.11

The traditional systems analysis approach.

Figure 4.12

Characteristics of the old system and the new system.

		APPROXIMATE NUMBER OF DATA				
		Records				
System	Structure	Physical	Logical	Relationship	Entities	Attributes
LS1	VSAM/virtual database tables	780,000	60,000	64	4/350	683
LS2	DMS (network database)	4,950,000	250,000	62	57	1478
PS-L	Client server RDBMS	600,000	250,000	1,034	1600	15000
PS-P	Client server RDBMS	600,000	250,000	1,020	2706	7073

architectural goals of both the old and new systems can simplify things. Why was "address" put in this place, and how might we manipulate data from the old system into a coherent data structure as it would appear in the new system? Understanding not only the hows, but the whys of systems is critical to making work as efficient and accurate as possible.

Let us take a look at a concrete example of what types of figures might be dealt with in terms of a systems migration effort. In this figure, we see that the old payroll and personnel systems are going to be replaced by a new system. The platform is changing; the operating system and even the core data structure are changing from a flat and hierarchical system to a client/server relational database management system.

One of the first things that catches the eye is the large disparity between the number of logical and physical records in the old system and the new. The old system has a total of more than 5 million physical records, with just over 300,000 total logical records. The new system seems to reduce the total number of logical records to 250,000, and the number of physical records is being reduced by a factor of 7! How is this even possible? On the other hand, the total number of attributes is ballooning from about 2,000 in the combined old systems to 15,000 in the new system. In many system migration cases, what we find is that the new systems may appear to have substantially more or less data than the old systems. This tends to make an attribute level mapping of data from the old system to the new extraordinarily difficult. But why the huge change in data storage statistics? There are several reasons for these changes.

- As systems age, they have more and more support code and data put into them to keep them running in response to changing requirements. Almost any system that is older than a few years will have typically required modification to allow it to perform some task that was outside of its original requirements. These modifications are rarely clean or elegant, and often require "strut" data structures that are not required in the new system, since it hopefully was designed from the start to accommodate that requirement.

- Different requirements for the new system sometimes cause extra data to be moved into or out of the system. For example, mappings between zip codes and state names, past client histories, and other information might be obtained from another source in a new system, so that the new system would appear smaller than the one it is replacing. This is due to a change in processes and a change in data flow.
- Typically, new systems implementation efforts are targeted rightly or wrongly to satisfy many data needs that the users may not have had satisfied in the past. This can cause "feature creep" in the design of new systems that leads to the appearance that they are larger or smaller than the original.

One of the problems that new system development frequently falls victim to is something akin to "data packrats." In many cases, attempts are made to bring all of the data from an old system forward to a new system, when no analysis has been done as to whether or not that old data is actually needed in the new system. This data can crop up in strange places. For each data item that a system captures and manipulates, it is always a good idea to know why that item is being captured, and what it will eventually be used for. In many cases, particular pieces of information are captured because they are needed for some small sub-process, for example, validating customer information or running a particular validation check on an account. As time moves on and processes change, that data might no longer have any reason for existing, yet still it is brought forward because everyone is "pretty sure that it is there for one reason or another."

If moving to a new system is starting with as clean a slate as possible, why not make an effort to minimize the amount of information the new system has to cope with by taking a hard look at whether or not data-capture requirements have changed since the architecture of the old system? Then again, sometimes data is captured simply because the organization thinks that it might have a use for the data sometime in the future. For example, one major national credit card company captures information on the shoe size of its customers where that data is available. Perhaps the data will be useful in some data mining effort in the future, but before adding large volumes of data that must be managed to a system, it is always wise to look at the proposed benefit relative to the very real current costs of managing that data.

The tendency is to capture as much data as possible, since the thinking is that no one ever got in trouble for having too much information on

Figure 4.13

Metrics of an "extreme" data engineer.

Terrific Data Engineers ...

- 2 person-months = 40 person days
- 2,000 attributes mapped onto 15,000
- 2,000/40 person-days = 50 attributes per person-day
  or 50 attributes/8 hours = 6.25 attributes/hour

and

- 15,000/40 person-days = 375/person-day
  or 375 attributes/8 hours = 46.875 attributes/hour
- Locate, identify, understand, map, transform, document, QA
- 52/60 minutes = **.86 attributes/minute!**

which to base decisions and actions. Unfortunately, that is not the case. Each piece of data that is captured has to be managed and dealt with, taking into account all of the quality issues that can arise in data. The only thing worse than not capturing a specific piece of data is thinking that the data you have is accurate when in fact it is not.

Now let us look at the proposed metrics of this attribute mapping process, which came from a professional systems migration project (Figure 4.13). Given the problem, a mapping of 2,000 attributes onto a new set of 15,000, it was proposed that two data engineers can accomplish the work in 1 month of constant work. Bearing in mind those numbers, we can look at the figure above and see that all of this work comes out to averaging 0.86 attributes per minute! In other words, we would expect these data engineers to be able to understand and map close to 1 attribute per minute, after they have successfully located the attribute. They would then of course be allowed the remainder of their 1 minute per attribute analysis of the document and do quality assurance on their work. Clearly this is not a sustainable rate of work. In fact, it is an utterly unrealistic pace for the work to proceed at for all but the most rudimentary systems migrations that involve a minimum of data. Perhaps these numbers could be thought of as an optimistic projection for simple projects.

Project Planning Metadata

Figure 4.14 shows a project plan that was submitted by one of the final four mega-consulting firms on a project. They told the customer that it would require more than $35 million to implement while the authors' organization brought it in for under $13 million. In this case, a copy of the

ID	Task Name	Duration	Cost	Work
1	**1000 ORGANIZATION**	**18.01d**	**$128,335.99**	**82.44d**
2	1100 Organize Project	18d	$42,585.33	27.36d
3	1200 Complete Work Program	18d	$71,739.42	46.08d
4	**Detailed Work Plan and Finalized Deliverable List**	0d	$0.00	0d
5	1300 Develop Quality Plan	18.01d	$14,011.24	9d
6	**2000 ESTABLISH DEVELOPMENT ENVIRONMENT**	**54d**	**$235,364.34**	**228.07d**
7	2100 Setup Application Software	18d	$51,310.67	49.86d
8	2200 Site Preparation	54d	$184,053.67	178.2d
9	**Comprehensive Backup Plan**	0d	$0.00	0d
10	**3000 PLAN CHANGE MANAGEMENT**	**72.01d**	**$347,901.67**	**249.13d**
11	3100 Develop Change Management Plan	18.01d	$39,821.00	21.97d
12	**Change Management Plan**	0d	$0.00	0d
13	3200 Implement Change Management Plan	36d	$123,597.00	91.08d
14	3300 Develop Impact Analysis Plan	18.01d	$17,485.42	12.96d
15	**Impact Analysis Plan**	0d	$0.00	0d
16	3400 Implement Impact Analysis Plan	18d	$166,998.25	123.12d
17	**4000 PERFORM CONFIGURATION TEST**	**72d**	**$93,585.25**	**76.14d**
18	4100 Prepare for Functional Configuration Testing	54d	$53,091.67	36.18d
19	4200 Perform Functional Configuration Testing	18d	$40,493.58	39.96d
20	**5000 PRELIMINARY SYSTEM & PROCESS DESIGN**	**108d**	**$1,248,758.99**	**1079.82d**
21	5100 Analyze Business Processes	54d	$621,386.25	511.92d
22	5200 Software Fit Analysis	54d	$568,447.16	505.44d

Jun
S S M T W

Project:
Date: Thu 9/28/00

Task | Summary | Rolled Up Progress
Progress | Rolled Up Task
Milestone | Rolled Up Milestone

Page 1

Figure 4.14

Representative project plan.

actual Microsoft Project document was taken and examined carefully before exporting it to a format where it could be repurposed—XML. Once available in XML, it was imported into spreadsheets, databases, and data-analysis tools. Analysis of this data enabled us to determine that the organization was attempting to bill customers for several full years of a single partner's time. It also enabled us to point out early on the infeasibility of their data conversion planning.

The original consultant's proposal was that the data conversion for the ERP would take 2 person-months. When we did the math, we found the following:

- Two person-months is equal to 40 person-days.

- In 40 person-days, the consultant was stating that they could map 2,000 attributes onto 15,000!
- On the source side, 2,000 attributes mapped in 40 person-days required a rate of 50 attributes each person-day; 6.25 attributes analyzed each hour.
- On the target side, the team would have to work to analyze 15,000 data attributes in 40 days—a rate of 375 attributes each person-day and 46.875 attributes each hour.
- To do a quality job, locating, identifying, understanding, mapping, transforming, and documenting tasks would have to be accomplished at a combined rate of 52 for each hour or .86 attributes for each and every minute!

There all sorts of reasons that these numbers are not credible, and it implies that the organization is either underbidding the project and hoping for an add-on contract to extend the work, or they are hopelessly naive about the process required. Whether organizations believe a metric of one attribute per hour or not, if they go to the trouble of analyzing the metadata they can collect about the project, they will be better informed as to the project's size and shape. Next, we will describe the process of repurposing the ERP metadata—wrapping it in XML and reusing it in a number of ways to help the project implementation.

Extracting Metadata from Vendor Packages

As this chapter is written in 2003, the war between Oracle and PeopleSoft that has also involved J. D. Edwards is being played out. It serves to emphasize the important ERP-derived data management products that can be managed using XML. Imagine the amount of resources that will be wasted converting from J. D. Edwards to PeopleSoft and then converting it again to others.

Figure 4.15 shows the first 23 of approximately 1,000 business processes contained in the PeopleSoft Pay, Personnel, and Benefits modules—a popular combination of products purchased to replace legacy systems. This metadata can be accessed relatively easily—a fact that is not well known. However, obtaining ERP metadata in an XML-based format is not difficult. Understanding the internal structures used by the ERP can vastly

Home Page	Business Process Name	Component Name	Step Name
Benefits	Administer Base Benefits	Manage Benefit Enrollments-US	Benefit Program Participation
Benefits	Administer Base Benefits	Manage Benefit Enrollments-US	Benefits Deduction Summary
Benefits	Administer Base Benefits	Manage Benefit Enrollments-US	Benefits Summary
Benefits	Administer Base Benefits	Manage Benefit Enrollments-US	Disability Benefits
Benefits	Administer Base Benefits	Manage Benefit Enrollments-US	Employee Data Summary
Benefits	Administer Base Benefits	Manage Benefit Enrollments-US	FSA Benefits
Benefits	Administer Base Benefits	Manage Benefit Enrollments-US	Health Benefits
Benefits	Administer Base Benefits	Manage Benefit Enrollments-US	Leave Plan Benefits
Benefits	Administer Base Benefits	Manage Benefit Enrollments-US	Life and AD/D Benefits
Benefits	Administer Base Benefits	Manage Benefit Enrollments-US	Savings Plan Benefits
Benefits	Administer Base Benefits	Manage Benefit Enrollments-US	Vacation Buy/Sell Benefits
Benefits	Administer Base Benefits	Manage Dependents/Benefs	Dep/Ben Comments
Benefits	Administer Base Benefits	Manage Dependents/Benefs	Dependent/Beneficiary Summary
Benefits	Administer Base Benefits	Manage Dependents/Benefs	Dependents/Beneficiaries
Benefits	Administer Base Benefits	Manage Leave Accruals	Report Leave Accruals
Benefits	Administer Base Benefits	Manage Leave Accruals	Review Leave Accruals
Benefits	Administer Base Benefits	Manage Leave Accruals	Run Leave Accrual Process
Benefits	Administer Base Benefits	Report Benefit Participation	Benefits Contribution Register
Benefits	Administer Base Benefits	Report Benefit Participation	Create Carrier Interface
Benefits	Administer Base Benefits	Report Benefit Participation	Deduction/Benefits Register
Benefits	Administer Base Benefits	Report Benefit Participation	Health Benefits Participation
Benefits	Administer Base Benefits	Report Benefit Participation	Life and AD/D Participation
Benefits	Administer Base Benefits	Report Benefit Participation	Load Carrier Reporting Table

Figure 4.15

A view of PeopleSoft businesss processes.

simplify the process of evolving your data into its new forms. Understanding the value of the XML-wrapped business processes is easier when viewing business processes as hierarchical structures.

Figure 4.16 Illustrates the PeopleSoft Internal Metadata Structure. Figure 4.17 shows the physical implementation of the hierarchy described below. This hierarchy of workflow, system, and data metadata and other structures play a number of roles in the implementation of the ERP, including

- Workflow Metadata can be used to support business practice analysis and realignment. This permits accurate representations of what exactly the ERP does, which can have important implications if the organization is planning to become ISO-9000 certified to do business in the EU.

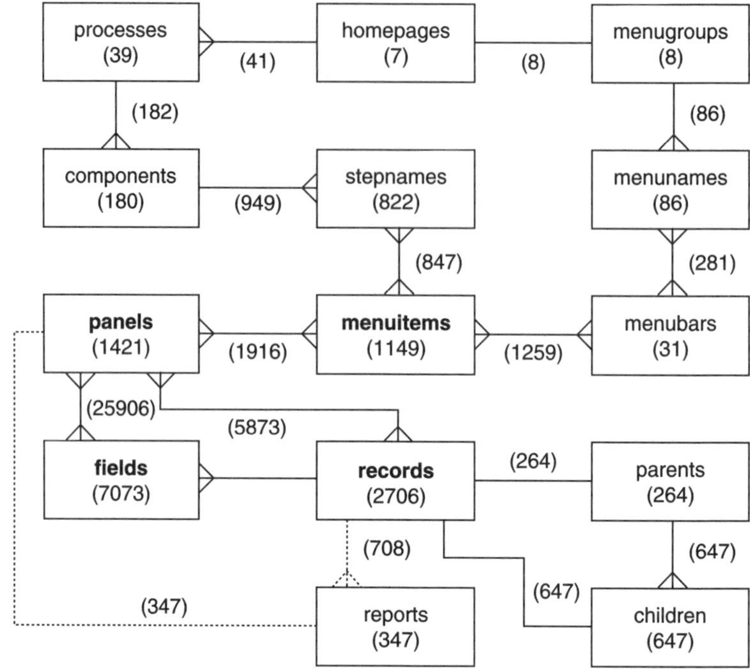

Figure 4.16

PeopleSoft internal metadata structure.

- System Structure Metadata can be used in requirements verification and system change analysis. XML-wrapped, system-structure metadata allow the development of more precise requirements validation techniques. We practice a requirements technique that shows how each requirement can be precisely identified as system functionality existing on one or more uniquely identified screens of the application. For example, panels X, Y, and Z are used to implement the hiring process.

- Data Metadata is data describing specific aspects of the implemented data, and it can be used to support data-related evolution sub-tasks such as data conversion, data security, and knowledge worker training. Expressing the metadata in XML permits them to be reused in support of data conversion by automating the building of extraction queries and organizing training sessions.

Figure 4.17

PeopleSoft process metadata.

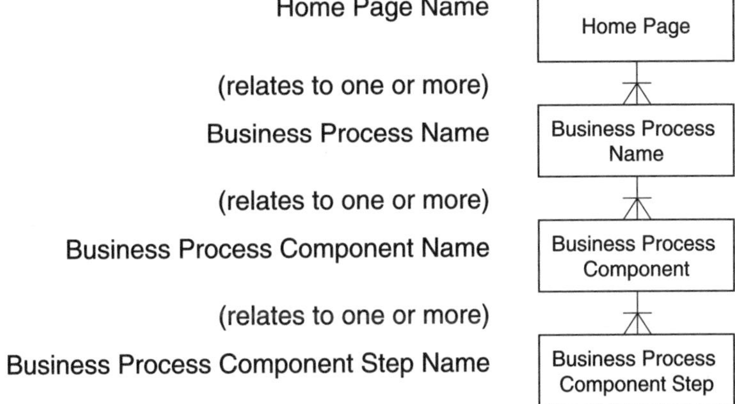

ERP metadata expressed in XML have many other novel uses. See Aiken and Ngwenyama (1999) for more technical details of these uses. Let us close this section on ERP metadata products by describing two products that are seen as useful by all managers.

The first is a quick tool developed for managers who are interested in exploring more about the new ERP. Illustrated in Figure 4.18, a small Java application reads the XML and allows the user to display summaries of ERP metadata depending on where the mouse is placed. The figure illustrates use of workflow metadata showing the processes in each home page and the Administer Workforce components. It indicates the processes associated with each homepage, particularly the two with the most: Develop Workforce, and Administer Workforce. The same tool was used to display why the recruiters were receiving separate training. In this manner, every manager who visited the web site understood that they were benefiting from the use of XML.

The second management oriented product is the ability to phase various cut-overs during the implementation. Figure 4.19 shows a chart that all management understood. XML provided a means of buffering users from transitions with high failure costs. Legacy data expressed in XML interacting with the ERP data can be managed using XML schemas, focused data engineering. As a data management product, all who have suffered through poorly managed cut-overs will welcome the phasing ability.

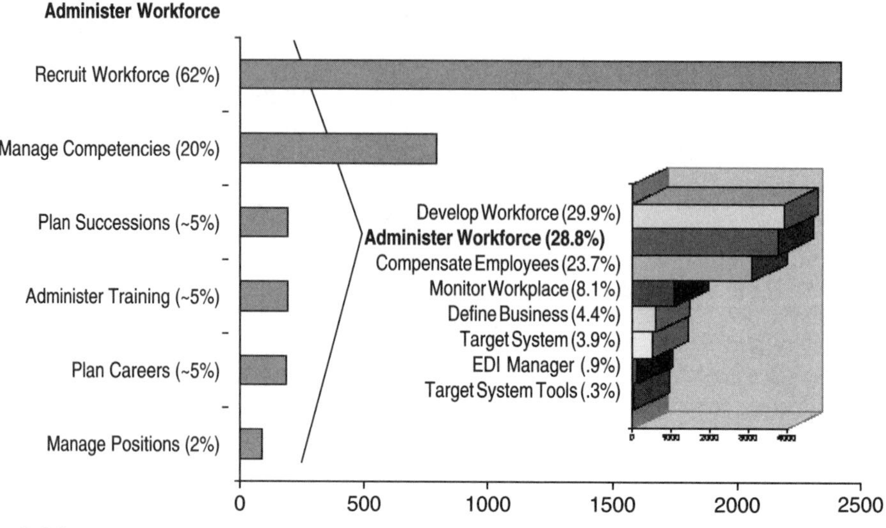

Figure 4.18

Tangible use of XML by management: XML wrapped PeopleSoft Metadata.

Figure 4.19

XML wrapping PeopleSoft Metadata. (TheMAT is short for The Metadata Access Technology.)

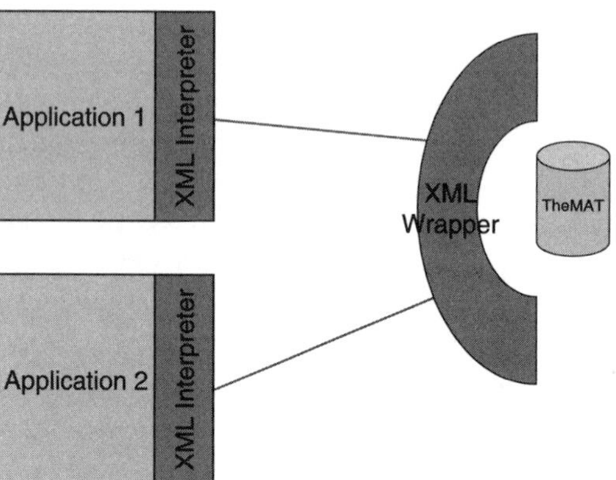

Real world projects, however, tend to be of a level of complexity that rules out the use of this information as a basis for estimations. In truth, the actual amount of time that it takes these efforts is many times this estimate. Given this information, it is not difficult to see why data-engineering projects of this type tend to run late and over budget. Even the engineer of a train bridge over a river is not burdened in his or her job with trying to figure out a way to take old architectural pieces of the previous bridge and somehow work them into the design. The task of simply understanding the complexity of systems migration in context is considerable. In some cases, that preliminary step may take as much time as an organization has allotted for the entire effort!

So the question arises, how is it exactly that we measure these data-engineering tasks? In order to effectively plan projects and understand what one is getting into before the project is launched, it is important to have some ability to measure what it will take.

Chapter Summary

We have described the interrelationships that exist between XML and data engineering. At the very least, we hope that you are motivated to begin reverse engineering your new systems in order to obtain an understanding of the data architecture of the target components. This discussion led to an argument for the importance of architecture concepts supporting the analysis. We have also covered the role of data quality in XML metadata recovery, development of vocabularies supporting metadata-engineering activities, and the approach to XML-based data engineering.

The purpose of these discussions is to get data managers thinking in the right direction about some of the projects currently going on inside their organizations. When looking at the Zachman framework, it is good for data managers to know that things they are doing in their projects today can work toward the goal of a more coherent overall architecture, even if management will not spring for an enterprise architecture initiative. Toward the end of the chapter, we discussed sizing components so that value could be shown from metadata engineering projects, and how to structure these engagements to get the most benefit out of the XML-based metadata.

Distilled into its simplest form, we hope the lessons of this chapter show that first and foremost, organizations need well-structured data upon which to build their XML structures. Attacking this issue at the global organizational level is too much and too expensive, so data managers need to take a bottom-up approach to building these solutions. Throughout these projects, there of course needs to be a way of fitting these components together, and this coordination of components can be accomplished through effective metadata management techniques we have discussed.

References

Aiken, P. H., Ngwenyama, O., et al. (1999). Reverse engineering new systems for smooth implementation. *IEEE Software 16*(2): 36–43.

Finkelstein, C., & Aiken, P. H. (1998). *Building corporate portals using XML.* New York: McGraw-Hill.

Merriam-Webster's unabridged dictionary. (2003), Springfield, MA: Merriam-Webster.

Spewak, S. H. (1993). *Enterprise architecture planning.* Boston: QED Publishing.

Zachman, J. (1987). A framework for information systems architecture. *IBM Systems Journal 26*(3): 276–292.

5

Making and Using XML: The Data Managers' Perspective

Introduction

Two trends are occurring in the XML and data management technologies that make it difficult to accurately sum up. First of all, because of the XML hype, practically all vendors are relabeling their offerings to make it seem as if they take advantage of XML. Some do; others have not gotten it quite right. The second complicating factor is that the use of XML technologies is still relatively immature. As our collective use of XML and data management technologies matures, the means by which we incorporate the technology will evolve as we move rapidly up a steep learning curve. In short, we need to know more before we can determine how best to develop XML-based support for data management processes.

In this chapter, we will attempt to describe major categories of XML-based technologies in terms of whether they are used to capture (input), process, or produce XML (output). This categorization reflects not only the main things that computers do (input, process, output) but also what is done with any type of data. Data can be created, consumed, or used. This is certainly not the only way these tools could be categorized, and there are some fuzzy boundaries as many tools perform more than one operation. The reason for this categorization is that data managers typically think of XML in terms of which of the three facilities are most needed. Some data managers are interested in XML in order to understand data coming from outside vendors. Others are interested in how it aids the process. Still others are interested in exporting XML for use elsewhere.

This chapter is important for data managers who want to get a glimpse of which classes of tools are available to work with today. There are plenty of software companies who will speak in glowing terms about what is coming around the corner, but the discussion of data management technologies in this chapter is intended to give data managers an idea of the kinds of functionality they can rely on now. This discussion refers not just to software that is used strictly for XML, but related software such as modeling tools that are already in many organizations. For some, working with XML-capable data management technologies understand that it is more about learning the new tricks of the software that they already have, rather than learning a new toolset altogether.

Input

There are three basic ways to get data into XML other than creating a new application capable of producing it. Each of the three we will discuss below.

- XML editors
- CASE (Computer Aided Software Engineering) tools
- Extracting metadata from negacy systems

XML Editors

An XML document is simply text. Therefore, it can be created in any text editor such as Notepad, Emacs, TextEdit, etc. Many people can and do craft their XML by hand using this type of editor. It is likely, though, that many data managers will graduate to editors that have been designed specifically for creating and editing XML documents. These editors, such as XML Spy and XML Pro and many others, provide graphical representations of an XML document to make the design process easier on the developer. While these editors have some of the features of computer-aided software engineering (CASE) tools, they are not meant to facilitate engineering directly, just to create documents, and are therefore classified as editors rather than CASE tools.

Figure 5.1 illustrates one basic feature supported by XML editors—the ability to visualize and manage the document's structure from a metadata perspective. The figure shows an XML document describing an XML structure called Bookstore. Bookstore is composed of a sequence of books and books are composed of title, author, year published, etc. This type of rudimentary metadata management is crucial to managing and evolving XML structures. By briefly looking through a document, an author can assess what the purpose of the document is, and what type of metadata is captured in it. If the document conforms to a particular vocabulary standard, much more information might be available, including the domain of various data items, and other extended information.

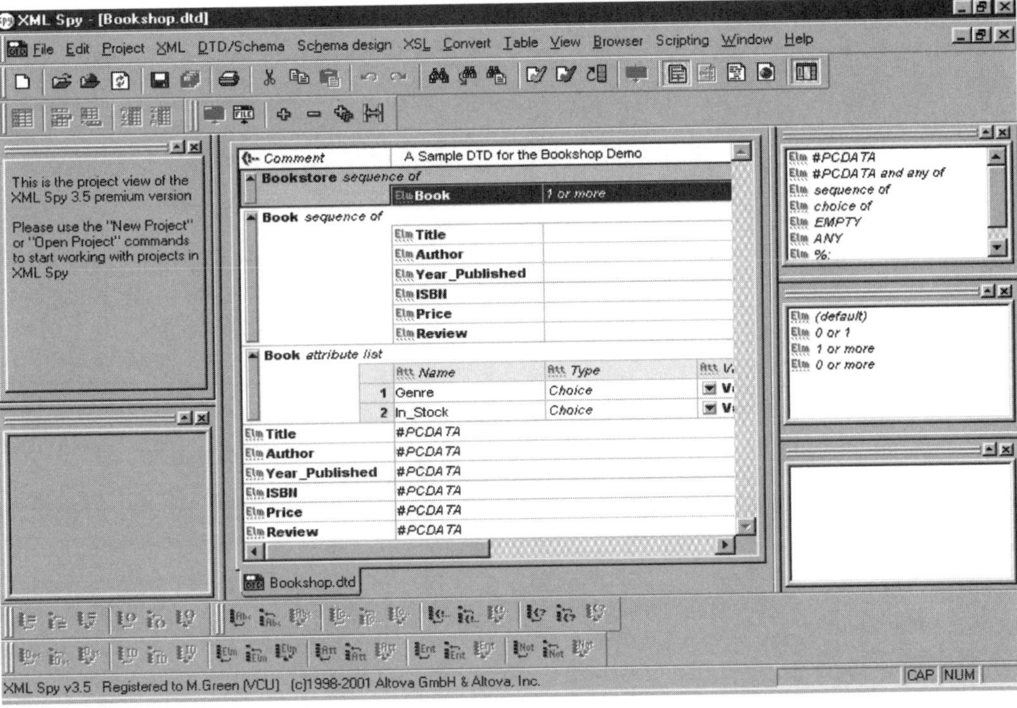

Figure 5.1

Screen shot from XMLSpy web site accessed 10/2001.

Figure 5.2 shows a demonstration screen shot from the XMLSpy web site. The illustration scenario is of an organizational chart, showing the tool's ability to integrate the management of the

- XML document's structure as an XML schema (OrgChart.xsd)
- Associated stylesheet (OrgChart.xsl)
- Integrated WSDL specification
- Document after it is rendered, using the stylesheet, into XHTML (OrgChart.xml)
- Error handling and debugging
  - SOAP debugger tool
  - XSLT debugging tool
- Governing XML structure for a related XML document (ipo.xml)

It makes sense to try out some of these tools because of their low entry cost. The cost is typically measured in hundreds of dollars rather than thousands, and many data managers find them useful if for no other purpose than to inspect and debug XML documents. A tool with integrated XML concepts will aid the learning process and typically covers its cost (and then some) in valuable learning experiences.

CASE Technologies

CASE, which stands for computer aided software engineering, is a class of tools that is already heavily used in every type of organization. This particular classification is somewhat broad, but for the purposes of this discussion we will try to restrict it to software packages that help in systems development.

Figure 5.3 shows the first instance of a CASE tool incorporating what we consider desirable XML support. Since Visible Advantage has its origins with Clive Finkelstein, who is known as the father of information engineering, it was not surprising that it was the first to provide quality XML support. The figure shows just how integrated the process of managing the CASE tool metadata could be. While the entity "Person" is

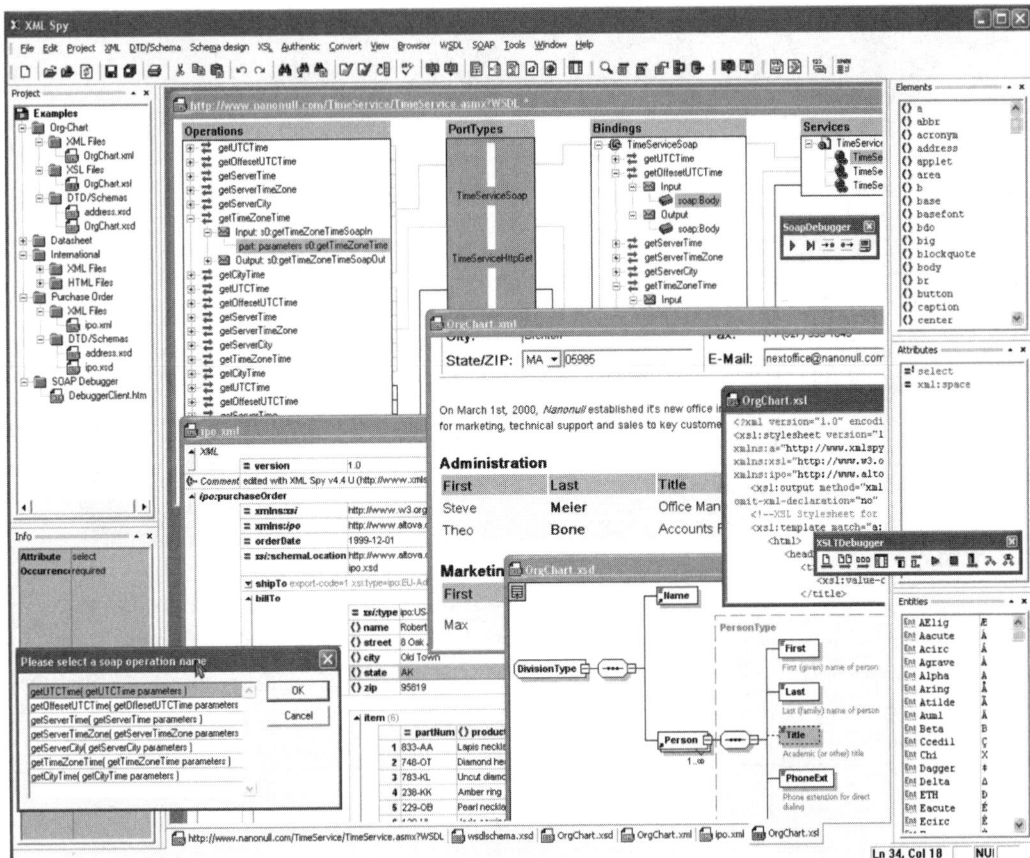

Figure 5.2

Demonstration screen shot from the XMLSpy web site. (From http://www.xmlspy.com/, accessed 9/2003.)

described in standard information engineering format, it can be simultaneously displayed and output as XML. This degree of integration is one of the most important aspects of CASE tool usage, specifically maintaining the model (in this case, the metadata of "Person") separately from the way it is represented. Figure 5.4 illustrates the same degree of integration, in this case managing schemas concurrently with design objects.

In many ways, the capabilities of Visible Advantage's products are not representative of the CASE tool industry. CASE tool usage peaked

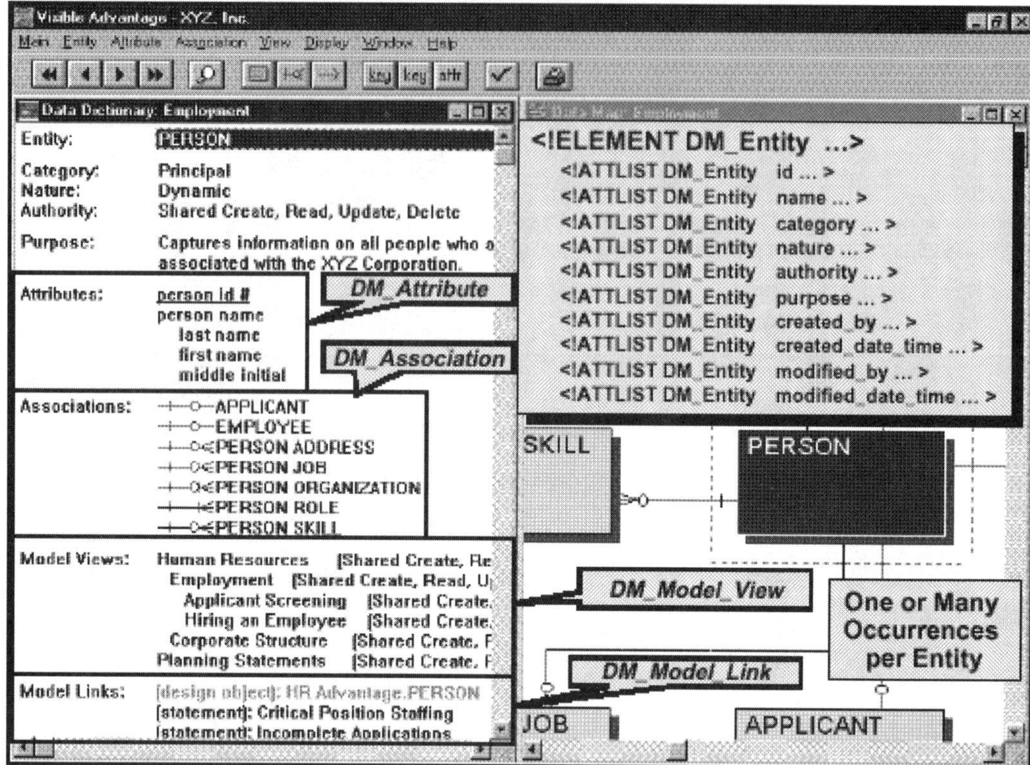

Figure 5.3

CASE tool support for XML provided by Visible Advantage. (From http://www.visible.com, accessed 10/2001.)

around 1992–1993 when more than two-thirds of organizations used the technologies to help manage their metadata. Since 1993, CASE tool usage has slipped to less than one in three organizations! A number of data modelers have professed to us that PowerPoint is now their current favorite "CASE tool." The reason for the decline may be due in part to the lack of products desired by the data management community.

The drop in CASE tool usage has also been due to the usage myth illustrated on the left half of Figure 5.5. The old belief has been that all organizational metadata must "fit" into a single CASE technology. The problem with this is that access to the metadata from outside of the CASE

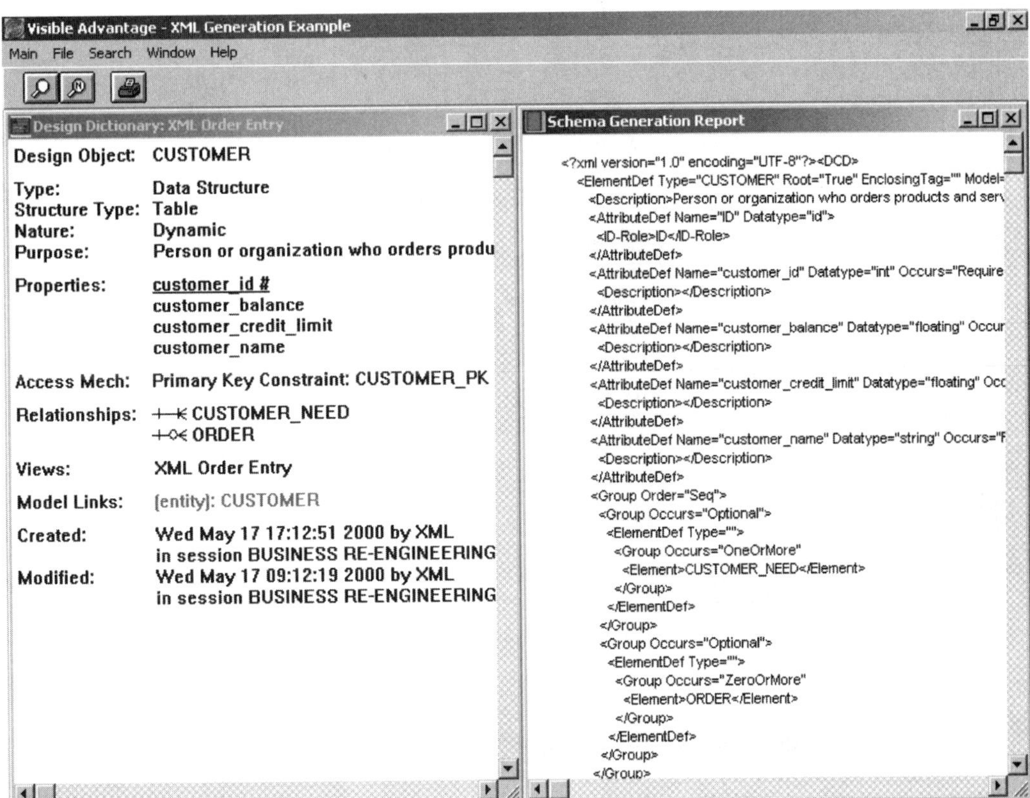

Figure 5.4

Managing schemas concurrently with design objects.

tool has traditionally been very limited, which discourages widespread use. So it comes as no surprise that the valuable metadata in these tools is of limited value when few actually use it. Perhaps one of the reasons for the CASE tool myth is that software vendors have been eager to represent their products as something that could handle any situation, and the price tags on the products have provided added impetus for organizations to try to fit everything into one tool.

The "new" model of CASE tool usage is shown on the right of Figure 5.5. Notice how XML-based integration of the metadata is both the input and the architectural basis. If integrating data using metadata works, then consider how managing metadata with additional metadata will also help out. Integrated metadata sits in an open repository, ready for a variety of

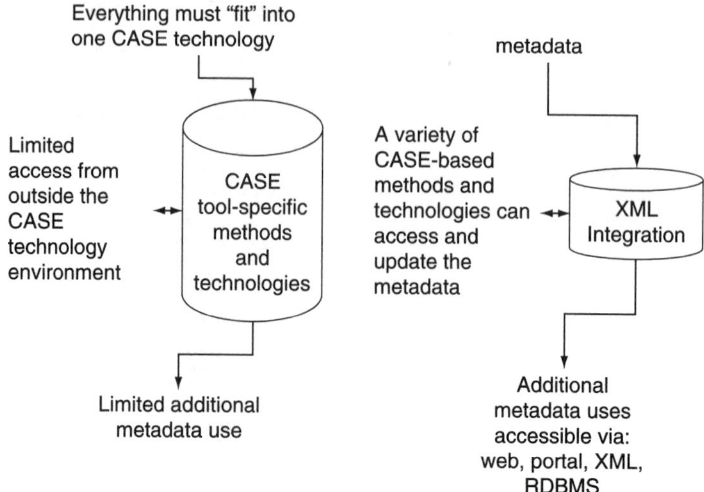

Figure 5.5

Competing models of CASE tool usage.

CASE-based tools and methods to operate on it as utilities. The subsequent metadata is widely accessible via web, portal, XML, database management system, and so on. The accessibility in turn drives continued use of the data.

Extracting Metadata From Legacy Systems

Figure 5.6 illustrates the reverse engineering challenge often encountered as organizations begin the process of integrating XML into their environments. The right-hand side of the figure indicates a realistic goal of identifying the size, shape, and other relevant capabilities of the various architectural components that comprise the current architecture. On the left side of the figure is information about the legacy environment—in this case, just counts of files, tables, and attributes. (This often comprises what is known about the current architecture.) What must be accomplished in order to make this metadata useful for XML and data engineering tasks is to obtain meaningful descriptions of the existing operational data architecture components so that they can be "wrapped" in XML.

Wrapping groups of data items together requires two specific considerations. First, wrapping must not invent new XML tags unless the noun (or the data object being referenced) is new. Data managers must find and assign the correct tag to each data item. Creating new tags must be the exception rather than the rule. A normal part of evolving knowledge of

Technology	Logical/ Virtual Databases	Subject Areas	Tables	Attributes	Unique Attributes	Records	Programs/ Copybooks	Lines of Code
Data Management Technology Type 1	44	20		13,067	6,600			
Global schema						1,049		
T01						5		
C01						4		
Data Management Technology Type 2								
R2			613					
R3			108					
R5			127					
R7			447					
R72			5,996					
R73			11,224					
Data Management Technology Type 3			1,227	9,000	2,514			
Application							10,970	15,700,000
Copybooks							5,518	498,966
Totals:	44	20	19,742	22,067	9,114	1,058	16,488	16,198,966

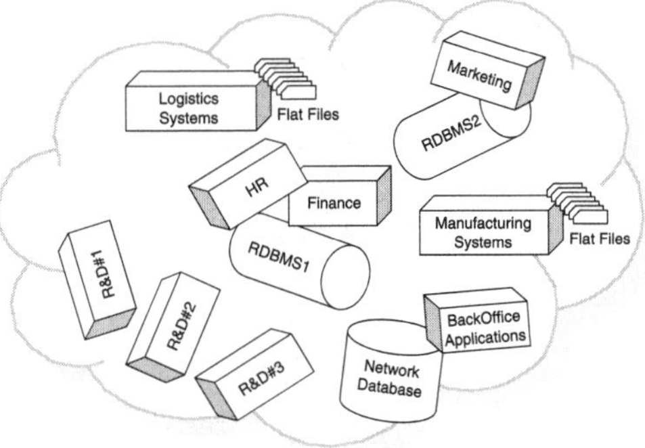

Figure 5.6

What we actually know and what we'd like to know about organizational data structures.

these structures will be to improve understanding by renaming attributes and structures as collective understanding matures. Second, notice must be taken of the organizing format and the process usage of the data structure in question. Understanding data structures variations and how processes use them opens another door; transformations to automate the mapping among the structures can be developed. These two points together mean that, overall, data managers should avoid reinventing the wheel with new tags. If, however, they are in situations where there is more than one tag for the same concept, as long as those concepts are well understood, it should be possible to build a bridge between them with a transformation expressed in XSLT.

In the future, when the metadata needs improvements or corrections, they can also be done because XML can be used both to maintain the structures, as well as to perform transformations between structures. Programmatic changes to metadata can be accomplished by applying the same transformations to documents containing the metadata! The goal is to create new metadata and capture it in XML as a part of ongoing system enhancement efforts. Limited, focused analyses with specific goals will be much more successful than efforts guided by a general belief that data managers are doing the "right" thing by recovering metadata.

Let us look at an example continued from the previous chapter where this metadata evolution would be necessary. Many organizations are facing the implementation of ERP. As part of the implementation effort, there is a need to move data from legacy systems into the ERP, which requires solid understanding of the source metadata from the legacy system, and the target metadata from the ERP.

Figure 5.7 shows how an ERP can be reverse engineered in order to develop a means of regularly extracting the metadata XML form to a repository. This XML-based metadata is then used in the effort to move data into the ERP. We developed a repeatable procedure so that whenever the metadata changed (in this case, we were dealing with a PeopleSoft system), we could simply regenerate our version with a little work, resulting in all of the data and process metadata being wrapped in XML. That XML is then available for reuse in a number of different ways. The lesson here is that there are effective semi-automated and automated means of extracting the metadata from systems, both new and legacy.

Since the previous means of extracting this information was manual and resource intensive, this is good news. In some instances, reverse engineering the metadata from an existing system in order to express it in XML will be trivial. Many CASE tools have newly added functionality permitting them to extract the data structures automatically in entity-relationship diagram (ERD) notation and sometimes in XML as well. In other situations, you will be faced with the need to develop a reverse engineering analysis without such aid.

But how is that done? Figure 5.8 shows the most common means of achieving the understanding required of architectural components—

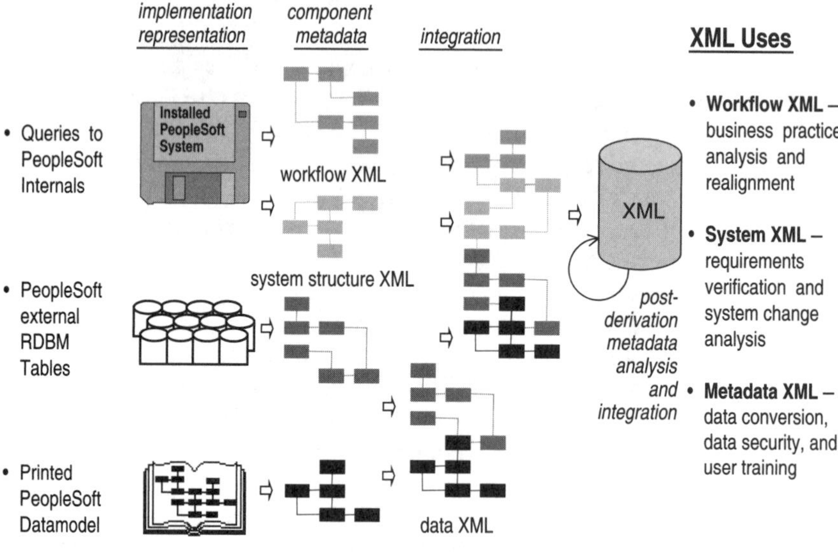

Figure 5.7

Reverse engineering new systems. (Adapted from Aiken and Ngwenyama, 1999.)

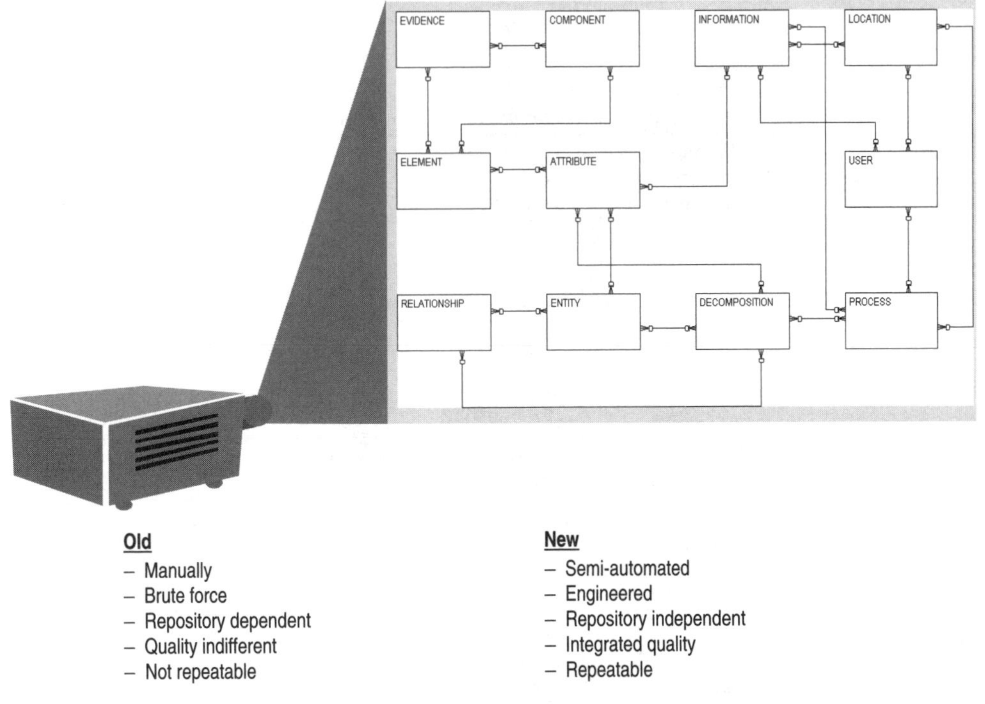

Figure 5.8

Invaluable data analysis technology used during XML development activities.

group analysis sessions (sometimes referred to as JAD or "joint application development" sessions) using a large-screen projector. This information is included along with our discussion of CASE tools precisely because it is often needed even when there is software automating some of the process. Using the developing model components, business users, subject matter experts, technical personnel, and management gain a collective understanding of the component in question.

The mode of operation in these sessions has been completely transformed by the increasing maturity of data analysis software. Comparing old and new approaches to reverse engineering data structures is like night and day. Prices for this type of software can start around $5,000 but will more typically rise to the equivalent of a full-time employee (FTE) if one is to obtain "industrial" analysis strength.

Figure 5.9 and Figure 5.10 illustrate that the key difference (less subject matter expert involvement required) in the process is the amount of time

Monday	Tuesday	Wednesday	Thursday	Friday
Morning: Model preparation	Morning: Model refinement/ validation session	*Morning: Model preparation*	Morning: Model refinement/ validation session	*Morning: Model preparation*
Afternoon: Model refinement/ validation session	Afternoon: Model refinement/ validation session	Afternoon: Model refinement/ validation session	Afternoon: Model refinement/ validation session	Afternoon: Model refinement/ validation session

Figure 5.9

Division of time and labor required using manual data analysis.

Monday	Tuesday	Wednesday	Thursday	Friday
Morning: Model preparation	Morning: Model preparation	Morning: Model preparation	Morning: Model preparation	Morning: Model preparation
Afternoon: Model preparation	*Afternoon: Model refinement/ validation session*	Afternoon: Model preparation	*Afternoon: Model refinement/ validation session*	Afternoon: Model preparation

Figure 5.10

Division of time and labor required using semi-automated and automated data analysis is significantly less than using manual methods.

and type of involvement required on the part of the subject matter experts (SMEs) and business users. Their role is to describe the use of data in their business environment and to verify that the data models accurately capture this understanding. Well, now we want to develop our understanding of the XML structures concurrently with the development of the data models.

Figure 5.9 shows that the majority of the weekly sessions were devoted to sessions held with the business users/SMEs. These sessions were unfortunately subject to the "terror of the blank screen" when modelers/facilitators would welcome everyone to the meeting and say, "Now tell me about your business!" Normally the business users were given only three mornings during the week to tend to existing duties—time when the modelers would refine the component models and formulate questions for the next joint session.

Figure 5.10 shows a different operation with just two afternoons reserved for joint business user/SME development activities. The data analysis software technologies (also sometimes called *data profiling packages*) are based on a powerful inference technology that allows data engineers to quickly form candidate hypotheses with respect to the existing data structures. During the two afternoon joint sessions, the modelers present the various hypotheses to the SMEs both business and technical who confirm, refine, or deny them. This allows existing data structures to be inferred at a rate that is an order of magnitude more rapid than previous manual approaches. From this point, the model component is just a few transformations away from a logical normal model. It is at the logical level that data redundancies are identified and exploited. Data analysis technologies provide a means of following a formal path to logical understanding by profiling the columns, across rows, and among tables (Olson, 2003).

After examining CASE tool approaches and analysis sessions as methods of creating XML input, we will now turn our attention to various data management technologies that process and interpret XML data. Processing XML represents the second of the three classes of data management technologies and their relationship to XML.

Processing XML

Once a data manager has handled the task of obtaining or creating XML data, there is a need for tools that aid the process of actually accomplishing meaningful work with that data. This section deals with various technologies available to process XML and what they mean to data managers—starting with XML databases and servers. These two types of technologies aid in the storage and use of XML data.

The following discussion of XML databases/servers has been adapted from Steve Hamby's *Understanding XML Servers* (2003) because it is difficult to identify a better way of organizing and presenting the material. XML databases and servers can be categorized according to three functions: integration servers, mediation servers, and repositories. Individual product offerings may include one or more of these classes of functionality.

XML Integration Servers

Think of a switchboard that can translate requests and data, both in the form of XML documents, and you will understand XML integration server technologies. The best way to grasp the difference between integration servers and mediation servers is the level of granularity that they are optimized to serve. Integration servers are optimized to support document exchange via physical connectivity and semantic mapping. XML mediation servers are generally focused on addressing format and structure transformations at the data structure and individual data element levels.

XML integration servers have been typically used to interface legacy systems with each other and with other environments. Conceptually, integration servers act as message-oriented middleware. Using XML schemas or DTDs as structure identifiers/validation techniques, XML integration servers provide translation and connection deliveries whose functionality and scope can be extended using various Enterprise Application Integration, or "EAI" adapters. Each legacy system could call the integration server to provide application program interfaces (APIs), document level message exchange, and mapping of document names.

Integration servers can issue queries to access messages from various interfaces providing interfaces to various legacy applications. They function as the hubs in some instances where they facilitate the exchange of documents such as "purchase orders" among diverse business partners—this is a topic that will be discussed at some length in the chapter on XML frameworks. For example, imagine an XML document called "Purchase Order" from company X that could trigger a rule transforming the metadata of the document into something that company Y knows as an "M242-purchase order." A document can actually carry around information that makes it possible for it to translate itself to be understandable by others.

Perhaps best of all, the integration multiplier goes from geometric growth in complexity to linear growth. As each application is added, it is accessible to other connected applications. The exchange cannot be valuable to the organization until the semantic understanding has been mapped from application to application. This can be accomplished using a series of XSLT transformations that are used to manage the transformation of data from one format and structure to another.

XML Mediation Servers

XML mediation servers are generally focused on document transformation—changing individual data items or document data structures. As organizations adopt XML technologies, they tend to implement them from a technical perspective instead of from a semantic understanding perspective. This harkens back to the earlier discussion of how organizations often start with XML by wrapping what they have in simple XML tags, rather than understanding the structure of what they have and expressing that in XML. We illustrate an important point in our lectures by leading a discussion that we routinely have with audiences, asking them to consider the following real-life situation. According to our survey of the industry, only about one in five organizations is formally specifying technology used to build new system functionality. The scenario that we ask others to consider is this:

> One year ago, an organization had literally hundreds of data items duplicated among dozens of applications. Because of book like the one you are reading, technical specialists within the operational support group become interested in XML capabilities, and spontaneously begin to develop standard vocabularies. Now, one year later, the organization has literally dozens of XML "standard" vocabularies, where the year before it had none. Question: Is the organization better or worse off than it was one year ago?

Often the first thought is to react to the silliness of having multiple "standards" and to think of the organization as worse off than it was a year ago before it spent the year doing duplicative, inefficient metadata engineering. However, please also consider the following positives that help to indicate the power XML has to assist with duplicative data problems—these in turn can help organizations to justify the cost of harmonizing duplicative data problems.

- The organization has gotten multiple person years' worth of working XML experience. Even if it was not coordinated, the short learning curve will make it very easy to coordinate and focus the newly acquired XML expertise.
- The organization now has good working knowledge of which data and data structures are more "valuable" to the organization, by identifying which were valuable enough for people to bend their efforts toward. Results of some of the mini projects implemented over the last year yield solid, reusable metadata. The Pareto subset of data should be easily completed.
- Most, if not all, of the XML name and structure changes can be made and maintained using XSLT and often can make use of namespaces. For example, for one type of change, the key is to change all instances of the use of the XML tag "person" to the tag "INDIVIDUAL." As discussed earlier, this is possible

when there is an understanding that they are one and the same for the purposes of the data structure.

- The most value has come from the past year's focus on developing understandings of the use of names by the business users. If we were to hold a data naming meeting, we might get folks to show up if we offer free cookies. Face it, data standardization discussions do not sound exciting. It works much better if you tell the business users, when they ask you to use XML on their application, that you need to have them name everything correctly. This they do readily, and once the initial vocabularies are implemented, they are tested right away. Feedback is sure and swift, so it is easy to make changes to the existing rules.

We contend that using XML and learning from the exercises far outweighs the negatives of having developed multiple standards. Indeed, the synergies are so apparent that this capability to reuse and manage metadata creates quite the business case for spending the additional 5% required to capture the metadata. Architecturally similar to integration servers, the mediation servers are easily extensible transformation engines. Frequently powered by GUI-based drag-and-drop functionality, the real goal of these systems is often to make the maintenance of the rules for transforming data items and data structures among various "services" a part of the business user's tasks and remove the support requirement from IT.

XML Repository Servers

XML repository servers are optimized to store XML metadata and documents. They are a relatively new technology designed to handle XML more efficiently than existing technologies that have not been built to support XML. The current crop of big iron databases (DB/2, Oracle, Informix, Adabase, etc.) has had XML features added or has been modified to incorporate XML. These are XML-enabled databases—defined as conventional databases that have been fitted with some kind of front-end XML adaptor to manage the storage of data from XML documents, system transactions encoded in XML, etc. The XML repository servers are typically native XML databases, architected from the ground up to manage XML and allow XML documents to be stored as XML internally.

This leaves data engineers with an important and difficult-to-reverse design decision that must be made: Will the fundamental data structure be fundamentally data-centric or document-centric? XML documents have hierarchical structures, resulting in the need for complex mappings and software tricks to store or retrieve the documents from an XML-enabled relational database. Systems are typically data-centric (think tabular data) versus document-centric (non-tabular data). The general rules seem to be that data-centric XML documents are more appropriate for XML-enabled databases while document-centric XML documents are more appropriate for native XML databases. This makes sense since XML-enabled databases will be able to store tabular data that happens to be represented in XML with ease, while the non-tabular data lends itself to more efficient storage in its native XML format.

XML repository server use is growing, reaching into one in three organizations. Repositories do have the distinct advantage of being able to store metadata using the same technologies that are used to store the XML documents. This means that standard vocabulary can be implemented at the same level as data access security, and that bad habits of using expired data item tag names can be avoided by enforcing the use of the standard vocabulary. The repository servers also offer services such as compression, automated XML wrapping, and XSLT transformation capabilities.

As you might imagine, the features of the XML frameworks (to which we have devoted a later chapter) are closely supported by XML repository (and other) server types. Figure 5.11 shows two popular solutions and how the various services can provide single-source data in output formats suitable for mobile phone, PDA, printer, browser and CD. These services are offered under a panoply of acronyms including:

- Web Services
- SOAP (Simple Object Access Protocol)
- Java and EJB (Enterprise Java Beans)
- DOM (Document Object Model)
- .NET (Microsoft's Initiative)
- HTTP (Hypertext Transfer Protocol)

These operate in concert with even more technologies and approaches, including query manager, e-commerce, content management, portals—okay, you get the picture.

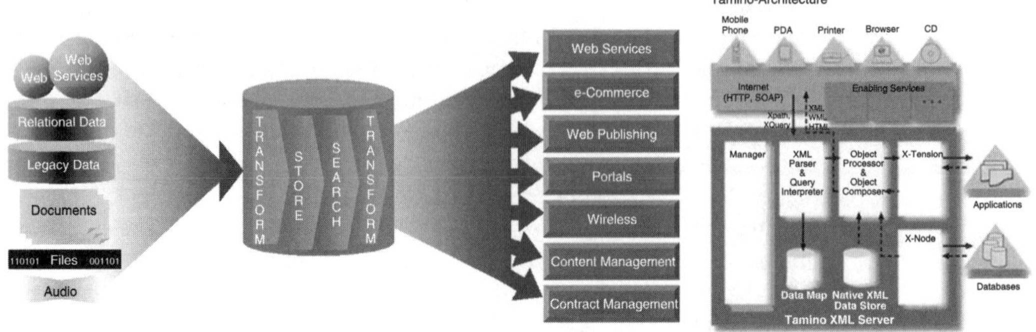

Figure 5.11

Ipedo (left) and Tamino (right) feature articulations from their web sites. (Courtesy of Ipedo, www.ipedo.com, and Software AG, www.softwareag.com/tamino.)

Outputting XML

Now that we have covered ways of inputting and creating XML, and also ways of processing it and consuming what was generated, it is time to take a look at data management technologies that address XML output. The first that we will examine are the XML converters.

XML Converters

XML converters focus on the development of XML documents that are specified by non-technical users via drag-and-drop GUIs. Figure 5.12 illustrates how one of these products facilitates transformation of documents to XML, and then further to a BizTalk framework or a Tamino server. Many organizations are faced with situations where they have to convert existing documents into XML, and the XML converters class of tools is an aid to the process. One typical approach involves a user highlighting a key portion of a document, and training the program about the context information around that piece of the document that makes it interesting. The XML converter then takes that context information and looks for it both within the sample document and in other documents

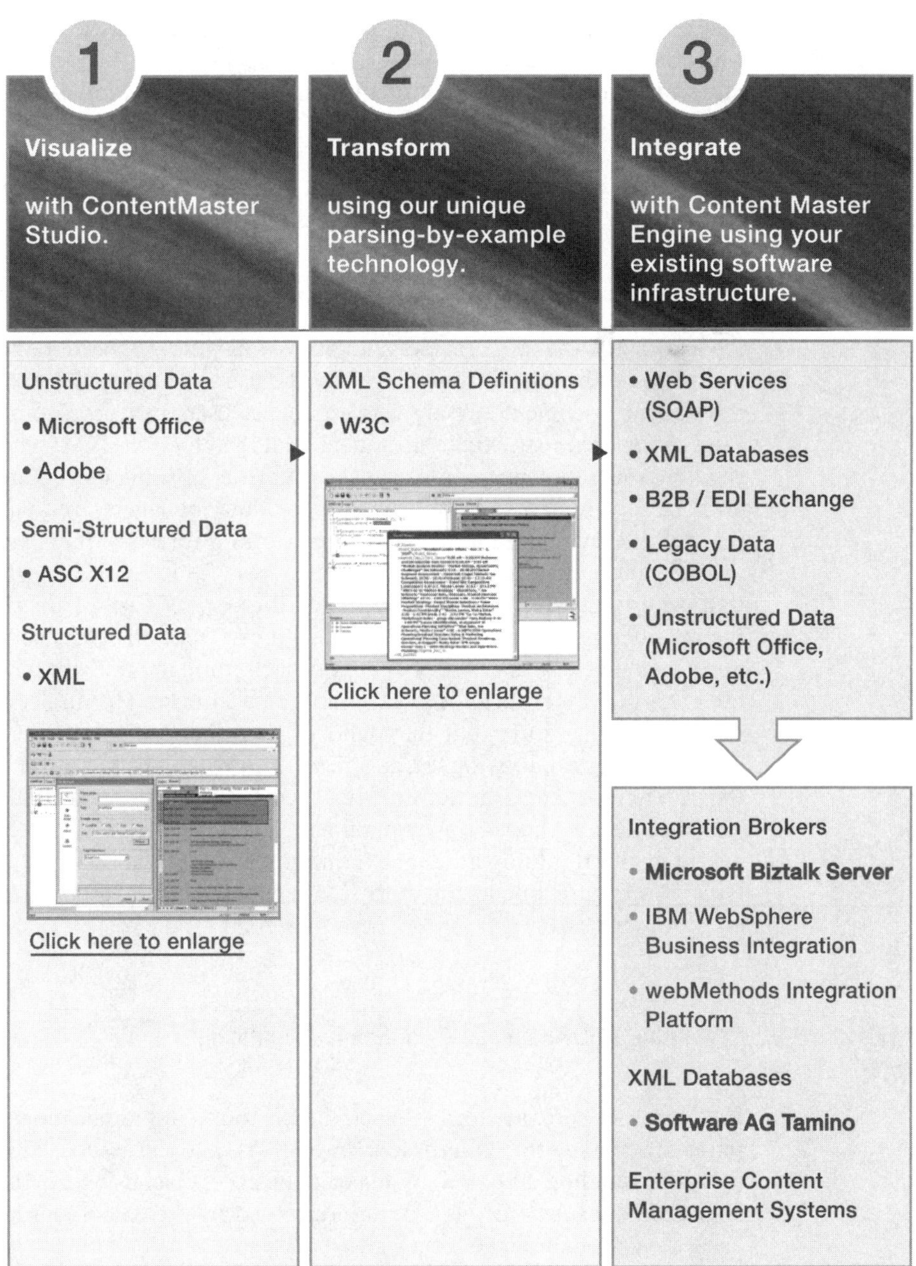

How ContentMaster Works:
1
Visualize
with ContentMaster Studio.
2
Transform
using our unique parsing-by-example technology.
3
Integrate
with Content Master Engine using your existing software infrastructure.
Unstructured Data
• Microsoft Office
• Adobe
Semi-Structured Data
• ASC X12
Structured Data
• XML
Click here to enlarge
XML Schema Definitions
• W3C
Click here to enlarge
• Web Services (SOAP)
• XML Databases
• B2B / EDI Exchange
• Legacy Data (COBOL)
• Unstructured Data (Microsoft Office, Adobe, etc.)
Integration Brokers
• Microsoft Biztalk Server
• IBM WebSphere Business Integration
• webMethods Integration Platform
XML Databases
• Software AG Tamino
Enterprise Content Management Systems

Figure 5.12

XML converter. (Courtesy of Itemfield, Inc., www.itemfield.com.)

that are fed to it. Structured information can be extracted in this way, which is then encoded in an XML format specified by the user and outputted to any number of different sources (in the case of Figure 5.12, Tamino and BizTalk).

XML conversion tools at the time of this writing tend to be less sophisticated than some users expect. Rather than presenting a tool that "figures out" what is in the document, the software packages provide more of an interface for users to teach the software which parts of the documents are meaningful, where those parts are located, and how they should be expressed in XML. In other words, the trained user is really doing most of the work. Still, the tool provides a number of facilities to speed the process, and to generalize the lessons taught by the user and apply them to many subsequent documents. Using this approach, users can develop a set of rules for one semi-structured document, and then have the XML converter run the same set of heuristics against documents of similar structure.

The advantages to these packages for data managers are that, as of this point, they represent one of the best options for extracting data from unstructured and semi-structured documents. Typically, if an organization were to develop a custom approach for a specific set of documents, the results might be slightly better than those from an XML converter. Given the time and expense of that approach, though, many find that the use of an XML converter is a reasonable compromise. The disadvantages to these packages are that they tend to be rather pedantic in terms of what data they are looking for, and there is quite a bit of variation among the different packages in terms of how accurately they can generalize the rules they were taught to new documents. Overall, this class of tools is definitely worth taking a look at for data managers who need to convert large numbers of documents into XML. However, they are not without their drawbacks.

Generating XML Automatically or Semiautomatically

Data analysis software technologies, CASE tools, and applications themselves are proving to be useful sources of XML and the associated semantic understanding required to make data accessible using XML. It is helpful to consider the metadata models used by the technologies as the basis for your mapping efforts.

When we refer to these XML generating tools, we are speaking of applications that already contain some data, which can then be represented or "exported" as XML. In some other cases, however, the application may not actually have data, but only a means to fetch it, such as in a report-writing application that connects to a database to pull data it reports on. The semi-automatic XML generators will typically ask the user a set of questions about how the XML should be structured, which tags should be used, and so on. The automatic XML generators create output usually according to a standard DTD or XML schema, with minimal user intervention. Automatic generation is not necessarily more desirable than semi-automatic generation. Data managers usually find that it depends on the situation, what they are generating, and where it needs to go afterward.

To make sense of the many types of software that generate XML automatically or semi-automatically, we can put them into two broad categories. The first and more desirable category is the tools that generate XML as a "view" of a competent data model that the application has internally. A good example of this would be Visible Advantage that was discussed at the beginning of the chapter. These tools have an excellent generic data model that is held in the application, and when it comes time to generate the XML, it is performed by outputting an XML description of that competent data model. In this way, the application knows how the182data is structured, and the XML is just one way of looking at that structure.

The other category of tools that generate XML are those that "tack on" XML support to an existing product. In contrast to packages like Visible Advantage, these applications have internal data models that may not be compatible with a useful XML description of the data. Still, these applications can export XML by having the application do something of an internal translation between the way it understands the data, and the way the user wants to see it in XML. In practice, this approach is much less desirable. Symptoms of this approach include:

- Data items that are visible in the application, but not in the output XML files. Alternately, data items that are specified in the XML documents do not show up in the application after the XML is imported. This happens when there is no way for the application to translate the items into the appropriate places between the internal data model and the XML description.
- XML "inflexibility." This happens when there are few or no options for generating different forms of XML, or when XML that is input into the tool must always have exactly the same

structure. Tools with appropriate XML support have at least some input flexibility, for example, the ability to add extra (perhaps non-standard) metadata fields that can later be manipulated in the tool.

- XML "exclusivity." Some tools generate XML output that is in a format that cannot be understood by anything but the tool that generated it, because of its odd structure (for example, a particular proprietary schema that nothing else interoperates with). This is clearly undesirable, since XML documents that cannot be understood by anything else defeat one of the central purposes of XML.

These symptoms typically indicate a mismatch between the way the application understands the data, and the way it is represented in XML. It is still possible to work with these applications; they are simply a bit less desirable. There is hope, however—some tools that offered initial XML support in this way have managed to mature over time to more useful methods of generating XML. Furthermore, the number of tools with good XML generation capabilities (such as Visible Advantage) is growing.

Data Layers/Data Services

The last class of XML technologies is a particular type of framework that supports data delivery. Called data layers or data service layers, these technologies permit programmatic delivery of XML data. Taking the capabilities of the servers described in the previous section, and then adding to them the data service layer, produces several distinct advantages:

- The layers can be directly model-driven in that changing the model produces changes to the XML, causing subsequent changes in the mapping.
- To the extent that your non-tabular data can be packaged with its metadata, there exists integrated support for its classification and reuse.
- Internal query integration capacities permit data of virtually all types, images, email messages, spreadsheets, streaming data,

HTML documents, XML documents, and web services to be accessed using common queries.

- The data abstraction layer approach enables developers to focus on information rather than data connectivity issues.

The combination of all three server capabilities provides additional synergies as data managers discover the productivity of having the features integrated with the modeling and transformation features. To really understand the power of this integration, consider a scenario that would illustrate how data management could change for organizations able to adapt to effectively utilize the technology. Organizations without the ability to document past successes and repeat the guidance gained from those successes will be unable to take advantage of these or other datamanagement technologies—more on this at the end of this section. One organization has placed online demos of the integrated accessible on the web describing them.*

Data Management Maturity Measurement (DM3)

To close this chapter, we would like to introduce an idea that is important to data management—that of differing levels of maturity. Data management is a complicated discipline, and there are clearly some people and practices that are ahead of others in terms of their data management ability. Throughout this book so far, we have discussed the need for well-structured and understood data. After going over the tools in this chapter, however, it is vital to point out that advanced metadata management and data transformation are difficult to take advantage of if some of the more basic aspects of data management have not been addressed.

How can we assess the data management maturity of a particular organization? The tool that was developed for this process is the data management maturity measurement, or DM3 survey. By assessing how advanced the efforts are within a particular organization, data managers can be in a position to know which types of efforts are likely to succeed, and which are likely to fail. In addition, such an assessment provides information about the types of things organizations need to do in order to get ahead with their data management. The discussion of the DM3 survey

*http://metamatrix.com/13_livedemo.jsp

here is intended to get data managers thinking about what their organizations can and cannot do, based on how mature their practices are.

Five levels of developmental maturity are applied to software in the capability maturity model and to data in the DM3. The DM3 is based on the widely appreciated capability maturity model (CMM) developed by the Software Engineering Institute.* The DM3 survey database contains data management maturity measurements of more than 250 organizations, enabling researchers to assess the current state of practice both between and within industries. Each organization is assessed relative to basic data management areas. Application of the XML technologies described in this chapter must be performed by organizations able to demonstrate data management maturity equal to the "Repeatable" level (Level 3) of the data management maturity measurement (DM3). Organizations not yet at Level 3 may not have as easy a time demonstrating savings derived from its application.

In Figure 5.13, the intersecting aspects of the DM3 survey are shown. The rows correspond to different tasks that are performed as part of an overall coordinated data management effort. The columns correspond to levels of maturity for each task. The "Initial" level is for organizations that have addressed a particular task, but in an informal or unstructured way. The "Repeatable" level means that at some point, the organization has taken the time to define a process for accomplishing a particular task, and that it is possible to repeat that process. The "Defined" level means that not only is there a process in place, but it is actually published throughout the organization and its use is encouraged. This is often quite a step up from simply having the process. The fourth level of maturity is "Managed," which deals with whether efforts are made to determine if the process is working or not. What this means is that having a process is not enough—the question is, Does the organization know that the process is and continues to be the right process? Finally, maturity level five, referred to as "Optimizing," addresses whether or not an organization uses a feedback loop to constantly improve the process that is used. Organizations that rank at maturity level five typically make a concerted effort to find out if the process is breaking down, and if so, what the alternatives are and how they can be fed back into the process to improve it. This is referred to as an "optimizing feedback loop."

The DM3 survey has shown itself to be an extremely effective tool in assessing data management maturity. There is a strong correlation

*http://www.sei.cmu.edu/cmm/

Figure 5.13

Five levels of developmental maturity and five data management areas of the DM3.

	Initial (I)	Repeatable (II)	Defined (III)	Managed (IV)	Optimizing (V)
Data Program Coordination					
Enterprise Data Integration					
Data Stewardship					
Data Development					
Data Support Operations					

between overall DM3 score and success in data management projects, as well as strategic advantages gained from use of data. We typically recommend that data managers take a look at issues that the DM3 brings up, simply because it is difficult for an organization's efforts to improve unless it knows where it stands.

Chapter Summary

The key to understanding how to effectively implement XML technologies is to see them as extensions of data management technologies. GUIs such as ItemField are really data rationalization tools. Now you can hand them to the knowledge workers and ask them to help you to understand their uses of data.

In this chapter, we have covered input, process, and output of XML data with discussions of various approaches to XML problems, and we have looked at the data management maturity that is necessary to apply these technologies effectively. When these technologies are tied together with coherent data structure and sound engineering principles, they can be tremendous assets. Going back to the architectural and engineering analogy, if the foundation of a building is well built and the architectural plans for the building are specified and understood, the technologies outlined in this chapter can act as the heavy lifting machinery that allows the construction of something truly astounding.

References

Aiken, P. H., Ngwenyama, O., et al. (1999). Reverse engineering new systems for smooth implementation. *IEEE Software 16*(2): 36–43.

Hamby, S. (2003, April). "Understanding XML servers." Paper presented at the DAMA/Metadata Conference, Orlando, FL.

Olson, J. E. (2003). *Data quality: The accuracy dimension.* San Francisco: Morgan Kaufmann.

Parker, B. G. (1999). Enterprise wide data management process maturity. *Auerbach Data Base Management.*[*]

[*]The data management program definitions are defined by and used with permission from Burton G. Parker.

6

XML Frameworks

Introduction

XML by itself is great, but better still is the assembly of XML tags into larger data structures, paired with a delivery mechanism to create larger solutions. The concept of an XML framework is an application of XML technology to solve a particular problem or set of problems. Generally these problems are more complex and larger than those addressed by some of the technologies described in the XML Component Architecture chapter of this book. Although defining one's own language is something that is well within the reach of XML's users, frameworks do not stop there, but go on to build a higher-level system that incorporates XML as a data interchange and specification language. The frameworks that are discussed in this chapter build on the main capabilities of XML to produce extremely beneficial systems. We will discuss the types of benefits that organizations see from the use of XML frameworks, along with the specifics of several example frameworks, including RosettaNET, ebXML, BizTalk/.NET, and Acord. At the end of the chapter, we will present an example of an XML framework in action as developed for the chemical industry, and close with a discussion of the common themes, services, and advantages that are found in XML frameworks' design.

Framework Advantages

The types of systems that operate using XML frameworks existed before the use of XML was widespread, but they tended to be very brittle and industry specific. As XML has matured, it has encouraged broader thinking in terms of how metadata can be used in systems. The fact that a number of XML-based frameworks have popped up over the past few years while the non-XML systems are languishing says something about the ease of adoption and benefits associated with using XML.

How did these frameworks come about in the first place? As more organizations began to use XML and its utility grew, efforts were mounted to create a set of components that would allow business information to be sent over the Internet. By using networking and XML, organizations could make sure that everyone was able to participate in the growing electronic marketplace by using a low-cost, reliable, and highly available technology as well as continuing interoperability. The issue of ongoing interoperability is quite important; with many thousands of businesses and almost as many unique systems for storing and manipulating business information, it is important to know that any technology selected would not quickly morph and change into something that would require complicated reconciliation.

This type of outlook requires a certain level of forward thinking. As data-management sophistication has increased, so too has the interest in these frameworks. Adoption started with the largest organizations that could achieve the economies of scale necessary to make the systems worthwhile in their infancy. Initially, the development of some of these frameworks was not cheap or fast. The frameworks and the software that use them are evolving, though, and the use of them is becoming more widespread since organizations no longer have to be huge to see the benefit. In some cases, organizations have adopted the frameworks not as a choice but out of absolute necessity; their competitors possessed such a strategic advantage by using the framework that they have had to adopt it in order to level the competitive playing field.

Since many of these frameworks attempt to accomplish many of the same goals, it is useful to first discuss the types of things these frameworks are trying to accomplish, and then follow that with a description of each of the frameworks in context. These frameworks have only come about as a result of organizations realizing the value of automated communication within and between industries. This section deals with characteristics of the frameworks, including standardized data formats, standardized process models, the connection of as many organizations as possible, the logical spoke-and-hub model used by the frameworks, security provisions, lowering the barrier to entry, and homogenized transactions.

Shared Vocabulary—A Standardized Data Format

The first quality that all of the frameworks have in common is a common or shared vocabulary (in data-management terms, this is a standardized data format). There are two ways of looking at the standard data formats. The first is by syntax, and the second is by semantics. For syntax, these frameworks use plain XML documents or snippets of documents that are exchanged back and forth between systems. Since XML is already widely implemented and software can easily be had that supports XML, no organization is shut out when XML is used. As an interchange language, it has all of the advantages discussed in earlier chapters.

The semantics aspect is also important and has long been a stumbling block for data managers—the XML documents that are being transferred back and forth are all compliant with a particular XML DTD or Schema. They all have the same set of valid elements, and meanings associated with those elements. This semantic similarity is absolutely crucial to the success of these frameworks. If the organization is able to figure out how the common semantic model maps to their interpretation of various data items, then there is no need to worry about additional data formats—systems only need know how to process the common XML format.

As an example, take the case of a major publishing house with many different partners that supply them with lists for customer solicitations. Every month, each vendor sends the publishing house a long list of customer names obtained through various means. Every month, the publishing house must undertake a substantial effort to manipulate the data from the form it was sent in by the vendor, to the form used in the publishing house's internal systems. In effect, this means that the vendors never really change the data formats that they use, and the publishing house must have the ability to translate data formats from potentially many different vendors, every single month. On the other hand, if an XML framework had been used, the publishing house would be able to have one piece of software that knows how to do one thing only—to take a standard XML document in a predetermined form, and translate it into the language of the publishing house's systems. Rather than translate multiple different data formats every month, the potential is to only have to worry about one data format, and automate that process as well.

Part of the standardization of data formats is putting together an actual specification of how everything will be done. These documents are sometimes referred to by name, such as formal Collaboration Protocol Agreements, or CPAs. Along with the specification of a CPA, many frameworks provide a shared repository for a number of data items that do not relate to any specific transaction, but rather relate to the structure of the overall network of trading partners. These shared repositories often include:

- Company names and profiles
- Information models and related data structures associated with message interchange
- Business process models for various trading partners
- Related message structures

Making sure that the data is understandable by all of the involved parties is only part of the challenge, however. The next part is to make sure that the business processes the data applies to also make sense between partners.

Standardize Processes

The second concept that the frameworks employ is the standardization of processes. Each organization tends to have its own way of doing things. For example, the purchasing process is different in every organization with respect to who has to inspect which documents, what information those documents must contain, and how the process flows from point to point. The differences in processes make it almost impossible to automate aspects of business effectively, since the specifics of dealing with each organization differ so greatly.

Standardized processes do not necessarily require an organization to change the way it does things internally, but they do force the organization to change the way information is put into the process, and taken out of the back of the process. The actual process internally may remain a "black box" that the users do not have to modify, but the standardized portion has to do with how external entities feed things into the process and receive output from the process. The "black box" of the internal process is taken care of for the user. The standardized input and output must be understood by the user in order to make use of the processes. The benefits from standardized processes are profound; all trading partners can be treated alike, which reduces the amount of complexity involved with trading. One theme that is encountered over and over in the use of frameworks is the attempt at minimizing the complexity needed to communicate with everyone else that uses the framework. If a group of trading partners could be considered a network, the idea is to establish a common communication ground that everyone can use, rather than setting up a mess of individual point-to-point systems.

To illustrate this point, take an example from the chemical industry. Every company in the industry may have a slightly different process for selling a chemical, from the exchange of funds, to the shipping date and method, to the way that the warehouse where things are stored finds out about the actual sale. Still, there are commonalities between all of these processes, namely that money and goods are changing hands, and that there needs to be some way of coordinating delivery. Rather than using point-to-point systems that in some cases require traders to take into account the idiosyncrasies of their trading partner's processes, the process is abstracted to what is necessary for everyone. The entire network of traders then uses that core process.

This example can be generalized a bit to give a basic definition of the functionality of frameworks—the way that trading is accomplished between partners is by the exercise of various processes. The purchase process has to be the same so that from the perspective of the buyer, it does not matter who the seller is—the process remains the same. Processes for querying inventory, returning goods, and requesting information must always be the same so that participants in the network can feel free to utilize the best trading partner without incurring additional overhead related to reconciling those processes.

Given standardization of data and processes, the framework starts to have some real value. Once the framework has been designed, the next step is to start to share it with other organizations to get the word out, and maximize the overall benefit of the design work that was done for everyone.

Connect as Many Organizations as Possible to Increase Value

One of the most interesting aspects of networks that form around the use of these frameworks is that the more organizations that are members in the network, the more value the overall network has. This is known as "the network effect." As it grows larger, it becomes more and more representative of the industry as a whole, and begins to comprise the electronic marketplace for goods and services in that industry. XML frameworks are akin to the early telephone system. The benefit of the telephone grew exponentially with the number of people who had one. If only 10 people had telephones, their utility was limited by whom the telephone could be used to contact, while widespread telephone use greatly increased its value as a common mode of communication.

To take advantage of the network effect, these frameworks were built to enable as many organizations as possible to use them. Again, if we look at a group of trading partners as a network, the benefits of 5 trading partners participating in the use and development of a framework might be worthwhile, but the participation of 10 makes the benefit substantial, due to the increasing number of data formats and processes that each individual member no longer needs to be able to reconcile.

Logical Hub-and-Spoke Model: Standards and Processes

The use of standardized data and processes forms a logical hub-and-spoke model for communication using a particular framework. Earlier, we discussed how the use of these standards reduces the number of connections that are necessary between organizations in order to get business done. Figure 6.1 shows the difference between these two communication models. When looking at the peer-to-peer model, we see that the number of connections is larger, and that the organizations must communicate strictly between one another. Communications that A sends to B could not be sent to C; this is because the process and data format differences between B and C would make messages bound for B unintelligible to C.

In the hub-and-spoke model, we see that all of the organizations can communicate through a central hub. In this case, this is not a physical device—it is not meant to stand for an actual piece of software or a server—it is representative of the common data and process format through which the communication must flow in order to reach the other end. In a previous chapter, we discussed that the peer-to-peer or point-to-point model requires the creation of (N * (N – 1)) / 2 agreements between trading partners, while the hub-and-spoke model requires only N agreements. Moreover, any agreement between three business partners can be adopted by more and more organizations as time goes on. In some cases,

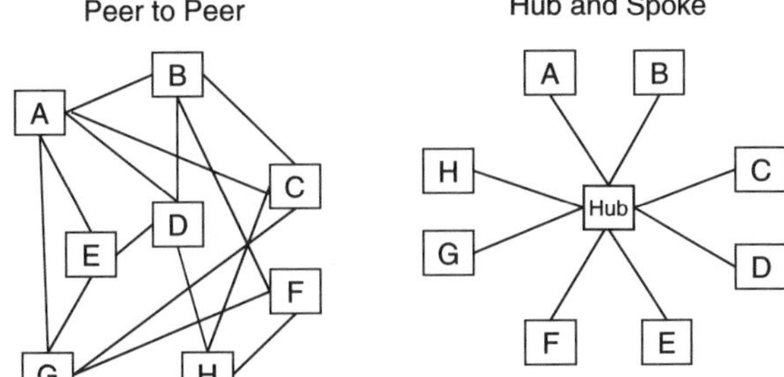

Figure 6.1

Compare and contrast the Peer to Peer model and the Hub and Spoke model.

frameworks for industry trading may develop as an expansion of an agreement between a relatively small number of "seed" partners.

Looking at the hub-and-spoke model, logically it means that every single organization must create only one data link—from itself to the hub. If another 20 organizations later join the model, each of the original organizations does not have to do anything in order to be able to communicate with the newcomers, since all communications go through the logical hub of data and process standards. In the peer-to-peer model, if another organization "X" were to join the group, the number of new links that would potentially have to be built would be equal to the total number of trading partners in the arrangement. This type of architecture is doable for small numbers of partners, but quickly becomes impossible when any reasonable number of organizations is involved, just as it would be impossible to effectively use a telephone system if connection to the network required creating an individual connection to everyone else using the network.

If an XML framework is going to be a preferred place to do business, it has to be reliable and trustworthy. Individual bank branches put a lot of work into making sure their customers feel safe putting their money in that location, and XML frameworks are no different, particularly when millions or billions of dollars in transactions have to flow through them.

Standardized Methods for Security and Scalability

Each of the frameworks in this chapter addresses standard ways of ensuring security and scalability of the system. These frameworks are built from the ground up to be scalable, owing to the previous point that the value of the total increases with the number of organizations that take part. Security is clearly also a very important consideration—provisions must be put in place that allay the concerns of trading partners, including threats such as data snooping, industrial espionage, corruption, misrepresentation, and so on. When it comes to security and scalability, the same approach is taken as with data formats and processes—standardization means that the designers of the framework only have to solve that problem *once*. All framework users then benefit from the solution, rather than each user having to come up with its own individual way of coping with these issues. Furthermore, the security model can be validated a single time, and strong evidence can be presented to the participating organizations that they are not exposing themselves to large amounts of risk by taking part in the group.

Frameworks Lower Barrier to Entry

One of the unexpected benefits of frameworks is that they tend to lower the barrier of entry for other organizations into particular networks. After all, anyone who can set up a system that can issue the appropriate standards-compliant documents and understand the result that comes back can take part in the trading community. When the frameworks were first being developed, they generally required large technology investments, but as they have grown, a number of other options have become available. Web-based systems exist that can automatically create and dispatch the XML documents sent using the framework, which allows smaller "Mom and Pop" operations to take part in the marketplace.

In other cases, organizations that purchase large ERP systems may require that their vendors and even customers use similar ERP systems in order to smooth the process of doing business. ERP requirements tend to greatly increase the barrier to entry since the investment needed to implement an ERP is substantial. By using XML, users of these frameworks have effectively minimized the technology investment required to use the framework, which will hopefully maximize the users of the framework and the value of it to all of the trading partners.

Commonly Available Transactions

One of the patterns commonly seen when working with these frameworks is the division of data exchange into various transactions between part-

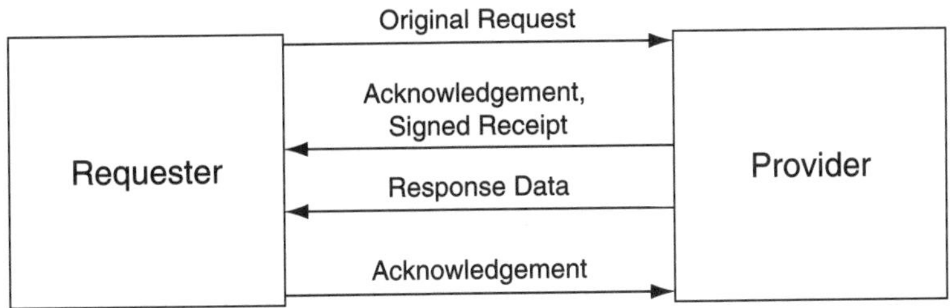

Figure 6.2

Typical exchange of messages in one logical transaction.

ners. A transaction might be a request for information about a particular product that is offered, an actual order for that product, or the exchange of administrative information. In most cases, though, the transaction is carried out with a sequence of events similar to those seen in Figure 6.2.

In Figure 6.2, we see that transactions can be broken down into a number of communications between the original requester of the information and the provider of the information.

1. First, the requester issues its initial request. This is a document whose format is dictated by the technical specification of whichever framework is in use. By virtue of the fact that both parties take part in the framework, the requester can be confident that the provider's systems will understand this request.
2. The provider then sends back an acknowledgement and/or a signed receipt. This lets the requester know that the original request was received, and that it was received properly. In some cases for security, the acknowledgement may be signed or otherwise contain some information that allows the requester to be sure that the provider is who it claims to be. Each framework has different provisions for security, but this is one of the ways that those provisions frequently show up in the actual message exchange.
3. Next, the provider issues the response data to the requester. Some frameworks might roll this data up into the previous step and accomplish everything at one time, while others separate them into two distinct steps. In either case, the provider must respond to the request and provide an answer, whether that answer is, "Yes, you have now purchased 100 widgets at a cost of $0.99 per widget," simple administrative information, or even an error.

4. Finally, the original requester sends an acknowledgement back to the provider. After this is accomplished, both parties can be confident that their messages were correctly received, and that the transaction has ended.

There are a few things to point out about this model. First, models of this type typically provide a reasonable amount of reliability. When each party must respond to the requests or information of the other, it becomes easier to guarantee that messages are passed properly. If a message were passed improperly, the acknowledgement would give the error away to the original sender of the document and allow for correction of errors. Second, sending acknowledgement messages allows for piggybacking of extra data that aids with issues such as security. Finally, communications models of this type can be easily formalized into a set of instructions that neither party should deviate from. Coming up with a solid set of rules for how communications should flow back and forth allows more robust implementations of actual software—there is never any question about what the next correct step would be in the process.

Now that we have covered some of the ideas that are common between frameworks, it is time to take a look at specific frameworks, where they came from, and what they have to offer, starting with one of the first to come on the scene—RosettaNET.

RosettaNET

One of the oldest XML-based frameworks is RosettaNET. The framework takes its name from the Rosetta stone, used to decipher hieroglyphics for the first time in history. Given the meaning and importance of the original Rosetta stone, the name indicates from the start that the designers realized the complexities involved with their task, and the importance of providing a translation between organizations, just as the original Rosetta stone allowed us to translate hieroglyphics into English. The target of RosettaNET is to automate supply-chain transactions over the Internet for the members that take part in it. RosettaNET was created in 1998 by a variety of companies in the electronic component industry including Intel, Marshall Industries/AVNET, Hewlett-Packard, Ingram Micro, Inacom, Solectron, Netscape, Microsoft, IBM, and American Express. The reason for its creation was to standardize a number of common information exchanges such as pricing information, product descriptions, product identifiers, and so on, throughout the electronic component industry. Today, RosettaNET is a nonprofit consortium of companies, much like the W3C or OASIS, whose goal is to streamline the high-tech supply chain by eliminating redundancies and improving flow of critical information.

The core of RosettaNET is defined by the use of PIPs, or Partner Interface Processes. These act as standard XML-based dialogs that define processes and vocabulary interaction between various trading partners. Each PIP may consist of multiple transactions that specify activities, decisions, and roles for each trading partner. For example, PIP3A4 Manage Purchase Order consists of three possible transactions: send purchase order, update purchase order, and cancel purchase order. PIP3A4 specifies two entities: buyer and seller. The "buyer" performs the "create purchase order" activity that is understood by all parties as "creating purchase order once acknowledgement of acceptance received from seller."

Each PIP contains a specification of a particular XML vocabulary, a list of which elements are valid in transmitted documents, and in what order they must be used. Also included with each PIP is a process choreography model, which covers how messages flow and in which order they should be sent and received. A simple choreography model for a purchasing transaction might be that the buyer initiates the transaction by sending a document requesting purchase; the seller sends a document back intended to confirm and verify the order. The buyer then responds again with payment information, and so on.

Figure 6.3 shows some example PIP clusters with sub-functions (segments) shown as bullet items. There are many processes that are covered by various PIPs in RosettaNET, and PIPs themselves are categorized into "clusters" that accomplish various tasks in specific areas. The clusters are supposed to represent various core business processes, and each cluster may contain many different PIPs.

RosettaNET also contains something called the RNIF, which stands for the RosettaNET Implementation Framework. The RNIF covers the way in which messages are actually sent back and forth. Information related to the specific transport protocols, security and scalability techniques, routing, and the way documents are actually aggregated and sent are all specified by the RNIF. The RNIF specification strives to be complete in its description of various behaviors, to leave as little as possible to chance and guessing on the part of the software creator who implements RosettaNET software.

The framework also provides two dictionaries—the RosettaNET technical dictionary, and the RosettaNET business dictionary. The business dictionary covers the various high-level business concepts that are used in

Partner, Product and Service Review

- Partner Review
- Product and Service Review

Product Introduction

- Prepare for Distribution
- Product Change Notification

Order Management

- Quote and Order Entry
- Transportation and Distribution
- Returns and Finance
- Product Configuration

Service and Support

- Warranty Management
- Asset Management
- Technical Support and Service Management

Inventory Management

- Collaborative Forecasting
- Inventory Allocation
- Inventory Reporting
- Inventory Replenishment
- Sales Reporting
- Price Protection
- Ship from Stock and Debit/Credit

Marketing Information Management

- Lead Opportunity Management
- Marketing Campaign Management
- Design Win Management

Administration

Manufacturing

...

Figure 6.3

Sample RosettaNET PIP and clusters.

RosettaNET, such as which entities are exchanged, and which business transactions members in the network may undertake. The technical dictionary, on the other hand, provides a lower-level description of the technical aspects of how some transactions are accomplished. With any good data structure, one usually finds an accompanying data dictionary that lays out exactly how things are put together. This documentation can aid individual organizations in deciphering the mapping between RosettaNET data items and their own systems, as well as provide them with documentation to view all of the different possibilities and capabilities of the framework as a whole.

Up until now, the partners involved in RosettaNET have been businesses in the information technology, electronics components, telecommunications, and semiconductor manufacturing industries. In many ways, RosettaNET has pulled these industries together, and created a number of interesting opportunities for all of the members. Participants in the network have found that RosettaNET allows them to inspect purchase orders from across their industry, and to perform data analysis that was not even

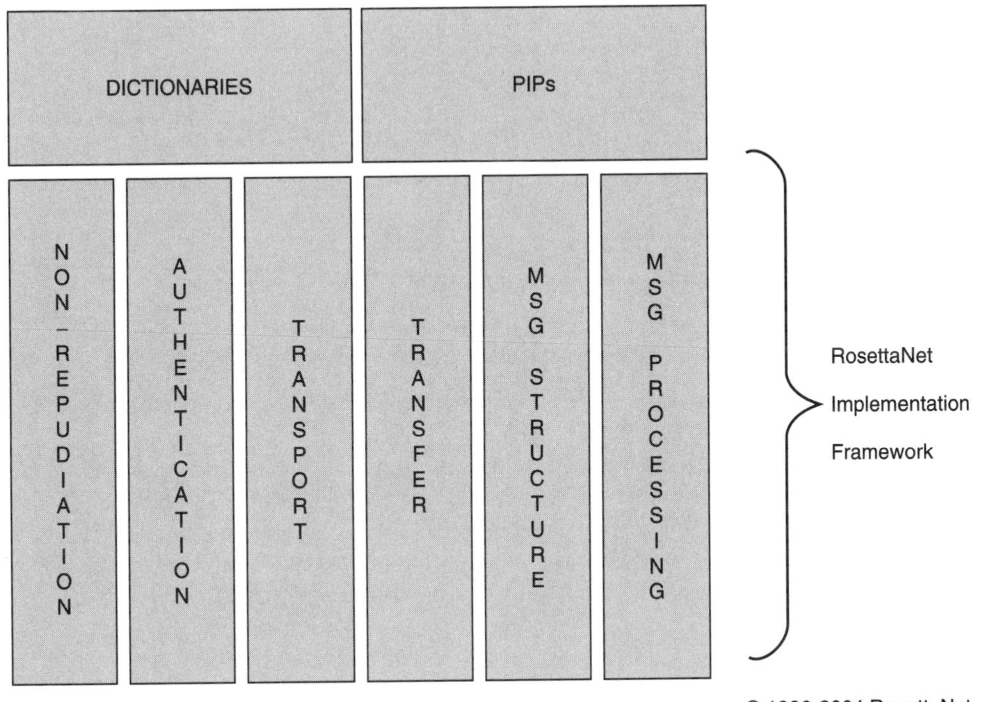

Figure 6.4

The RosettaNet Implementation Framework and related structures.

possible before, since no common marketplace existed through which the data might flow. The existence of the network has also provided opportunities for new revenue streams—industry data can be aggregated and resold to third parties that might be interested in future interaction with the industry. Bulk discounting and larger sales are possible with automation, and partners have generally found that productivity has increased while the cost of business has decreased as a result of their use of the RosettaNET framework.

XML can be thought of as the blood and bones of the RosettaNET framework. The concepts that went into the architecture of the XML standards from the start allowed the RosettaNET architects to design a system for flexibility and interoperability. RosettaNET can be thought of as a success story of XML frameworks, and it actually represents one of the earlier efforts in this area. As new frameworks are developed in the future that have the benefit of past experience in terms of what has worked and what has not worked in RosettaNET, the advantages of these frameworks will only grow.

The next framework has a lot in common with RosettaNET, while providing more generic facilities for accomplishing trading relationships. While the desired outcome of RosettaNET might be similar to that of the next framework (ebXML), the way that it was accomplished is quite different.

ebXML

The stated goal of the ebXML project was "to provide an open XML-based infrastructure enabling the global use of electronic business information in an interoperable, secure and consistent manner by all parties." Other descriptions include the term "single global marketplace," "facilitating the ability of enterprise of any size in any geographical location to conduct business," and "enabling modular, yet complete, electronic business framework that comprise the 'rules of the road' for conducting electronic business."*

ebXML standards were created and supported in conjunction with OASIS and UN/CEFACT, and are credited as having created a single global electronic marketplace. Two of the architectural goals from the start were to leverage existing XML components wherever possible, and to provide a ready-made library of commonly used business objects. These architectural approaches are reminiscent of object-oriented software development. Using existing XML components wherever possible essentially amounts to using existing software rather than recreating it from scratch, and providing a library of commonly used business objects is another way of making sure that the output of the effort itself is as reusable as possible in the future. Reuse is also encouraged. Because the design of the framework ensures data communication interoperability, the common semantic framework ensures commercial interoperability. Furthermore, publishing mechanisms allow enterprises to find each other, agree to establish business relationships, and conduct business. These are maintained via a formal Collaboration Protocol Agreement (CPA) and shared repositories for company profiles, business process models, and related message structures.

*http://www.ebXML.org, accessed in 10/2001.

Like other frameworks, ebXML does specify XML documents that are sent back and forth between organizations to accomplish particular tasks. The actual full ebXML specification goes further than just defining a type of document that organizations can exchange. It is intended as an actual suite of different technologies that allow many types of functionality, including exchanging business information, conducting business relationships, and registering business processes. All of this is done in a common format that all organizations can easily understand. In addition, a large amount of ready-made software is already available for exchanging ebXML messages with other organizations. In some ways, this standard provides out-of-the-box solutions for some problems rather than just a data specification. The set of standards that comprise ebXML are fairly far reaching; while there are a number of other XML components that solve similar problems for specific industries, ebXML is one of the only technologies that provides the representational flexibility to deal with many different industries, despite their different terms and procedures. RosettaNET and other frameworks have grown quite a bit over time, but there may still be some artifacts left in these frameworks that identify them as having come from a particular industry or sector—ebXML was engineered from the start to be more general in its applicability.

The following are some of the metamodels included in ebXML:

Business Process Model

- Represent "verbs" of electronic business
- Define "how" business processes are described
- Use a common language to express business processes

Information Model

- Represent the "nouns and adjectives" of electronic business
- Define "what" reusable components can be applied
- Enable users to define data that is meaningful while also maintaining interoperability

Messaging services define services and protocols such as the following that enable data exchange:

- Common protocols such as SMTP, HTTP, and FTP
- Cryptographic protocols such as HTTPS/SSL
- Digital signatures that can be applied to individual messages

Registry and Repository

- Store company profiles
- Store trading partner specifications
- Includes final business process definitions

Among its many components, ebXML specifies a business process representation schema, a message service specification detailing how ebXML messages move between organizations, and a registry services specification. In keeping with the requirements of an open platform, all relevant

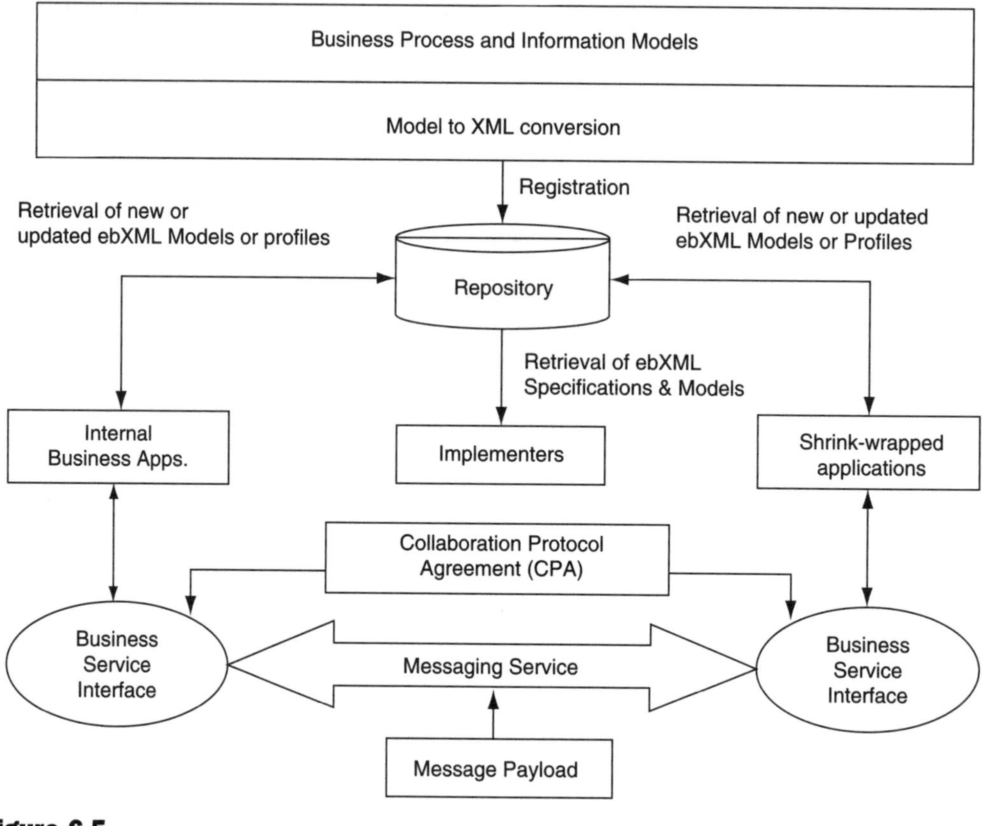

Figure 6.5

The ebXML technical architecture.

technical and procedural documents are available through the ebXML project web site. If ebXML has any downside, it might be the complexity of the interrelated standards. Unlike some of the other XML technologies, the entirety of ebXML is likely not something that could easily be understood in an afternoon, but then again, neither is the complex set of processes that it is trying to represent.

While the steps to implement ebXML are not quite as simple as those described by the ebXML literature, the general outline is useful to understand.

Step 1

- Design and register business processes and information models
- Implementer browses the repository for
  - Appropriate business processes
  - Process that intended partner is registered to support

Step 2

- Implement business service interfaces and register Collaborative Partner Profiles (CPP)

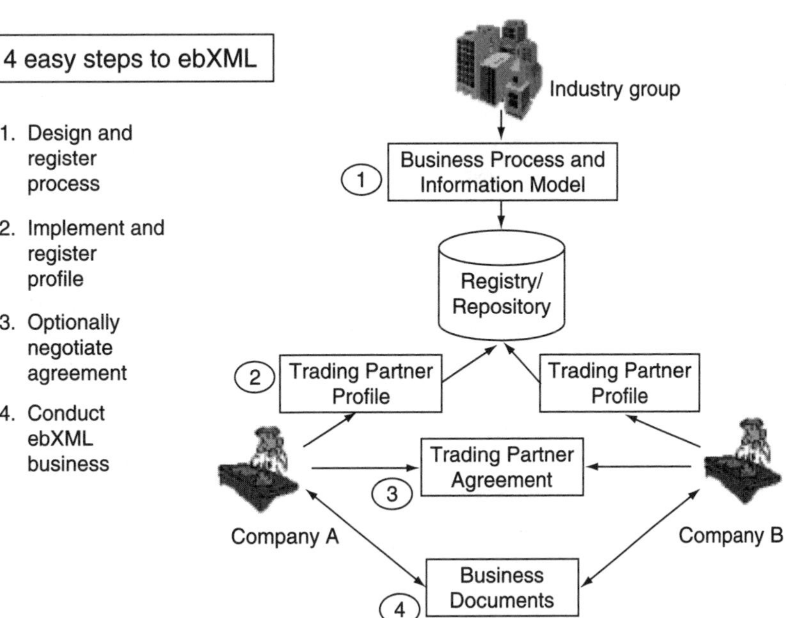

Figure 6.6

Steps toward using ebXML presented in a light-hearted manner from its proponents.

- Implementer buys, builds, or configures application(s) capable of participating in selected business process
- Implementer registers capability to participate via CPP

Step 3 (Optional)

- Negotiate and define CPA (Collaboration Protocol Agreement)
- Two parties negotiate
  - Technical details and/or functional overrides
  - Draw up the result in the form of a CPA
- Register the CPA

Step 4

- Exchanging messages between business partners
- Software sends and receives ebXML messages
  - Messages contain ebXML business documents
  - Messages are sent via secure and reliable ebXML Messaging Service

Several companies are currently pushing adoption of ebXML as a "lingua franca" for electronic business on the Internet, and its popularity has been growing steadily, enticing many organizations with the prospect of replacing several incompatible and brittle communications interfaces with one system that can handle interbusiness communication. It seems also that some convergence of other frameworks with ebXML might be on the horizon. RosettaNET has plans to include ebXML's messaging services specification in the RosettaNET Implementation Framework (RNIF). ebXML represents a strong standard that many are interested in to promote communication *between* industries rather than just *within* industries. Later in the book, we will talk more about communication within and between industries, and how frameworks like ebXML, in conjunction with other standards, might make wide interindustry communication possible.

The next framework that we will discuss is quite a bit different from the first two, and represents one of the most recent major approaches to the topic.

Microsoft Offerings: BizTalk and .NET

BizTalk was Microsoft's first offering in the XML frameworks. While attention is now focused on Microsoft's .NET product suite, it is worth spending a few minutes on BizTalk to see how its architecture was organized to provide common business services.

BizTalk

BizTalk is intended to be a platform-independent solution that handles document transfer within and between organizations. Developed by Microsoft and transferred to BizTalk.org, the framework has five areas that are intended to aid in application integration:

1. Document Routing and Transport
2. Data Transformation
3. Application Integration
4. Process Automation
5. Scalability and Manageability Services

Almost all frameworks handle some aspect of the document routing and transport function. Process automation is one of the core missions of an XML framework, and scalability and manageability services are also characteristics that most frameworks share in common. The data transformation and application integration pieces of the BizTalk functionality are what set this framework apart from the others. Many different plug-ins or adaptors are available for BizTalk that take the core framework and extend it by making data interchange with various ERPs, databases, and web services possible.

BizTalk was originally developed by Microsoft, and has since developed into two separate entities, depending on what is being discussed. Microsoft sells the BizTalk server, which is an actual software implementation of the ideas behind the framework, but there is also a BizTalk specification, similar to the RosettaNET RNIF, that lays out exactly how the heavily XML-dependent technology functions and accomplishes the tasks that it does.

The technology of BizTalk is structured around a server model. Some frameworks tend to be spoken of as a network that messages flow through, but BizTalk is usually referred to by its various BizTalk servers, through which messages flow—a slightly different focus. The server focuses on a number of areas, including:

- **Business-to-Business and E-Commerce.** This includes trading-partner integration, supply-chain integration, order management, invoicing, shipping management, etc.
- **Automated Procurement.** Some of the areas involved here are Maintenance Repair and Operations (MRO), pricing and purchasing, order tracking, and government procurement.
- **Business-to-Business Portals.** This large and growing topic encompasses catalog management, content syndication, and post-sale customer management.
- **Business Process Integration and Exchange.** This area usually deals with integration of E-Commerce, ERP, and legacy systems.

In Figure 6.7, an example is provided of the layered protocol model of BizTalk. This layering of protocols is based on the OSI model for networking. The process of layering protocols involves creating a particular protocol to do something very specific and small (for example, ensuring that data is correctly moved through a physical wire or existing logical network), and then creating new protocol layers above it with higher-level functionality, each building on the services provided by protocols at lower

Figure 6.7

Example of message passing in BizTalk systems.

layers. Figure 6.7 shows a simplified version of this protocol layering at several levels: First, the application talks to the BizTalk server. Then, the server uses a data-communication layer to transfer data back and forth. The data-communication layer handles technical details such as whether SOAP via HTTP or MSMQ is used to transfer the messages. On the other end of the transaction, another data-communication layer receives and interprets the messages coming in over the network, and passes them up to the BizTalk server. Finally, the server makes the information sent and received accessible to the application at the highest level. In this way, the application does not need to bother with the details of how all of this works—from its perspective, it can speak to the BizTalk server and accomplish many things simply.

But how is the sending and receiving of that data accomplished? In Figure 6.8, we see the structure of a BizTalk message. These messages are exchanged between BizTalk servers to accomplish the tasks described earlier as capabilities of the server. Note that while this information could certainly be represented in a non-XML format, the way the message structure is laid out here even *looks* like a rudimentary XML document. The overall BizTalk message acts as the parent wrapper to two items—the transport envelope and the BizTalk document. The document in turn contains

Figure 6.8

The structure of a BizTalk message.

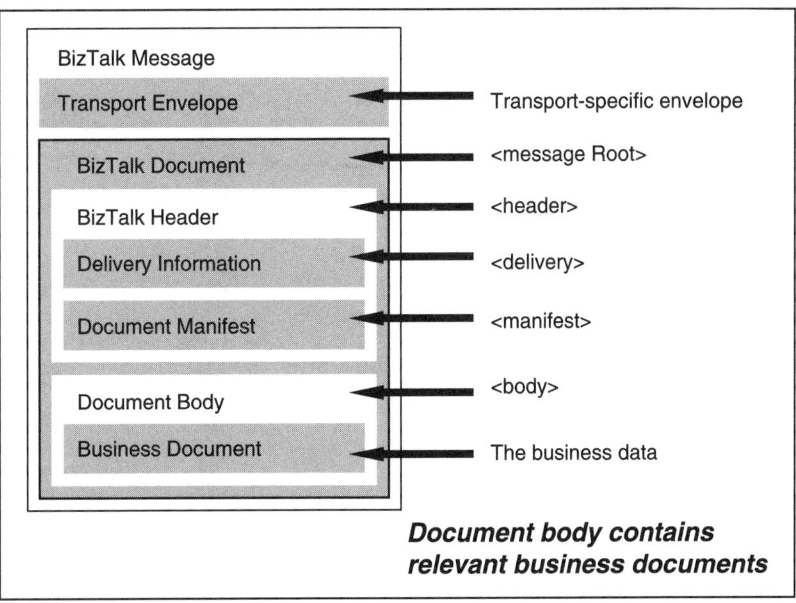

its own children—the BizTalk header, and the document body. This message structure is typical of many XML frameworks—the "Transport Envelope" and "BizTalk Header" portions of the document usually contain various types of metadata about the document and the process that it represents. This information might contain source and destination addresses, information about the specifics of the protocol used to send it, digital signatures or security information, and information about the types of additional data the body of the message contains.

Taking a look at the message structure only provides a low-level view of what is possible with the framework. Next, we will investigate the various tools that BizTalk provides to add higher-level functionality to the base technology described above.

Given the various tasks that BizTalk servers perform, a number of tools are needed to facilitate the process. These tools help users build business processes, and the corresponding BizTalk representations of those processes. The optional tools available with BizTalk include:

- **The Orchestration Designer**. This tool provides a common visual interface to BizTalk, and aids in building integration layers for existing processes.
- **XML Editor**. For the creation of individual XML documents, an editor is provided. It also contains some capabilities that help reconcile different types of schemas.
- **The Mapper**. This tool helps in the process of mapping one data set onto another, and can generate XSLT programs that express the mapping operations that were performed.
- **The Messaging Manager**. This helps automate the trading of profiles and agreements, using a GUI interface.

These various tools support the facets of the tasks that the BizTalk server performs, and they really show how XML can shine, from defining processes and organizations as XML-based documents, to transforming data from a source to a target specification. XML documents permeate the system, but more importantly, the architectural perspective that XML provides makes the system's flexibility possible in the first place. Some of the power behind BizTalk has been biztalk.org whose value-added services (such as use of open-source code and automated schema submission and testing) are designed to facilitate growth toward a critical mass of information.

.NET

First a few words from Microsoft to describe .NET:

> Microsoft® .NET is a set of Microsoft software technologies for connecting your world of information, people, systems, and devices. It enables an unprecedented level of software integration through the use of XML Web services: small, discrete, building-block applications that connect to each other—as well as to other, larger applications—via the Internet. .NET-connected software delivers what developers need to create XML Web services and stitch them together.

Another way to look at the overall .NET initiative is to examine three of its levels :

- Everything needs to be a *web service*. This applies to both pieces of software and resources in the network like storage.
- You need to be able to *aggregate* and *integrate* these web services in very simple and easy ways.
- The system should provide a *simple* and *compelling* consumer or end-user experience.*

The most telling phrase in the above description is, "Everything needs to be a Web service." Microsoft hopes to turn all applications including its own software into web services. Already you will notice how the properties tag reveals document-specific metadata tallying the number of minutes you have spent editing the document—this in preparation for charging for software rentals. One cynic describes the move as follows:

> Once your spreadsheet talks XML, it can link across the Net into other spreadsheets and into server-based applications that offer even greater power. .NET puts little XML stub applications on your PC that do not actually do much until they are linked to the big XML servers Microsoft will be running over the Internet. You can do powerful things on tiny computers as long as you continue to pay rent to Microsoft. The effect of dot-NET is cooperative computing, but the real intent is to smooth Microsoft's cash flow and make it more deterministic. .NET will move us from being owners to renters of software and will end, Microsoft hopes forever, the tyranny of having to introduce new versions of products just to get more revenue from users. Under .NET, we'll pay

*http://Microsoft.net/net/defined/default.asp, accessed 10/2001.

> over and over not just for the application parts that run on Microsoft computers, not ours, but we'll also pay for data, itself, with Microsoft taking a cut, of course.*

.NET makes use of five additional tools. In Microsoft's own language; they are

- **Developer Tools**: Make writing Web services as simple and as easy as possible using .NET Framework and the Microsoft Visual Studio toolset.
- **Microsoft Servers**: Best, simplest, easiest, least expensive way to aggregate and deliver Web services
- **Foundation Services**: Building a small set of services, like identity and notification and schematized storage, that will make it really simple for consumers or users to move from one service to another, from one application to another, or even from one environment to another
- **Devices**: We're building a lot of device software so that people can use a family of complementary devices . . . to make that experience as compelling and immersive as possible.
- **User Experiences**: Building some very targeted end-user experiences that pull together the Web services, and that pull together and integrate a lot of functionality to deliver a very targeted experience. So we're building: MSN for consumers, bCentral for small businesses, Office for knowledge workers, Visual Studio .NET for developers.

Some have correctly stated that the entirety of .NET is difficult to describe. The .NET initiative is a combination of a number of different elements whose relationships are as complicated as the elements themselves. Really, .NET is an initiative, not a single technology. The initiative contains a programming language (the new C# language), a virtual machine like the one used to run Java programs, a web services push, a system of allowing different programming languages to be used in conjunction with one another, a security model, a just-in-time compiler, and an object hierarchy, to name just a few. Intertwined through all of these technologies is a common thread of XML used to represent data, but it would not be accurate to say that .NET

***Data, Know Thyself* by Robert X. Cringely (http://www.pbs.org/cringely/pulpit/pulpit20010412.html), accessed on 10/2001.

is XML or that XML is .NET. Rather, XML is used as a small but important part of a much larger initiative called .NET.

When people refer to XML and .NET, frequently what they are talking about is the extensive set of XML APIs (Application Programming Interfaces) that .NET provides for programming language access. The goal of these APIs is to make XML access as simple as possible for two reasons; first, as XML is used in many areas of .NET, tools need to be provided to work with that XML, and second, to encourage the use of XML within applications for data-representation needs.

Both BizTalk and ebXML aim at providing capabilities with XML that are not specific to any particular industry. Next, we will take a look at an XML framework that was created and grown with a specific industry in mind. Industry-specific frameworks often contain a trade-off—this next framework, Acord, sacrifices a bit of general applicability that ebXML or BizTalk might provide, in exchange for a system with preexisting components that match industry-specific needs.

Industry-Specific Initiatives

Acord

The Acord group is a non-profit organization that works to develop and promote the use of standards in the insurance industry. Created in 1970, Acord first dealt with the development of a set of forms for information gathering by insurance companies. In the 1980s, it began focusing on data standardization and is currently working on a number of XML standards related to lines of business related to insurance of various kinds. Specifically, Acord is working on standards related to property and casualty insurance, life insurance, and reinsurance. One of the reasons that Acord became involved in data standardization was to help prevent the development of many different, incompatible XML DTDs in different areas of the industry that would later have to be reconciled. Instead, Acord wishes to act as a central industry broker for these standards in a way that can build consensus among member companies. The interoperability of these industry-wide standards allows all involved parties to reap maximum benefit. Doing it right *once* at the industry level (instead of many times at the company level) reduces the total amount of effort needed to build the standards and allows all members to take part.

As with any good framework, Acord starts with a data model that details the metadata needed in order for effective communication to happen. Different insurance companies have different ways of storing and referring to various data items, but the central Acord data model relating to life insurance is the basis for later XML documents used to describe various data or phenomena in the insurance industry. The data model was created to allow interoperability, but was also built with an eye toward expandability. The creators of good frameworks always factor industry change into all of their decisions to prevent having to solve a similar problem again at a later date. Finally, usage of this data model allows organizations to achieve some type of consistency in representation, as well as reusability. Data models that become the de facto method of representing specific concepts can be reused in new systems so that as legacy systems are updated and replaced, the translation component can be eliminated as the new system is brought online to understand the data model natively.

Acord represents an effort by a large portion of the insurance industry to come together and develop standards to reduce costs and improve efficiency not only within companies, but across the entire industry. At the date of this writing, Acord has over 1,000 member insurance companies (including the majority of the top 25), 27,000 agents, and 60 software vendors. Acord has also recently been working with the Object Management Group (OMG), a body that helps to set data standards for a number of different industries. The work that Acord has done within the insurance industry is becoming the acknowledged and adopted standard for that industry.

Along with an XML format, Acord also specifies a series of forms that allow for the collection of standard data related to various types of insurance. Predictably, these forms are based on the Acord data models, and attempt to gather standard information that will be needed regardless of the type of policy or company with which a customer is doing business. At an industry level, Acord can take steps to make sure that these individual forms are compliant with various information-collection laws and regulations. They also ensure that information collected by an Acord form in one organization will be transferable to another organization that uses the same forms, rather than requiring a complicated data-reconciliation process.

Acord also has developed and maintains its own EDI standard, called AL3 (Automation Level 3). It tends to focus on communication between property and casualty insurance companies, the agents of those companies, and other industry trading partners. The system is currently being used for exchanging accounting, policy, and claims submission and processing information. The AL3 standard also delves into some standardization of business processes, as with other XML-based frameworks. The flow of data and the business processes that require it often go hand in hand, so it is not strange to see data standards next to business-process standards.

Envera

The Envera Hub is a good example of a mature framework usage for the chemical industry. The industry achieved a strong start toward development of a common XML-based framework-based approach to information exchange. The Envera Hub was developed to be a business-to-business transaction clearinghouse with an in-depth menu of value-added services for its members. Implemented by a consortium of multinational chemical-industry players, the hub facilitated transaction exchange with other members. This provided an incentive to join the hub.

Envera developed a Shockwave presentation describing both the business case and the utility of the hub model. Unfortunately, the demo is no longer available. We will present some shots from the demonstration to illustrate the type of technological sophistication achieved by this XML framework.

Members were equity partners in the venture and all were supposed to realize cost savings and begin to learn more about their industry using the metadata collected by the hub. For example, the hub accumulated volumes of data on one of its consortium members' product-shipping logistics. This included data on specific product orders, quantities, warehousing requirements, shipping routes, and schedules. Hub operators "mined" this data on its members' behalf—for example, offering residual space in containers to the market as well as cargo vessels not filled to capacity, or warehouse space that is about to become vacant. Members also realized savings from reduced complexity in order fulfillment, lower working-capital requirements, and revenue boosts through re-engineered distribution channels. Figure 6.9 lists the various areas of the enterprise where savings were made possible.

Figure 6.10 shows just some of the ways that organizations might attempt to work together as partners. Organizations must become good at managing procedures in order to use them effectively. Figure 6.11 shows various types of cross-organization communication used to complete a single transaction. The hub replaces much of this variability both in terms of business processes and technical complexities.

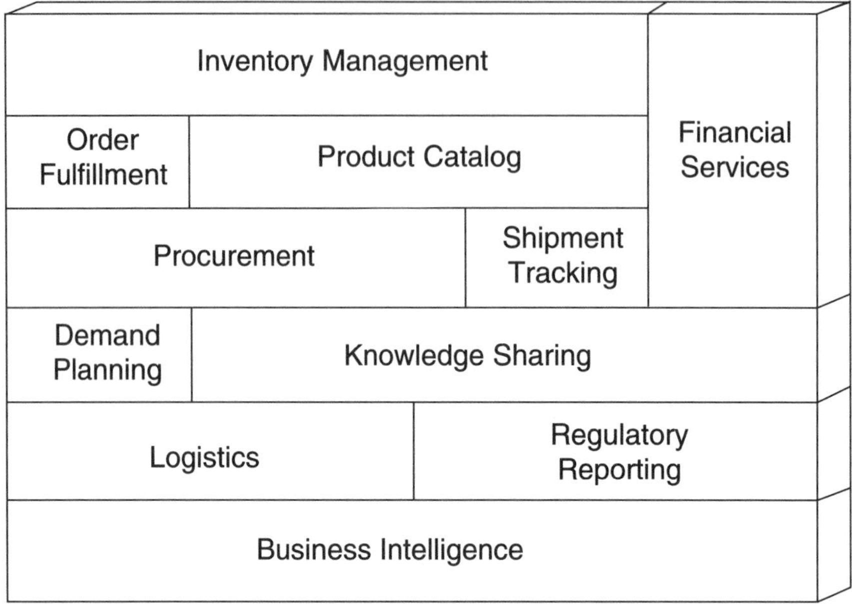

Figure 6.9

Metadata uses maintained by the clearinghouse.

The Envera Hub "learns and/or is taught" Member A and Member B's metadata. Once this is understood, the Hub can develop translation rules required to make Member A's document understood by Member B's system. Figure 6.12 shows how the XML translators work.

All of this is achieved via a commonly understood XML vocabulary, which enables members to reap online business-to-business efficiencies regardless of their IT sophistication. The hub permits XML-based transaction exchange across many different types of organizations involved in the chemical business. Using XML as the basis, the Envera group developed detailed understanding of the data structures and uses within the industry.

Figure 6.13 shows the use of the translators reformatting an XML purchase order-acknowledgement document. Best of all, the interfaces can be maintained by XML because the translation rules themselves are stored as XML documents. This means that maintenance can be per-

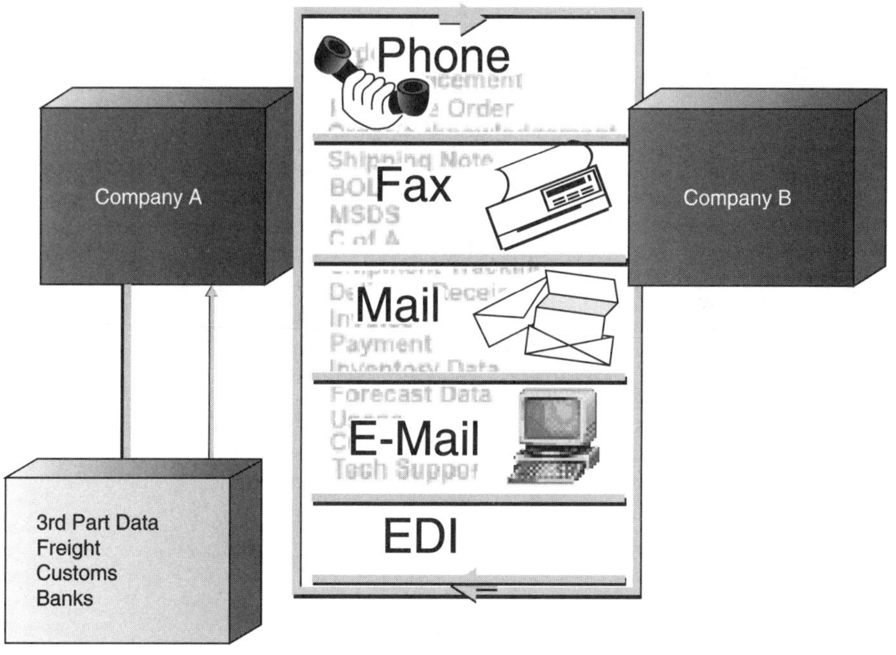

Figure 6.10

Organizational connectivity variations eliminated by use of Envera Hub.

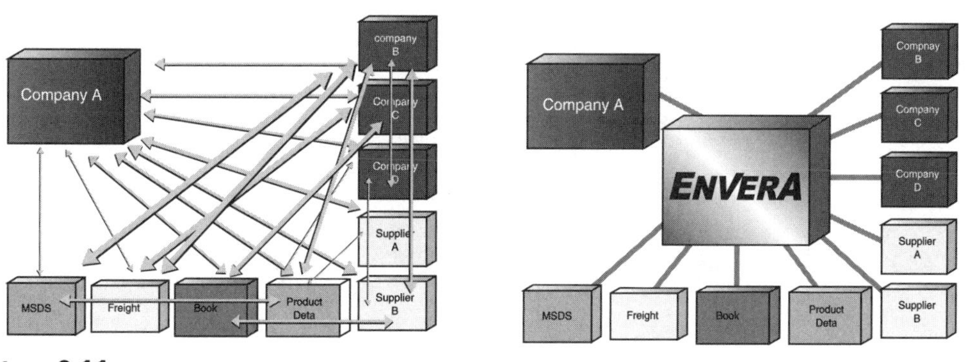

Figure 6.11

Cross-organization communication used to complete a single transaction and replaced by the Envera Hub.

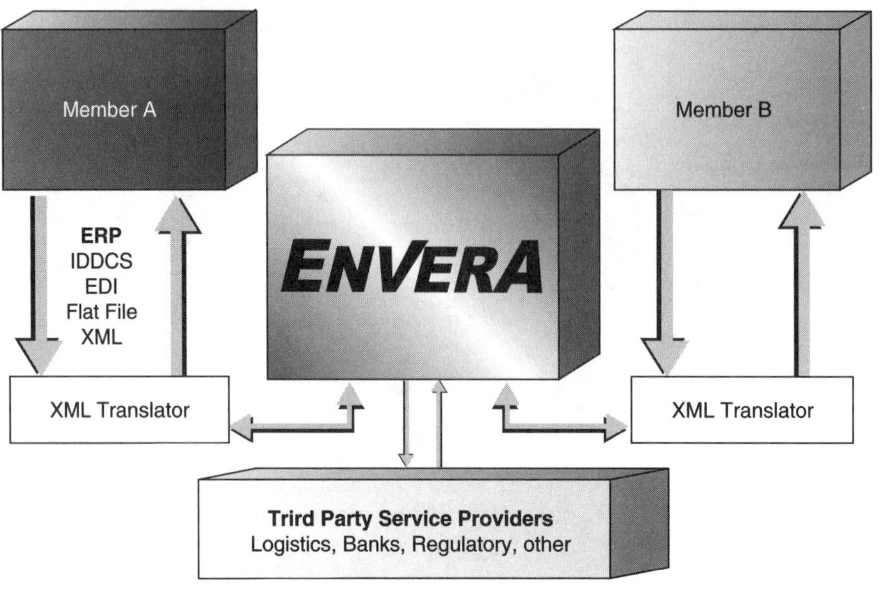

Figure 6.12

XML translators at work.

Figure 6.13

Translators reformatting an XML order acknowledgment.

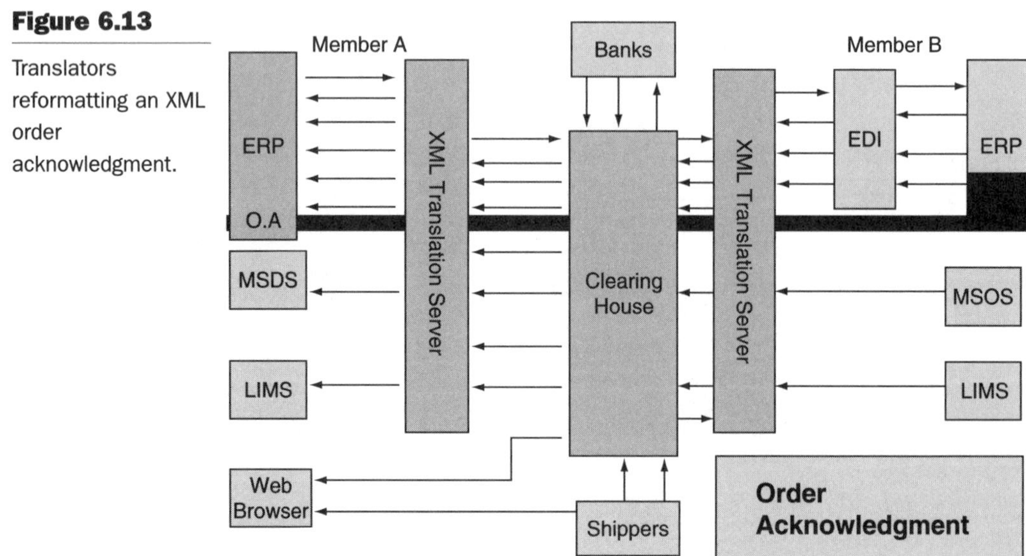

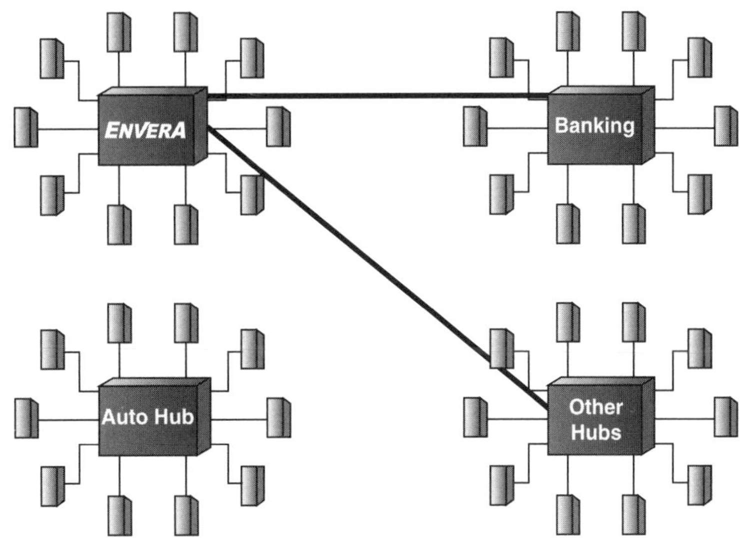

Figure 6.14

Connections between hubs enable wider communication between industries.

formed using modern Database Management System, or "DBMS," technologies instead of reading through custom programs of spaghetti code.

Figure 6.14 illustrates a final significant ability of the hub, that it could link to other hubs and types of systems. Once Envera learned how to translate between any two systems (say a logistics and a cash-forecasting system), new systems of either type could be added with virtually no additional effort. By the same sort of leverage, once Envera was hooked to other hubs, the connectivity multiplier was enormous. New companies could often be added to the hub with little or no new development.

The fact that the Envera hub has not received wider recognition has been more due to the pre-dot.com bust than to any technical issues with the hub. As this book is being finished, in the fall of 2003, the Envera hub seems to be an underappreciated asset that comes as a bonus to a corporate merger.

Common Themes and Services

At this point, we have taken a look at a number of different frameworks. While the approach to solving problems is different from framework to framework, they do have quite a bit in common. The common themes of these XML frameworks include:

Integration of applications and business partners

- Framework servers exchange using open W3C-standard XML
- Framework document transformation is done in W3C-standard XSLT
- Reduced cycle times
- Lower production costs
- Improved operating efficiencies
- Strengthened customer relationships and service
- Better-informed decisions
- Tighter supply-chain integration
- Actualized new-revenue channels
- More immediate return on investment

Framework servers support multiple protocols and common services, including:

- Electronic data interchange (EDI)
- Extensible Markup Language (XML)
- File Transfer Protocol (FTP)
- HTTPS/SSL
- Hypertext Transfer Protocol (HTTP)
- Multipurpose Internet Mail Extensions (MIME)
- File sharing
- Simple Mail Transfer Protocol (SMTP)
- Transmission Control Protocol/Internet Protocol (TCP/IP)
- Unified Modeling Language (UML)

Common XML-based framework advantages include:

- Relatively less technical expertise required
- Flexible and open architecture
- Inexpensive public network
- Low deployment cost
- Open to businesses of all sizes
- Open binding architecture (allows any developer to build adaptors that allow their products to be accessed from the framework server)

Security

- Public-key infrastructure
- Digital signatures
- Encryption
- S/MIME v. 1.0, 2.0, and 3.0
- Pluggable architecture for third-party security products

Server Document Delivery

- Sends, receives, and queues messages with exactly-once semantics
- Supports synchronous and asynchronous interaction
- Supports document tracking and analysis

Scalability

- Servers can be clustered
- Administration tools handle clustering and server replication

These themes are also shared by additional offerings beyond those discussed, such as the Sun ONE framework pictured in Figure 6.15.

XML frameworks in general frequently attempt to take the emphasis off of data structures and specific platforms by standardizing the data-interchange aspect of trading, and instead try to focus on the business

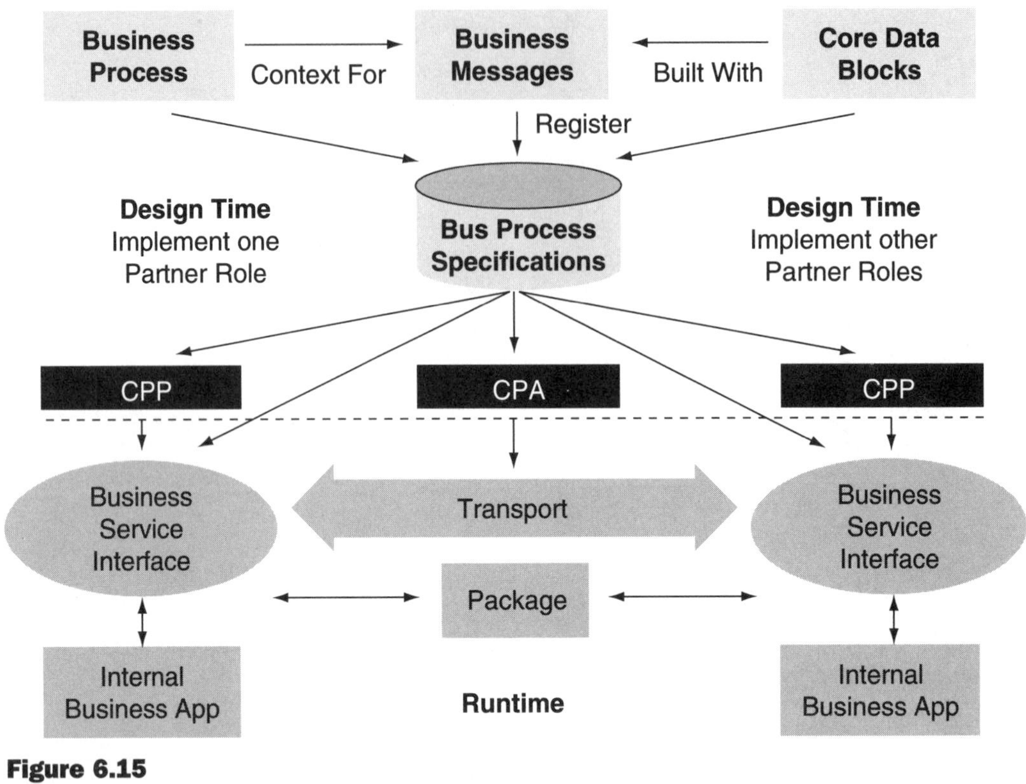

Figure 6.15

Sun One XML-based framework. (From *Sun ONE Architecture Guide: Delivering Services on Demand.* Courtesy of Sun Microsystems Inc., www.sun.com.)

processes behind the flow of information. After all, the reason why businesses have information systems in the first place is to facilitate their business processes. One of the most frequent problems with any type of technology is that the user gets distracted by the minutiae and details of the technology and does not spend the necessary time thinking through the business rules and logic behind what the technology is doing. By setting up automated systems for carrying on business transactions, these XML frameworks are trying to put as much focus on the business process as possible.

These frameworks all share the concept of the "metamodel"—a technical description of a business process. These models represent the "verbs"

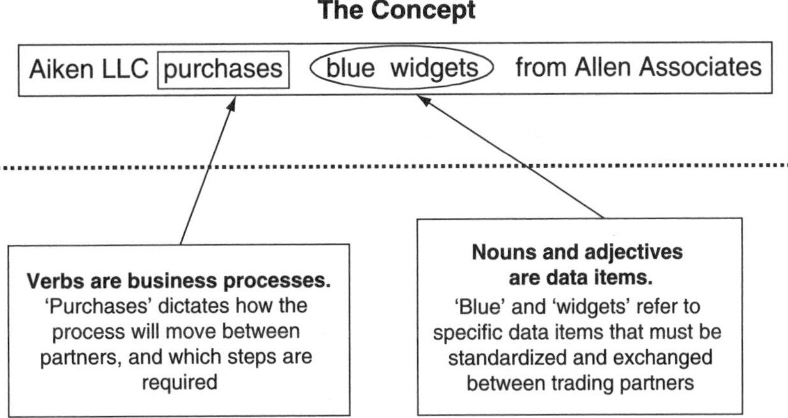

The Concept
Aiken LLC purchases blue widgets from Allen Associates
Verbs are business processes.
'Purchases' dictates how the process will move between partners, and which steps are required
Nouns and adjectives are data items.
'Blue' and 'widgets' refer to specific data items that must be standardized and exchanged between trading partners
Interpretation in an XML Framework

Figure 6.16

Interpreting high-level business requests in terms of the framework and concepts of level business requests.

of electronic business, and provide a common way for specifying processes. For example, one organization might wish to purchase goods from another. The business process is represented at its core by the use of the verb "to purchase." The information models, on the other hand, represent the "nouns" and "adjectives" of electronic business. They define what reusable components can be applied to various processes. Taking the example of purchasing, when a purchasing process is invoked, it must have some object on which to operate—the organization itself and the item that is being purchased represent nouns. Adjectives frequently modify the nouns to give a clearer picture of exactly which type of item is being described. The information models allows users to define data that is meaningful while maintaining interoperability. The interplay of these two ideas is illustrated in Figure 6.16 by taking a business request (purchasing a particular item) and showing how different parts of the request are understood and dealt with by an XML framework.

Conclusion

The benefits of using the frameworks described in this chapter have become a compelling argument for organizations to move toward more extensive use of the frameworks and other components of XML as well. Interestingly, these frameworks seem to be methods of creating rallying points for entire industries—the industry comes together to create a set of data standards and a way of exchanging them in XML for the benefit of everyone involved. As competition within industries has intensified, in many situations competitors find themselves linked by supplier/purchaser relationships. Facilitating more efficient communication within industries increases efficiency and allows for even more vigorous competition. Even before XML became popular, the trend was toward increasing contact and involvement between organizations and industries. In many cases, the adoption of these XML frameworks is just a signal of the acceleration of that trend.

The frameworks presented in this chapter represent concrete examples of how XML is delivering on some the things that were always promised of it. XML-language documents and the architectural directions that XML opened up for the information world are the bones of these frameworks. These bones are what make the difference between the one-off solutions for solving specific trading problems, and the general, flexible, and elegant solutions described in this chapter. It is probably a safe prediction to say that the value of XML frameworks will increase along with their overall use over the coming years.

Not everything about XML frameworks is absolutely perfect, though. Just like any technology, XML frameworks can in some situations raise as many questions as they answer. One of these questions is the way in which the frameworks will be integrated. As we have seen earlier, some frameworks are starting to collaborate, as is the case with RosettaNET and ebXML. XML frameworks are proliferating, and not all of them interoperate correctly with one another. Larger organizations that take part in a number of different industries may find themselves still facing the issue of maintaining multiple interfaces (representing various different frameworks) with different trading partners. Interoperability between frameworks, and something of a meta-framework that represents the metadata, business process standardization, and document-exchange methods that would tie frameworks together would be most valuable. Frameworks have shown the myriad benefits that are to be had when intraindustry communication can be automated and managed effectively. Reconciling those frameworks and bringing the same benefits to the larger community of industries may well represent another level of gains of a similar magnitude. Later in the book, methods for how these frameworks might be reconciled will be discussed along with the potential implications for the industries that take part.

7

XML-Based Portal Technologies and Data-Management Strategies

Chapter Overview

Chapter 7 discusses our use of a specific type of portal—an XML-based portal—as a foundation upon which to build an organizational data-management practice. After dodging a fast-moving hype bullet, we describe how the legacy code maintenance burden moves inversely to the degree of information engineering that organizations are able to implement. The pain inflicted by the legacy code maintenance burden can be reduced by reapplying information-engineering principles in an XML-based portal environment. XML-based portals (XBPs) are a specific type of portal technology that greatly facilitates the implementation of specific data-management functions through the careful application of specific architectural enhancements, integrative solutions, extended data management reach, data preparation techniques, new technical reengineering projects, and maintenance burden reduction strategies.

A portal is essentially an application that allows for rapid integration of data from internal and external sources, and provides the user with a standard interface for accessing many different resources. When we use the word portal, we do *not* mean the type of web portal seen on the Internet, such as what Yahoo! provides. Still, there are some distinct similarities—Internet portals typically aggregate news, stock quotes, weather information, search capabilities, comics, and all forms of other information into one customized page that is specific to a user. In this way, the portals we will discuss in this chapter are indeed similar to web portals, only with different sources of data being provided to the user, and very different internal operations and capabilities.

Portal Hype

Unfortunately, when discussing portals, it is necessary to contend with the hype surrounding the concept. One of the authors of this book helped to start the portal wave by co-authoring with Clive Finkelstein the first book on corporate portals. Thanks to Clive, we had the sense to discuss the huge role that XML should play in this new technology. But most writers on this topic do not specifically address the XML capabilities of their portal examples, and thus readers have been unable to assess the technology's features properly.

It may appear as if we ourselves are resorting to hype by titling this chapter "XML-Based Portal Technologies and Data-Management Strategies." However, our goal with this chapter is to illustrate how the use of XBPs can effectively support the expansion of an organization's existing data-management efforts. First, we need to explore and review the business problem that careful application of XML-based data-management principles can solve—exactly how this approach can reduce the burden of legacy code and help data managers. Since the amount and varying types of data that organizations need to store is increasing, so too should the scope of data management be extended to meet those demands. In this context, we will cover material that offers a reason to be excited about what portals have brought to the market. But before we define portals in further detail, we must explain our use of another buzzword.

We will be using a term in this chapter that has sometimes been considered a "bad" word—*reengineering*. The term was misused so frequently throughout the late 1980s and 1990s that it has become the source of much misunderstanding and, frankly, disgruntlement. A prime example occurred in the business community as both management and workforce came to understand the term reengineering to be synonymous with cost cutting, job loss, and turmoil. This could be thought of as the "Dilbert" definition of reengineering. Earlier in this book, we defined "metadata" in order to provide a common frame of reference and otherwise reduce confusion. For the same reason, it is necessary to offer a good definition of reengineering here.

In this chapter, we will use the definition of the term as formalized by Chikofsky and Cross (1990) and later adapted by Aiken (1996):

> Reengineering is the examination and alteration of the target system to reconstitute it in a new form. The target system is the system to be reengineered. Reengineering can only result from the coordination of forward and reverse engineering efforts. An important point to understand is that reengineering generally involves first some reverse and then some subsequent forward engineering.

One of the interesting things to note about this definition is that a source system (that which is being reverse engineered) and a target system (what we are forward engineering toward) are assumed. In other words, there needs to be a "before" and an "after." Too often in the past, *reengineering* has been used as a term not for changing existing systems, but as a metaphor for essentially throwing everything out the window and starting over, usually at tremendous expense. There is a very specific reason for using a formalized definition of the term. Our use of *reengineering* is intended to help readers understand that the methods described here are based in sound, repeatable, predictable, and standardized engineering principles. Engineering in the physical world cannot be accomplished without understanding the meaning and properties of the components being used. In this respect, data engineering is no different. The principles described here can be used in implementation work in virtually any organizational context.

Now that we have primed the pump by learning about a subject that some did not think they wanted to learn more about (portals) in the context of an un-useful business term (*reengineering*), we will next explain how organizations can save millions annually by focusing on XML-based portal development. This development is aimed at providing a synergistic combination of data management, portals, and XML for implementing a generalized access to cross-functional data. (Note that many organizations provide excellent cross-functional data access without XML; this guidance is for organizations desiring to catch up.) Next, an exploration of how data-management roles will expand is presented, followed by a description of the growing importance of data preparation. The chapter closes with a few case studies, including a description of how portals work with an ERP.

The Need: Legacy Code Maintenance Burden

Whether it is called legacy, heritage, or some very bad explicative, code, organizations maintain huge amounts of it. Until recently, outsourcing and ERP implementation have been considered the primary means of reducing legacy code burden. ERP implementation statistics are not good (see Figure 7.1), and outsourcing requires the organization to lose responsiveness and control over intellectual capital.

With the advent of web-service standards and recommendations, organizations can plan to use legacy functionality by wrapping web services around existing systems as an alternative to maintaining a large code inventory.

Let us begin by examining the legacy system characteristics that often drive organizations to consider ERP implementation or outsourcing of this functionality. The example we will use is one published by Michael L. Brodie and Michael Stonebraker in their 1995 book *Migrating Legacy Systems* (see References for publishing information). In the example they use, they describe and represent relevant characteristics of a rather typical legacy system. Given the authors' combined experience with more than 50 major legacy systems, this does present an accurate if disconcerting picture of the state of systems.

This cash-management system supported check processing and other specialized services for large corporate customers, including such functions as:

- Zero account balancing
- Reconciliation of cleared checks
- Electronic funds transfer (e.g., Swift)
- Lock box operations
- Online query facility

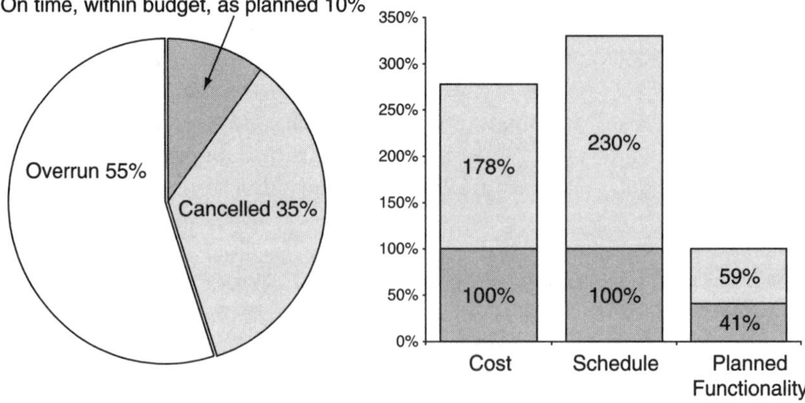

Figure 7.1

ERP implementation statistics—most implementations result in cost and schedule overruns. (Adapted from statistics on the Standish Group web site, www.standishgroup.com, accessed 10/2001).

The system cost the organization more than $16 million to put into place. Developed in 1981, the system ran on an on IBM 3090 and was used to manage more than 100 gigabytes of VSAM files. Composed of 40 software modules and 8 million lines of COBOL/CICS code, the system maintained the Federal Reserve Bank connection and processed 300,000 transactions daily, as well as anywhere from 1 to 2 million checks nightly.

The first figure to examine for opportunities is the 8 million lines of code. Organizations might spend approximately $0.10 to maintain one line annually, given the costs of paying programmers to debug and document the code. Multiply that figure by 8 million, and it will be clear why reductions in the amount of code that organizations are required to maintain would be welcome indeed. It should come as no surprise to discover that Pareto principles apply to application code. Analysis of the 8 million lines reveals that three software modules that comprise just 1.7 million lines of code perform the key application functionality. Figure 7.2 shows how the core functionality of the system requiring reengineering accounts for 22% of the application code; the remaining code can be sliced away, as it is not key to the application functionality and consists of interfaces to other organizational parts, interface code, interfaces to data-management routines, and interfaces to hardware, such as for check sorting.

This is another feature of the stovepipe manner in which systems have been traditionally developed that is not often reported. Each application

Figure 7.2

Core functionality accounts for 22% of the application code.

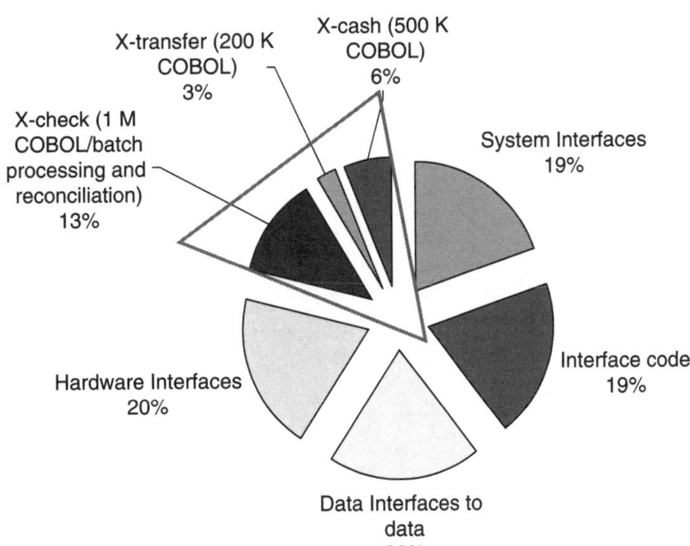

was developed as a stand-alone system and contains as much as five times the code that would have been required if the application had been developed as part of an integrated system. That represents only a portion of the problem. Stovepipe systems also have other serious drawbacks; typically, they lack integration with other applications, or what integration does exist is insufficient or ad hoc, and their data structures are highly dependent on the code behind them that manipulates the data. This inherent complexity causes problems when it comes time to change and evolve these systems. Organizations can clearly benefit from a new approach to information delivery.

Aiding Implementation of Information-Engineering Principles with XML-Based Portal Architectures

XML-based portals can help organizations to implement information-engineering (IE) principles as originally postulated by Clive Finkelstein (1989, 1993) in the late 1980s. In order to expand on this, we will first explore the mathematics of portals. While most legacy applications can be reengineered to take advantage of portal capabilities, the conservative figure that only one in five are can be transformed into portal-based applications. In this situation, the math works out as follows: Take an organization with 5 million lines of legacy code and apply the $0.10 annual maintenance cost per line of code, which gives us an annual maintenance cost of $500,000. Reducing 80% of the code by just 20% would permit savings of $80,000 annually. The 80% figure represents the application code that covers the necessary infrastructure of the application that does not have anything to do with the business logic, such as creating database connections, formatting queries and response sets, and a plethora of other technical details. If we take a more realistic approach, that many more than just one out of five systems can be evolved into this format, what occurs is an increase in the annual savings paired with a substantial decrease in the legacy code maintenance burden.

As with most technologies, there are places where a portal could be implemented from which the organization will not experience a positive return on investment, as well as places where the organization will experience diminishing returns. The portal capabilities focus on trying to reduce as much of that 80% "infrastructure" code as possible. Reducing this code by 20% is certainly a conservative goal. More is likely achievable, but pushing to extend savings beyond 50% or 60% may yield only marginal additional gains.

Code reduction is only one benefit of portals. Other tangible savings can accrue in the first year from:

- The reduction of computing time required to maintain and run the code that is no longer needed
- Savings from avoiding the storage of redundant datasets
- Measurable knowledge-worker productivity gains. These gains stem from the benefits of increased information integration.

Longer-term savings come as the portal gains critical mass with respect to other integration challenges. It will be clear when this happens because application users who have not yet reengineered their systems for the portal will be asking the data managers to help them move their applications into the portal. In order to accomplish the integration, they will offer some of their resources, such as subject matter experts (SMEs) and direct fiscal support to pay for the reengineering. This happens when the users realize that it is an investment in technology that will directly pay off. It is often difficult to get portal technology in the front door for the first time. Once projects have been successfully implemented, it is common for other users to want a piece of that success for their area of operation. Since the portal functionality essentially removes the maintenance burden of a substantial portion of systems, as more systems are migrated over to use a portal that has been implemented, the savings tend to accumulate quickly, due to the use of a shared portal.

Finally and most importantly, these savings can and should be claimed by the data management group, as the savings result from the work of data managers and good data management principles. The trend is toward helping data managers transform their business units into something that shows positive return on investment. That sounds great, but how is an organization supposed to go about picking a target on which to try this approach?

Figure 7.3 shows how careful examination of a legacy environment can identify a number of stovepipe applications, typically the most suitable for evolving toward a portal architecture. These applications must be stripped of features and code that do not add value and repackaged as web services invoked from the XML-based portal. What is useful in the applications is the business logic. The portal should handle as many other technically necessary aspects as possible. The applications identified here represent "low-hanging fruit"—those systems where savings can most

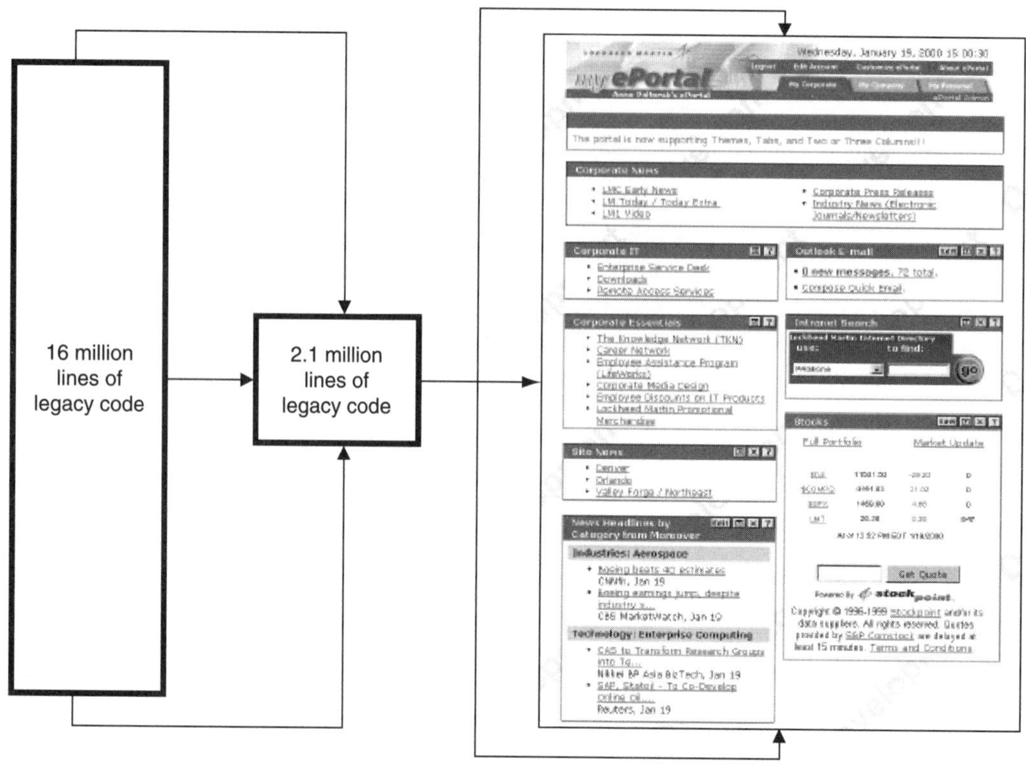

Figure 7.3

Evolving applications from stovepipe to web service-based architectures.

easily be realized. Once the process has been completed one time, organizations become increasingly adept at this type of system reengineering and more applications will be seen as candidates for web service-based portal wrapping. Earlier, we talked about the conservative estimate that only one in five systems could benefit from this process. This figure represents the low-hanging fruit described in this section. Once the most obvious problem applications have been helped, data managers often come to realize that the approach can be applied to many more than just one in five systems.

As a result of careful reengineering, it will be easier to understand and evolve the portal-based services. Figure 7.4 shows how organizations with experience can apply variations on the initial tech-

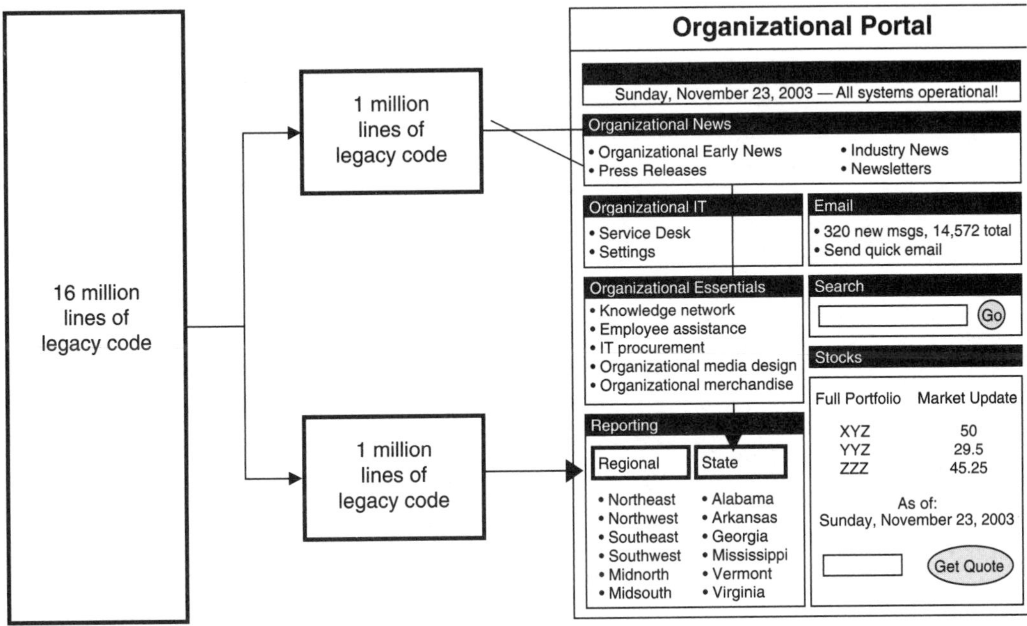

Figure 7.4

Alternative and more sophisticated means of application reengineering legacy applications into an XML-based portal context.

niques to create a more useful service. These are the "one-to-many" and "many-to-one" techniques:

- Take a single legacy application that provides two or more services and break it into several applications providing each of those individual services
- Combine one system's services with those of another existing system's services to produce one system where there were previously two

These approaches can be more easily implemented because the XML-based portal services are better understood. They provide a single type of service that can be used in many different places.

Portals are typically implemented by IT organizations to provide a uniform gateway or entryway to enterprise applications. The upper half of Figure 7.5 shows the flow moves from portal to application and from

Figure 7.5

XBPs can be used to access legacy data directly, as shown in the lower half of this figure.

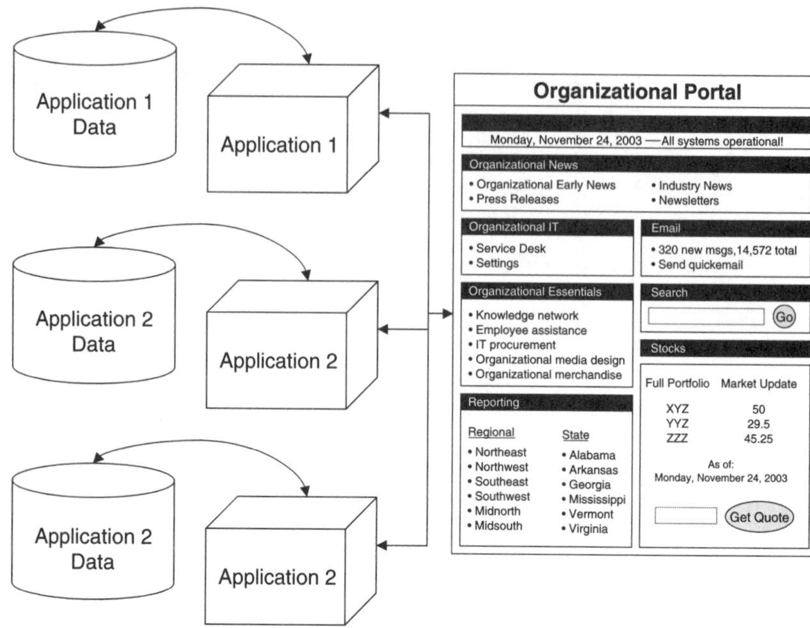

(Above: Assessing data through existing applications)

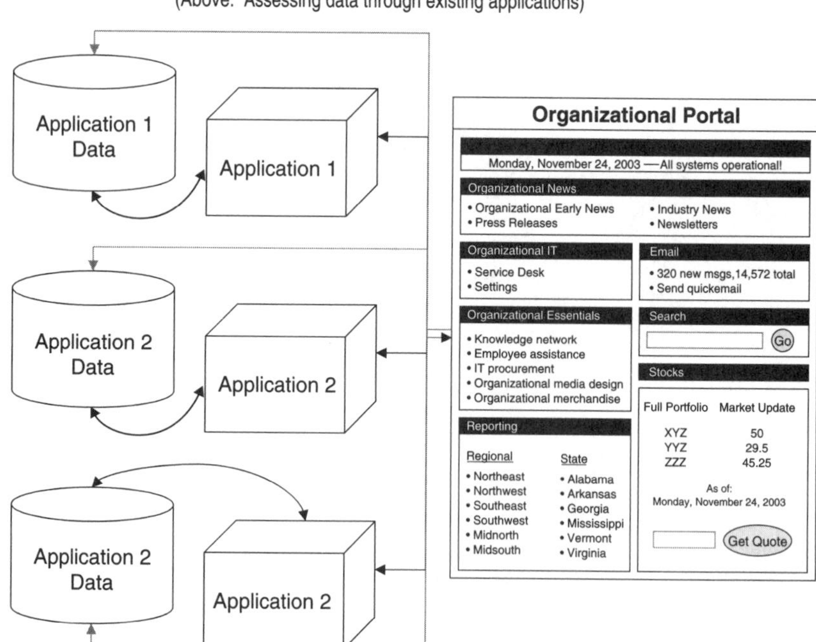

application to data. The lower half illustrates that by adding XML capabilities to those of the portal, organizations can connect their legacy data directly to the portal without relying solely on access provided by the legacy applications.

Reengineering legacy applications into XML-based, portal-wrapped web services allows organizations to move toward the original promise of information engineering (IE). Clive Finkelstein's premise has always been that well-structured data should be at the heart of all technology systems. The term "well-structured data" has always meant in part that the supporting data structures should be flexible and adaptable. Organizations gain three advantages by implementing well-understood data structures:

1. **Before data assets can be managed, they must be understood.** As Michael Brackett (a past president of DAMA International) has stated many times, "Data is the one organizational asset that cannot be used up." It makes sense to develop a good working knowledge of your organizational data. There are many good reasons that data has been implemented in a stovepipe manner—time and budget pressures, lack of skilled data managers, lack of understanding of data-management principles, industry-wide lack of understanding as to the costs of these approaches, and many others. The result is that data managers often spend time trying to understand their own data, rather than managing it. The advantage here is that by understanding data, it becomes *possible* to manage it.

2. **Organizations that understand their data, better understand their organizational capabilities.** If the strengths and weaknesses of data assets are known, the picture of what capabilities an organization has is clearer. This aids in the recognition of opportunities that the organization might not have previously known were within their grasp. It also prevents attempts at implementing technology-based solutions that are dependent on or contain badly designed data. Frequently, implementation projects (such as ERPs) have failed due to incompatibility between data structures, and poor data quality. Once capabilities are understood from a data perspective, data managers can consolidate redundant data. Reducing the amount of data managed by the organization is often a necessary prerequisite to marshaling it in support of organizational strategy. While reduction of the amount of data is significant in its own right, it also greatly helps the process of

creating reusable assets—a necessary and too-often overlooked complement to implementing application code reuse.

3. **Knowing and understanding data permits data managers to control this asset in support of larger strategies.** It is only when data is well understood that organizations can effectively utilize it in support of strategy. All systems exist to support aspects of strategy. One revealing exercise is to formally identify the elements of strategy supported by each application. Data that is organized in stovepipe fashion is often brittle, meaning that changes often require unanticipated modifications to the application code and business processes that use the data. Flexible data stores make it significantly easier to repurpose data in other applications and processes. This makes it cheaper and easier to use data assets in support of strategies. Simultaneously, it simplifies planners' understanding of how to use data assets in support of strategy.

The astute reader will have noticed here that XML may not seem to be a key component of this scheme. It can and has been successfully implemented by organizations that do not use XML. XML is most helpful in providing lower metadata development costs for organizations that have low data-management maturity.

To summarize, implementation of IE requires understanding data assets before understanding how their properties support and impede strategies. With a collective 30 years of consulting practice and research into data-management practices (Aiken & Mattia, In press), we have seen only 1 in 10 organizations that are ready to implement IE principles. Organizations that want to improve their data-management practices can use empirically derived measures that already exist. Understanding where and in what order improvements can be effectively applied is key.

The good news is that those who are able to sustain IE, quickly reap the benefits; applications require less time to understand, code maintenance costs are lower, applications are engineered from the start to require less code, and more strategic dexterity results from implementing IE principles. The fundamental challenge of information engineering has been how to move legacy infrastructure forward to take advantage of these principles. The burden of legacy systems has increased to the point that maintenance is consuming up to 80% of IT budgets. Before the introduction of XML-based portal technologies, it was cheaper to pay for maintenance than to implement a true IE program. Now things have reached a point where there is almost nothing more expensive than status quo maintenance.

Given the introduction of XML-based portal technologies, the future of data management is changing in three important ways:

- The definition of data management is being expanded to include management of unstructured data. Examples of unstructured data would be Word documents, emails, presentations, and notes.
- Applications development will change due to the use of portal technologies and the benefits they provide.
- Data will likely be prepared with e-business in mind from the start, rather than preparing and cleansing data, only to later add an e-business interface.

These three points are described in the chapter subsections that follow. First, though, a precise definition is needed of what we mean when we say "XML-based portals" (XBP).

Clarifying Excitement Surrounding XML-Based Portals (XBPs)

Just as the hype surrounding the terms "reengineering" and "metadata" requires us to use a precise definition, the same is true of the term "portal." A firm definition is needed before we can present XBP solutions. First, we will define portal and its basic capabilities, and describe the initial excitement portals have engendered.

Portal technology alone can be considered a significant advance in organizational capabilities. Unfortunately, due to the economic slowdown around the year 2000, the case for portals became buried in hype. Forecasts from the late 1990s before the dot.com bust predicted a rosy future for portals, and everyone tried to jump on the bandwagon, which subsequently collapsed under the weight of its own hype. Here is an example:

> *We have conservatively estimated the 1998 total market opportunity of the EIP (Enterprise Integration Portal) market at $4.4 billion. We anticipate that revenues could top $14.8 billion by 2002, approximately 36% CAGR [Compound Annual Growth Rate] for this sector.*[*]

---

[*]InfoWorld Electric web site <ETH> http://www.infoworld.com/cgi-bin/displayStory.pl?/features/990125eip.htm

This rosy scenario was given during the high-rolling days before the dot.com bust. Keep in mind that Hollywood and the entertainment industry would think of $8 billion annually as a good year, and this will help to calibrate your thinking. Portals were seen as a source of growth, so a lot of attention was paid to the sector. Descriptions of portal visions include the following:

> Envision the enterprise information portal as a browser-based system providing ubiquitous access to business-related information in the same way that Internet content portals are the gateway to the wealth of content on the web. (InfoWorld Electric web site, accessed in 1996)
>
> Portals are applications that enable organizations to more rapidly interchange internally and externally stored information, and provide users a single gateway to personalized information needed to make informed business decisions. Portals are an emerging market opportunity; an amalgamation of software applications that consolidate, manage, analyze and distribute information across and outside of an enterprise (including business intelligence, content management, data ware-house and mart, and data management applications). (Merrill Lynch: SageMaker web site, accessed in 1998)

For all its hype, the initial portal goals were limited to attempting to provide a consistent user interface to the knowledge worker. But even the implementation of a common, well-designed interface alone would help organizations for a number of reasons described below.

- **Better user/product understanding**—users properly trained in the portal interface can be more intelligent, creative, and powerful in their use of the system.
- **Lower cost to develop**—significant up-front savings on development costs and interface maintenance costs are possible. In addition, improvements in data quality due to implementation of a consistent user interface are also realistic (see Aiken & White, 2004, for example).
- **Lower organizational cost to implement and maintain**—implementation of a consistent user interface can reduce costs from current levels of about 30% of the total development costs to less than 3% through the use of portal technology. The portal gets the user interface *right* in 1 place, rather than having application programmers get it *almost* right in 10 places.
- **Faster time to implement**—organizations are able to implement user interfaces and subsequent modifications more rapidly, significantly reducing the barriers to implementing changes to processes and technology.

- **Lower training costs**—savings in technology training can be achieved though use of consistent user interfaces. Why train workers on many different interfaces?

Figure 7.6 shows how knowledge workers may have to navigate and understand numerous interfaces to obtain information supporting their work. We recall fondly the desk of an action officer at the Defense Information Systems Agency (DISA) whose desk (in 1992) was crowded with the following items:

- A vintage DOS machine (386)
- A Windows 3.0 machine

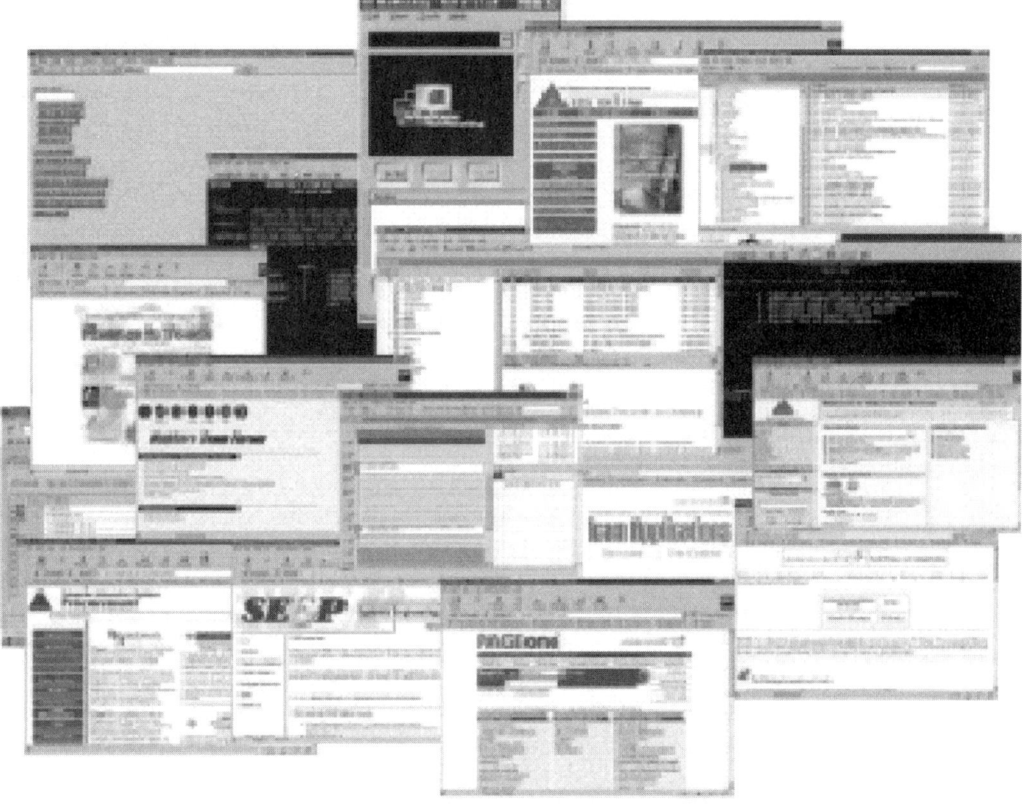

Figure 7.6

Adapted from Terry Lanham's articulation (Lanham, 2001).

- A Macintosh
- A 3270 Terminal
- 2 UNIX machines—one to run native UNIX, the other a UNIX environment permitting a DOS shell to be opened

These six machines were required in order to accomplish the required tasks, which were specifically to act as the systems integrator by reading information from one machine and re-keying it into one or more other machines. In the same manner that Windows was designed to provide a consistent user experience for applications within its environment, a portal is an attempt to provide a consistent user experience across all applications. How many web sites does the average worker use in a day, each of which has a different way of logging in, logging out, and getting information?

For the DISA action officer, a portal solution—had it been available in 1992—would have combined all of the applications together under a single portal, as shown in Figure 7.7. When an application is provided over the web, a single computer can be used as the front end, and the officer would have accessed the various applications from a single application, namely the portal. Perhaps Terry Lanham stated it best when he said, "Portals do for systems what Window did for applications." Terry, incidentally, presented one of the first portal ROI case studies where the savings amounted to $100 million annually (Lanham, 2001).

There is one very important quality-control caveat. With Windows, there are varying degrees of how well the applications conform to the typical user experience. Similarly, a wide variety of things can happen when a knowledge worker clicks on any of the links shown in Figure 7.7, depending on whether the system was properly reengineered. The range of possibilities is presented in Figures 7.8 through 7.10.

At the positive end of the quality spectrum, the link selected by the user might call up a screen designed according to standards containing the usual error-checking routines. The knowledge worker would use this screen to specify the information desired and submit the request. The system would return the information according to reasonable expectations and in a form that is most useful. A poor user experience with the portal might occur when the screen that is accessed from the portal link leads immediately to an old-fashioned "green screen" on which the knowledge worker is expected to enter cryptic codes and communicate with the system in a non-intuitive manner. In this case, very little has been done to reengineer the "old" application—as soon as the knowledge worker

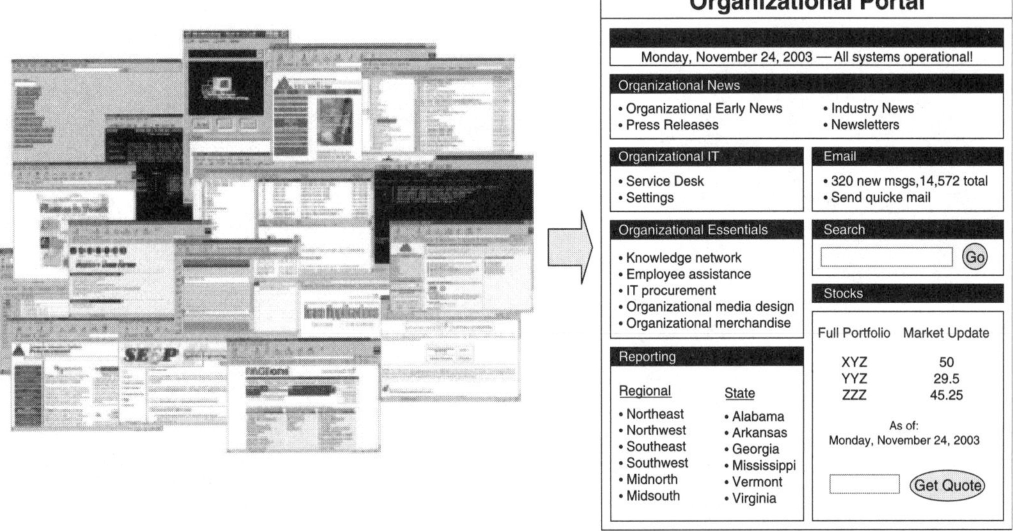

Figure 7.7

Adapted from Terry Lanham articulation (Lanham, 2001).

requests the service provided by the mainframe application, he or she is "in" the terminal emulator communicating with the application. Of course, practical integration features such as the ability to cut and paste across various applications typically correlate with the soundness of the reengineering task. Better reengineering results in better integration and user experiences.

With the caveat of the variability of the reengineering done to the application, we can see how a number of portal types were developed in order to address obvious information-dissemination needs. These portal types include:

- **Enterprise Portal.** This would be a single gateway via corporate Intranet or Internet to relevant workflows, application systems, and databases—integrated using XML and tailored to the specific job responsibilities of each individual.
- **Employee Portal.** All employees can access processes, systems, and databases via Intranet or Internet to carry out job responsibilities with full security and firewall protection.

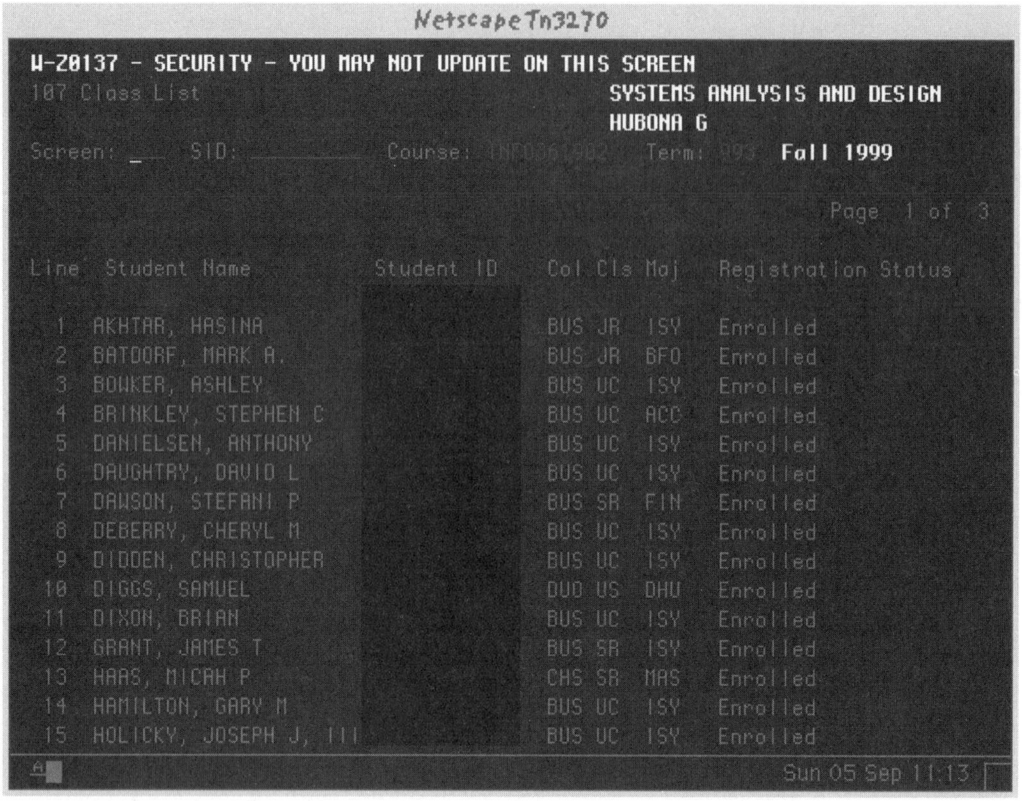

NetscapeTn3270

```
W-Z0137 - SECURITY - YOU MAY NOT UPDATE ON THIS SCREEN
107 Class List                                   SYSTEMS ANALYSIS AND DESIGN
                                                 HUBONA G
Screen: _   SID: ________   Course:            Term:      Fall 1999

                                                                 Page  1 of  3

Line  Student Name            Student ID   Col Cls Maj   Registration Status

  1  AKHTAR, HASINA                        BUS JR  ISY   Enrolled
  2  BATDORF, MARK A.                      BUS JR  BFO   Enrolled
  3  BOWKER, ASHLEY                        BUS UC  ISY   Enrolled
  4  BRINKLEY, STEPHEN C                   BUS UC  ACC   Enrolled
  5  DANIELSEN, ANTHONY                    BUS UC  ISY   Enrolled
  6  DAUGHTRY, DAVID L                     BUS UC  ISY   Enrolled
  7  DAWSON, STEFANI P                     BUS SR  FIN   Enrolled
  8  DEBERRY, CHERYL M                     BUS UC  ISY   Enrolled
  9  DIDDEN, CHRISTOPHER                   BUS UC  ISY   Enrolled
 10  DIGGS, SAMUEL                         DUD US  DHU   Enrolled
 11  DIXON, BRIAN                          BUS UC  ISY   Enrolled
 12  GRANT, JAMES T                        BUS SR  ISY   Enrolled
 13  HAAS, MICAH P                         CHS SR  MAS   Enrolled
 14  HAMILTON, GARY M                      BUS UC  ISY   Enrolled
 15  HOLICKY, JOSEPH J, III                BUS UC  ISY   Enrolled
A                                                      Sun 05 Sep 11:13
```

Figure 7.8

When a link is accessed—a 3270-based screen and interaction results.

- **Customer Portal.** A single gateway across the Internet, or via secure extranet, to details about products and services, catalogues, and order and invoice status for customers—integrated using XML and tailored to the unique requirements of each customer. Opportunities exist for one-to-one customer personalization and management.
- **Supplier Portal.** A single gateway to purchase orders and related status information for the suppliers of an enterprise.
- **Partner/Shareholder Portal.** A single gateway for business partners or shareholders. (Finkelstein & Aiken, 1998)

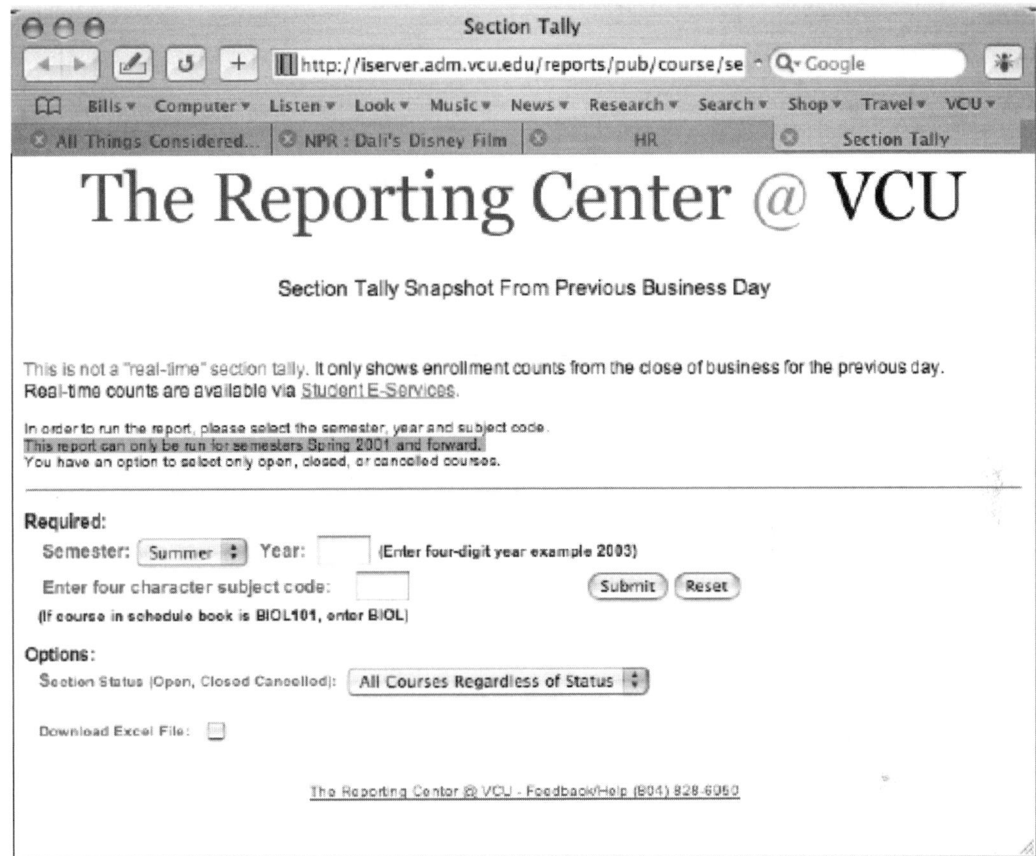

Figure 7.9

When a link is accessed—a browser-based screen and interaction results.

XML-Based Portal Technology

So the question arises, is it not good enough to provide a consistent user interface? What else is needed? More importantly, why do data managers need to learn about portals? First, if you let the applications people develop their portals without data-management participation, you will miss a splendid opportunity to implement some data-quality and data-integration principles. These are the principles that will establish data managers as contributors to the solution of specific problems in a

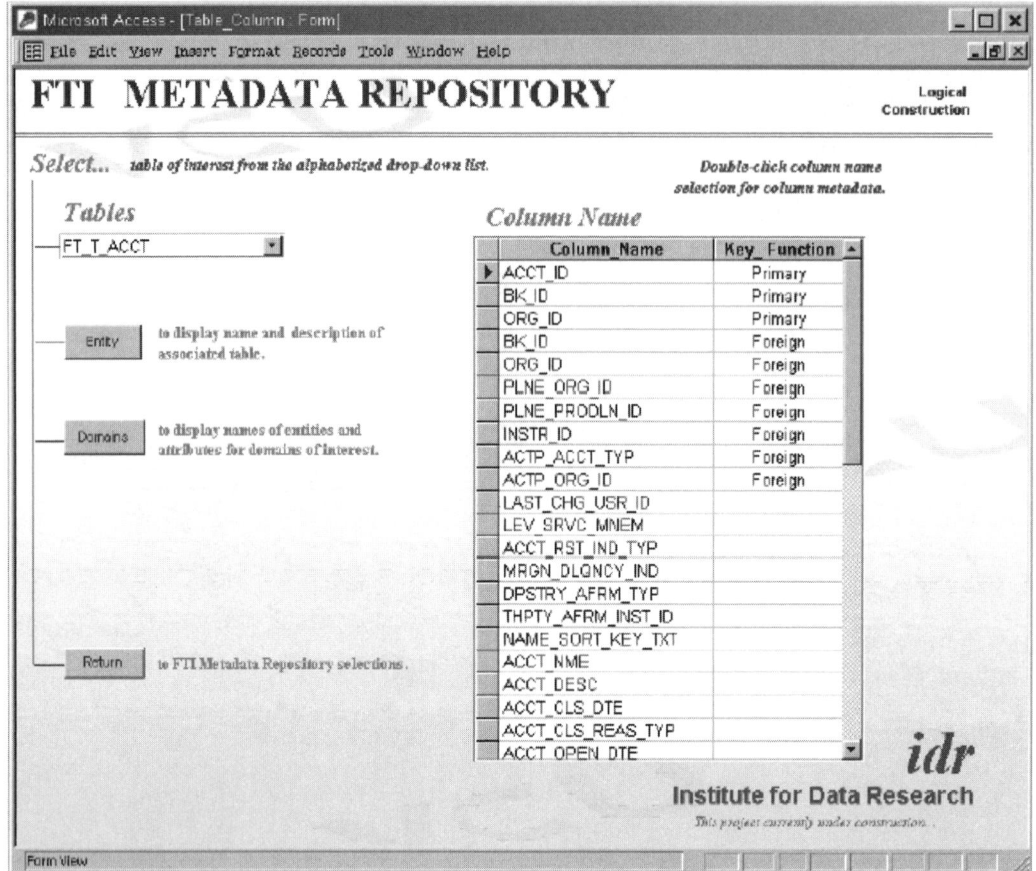

Figure 7.10

When a link is accessed—a Windows-based screen and interaction experience results.

cost-effective manner. Second, application developers do not necessarily know about IE principles, and may require guidance with the reengineering of the applications and the structuring of services. This reengineering and structuring is important so that the applications fit into an architectural pattern that best supports the organization's strategy. After all, if the application is not supporting some aspect of the organization or its strategy, why does it exist? Figure 7.11 illustrates specific portal advantages discussed previously and compares these to the advantages accruing from use of XBP technologies, discussed next.

Figure 7.11

Advantages that accrue from use of XML-based portal technologies.

Common User Interface	XML
1. Lower cost to develop	6. Standards-based Implementation
2. Lower training costs	7. More integration depth
3. Better user/product understanding	8. Wider integration
4. Lower organizational cost to implement	9. More rapid implementation
5. Faster time to implement	10. More architectural flexibility
	11. Better architectural evolvability
	12. Extended data-management reach
	13. Expanding data-management roles
	14. Novel data preparation opportunities
	15. Greater business and system reengineering opportunities

So what is an XBP? There is a continuum of how much an application is like a portal just as there is a continuum of how well or poorly an application sticks to human-computer interaction standards. The degree to which various portals incorporate XML will range from simply paying XML lip service (almost no support) to support at every level of the portal. A typical XBP product supports a specific *style* of developing information-delivery systems. XBP products contain three key elements:

1. **Engineered, XML-based and metadata-based data integration.** The portal is designed to support IE principles of well-defined, flexible, and adaptable data structures that can inherently be wrapped in XML. These structures are used in a variety of ways as metadata within the portal.
2. **Internet, Intranet, TCP/IP-based interfaces and delivery.** Adopting all of the advances on the web, portals should not attempt to reinvent the wheel but instead build on the access, security, and scalability of existing web technologies. There is nothing mysterious about this technology, and its maturity enables vendors to build portals on top of existing web technologies. This is a true advantage of portals over non-portal applications—portals can benefit from all previously developed web technologies.
3. **Extensive use of new technologies, including**

   – 4GLs (4th-Generation Languages). These languages are used to format and facilitate information into and out of the portal.

- Data-analysis tools. These tools are used to help derive correct data structures.
- Business rule engines are used to extract, formalize, and apply business logic.
- Data logistic networks are used to format and deliver data to the right place at the right time.
- Finally, XML-based model and repository manipulation involves having access to multiple levels of metadata, and making them available for manipulation.

As with all well-designed systems, knowledge workers who use the product will not know or really care about any of the above! What the knowledge worker will care about is his or her gain in productivity as a result of navigating the portal in particular ways. There are seven specific types of portal navigation as described by Joe Zarb (personal communication, March 2001):

1. **Any-to-any relationships.** Any-to-any indicates that any object in the portal may be combinable with any other item on the same screen. As a simple example, a customer identification number would be combinable with an "order" data structure to display the orders placed by that customer. This encourages users to try other combinations they hadn't previously thought of, like combining peanut butter with chocolate. Equipped with a browsing interface, this capability sets up a "teach a person to fish and you will feed that person for life" situation. If a person is taught how to relate different types of information via a reporting mechanism, he or she can later create their own custom reports by themselves. Any-to-any relationships encourage the knowledge worker to attempt to combine items of interest in the same spirit as the reporting centers and fourth-generation reporting tools such as Crystal Reports. In the purest sense, this is what the original promise of end-user computing was all about—giving knowledge workers tools they can use to obtain information in any source and easily combine it into ways that support their individual work styles.
2. **Drag-and-relate interaction metaphor.** This encourages users to make and use one of the biggest productivity improvements that the interface-development community has ever come up

> with: drag-and-relate. This interface concept permits users to create an "any-to-any" relationship by dragging one object to another to determine how the two objects are related. Like its predecessor, drag-and-drop editing, drag-and-relate encourages users to become even more immersed in individual tasks. When a user is dragging something, there is a feeling of heightened tension in carrying or dragging some object across a screen. The user is more immersed in the task since it requires attention, and less experienced workers learn their respective tasks more rapidly.

Any-to-any is supported by drag-and-relate and vice versa—one is needed for the other. Figure 7.12 shows how they combine to increase the access options for the "sample" dataset. On the left, primary/foreign key relationships are used to access data; on the right, additional links are created allowing access from almost any point to any other point. Using a variety of means described in the next section, even more access can be achieved.

> 3. **Point-of-view navigation.** A technique enabled by storing settings that permits a portal to be viewed from various perspectives, including Enterprise, Employee, Customer, Supplier, and Partner/Shareholder Portals. In some cases, different parties viewing the same data should have different views of it. For example, the "partner" view of customer information would likely be far less detailed than the employee view.

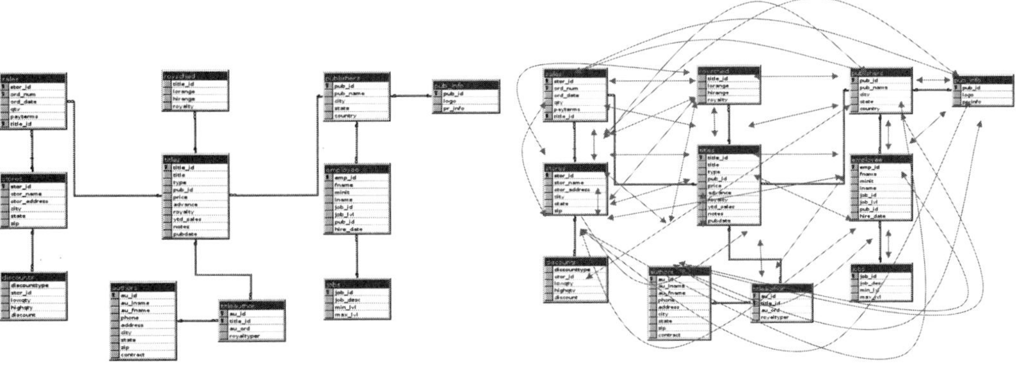

Figure 7.12

One vendor's version of drag-and-relate.

4. **Metalinks.** A link-management system using new linking facilities. These linking facilities are described in detail in the section on the XLink protocol in the XML Component Architecture chapter.
5. **Three-way scalability of objects, users, and records.** These three options for navigation of information are built in a very scalable way. This presentation encourages vendors and developers to incorporate the scalability concepts from the web-based information delivery world that have been so successful in the past.
6. **Integration from different data sources and different data stores.** This offers opportunities for standards-based data integration that is more rapid and accurate than what was previously available. This particular point will be covered more in depth in an upcoming section.
7. **Confederated Components Model.** This navigation permits workers to integrate data across differing models from different units without losing their context. The ability to integrate information from different models on the fly supports a higher level of cognitive momentum than was previously available. One example of integration is shown in Figure 7.13.

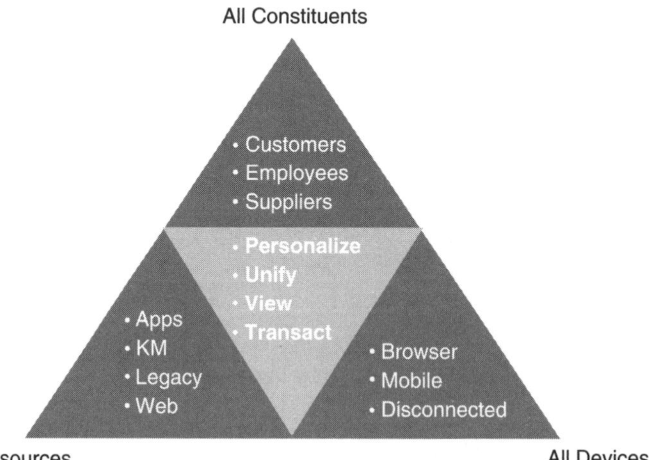

Figure 7.13

Illustration of possible portal component confederation from Zarb (Personal communication, March 2001).

XML-Based Architectural Enhancements

The architectural benefits of using XBP components fall into the categories of flexibility, ability to evolve, and maintainability. Each is described below.

Better Architectural Flexibility

By adopting XBPs, the organization instantly acquires an excellent set of integrated data-management technologies. By using these same technologies to manage its metadata, the organization can immediately realize more tangible ROI from reuse than most object-oriented implementations realize in a lifetime. The portal capabilities can be used directly as metadata management technologies—this saves having to invest in, implement, train on, migrate to, and maintain a separate metadata-management technology. As you will soon see, XBPs can implement broader data-structure categories, and since they can easily handle organization-sized data-delivery solutions, XBPs make excellent metadata-management technologies.

Using the XBP as a metadata-management tool means that you can use metadata and portal capabilities to manage your organizational metadata. Many of the various enhancements described from this point on are due to the fact that by implementing an XBP, all of the revolutionary operations such as drag-and-drop can be implemented in support of your metadata as well as your data. Knowledge worker training in the use of an XBP applies in two ways; to metadata and to data. All of this combines to increase the flexibility of the architecture now able to be implemented on a component-by-component basis within the framework provided by the XBP. As a result, the architecture can be maintained in formats most directly supporting strategic and tactical requirements. As long as they are designed according to good architecture-development principles, the various components can be implemented in different ways to support different organizational strategies, permitting the most architectural flexibility.

Finally, by using the XBP to maintain your enterprise data architecture and affiliated components, you are increasing the integration between your organizational data and its metadata—the subject of the next chapter sub-section. Consider how the knowledge workers of the organization will benefit as they simultaneously learn to access and manipulate data and its metadata—all actions applying to data also applying to metadata and vice versa.

Better Architectural Evolvability/Maintenance

All architectures evolve over time as the organization, its mission, its environment, its competitors, and many other things change. If they are maintained using XBP capabilities, making changes can often be accomplished globally. For example, changes from one set of competing XML standard names could be accomplished using "batch parsing" capabilities and relational database management systems (RDBMS). Instead of manually locating all instances of specific tags, metadata maintained in the XBP environment would allow users to make direct changes to data and the associated metadata—changing, for example, all instances of "southwest" and "southeast" to "south" as a result of expanded region definitions. The metadata would be maintained using the XBP and would be simpler to evolve.

Metadata managers and knowledge workers also have access to XSLT capabilities that are embodied in the XBP. As shown in Figure 7.14, one example of a better way to evolve can be seen in a situation where a stovepiped system finds itself managing multiple sets of tags to describe the same business areas. This occurs frequently after mergers and acquisitions. In order to disrupt processing as little as possible, both sets of XML tag structures are "learned" by the XBP. Once made accessible to the XBP, any data will carry with it a tag indicating which of the two mappings for this data is the correct one so that the XBP will associate the proper metadata. In instances where the data is being mapped from one tag set to another, XSLT transformations can be developed, providing transformation from one set of tag structures to the other automatically. This is an example of XML's malleability of data in action.

Since the XSLT transformations are implemented as XML documents, transformations themselves can be operated upon. When the organization is ready to eliminate one of the two sets of competing XML tag structures, it can do so by implementing changes to the mapping transformations as well as to the existing tag structures. Now recall that the portal is managing the data and the metadata using an RDBMS, and the metadata can be queried based on criteria such as pattern matching, similarity, and text-matching patterns. Potential changes can be more easily identified. Fixes can be applied more comprehensively and reliably. Links can be more easily managed using XLink, permitting links to destinations previously not thought

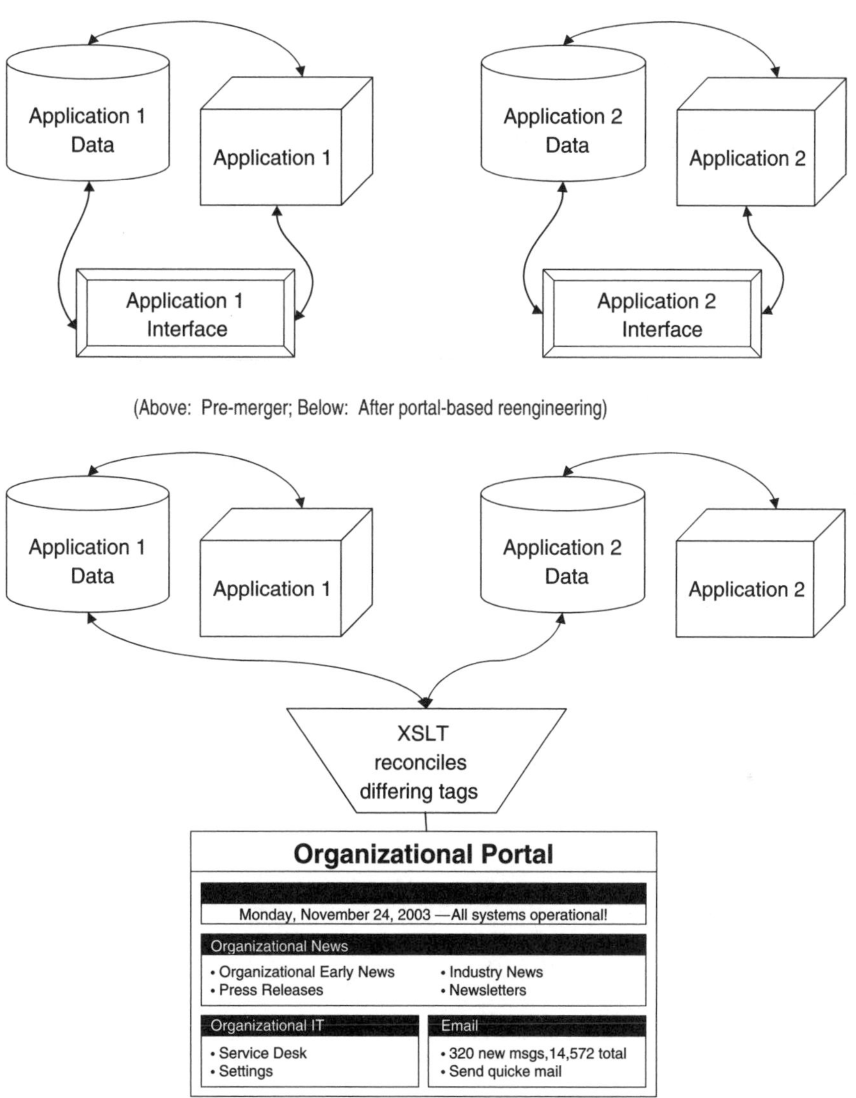

Figure 7.14

XBP and automated XSLT capabilities applied to metadata management.

of. By maintaining architectural components using the XBP, organizations can easily incorporate other XML architectural components such as XSLT and XLink into their metadata-management capabilities.

While the above description makes it seem as if XSLT is a wonderful solution that can be easily implemented, the reality is that XSLT is not a silver bullet, but simply another tool for data managers to add to their existing toolkits. Just as whenever any new technology is introduced, XSLT must be carefully evaluated and applied where cost effective and appropriate. XSLT coding can be difficult and involved—what we lightly refer to as "non-trivial." And nothing about the technology will permit data engineers to relax the rigor of their practice. Good practice can be extended by XML but not the other way around.

Enhanced Integration Opportunities

The next advantage that XBPs have over non-XBPs is increased standards-based integration, more integration depth, wider integration, and more rapid implementation. Each is discussed below.

Standards-Based Integration

One of the nicest things about XML is that it is often driven from outside of the data-management area. Because of the hype, business users are quite interested to find out if XML can help them in any number of ways. Many savvy business people are creating XML-based solutions. More often than not, though, they are starting by adding XML capabilities that help but do not fully realize its potential. Since the requests and resources for the XML implementations often come from the business users, data managers are in a powerful position to put together something that they have not previously been able to pull off: functional data standards. By the way, data managers might be wise to avoid telling their business partners about "data-standardization efforts," since the words might scare them off. Instead, just tell them that before XML tags can be applied to data, each tag must have a name. In this manner, data managers can get partners to name their data, and XML structures with tags arranged according to their best representation can be created.

The tag and structure combinations may be imperfect and might be changed in the future, but that will not be a barrier to using the structures in the XBP. Changes to the tag names and tag structures can be accomplished with provided features discussed earlier, such as XSLT. Calling something by one name one week and another name in subsequent accesses is done using a combination of direct manipulation, link changes, and transformations. The implication is that the standard vocabulary can be changed with little disturbance to the system operation. The actual naming of the tags is of little importance. What is critical is that the tags receive names so that the data can be wrapped in XML and made into meaningful data structures.

More Integration Depth

XBPs permit greater integration depth to be achieved among data stores because of their inherently flexible and adaptable structuring options. By depth, we refer to the penetration of the standardization into different areas. XML-based metadata can be created to support more flexible structure because of its support of a great variety of structure types. Consider that XBPs have virtually all major relational database-management systems available for connectivity, and thus XBP users can access any type of tabular data occurring in DB2, Oracle, Informix, etc. Given this wide support, there are few if any areas the XBP cannot penetrate due to lack of support for the data platform.

Many tend to forget, but data is also still frequently stored in hierarchical structures such as IMS. Essentially, hierarchical data structures in XBPs provide direct support for hierarchically organized data stores. Other variations in structures can be handled using features such as direct and indirect linking. The ability to use a wider array of data structures and access a range of databases permits integration to occur at a greater depth and strengthens the argument for using the XBP as a metadata management technology.

Wider Integration Scope

Hub-and-spoke integration permits wider integration because of the ability to enhance transformation engines by classes of systems as well as by individual system. For example, Figure 7.15 shows how a network of hubs

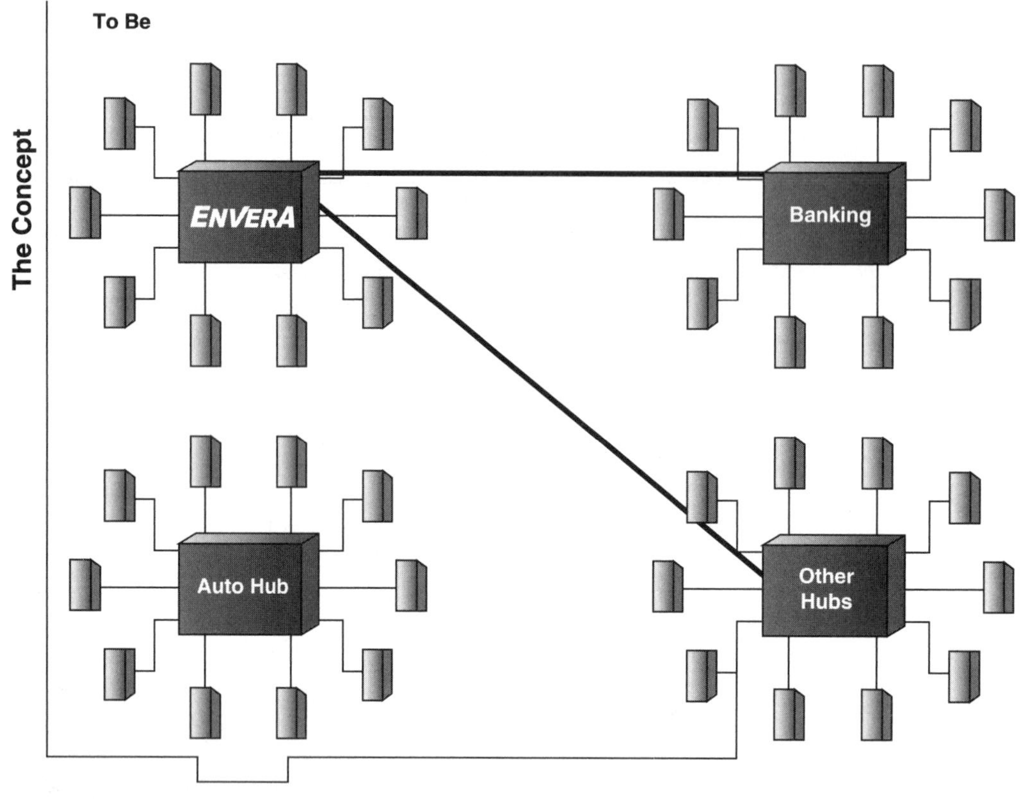

Figure 7.15

Integration, hub by hub.

can be used to maintain interconnections among various collections of XML tags and structures. Once the hubs can talk to each other, partners can not only communicate within a hub, but hubs can also communicate amongst themselves—this represents a new class of systems rather than another individual system.

More Rapid Implementation

The final asset is the speed at which new partners can be brought into the fold. Bringing on entire communities at a time as shown in Figure 7.15 makes for very rapid implementation of the actual data-integration possibilities. One central concept occurs repeatedly with portals and XML; just as portals are an attempt to get user interface and data integration challenges solved in one place so that others can reuse those solutions, XML does the same with data representation and manipulation. Much of the added speed of implementation is due directly to this approach—solve the problem in one place, and then exploit that solution in other places, avoiding reinventing the wheel wherever possible. The added speed is something of an illusion; it is not so much that XML and portals are revolutionary in this sense; rather, they are simply making sound architectural decisions, such as solving a problem correctly in one place, and letting everyone else benefit from those decisions. So it would be accurate to say that XML and XBPs are not faster, just that everything else is simply slower and more cumbersome.

Extending Data-Management Technologies/Data-Management Product Examples

XBPs allow the creation of exciting extensions to data management. Much of the work that has gone into data management has typically applied to tabular data stored in a relational database-management system. Although this seems to be where the most effort is spent, experts estimate that only 20% of data is in systems such as these. In Figure 7.16, we can see the dichotomy of data—structured and unstructured and also referred to as tabular and non-tabular data. Typically, data-management efforts are almost exclusively above the thick line in the "structured" category of data. The remaining 80% of data is stored in such forms as purchase orders, PowerPoint presentations, legal contracts documents, emails, and of course the ubiquitous spreadsheet.

Unstructured data is literally data that does not have an explicit structure. Take as an example an email written between colleagues. The documents are in fact full of structure—there are breaks between sentences, logical paragraphs, a title, and many other markers that to the human eye impart structure. For computer systems, though, it is difficult to extract data from these documents because the structure is not formalized in the way that a computer expects to see it. As a result, unstructured documents tend to be difficult to search and query. Somewhat obtuse plain-text searches are of course possible, but contextual searches are more difficult, such as, "Display all emails where the second paragraph makes reference to Bob Jones." The best that can be done is a wider

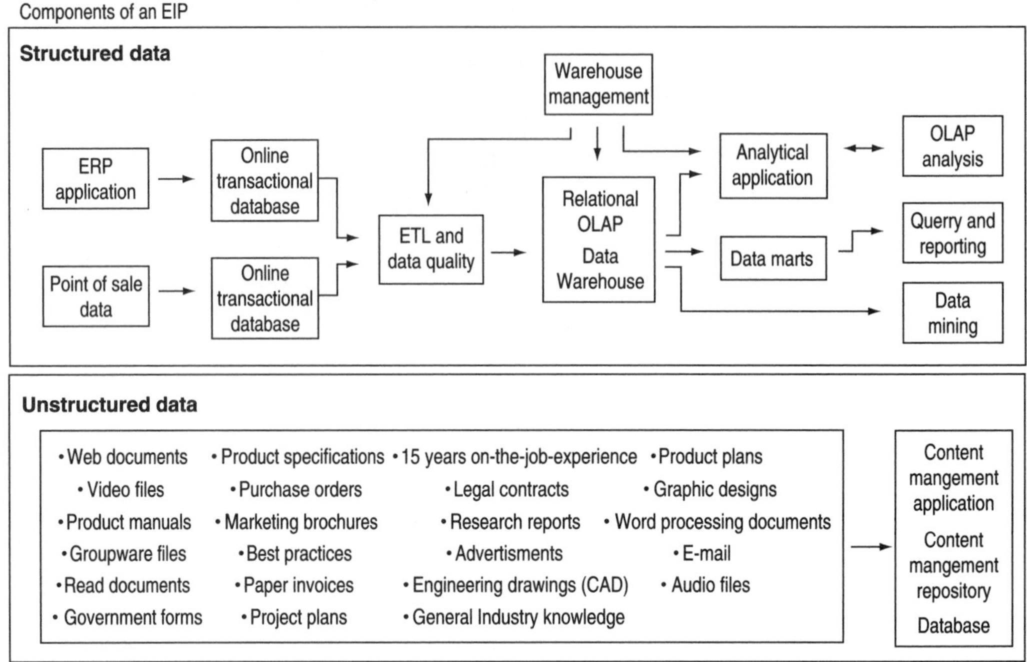

Figure 7.16

The dichotomy of structured versus unstructured data. (Adapted from Finkelstein and Aiken, 1998).

search, perhaps for "Bob Jones," the results of which would then be narrowed manually.

XML provides a number of possibilities for including more structured contextual information along with these documents. For example, the Office 2000 and Office 2001 suites set a standard, pointing toward the necessity for future document management technologies to include XML as part of the data-management baseline. Saving an Office 2000+ document to a BizTalk (by Microsoft) server now makes the wealth of automatically created document content and metadata accessible to searchers. Figure 7.17 shows the Properties Tab of a PowerPoint MS-Office Document, viewable by accessing the "File → Properties" menu.

This development alone greatly extends the reach of modern data-management practices. At least on a limited basis, it is now possible to include previously unstructured data in searchable intranets by using XBPs.

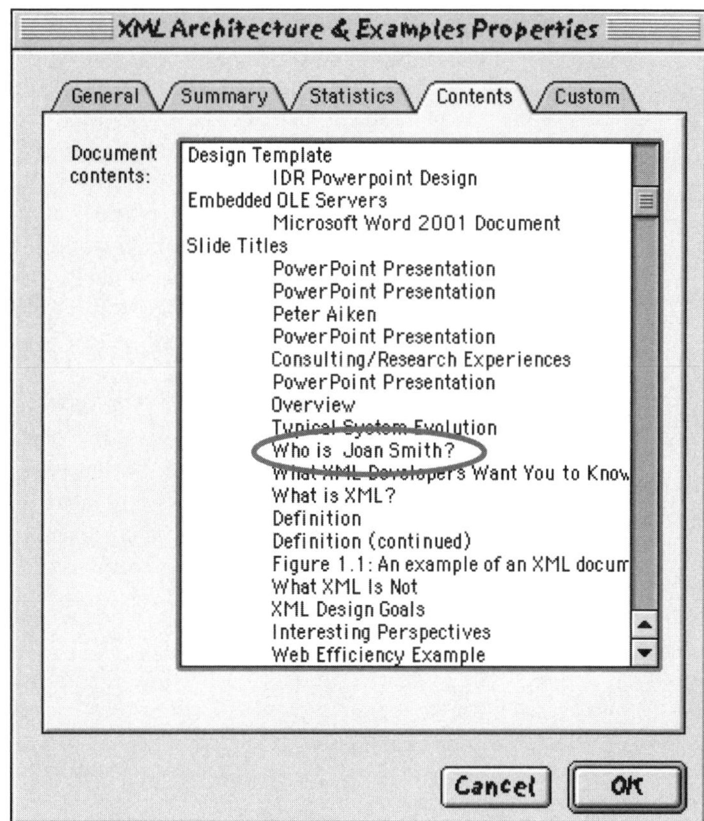

Figure 7.17

Contents tab of a PowerPoint MS-Office document.

The reach of current data-management knowledge, skills, and abilities can be extended to include this vast new array of valuable data once it is in a form that allows computer systems to effectively process it. Consider just the wealth of information that could be uncovered by integrating office and email documents with the existing tabular data. Queries can be written to ask for the PowerPoint slide with the title of "Who is Joan Smith?" modified by "Peter Aiken" in "March 2003," and the possibility exists to track its use throughout a defined pool of PowerPoint presentations. People who were referenced in internal documents could be linked to tabular data about their employment or activity on various projects. By tagging the metadata inside of unstructured documents, data managers could use those documents in the type of "any-to-any" relationships discussed earlier.

Extending data management to unstructured data also expands the role of information managers, not just the definition of data management itself. Data managers would be capable of delivering information by searching through the larger, formerly unstructured data. The domain potentially increases by a factor of four according to most experts. In addition, as the return on investment associated with XBPs becomes more widely known, users will increasingly demand that their existing environment be migrated into XBP environments. Beyond the metadata engineering is the application engineering—possible in the XBP environment because of metadata tagging. For application developers, this will be an unfamiliar paradigm at first, and they will require leadership and training in order to succeed.

We have discussed some of the ways that XBPs will change the role of data management. One of the opportunities this leads to is the possibility of creating "data-management products"—that is, data products that are of use to the organization, and that were created through effective data management. This is an important topic to discuss in conjunction with portal material in part because it speaks to the return on investment possible with portals, and also because it addresses the payoff of mature data-management practices making use of portals.

Selected Product Examples

Data-management products are usually seen as more valuable than the original information or source data. This is of course the classic value add-on, when the output of a process is more valuable than its input. XML's ability to rapidly repurpose existing data for new uses and the knowledge to manage it well puts data managers in the enviable position to develop new products specific to their organization (with support and input from the business community). Most of these examples are easiest to realize within the context of a portal, due to its unique functionality and reach. Let us look at some examples of what is meant by these new products.

- **Profiting from data quality.** Several forward-thinking organizations have invested in individuals to champion data-quality initiatives. XML permits the development of new and innovative ways to achieve higher-quality data using data-quality portals. The key is to provide data rapidly whose quality can be defined and quantified, enabling a distinction to be drawn between data that the organization *knows* is correct, and data it simply *hopes* is correct. In addition, making data more available and accessible via a portal encourages the use of the data. With more eyes on the data, problems become rapidly apparent. Public and private institutions have saved millions by illustrating how investments in data quality can easily demonstrate ROI. Data is used to make decisions every day. It is critical to know that the data being used as the basis for those decisions is sound.

- **Profiting from data analysis.** More data profiling technologies are incorporating XML, enabling them to achieve integration and complete mapping using GUI-based mapping instead of more labor-intensive means. Take the example of a utility company that was ready to spend the money for an upgrade to the hardware base of their data warehousing operation. An investment in XML-based data profiling technology was able to produce results quickly, revealing that a small adjustment to the data structures maintained by the warehousing group permitted the hardware upgrade to be postponed for more than a year. The group divided among themselves the upgrade savings for the year.
- **Small-scale information engineering.** In another capacity-planning example, a data-management group developed a novel means of demonstrating positive ROI in what is called small-scale information engineering. Consider an application where users request information for something that is not well defined, such as travel planning: "I am leaving on this day or that—depending on the flight times . . . " Traditional interaction consists of the user refining the desired information until it matches the description of the product he or she wishes to purchase, carefully weeding out the irrelevant information. In this case, data management convinced the application-development group to co-develop a more efficient solution. The data group first used mining, statistical, and predictive modeling to develop a clear picture of what the initial request was trying to accomplish. When the exact request was specified, the server sent the client the requested data wrapped in XML. This was done with the awareness that the knowledge worker would refine the query an average of 12 times. The applications group developed code that could perform the requested manipulations on the client side, which was only possible because the data was sent to

the client in XML, providing the extra information needed to manipulate it rather than just presentation formatting. This architecture is illustrated in Figure 7.18. Often, this powerful combination could solve a query with the initial set of data delivered. In most instances, it required fewer server accesses, and the reduction in the resulting overhead was measurably positive. In this case, the use of XML really only saved the server a few extra requests. But when the millions of hits the site usually receives multiply the savings, the benefit in hardware, network capacity, and support becomes clear. This is, in a nutshell, what small-scale information engineering is about—multiplying small savings into enormous savings.

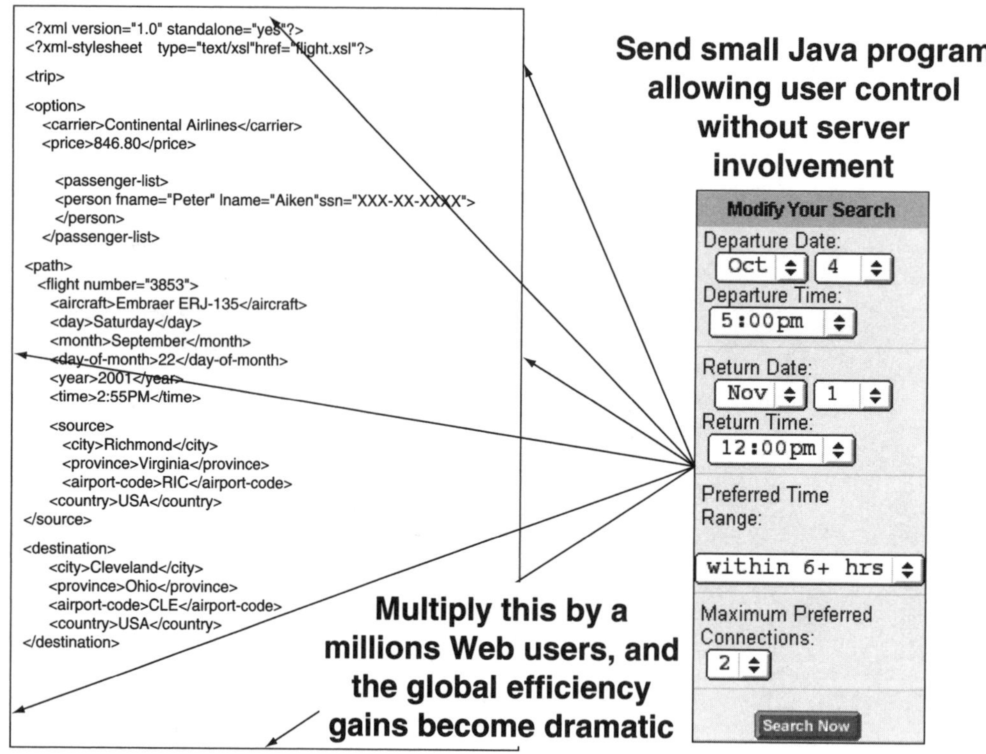

Figure 7.18

Illustration of small-scale information engineering.

Other data-management groups have developed products based around services that they provide internally, to competitors, and to partners. Certainly there is a wealth of other opportunities once the general concepts are applied to specific industrial problems.

Newly Important and Novel Data-Preparation Opportunities

"At the speed of the Internet" is a new phrase indicating very rapid movement of data and the triggering of associated processes. Data movement can only be rapid when it is fully automated—human interaction and validation is almost always the bottleneck. Over several years, organizations surveyed continue to report an increase in both the amount and kind of data that is truly exchanged automatically. Increasing automation of data is not really a choice, but a necessity. As the volume of data expands at a rapid rate, it is usually not an option to hire additional staff to keep pace. Data automation is enabled by XML, and yet it is a mixed blessing to some organizations that are not technologically up to the challenge. Other organizations have problems when they are forced by industry competition to embrace these processes rather than choosing it of their own volition.

Only 5% of organizations surveyed indicated that they did not see an increase in the number of automated decisions processed by their organization in 2002. Strangely, only 1 in 3 is approaching the process in a structured manner. They do not trust each other's data—only 1 in 3 companies are very confident in the quality of their own data, and only 15% of companies are very confident of the data received from other organizations. The dangerous trend seems to be that organizations are increasingly automating decisions with data with which they are not even comfortable!

Data quality issues are becoming more important as the demand for accessing data is increasing. Yet just 20% of organizations have ongoing data quality initiatives as of 2004. For e-transactions where errors move at the speed of the Internet, data preparation will become an automated activity and the price of errors will multiply. The price multiplies as the amount of human interaction decreases because it generally takes longer for the error to be recognized as it flows through multiple systems without the interference of rational thought.

The XBP gives organizations an opportunity to begin branding data as meeting certain quality standards. It seems strange that several human signatures are usually required for small purchasing decisions, but multi-million-dollar electronic purchases with trading partners are executed with no required standards on data quality. Using the proper semi-automated data engineering analysis, evolution can be properly supported to avoid data quality errors from eating away at the savings produced by automating processes in the first place.

The evolution we are describing can be understood in terms of the four specific activities described below:

1. Understanding Legacy Structures
2. Data-Quality Portals and Data Cleansing
3. Data Accuracy Assessment
4. Creating a Transitional Data Model

Understanding Legacy Structures

XML is about transferring and transforming data structures. This means that in order to wrap part of any legacy system, understanding is required. Understanding is a shorthand reference for using a data-centric perspective to represent the core metadata of the system. This formal understanding is required for effective implementation to occur. Metadata models are represented using standardized notation and are detailed enough to allow business analysts and technical personnel to read the same model, and come away with a common understanding. The model then forms the basis for developing new components, as well as the ongoing description of the overall enterprise architecture and how this particular metadata model fits into it.

In order to achieve this level of understanding, business analysts and technical personnel must share an understanding of the environment in which they work. New components should also be developed using specific approaches that allow the creation of objective measures. The alternative of course is ad hoc development, which is difficult to measure and even more difficult to document. Taking a look at how many components have been developed and how many are left, along with their various levels of testing, provides an organization with concrete facts about development process and quality. Cultivated with an understanding of the system metadata, the model becomes the basis, the language, and the currency for achieving understanding among team members, technologists, and knowledge workers.

As discussed in Chapter 5, there are a number of tools and technologies available, ranging in cost from $5K to more than $1 million, to aid the process of understanding legacy structures. All of them help to transform the older, manual method of reverse engineering the logical data structures.

The process of moving to logical models of the enterprise architecture components is critical to achieving what has been called "practical" or "good enough" data engineering. The older methods of driving straight at logical data models using Joint Application Development (JAD) sessions have been popular methods of deriving them: A group of SMEs would gather around the projection equipment and a data model would be reviewed in real time. A scribe would get notes of improvements/corrections, etc., and these changes would be applied at break or end of day. The model updates would be accomplished offline and after hours. The upshot was that the process was taxing on the SMEs, who were needed as much as 30 hours a week during peak analysis times.

The modern method uses tools that profile the data, making it easier to understand and thus infer the proper architectural components—first physical, then logical. These profiling engines are based on inference engines and replace the human knowledge extraction processes required by the manual methods. The SME's role can be reduced to confirmations and explanations rather than acting as the primary source of knowledge. Profiling engines allow analysis of the data and identification of specific hypotheses. These hypotheses are presented to the SMEs during model refinement/validation [MR/V] sessions, resulting in more efficient progress. Some of the high-end tools can even be used to generate the XML required to manage the metadata. This is accomplished in much the same way as CASE tools create data definition language [DDL] files.

When the use of software is combined with limited MR/V sessions, the process is always a more efficient use of the SMEs' time. This is a perfect example of what we mean when we refer to a semi-automated solution; it contains elements of automation and manual work, allowing the humans to do the important thought work while the machines are left to the time-consuming drudgery.

XBPs and Data-Quality Engineering

XBPs offer an opportunity to demonstrate positive return on investments in data-quality engineering. To illustrate, we will describe the tale of a courageous data manager's effort to make the organization aware of the costs of data quality problems.

Consider this example: A pharmaceutical maker maintained a master list of all of the physicians considered as customers. This list consisted of 2.4 million physicians and was used as the primary list for developing phone, mail, email, and package delivery lists. Twice-monthly mailings were made to each physician on the delivery list. The hitch was that SMEs within the organization privately estimated that the actual pool of physicians considered as customers consisted of 800,000—about one-third of the number on the list! In other words, three times as many materials as were actually needed were being sent out—twice a month!

The more the data manager learned about the problem, the stronger the case for taking action became. A data quality portal was created. The data manager placed a link to the "Master Customer List" (MCL); clicking the link retrieved an XML-wrapped flat file of 2.4 million organizational customers. The XML wrapper was standardized using an XML schema, and the data manager made arrangements with the known users of the data to be able to utilize the MCL. Each time the link was accessed, the user was asked to acknowledge a statement to the effect that this list was not the right list but it was the best list available. It was a simple click, but it forced acknowledgement of the problem, and many workers began asking what could be done to improve the quality of the data in the dataset.

Using the cookie data generated by the web interface, the data manager collected access statistics. The combination of publicly stating that the data was of potentially poor quality and the evidence of the widespread usage created a consensus to address the problem. Unfortunately, the only available resource to work on rectifying it was a clerk-level position—no software could be purchased due to the pricing of software for that specific purpose and budget restrictions on new software.

The data manager hired a college intern with good data skills to fill the clerical position, and after one year was able to report that the intern had reduced the list by 200,000 bad records. The savings were calculated by assessing the savings on mailings at the lowest postal rate of $0.20 per letter, presorted. Avoiding postage on 200,000 letters 24 times each year at $0.20 per letter amounted to more than $200,000 in savings even after taking into account the clerical salaries and benefits.

The well-articulated savings resulted in creating a second clerk position the following year. During that year with two people working on the problem, another 600,000 physicians were removed from the MCL. The second reduction resulted in more than $800,000 in savings. It was quite obvious to the company that the investment in data quality was paying off. For the third year, the data manager understood that as the target number approached, it was necessary to manage expectations. The savings could not be made infinite by decreasing the number of physicians in the MCL.

And then a funny thing happened.

A business process owner approached the data manager with a simple question: "Could the pharmacy data be put into the XBP just like you did with the MCL?" The pharmacy data had similar problems to those experienced in the MCL. "If we pay for the salaries, can you put some more interns on the problem and achieve similar results?" The answer was of course yes, and the demonstrated savings were substantial. Earlier we talked about how successful adoption of an XBP would cause internal pushes for further adoption, and this is a great example of just that phenomenon. Then an even stranger thing happened.

Someone noticed that the MCL and the MPL (Master Pharmacy List) datasets could be combined in new ways now that duplicates and incorrect entries had been removed. The combination was possible before, but the data had been so questionable that the result of the combination was worthless. The new combinational capabilities were adopted by the marketing and sales forecasting groups who loved their new capabilities, and made several important breakthroughs in understanding their customers without any data mining or other sophisticated data analysis techniques! The request for the MPL was followed almost immediately by another business-generated request, this time for the Master Distribution List. The resulting new combinations of data appealed to a broader group within the company, including the logistics/distribution group. Imagine at this point if the company had proposed removal of the XBP—the users would have howled in protest.

As the process began to snowball, another part of the business became eager to get their data into the XBP, because they saw that it saved them money, time, and effort. Data was quickly becoming known as either good or bad. Data moved into the XBP was seen as good because its characteristic metadata was published, including estimates of quality, in a manner similar to the travel web sites providing on-time records of various flights. Data outside of the XBP was seen as potentially questionable.

It is hard to imagine a better way to introduce organizations to data quality than through the use of XBPs. They permit organizations to quantify the problem and provide a means of helping users to understand the difference between good- and bad-quality data. XBPs represent an important tool in our approach to developing long-term products from data management.

Creating a Transitional Data Model

The last category of data management products is something that the business users must be trained to ask for and data managers to produce. Projects of most sorts involve transitioning from one data source, structure, or format to another.* The major classes of transformation include the following:

- *Data exchange* is the process of sharing data with other groups within and external to the organization.
- *Data evolution* is the process of changing the association of data from the target systems to the reengineering system.
- *Data integration* is required to achieve both data exchange and data evolution.

All of these tasks benefit from a very tangible data-management output called the Transitional Data Model (TDM). The TDM is a narrowly focused model that accounts for the four stages of data understanding that must be considered for all data evolution projects. The four stages are illustrated in Figure 7.19 and are described below, in implementation order:

Existing physical → Existing logical → Desired logical
→ Desired physical

They correspond to (from lower left) "As-Is Data Implementation," "As-Is Data Design" (upper left), "To-Be Design" (upper right), and "To-Be Data Implementation" (lower right) quadrants of Figure 7.19—illustrating the evolution of TDM. The transformations are performed by the data management team and presented for validation to the SMEs. The data management team begins by focusing on selectively extracting existing processes and technology components and representing them on a one-for-one basis in a physical model.

The scope of this effort is confined to data being evolved and required contextual data elements. It is an enterprise architecture component, but not the architecture itself. The next activity concentrates on taking the physical representations and stripping them of their technological aspects and characteristics: conceptually evolving the components to a logical existing representation that is technology independent. For example, in

*For additional reading, see *Data Reverse Engineering* Chapter 13, Indirect Outputs.

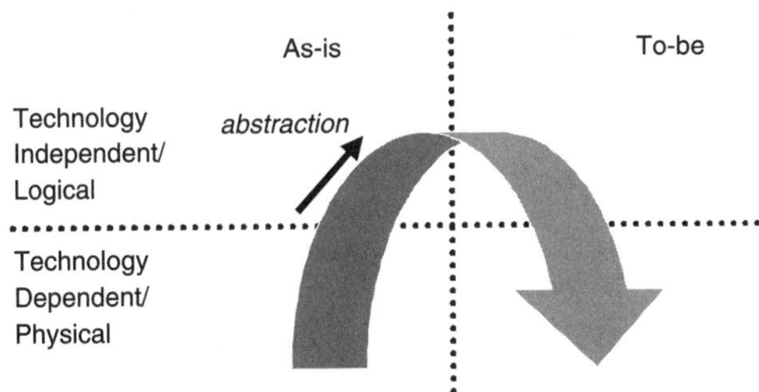

Figure 19

Four stages of transformation in data models.

Oracle, a field might be implemented as a 35-character area to store a last name, but the important part is that last name is being captured, and that it is a string—this typifies the difference between physical and logical representations. The goal is to focus the model components on what functions they are supporting, as opposed to how technology provides the support below the technology line.

As an example of the need to incorporate these stages into the TDM, consider how the first telephone voice response units (VRUs) were used. Typically, they determined which operator to route a call to, based on your last name, state of residence, product type, and so on. This was done because the capacity of user workstations was measured in the tens of megabytes instead of gigabytes as it is today. Data strictly segmented by the codes above are generally not flexible enough to re-implement in new systems without reorganization. Data must first be reorganized when, as in this example, the technical details of its implementation cause it to stray quite a bit from how it is used in the business context. Companies also exist that move VSAM files directly into database structures with poor results. In one case, a daily job required 45 hours of runtime! In the past, data-management teams have tried for perfection, but in today's business environment, it is more important to be good enough and rapid enough to contribute rather than theoretically perfect. TDMs, while conceptually simple, are underused tools that business users need to learn.

Greater Business and System-Reengineering Opportunities: Reduction of Maintenance Burden Strategies

In Chapter 4, we presented a detailed description of an ERP implementation example and illustrated the potential synergies that exist between the two individually perceived opportunities. In this section, we will present a second example of greater business and system-reengineering opportunities. It illustrates how an XBP can be used to reduce legacy maintenance costs by up to four-fifths. These represent solid examples from case studies of the return on investment that we have been discussing in the previous sections.

Earlier in the chapter, Figure 7.7 showed how portals are used to reduce the cognitive burden placed on knowledge workers accessing different systems. While portal technology focuses on common user interfacing, XBPs supplement the interface with a common data vocabulary. This capability is easily implemented in XBPs, but it is also possible for them to exist in non-XML-based portals—however, the overhead is much higher. The message is simple: get rid of code that is expensive to maintain and create increased demand for portal services. These are described below.

Get Rid of Expensive-to-Maintain Code

Projects often sound easier than they are to actually achieve. Before code can be eliminated, one must first find out how much is spent on maintenance annually and then discover where staff spend most of their time. Only then can one claim to have identified code that is expensive to maintain—that usually translates into specific program or system groupings. A goal statement is then formulated to focus the analysis. Once identified, a trained application-reengineering team examines the code using reengineering methods (see ongoing research at http://reengineering.org). A decision is made on the approach, and the "business rules" are extracted from the code. Business rules represent the portion of an application that directly support the organizational goals. This code is repackaged as a web service and installed under the portal. That takes care of the common user interface, given the caveats we described previously in this chapter.

The next task is to increase the scope for subsequent cycles of the data enterprise architecture. Using the bottom-up approach described in the chapter on Revised Data Management Goals, the components are developed with narrow foci applied to specific projects. Each application added to the XBP also has its data integrated via XML schemas. Automated management of the schema metadata means that when data-management challenges such as homonym and synonym questions arise, they can be easily identified and corrected through the XBP's technical capabilities.

Increased Integration Creates Demand for Portal Services Instead of Coded Applications

Rapid access to information is key to acquiring the support of the knowledge workers who use the XBP. The workers quickly gain appreciation for the advantages of the common interface. Perhaps a bit more slowly, the worker gains appreciation for the portal's ability to connect or prohibit connections between data items.

Any data item within the portal can be integrated with any other data item, or the XBP can report them as "not able to be integrated." Figure 7.20 shows how data from System A, an SAP system, can be integrated

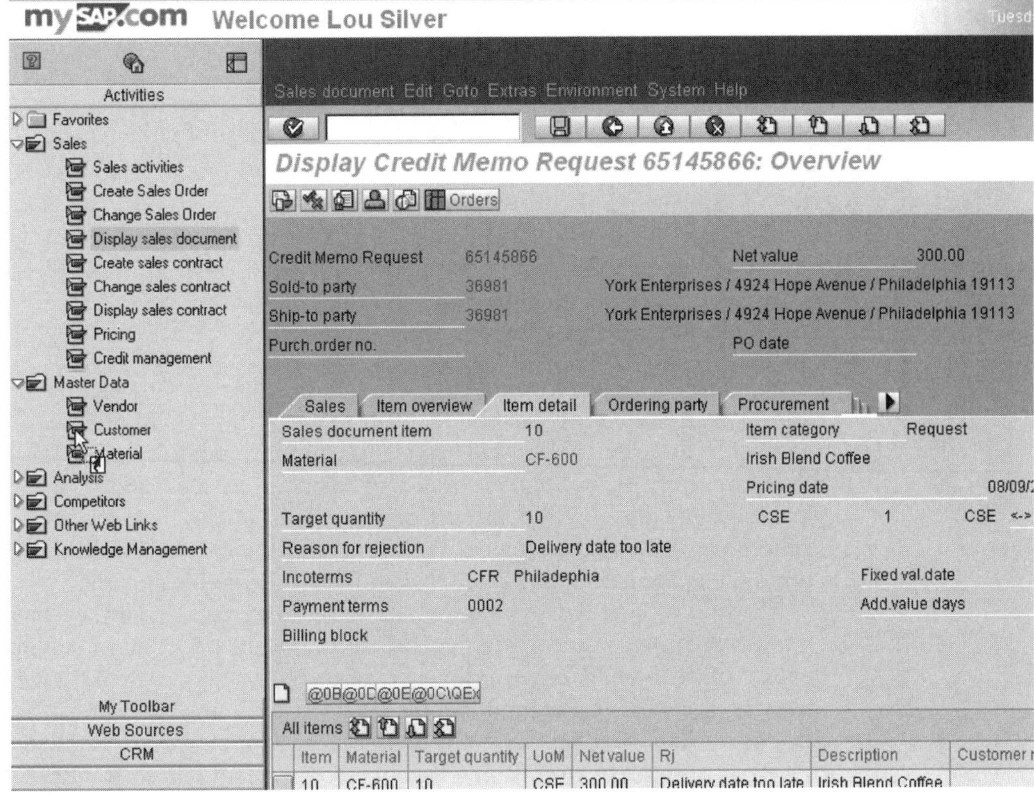

Figure 7.20

Top-tier portal demo.

with data from the sales system, even though the developers of the systems did not plan to integrate the two. Any knowledge worker with proper access can attempt to connect any two data objects without requesting that some connection be specially developed.

Each item added is integrated with the portal and thus with the existing collection of data. The XPB can answer any integration question by dragging and dropping items from one application onto another to see if they are connectable. If they are, the user is presented with a range of choices. The connection happens via XML transformations. The outputs can be reports, datasets, HTML pages, and XML. Increased quality attributes mean that knowledge workers will begin to desire data from the XBP.

Conclusion

At this point, we hope it is clear that XBP efforts are focused on incorporating appropriate XML. After all, who wants to do it the first time, knowing it will have to be repeated? XBP represents a very powerful technology, capable of benefiting many groups simultaneously.

Recent developments in portal technology that we have discussed in this chapter are combining to make this one of the most opportune times to work in information management. The three vital pieces are falling into place—the tools (XML-based portals), the techniques (data engineering), and the technologies (web-based information delivery). This chapter is meant to act as a guide for how these three fit together into the picture of better data management. We have gone to some effort to point out that it need not be an issue of reworking everything in the organization, but that it can be taken step by step, according to what can be cost- and feature-justified along the way. Regardless of the merits of any technology, it would be foolish to suggest anything other than a step-wise approach at refining data management, given the complexity of existing systems.

Hopefully, those data managers that started with distaste for the term "portal" will now be able to see the XBP as a fantastic opportunity in the context of real-world organizational data-management problems. Like any other technology, it cannot be implemented willy-nilly without planning, or it will be rendered as ineffectual as the last over-hyped technology that never seemed to work out. This chapter stresses the need to understand data structures as a way of pointing out that, in many cases, work must be done before organizations can start saving untold millions of dollars by implementing portals—they do not represent a quick fix or easy way out. What they do represent is opportunity; to the extent that any organization would like to reduce their data management costs, improve their decision-making ability, or tailor their data resources to aid strategic moves, it should be interested in closely examining XBP technology.

References

Aiken, P., & Mattia, A., et al. (in press). Measuring data management's maturity: An industry's self-assessment. *IEEE IT Professional.*

Aiken, P., & White, E. (2004). Organizational data quality approached from the user interface. *IEEE Computer*.

Aiken, P. H. (1996). *Data reverse engineering: Slaying the legacy dragon.* New York, McGraw-Hill.

Aiken, P. H., & Ngwenyama, O., et al. (1999). Reverse engineering new systems for smooth implementation. *IEEE Software 16*(2): 36–43.

Brodie, M. L., & Stonebraker, M. (1995). *Migrating legacy systems: Gateways, interfaces & the incremental approach.* San Francisco: Morgan Kaufmann.

Chikofsky, E., & Cross, J. C. II (1990). Reverse engineering and design recovery: A taxonomy. *IEEE Software 7*(1): 13–17.

Finkelstein, C. (1989). *An introduction to information engineering.* Boston: Addison-Wesley.

Finkelstein, C. (1993). *Information engineering: Strategic systems development.* Boston: Addison-Wesley.

Finkelstein, C., & Aiken, P. H. (1998). *Building corporate portals using XML.* New York: McGraw-Hill.

Lanham, T. (2001). Designing innovative enterprise portals and implementing them into your content strategies—Lockheed Martin's compelling case study. Paper presented at the Web Content II: Leveraging Best-of-Breed Content Strategies meeting, San Francisco.

8

Focusing XML and DM on Enterprise Application Integration (EAI)

Introduction

Enterprise Application Integration, or EAI, is yet another one of those buzzwords that we in technology have heard repeatedly over the years. Everyone was going to work on large EAI projects that would yield astounding results. A number of promises were made about EAI, but the end products were decidedly mixed. As with many ideas and technologies, ultimately the benefit derived is closely related to the way in which the idea is implemented. Throughout this book, we have talked about the importance of good data management as part of an XML-based approach to a problem. This chapter will continue along those lines with a discussion of the way EAI and XML work together, the pitfalls that others have encountered in the past, and what data managers can do to avoid those problems.

Even if EAI has been over-hyped in the past, it is still an important topic for a number of reasons.

1. As many systems develop along different paths over the life of an organization, the need to integrate those different sources of information and functionality becomes inevitable.

2. EAI is frequently found as a component of reengineering efforts. Reengineering is an attempt to realign existing

resources more efficiently, and changing the way things communicate and the results of that communication typically requires EAI work.

3. Since the amount of money spent on integration in the past has been so substantial, it is worth looking into more efficient technology to reduce the total expenditure necessary to connect systems within an organization.

Let us also look at a few key points that we can call the "IT Facts of Life," since they are relevant to the discussion of EAI in this chapter, and many other situations as well:

- No single vendor can provide all of the products and services to run an organization. This is intuitive, since vendors necessarily have to develop generic software that will run for many clients, and that does not take into account the specific challenges of a particular organization.
- Technologists are frequently left with the task of cobbling together solutions from many different packages.
- Companies are increasingly unprepared to effectively integrate as they shed in-house developers. For cost reasons, development often moves out of the organization, ultimately meaning that integration work must be done by external sources that know little about internal systems and integration needs.
- Buying more COTS (commercial off-the-shelf) software packages increases the dependence on software vendors and their support.
- The integration work being done is crucial. If links between the warehouse operation and the financial system break down, the ability to move goods and close out the books grinds to a halt. Many large companies have recently found that the inability to master links between complicated software packages can put their survival at risk.

The process of integrating systems and applications frequently involves shuttling complex data back and forth between various systems. While XML was not developed specifically as a technology to aid EAI, its utility within the field rapidly became apparent as developers of new EAI systems and ideas looked around for existing components with which to

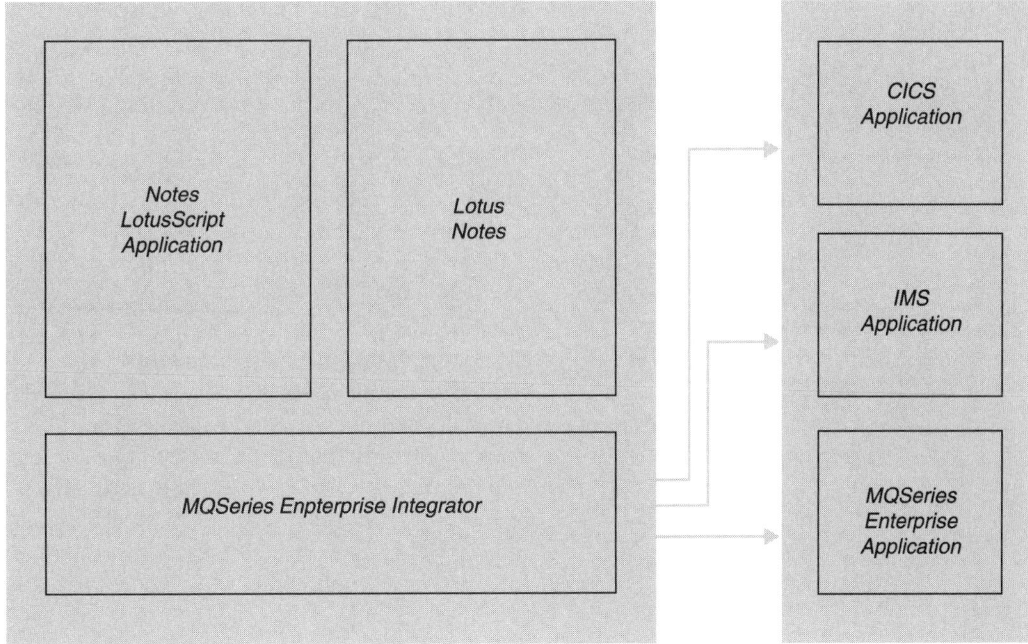

Figure 8.1

A typical EAI example—moving data between Lotus Notes and mainframe applications.

build. The flexibility, extensibility, and semantic richness possible with XML made it a natural choice as a vital part of the overall EAI picture.

Traditional EAI approaches create a message bus between two applications, and then spend a lot of time and energy focusing on the low-level technical aspects of putting messages onto that bus, and decoding them on the other end. That type of drudgery is precisely one of the areas where XML can help the most. Where the previous technical solutions were specific to the integrated applications, XML provides a framework that can be evolved to fit the needs of new data syntax and semantics.

Some of the first adopters of EAI were those who had large mainframes and who needed to move data to client/server applications. Perhaps the mainframe would house the authoritative source of information, while other machines would serve it up in different formats for various purposes. This tended to create point-to-point interfaces between all of the applications that were not always the same. In extreme situations, if there were 10 systems within an organization, there would be 10 corresponding applications, all of which had to be separately maintained and whose job it was to move data from the central mainframe to the systems surrounding it. In Figure 8.1, we see an example of this type of integration, with data being moved back and forth from a mainframe system using IMS and CICS to Lotus Notes.

More recently, when people refer to EAI, they are often talking about various toolkits and approaches commonly used to build EAI solutions. Specifically, the Distributed Component Object Model (DCOM) and the Common Object Request Broker Architecture (CORBA) have been the popular technologies used to integrate applications. While these technologies certainly have their place, they have tended to focus attention on the wrong level of integration. Many organizations have successfully put EAI solutions in place using DCOM or CORBA. On the other hand, others have put something in place only to find that it is brittle, difficult to maintain, and limited in functionality. Certainly there are some positive aspects to these technologies; for one, they encourage building connections in a hub-and-spoke model as opposed to a point-to-point model, and they put in place the basics of a common metadata model that is so important to this work. Still, the reality of implementation did not live up to the hype of the idea.

One of the drawbacks of the DCOM and CORBA approaches to EAI has to do with the way those technologies are structured. Both based on the object-oriented programming paradigm, they tend to suggest a pairing of data structures with functionality that may or may not accurately represent the way the data was stored. Since object-oriented development involves designing data packages (objects) with their associated operations, it is easy to see that the way data was represented within a CORBA- or DCOM-based application might be radically different from the way the source or target systems dealt with the data.

This creates another mapping and interfacing problem. Now, not only must the EAI solution move data from one application to another, it must first figure out how to move the source data into its own transport format, and then back out again once it arrives at its destination. Converting non-normalized mainframe-based flat files into dynamic CORBA objects can be quite a challenge. While this is appropriate in some instances, in others it has created a situation where developers were forced to pound a square peg (the source data) into a round hole (the object model and design of a CORBA-based EAI solution). Add to this problem the fact that most programmers doing this work are not trained in data design to begin with, and cost overruns paired with less-than-desired functionality start to become more understandable.

This often created the strange situation in which the EAI solution in question just sent data from one application to another, without much logic or processing in the middle. The result was that some EAI solutions ended up reinventing the wheel, doing something with complex and expensive software that could have been accomplished with an existing technology such as automated FTP, or secure copy.

For example, this type of middleware might have been used to send payroll data to the personnel department, and then shuttle personnel department data back the other way. In effect, this was an automation of flat-file transfer that might have been more appropriate for a simpler technology. The reason that these situations arose is that the data managers in question did not know what they needed in order to do the job correctly. The problem was not only that the simple functionality might have been better implemented with other technologies, but also that a large amount of opportunity was missed since data-engineering concepts were not applied throughout the process.

Figure 8.2 illustrates the topological complexities of the EAI game. Requirements are expressed in terms of point-to-point connectivity. Certain data sources must connect with other sources using specifically developed and maintained point-to-point connections. As an illustration, Figure 8.2 works at multiple levels that we will label as micro, mid, and macro.

- On the micro level, the application architecture would dictate that the applications shown in the figure would instead be sub-routines passing data back and forth. An ERP software package would be an easy-to-visualize example of this type of point-to-point connectivity below the application level.
- One the mid level, the separate application programs communicate with each other. A good example of this is just about any environment within a mid-sized or larger organization, for example, a payroll system communicating with a human resources system.
- One the macro level, the systems connect with each other across organizational boundaries. For example, take a common situation where payroll is outsourced, and data has to flow over lines into and out of the company.

Generally, the same principles apply for each level.

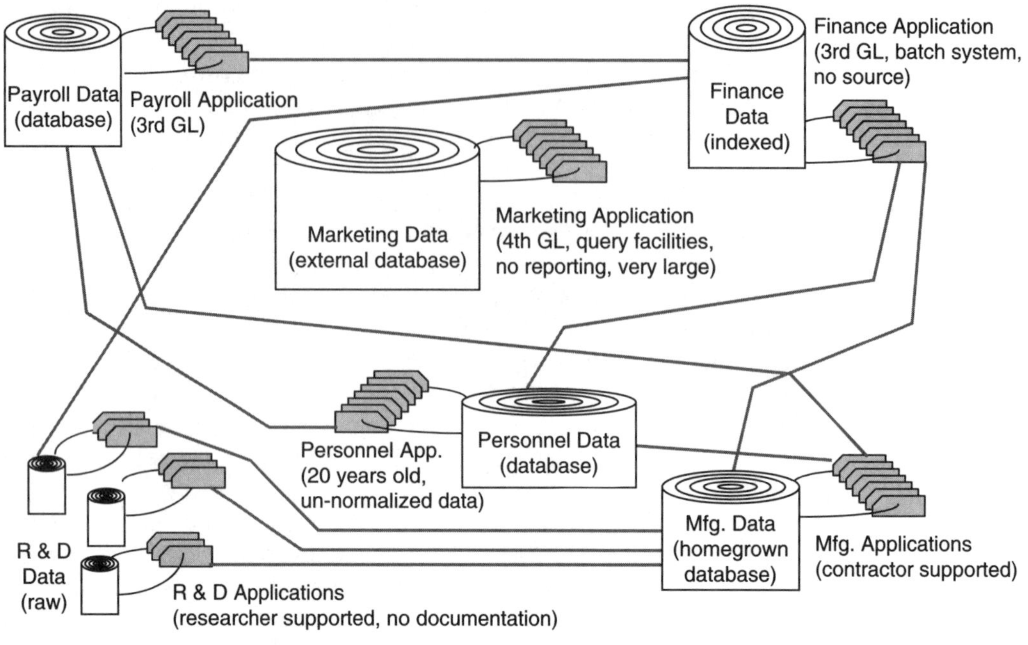

Figure 8.2

Gordian knot of legacy application interconnectivity.

What Is It About XML That Supports EAI?

Effective EAI requires semantic information about the data structures that are being moved back and forth. We have seen examples in previous sections of why it is beneficial to use data structures rather than data fields, and why semantics are important. XML supports EAI in that it provides metadata along with the actual data that is being sent, and allows the semantics that are so critical to the process to move right along with the data.

Frequently, when data managers ask their workers for the first time if they are using XML or not, they are surprised to find that its use is widespread. This turns out to be the case even if XML was not officially sanctioned within the organization. The next step in finding out how XML may already be used inside the organization is the discovery that two different groups have created two different sets of labels for various data items that must be reconciled if either is to be used. The good news is that not all of this effort will have been wasted. The syntax and semantics of tags can be translated back and forth to allow this reconciliation to occur. Just as this process can be used to take advantage of preexisting XML work, it is also possible to use it in EAI.

Flexibility and Structure

Technology is constantly moving and changing, and whatever EAI solution is put in place must have maximal flexibility to evolve along with the systems that it supports, so that when the inevitable change happens, the solution can adapt. For example, when data structures and semantics in one of the two applications begin to change, suddenly there is a need to translate that semantic difference between the two systems. Using purely technical approaches that only shuffle data back and forth, semantic translation is very difficult because the information is not aggregated at that level to begin with, and there is no additional contextual data about the structure. Rather than having information on an employee, the system might only have a bunch of strings labeled "first name," "last name," or "title."

When EAI is developed using XML as the lingua franca, XML's power can be used to refine things, even to the point of changing underlying semantics, within reason. Some elements of EAI implementation are ultimately going to be done right, while others will be done wrong. Looking to the future, putting in place a structure that is malleable, and that the organization is not permanently married to, will create cost savings right away, as well as down the line when the inevitable change becomes reality. Aspects of change, flexibility, and metadata malleability are the strategic applications of XML within the area of EAI. Next, we will take a look at the specific technical components of XML most frequently used in EAI.

From a more technical perspective, XML has two main "branches" that are most frequently used in EAI. The first we will call "XML Messaging," and the second we will call "Domain-Specific Languages." In Figure 8.3, these two branches are shown along with common examples of specific technology components.

XML Messaging

For projects that are more focused on loose integration of systems, typically what is needed is something of an XML messaging bus, across which

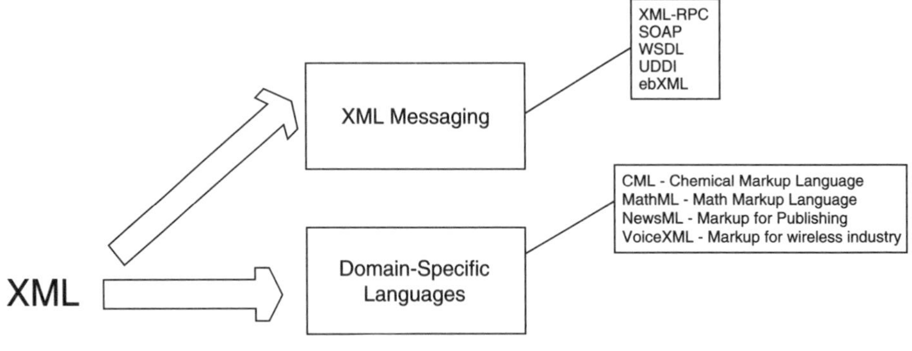

Figure 8.3

Two typical use "branches" of XML within EAI.

data is sent to and from the various systems. From this perspective, XML can provide a facility at a technically low level for getting data back and forth. The actual data interchange format is XML, and the transport protocols and associated technologies are those that have sprung up around XML. The examples of these seen in Figure 8.3 are XML-RPC (Remote Procedure Calls), SOAP, WSDL, UDDI, and ebXML. In these situations, the total solution is bound to be a mix of XML, the use of TCP/IP communication, and various pre-fabricated software components on either end that handle the connection and interpretation details of XML.

Figure 8.4 shows one possible representation of the common use of XML messaging in EAI. In the center of the diagram, there are various cubes stacked on top of one another, representing aspects of applications and systems that need to be integrated. Surrounding the entire cube is an XML messaging bus that can take information from various components and transport it to others. The third aspect of this diagram is the external object-based components. Frequently in XML messaging situations, it is possible to take common bits of functionality out of the applications and systems being integrated and put them inside object-based components, which are then reused by attaching them to the XML messaging bus. Rather than having functionality duplicated in multiple systems, these components can communicate with any system via the XML messaging bus. In this situation, XML provides a common way for system components and applications to communicate, while reducing the duplication of functionality in different applications represented by those common components.

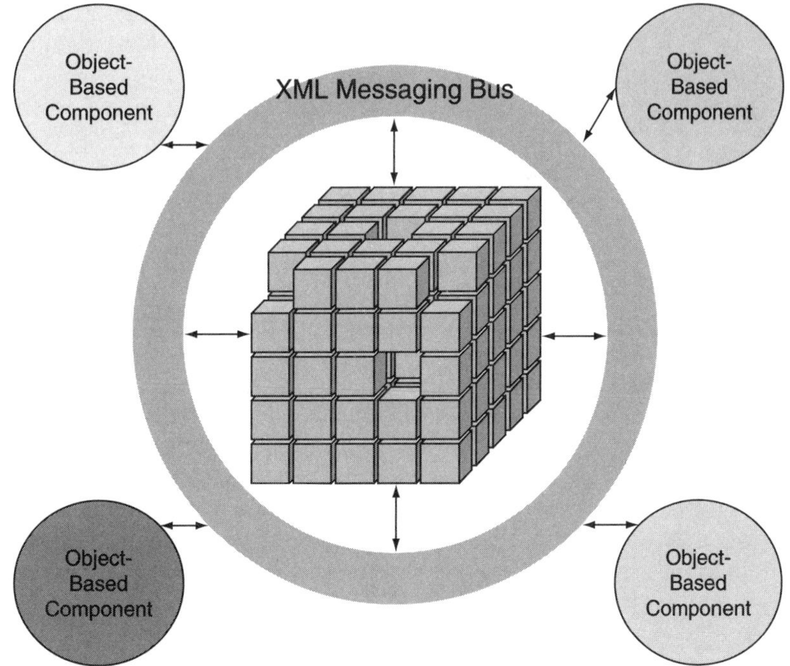

Figure 8.4

Using an XML messaging bus to communicate with various components.

Messaging is one of the most frequent XML tools used as part of EAI, but the next one that we will examine is almost as often encountered: the use of domain-specific XML languages.

Domain-Specific Languages

Domain-Specific Languages are ready-made XML languages that come with a set of definitions and a metadata model. These languages are also known as industry vocabularies. They are popular in XML-based EAI work because they present mature solutions to problems that data managers encounter. The examples listed in Figure 8.3 cover the areas of chemicals, mathematical formulas, and news releases, but there are many other accepted vocabulary standards available in just about every area imaginable.

To understand why domain-specific languages are attractive for XML EAI work, let us examine the situation of a media company that needs to distribute documents such as press releases. After being created in a particular application, these press releases are put into systems that distribute them via web sites and other mediums. The data manager is presented with a situation in which an EAI solution must be created to connect the publishing and distribution applications. Rather than going through the lengthy process of developing a common metadata model for the data that must be transmitted, he or she can use ready-made XML components such as RDF and NewsML to do the representational work. The use of these languages has several key advantages:

1. Using a domain-specific language obviates the need for an organization to develop its own XML component serving the same purpose. The readily available components prevent having to "reinvent the wheel."
2. Since the languages are already peer-reviewed and mature, they come with a pre-identified set of advantages and pitfalls. Data managers can make their decisions based on the requirements, rather than the hypothetical good and bad points of something they might develop themselves.
3. The fact that these languages are also used elsewhere aids further integration down the line. Tools already exist that understand standard domain-specific languages, while there is no existing software support for home-brewed XML languages that are specific to one or two EAI solutions.

Given these advantages, it is easy to see why preexisting XML components are attractive for integration work. Using them in concert with XML-messaging technologies is a solid instance of the cardinal IT rule—"Work smarter, not harder."

The Pundits Speak

Many different writers in the business media have also addressed the potential benefits of XML in EAI environments. We have taken a few of their perspectives and presented them here to provide different angles on the discussion. Frank Coyle of the Cutter Consortium made reference to the older, object-based models and to the XML messaging-bus concepts we have covered when he said,

> XML is revolutionizing distributed computing by providing an alternative to the object-based models of CORBA, RMI, and DCOM. XML in com-

> bination with HTTP opens the door to making remote procedure calls (RPCs) using the same basic web technology used to pass HTML data across the web. [This] simple but profound concept has revolutionized the distributed computing landscape and forced a rethinking of distributed protocols.*

We also present statements, made as part of a Gartner Group report from October of 2000, related to XML:

> XML represents a critical future direction for the management of metadata, data, [and] business rules and will play an increasingly important role in business and systems engineering. . . . Loosely coupled, asynchronous XML messaging infrastructures will dominate as the mode of communication for B2B integration.†

EAI Basics

What Is Integration?

Integration means different things to different people. The dictionary definition of integration tells us that it means to "join or unite" two things, or to make part of a larger unit. For our purposes, there are two different levels of integration that have very different characteristics.

1. Loosely coupled integration. This is the process of interconnecting two applications, and allowing for communication between the two. It is a cheaper and less complex level of integration that typically moves slowly and is error prone. Errors occur in loose integration because the two applications are different and only communicate for mutual convenience—they may have radically different ideas about what some pieces of data or processes mean. Applications are typically loosely integrated when they retain a degree of independence, but occasionally work together.
2. Tightly coupled integration. This is integration in its truest sense—two applications that are built using the same technologies and a common metadata model. This tends to be far more

*http://cutter.com, accessed 10/03.
†http://cutter.com, accessed 10/03.

> complex. One might say that this integration is the point at which the two applications have more similarities than they do differences. The functionality need not be similar, but the mode of operation, data concepts, and semantics are the same. Two applications are tightly integrated when each of their individual processing is dependent on the other.

It is important to note that tight integration is initially more expensive than loose integration. The initial investment has to do with thoroughly understanding and reconciling the data structures of the applications that are being integrated. In the loose-integration scenario, two applications with different data structures can only be integrated by creating a third data structure that maps between the two.

Like most other distinctions, the polar states of loose integration or extremely tight integration ultimately have many shades of gray between them. Regardless of which point in the continuum is ultimately chosen for a particular situation, it is important to have the two opposites in mind, along with their relative advantages and disadvantages. This perspective helps to identify which problems in EAI solutions come as a result of the architectural decisions, and which can be more immediately addressed. Now that we have seen the two extremes, we will take a brief look at the different components of an EAI solution, regardless of how tight or loose the integration is.

EAI Components

One of the most common factors that determines if IT projects succeed or fail is whether or not the project takes into account all of the different facets of what needs to be done. For example, some projects take a strictly technical approach, ignoring the data-architecture portion of the project, and end up with a corresponding set of drawbacks. In other situations, project teams become enamored of specific technical solutions and miss the larger context that the solution needs to operate within.

Figure 8.5 displays the three critical components that need to be considered in order to deliver successful EAI solutions. While it is possible to deliver a solution without considering all three aspects, such systems often are delivered either over budget, past deadline, with less than expected functionality, or all of the above.

Figure 8.5

Three critical components required to deliver EAI systems.

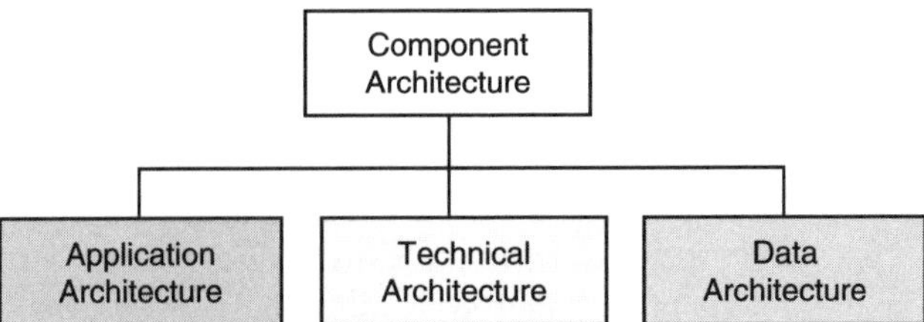

- **Application Architecture.** The Application Architecture component of an EAI solution takes into account the "style" and approach of the solution. Will the solution be client-server based? Will it be built in an object-oriented way? With a fourth-generation programming language? How will the application be put together, and how does it logically attack the core issues of the problem it is trying to solve?
- **The Technical Architecture.** This component is the one that project teams often spend too much time considering. The technical architecture deals with questions of what operating systems, hardware, platform, and network facilities will be used. It also encompasses a host of other non-software, non–data-related system and infrastructure questions. Technical facilities are the bricks that are used to build larger systems. While care should be taken to make sure that the right bricks are selected, the form and characteristics of the brick definitely should not dictate how the finished building or solution will be created.
- **The Data Architecture.** This component is typically the one that too little time is spent considering. The data architecture component of an EAI solution addresses issues of which data structures will be used, which access methods will be employed, and how data is coordinated throughout the system.

Throughout this chapter, XML is discussed particularly as it applies to the data architecture component of EAI above. Traditionally, when building systems that were focused around the use of toolkits like DCOM and CORBA, the most focus was put on the application architecture component. XML encourages architects to take a hard look at their data architecture through the facilities that XML provides, and to spend the appropriate amount of time in each area. For an EAI project to be a true success, focus is needed in each of the areas, rather than skewing analysis to one particular part of the picture.

The difficulty here is that focusing on three different areas requires three different sets of expertise. IT and systems infrastructure people are best suited to deal with the technical architecture; programmers and program architects are best equipped for the application architecture component; while data managers are in the best position to take care of the data architecture. Given these three areas of expertise, data managers still seem to be the ones who end up leading these efforts, for several reasons. Data managers typically have a higher-level view of the business and its technology needs, since they coordinate data resources in many different places. They also are often better suited to understanding the issues of integration that frequently come down to sticky data architecture questions.

These components come together to form the basis for technically effective EAI—in other words, an EAI system that delivers what was promised in the way of system integration. There are other definitions of a successful EAI system, however, particularly from the business and financial perspectives. In the next section, we will take a look at the motivation for why businesses want to approach EAI in the first place, and what financial incentives and pitfalls surround its use.

EAI Motivation

Despite some EAI promises that have not panned out, interest remains high and continues to grow. This is because data managers and their respective organizations are just now starting to measure how much lack of effective integration is costing them. In the past, data managers have frequently been aware of the consequences of poor or non–existent integration, but have not been able to make the business case to fix it, lacking solid numbers. This short section is intended to give data managers the ammunition they need to make just this case.

According to John Zachman, organizations spend between 20% and 40% of their IT budgets evolving their data.* Other sources say that 80% of data warehouse development costs are spent configuring the extraction, transformation, and loading (ETL) aspects of the warehouse. This includes three key components:

1. Data migration, or moving data from one system or application to another
2. Data conversion, or moving data from one format to another

---

*John Zachman, Personal communication, May 2003.

3. Data scrubbing, or the process of comprehensively inspecting and manipulating data into another form or state for subsequent use

This data evolution in many cases is not adding additional value; the data is simply being changed or moved to fit the peculiarities or specifics of another place in order to add value down the line. That these activities take up 20% to 40% of IT budgets means that they are an area to focus on in search of savings. In fact, all of these activities are heavily involved in the process of EAI, and reducing expenditures on them ultimately means saving on IT.

In Figure 8.6, taken from a Gartner Group survey report, we can see the breakdown of IT spending by activity and function in 1999 and 2000. Typically, EAI costs will fall into the first three categories: new development, major enhancements, and applications support, as well as the last two: administration and IT planning, and "other." All together, these represent more than 40% of IT spending. While there are other activities funded by these categories, it is typical to see the support and evolution of less-than-adequate EAI solutions eating up a good portion of the budget. This is one perspective on the different cost areas involved in EAI and their associated allotments. Another perspective would be to look at how much money will be spent across all industries on integration within a particular year.

Figure 8.6

IT spending distribution by activity for 1999 and 2000.

IT Spending Distribution by Activities/Department/Function (%)	**1999**	**2000**
New Development	12.3	12.4
Major Enhancements	9.2	9.4
Applications Support and Maintenance	10.6	10.6
Mainframe	7.6	7.4
Midrange Servers	8.7	8.6
Distributed Computing	11.1	11.1
Help Desk/End-User Support	5.5	5.9
Wide-Area Data Network and Charges	6.8	6.9
Voice Network and Charges	6	5.9
Administration and IT Planning	5.6	5.7
Other	16.5	16
Total IT Spending	100	100

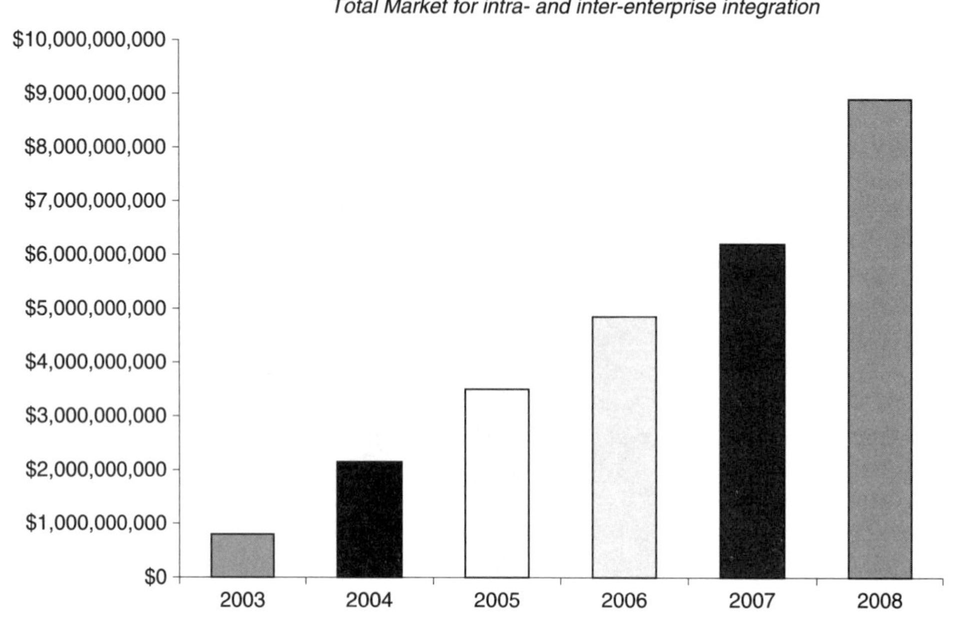

Figure 8.7

Total market for integration. (Taken from International Data Corporation's DM Review, 8/2001.)

In Figure 8.7, we can see that the total market for integration technology will grow from an estimated $1 billion in 2003 to $9 billion or more by the year 2008. With the importance of EAI within organizations and the amount of money being spent, it is worthwhile to take a hard look at the cost effectiveness and functionality of existing systems. EAI can become a component critical to keeping an organization running. Older systems built without the benefit of a data engineering perspective typically cost quite a bit more to maintain, just as a rental car company will spend more to maintain a fleet of older vehicles. One key to getting the maximal return out of an investment is minimizing the recurring maintenance costs that eat away at the savings the system should be providing in the first place. The economics of XML are such that this technology will appeal to small and mid-size organizations as well as large ones.

Typically, when data managers successfully sell EAI projects internally, it is based on standard return on investment calculations, like many other business decisions. Specifically, the investment can be justified by demonstrating that the proposed system has a lower maintenance cost, and that the difference between the current maintenance cost and that of the proposed system is enough to recoup the cost of the project within a particular time frame. In the past, organizations have not made much of an attempt to show a return on investment related to EAI. With figures related to how much is spent maintaining existing systems internally, data managers can make a financial case for their ideas as well as a technical and functional case. In business, new things are done for three core reasons:

1. The new way costs less than the old way. Given current EAI expenditures, this case can now be made.
2. The new way can do something that the old way could not. Combining EAI with XML opens up a multitude of new possibilities.
3. The new way does something faster than the old way. Reusing XML data structures in EAI systems allows proposed systems to be put together more quickly than their predecessors.

EAI implementation should not be done simply for its own sake, though. The best approach is to pick an area where the organization is experiencing quite a bit of pain, either financially or functionally, and attempt to find a solution. Often these solutions may take the form of EAI, since making the most of existing resources frequently means piping the output of one application or process into the input of another to provide more functionality. This piping is integration work focusing on coupling components more tightly—in other words, everything that EAI is about.

The major pitfall to avoid is creating a solution that is primarily focused on the technical level. Certainly the technical aspects of how integration is accomplished are important, but they should not drive the architecture and design of the solution. The real reason why EAI is needed rarely has anything to do with data formatting or transport details. Rather, the motivation is more at a semantic level: the meaningful outputs of one application need to be communicated to another to continue the value chain. When organizations focus on the semantic aspects of their EAI investments, the true expressive power of XML begins to shine through, and it distinguishes itself from other technologies.

EAI Past and Current Focus

The earliest authoritative academic definition appears to have been from 1992, and it stated that EAI was about "improving the overall performance of large, complex systems in areas such as

- Processing efficiency
- Unit responsiveness
- Perceived quality
- Product differentiation

Enterprise integration efforts seek to achieve improvements by facilitating the interaction among: Organizations, Individuals, and Systems" (Petrie, 1992).

As we have briefly addressed earlier in the chapter, the past focus on EAI has been at a rather low level technically. The questions EAI has been used to address have involved, for example, how to make an SQL server instance talk to CICS, or how to connect a Power Builder application with another program running on the company's mainframe. While those are important areas, they have tended to redirect focus from important issues of data semantics toward issues of data syntax. Technical integration of different products can often be accomplished either with ready-made tools that come with those products or with drop-in components.

It is vital that the semantic issues that prompted the integration effort play a primary role in the architecture of the solution. Too often, organizations build an extremely competent and technically sound EAI solution, only to spend the rest of their time doing technical acrobatics to make it actually accomplish what they want. The construction of an approach should be focused on the data structure level and the semantic level of the issue at hand. If a solution is based on a great way to transmit individual fields back and forth between applications, another layer of work must be done to package together various fields in some way that the solution can handle so that entire structures can be sent back and forth. What we are suggesting here is simply this: the form of the solution should follow the form of the problem; moving semantic data structures rather than building the solution based on the form of the source and the target systems.

Let us take a look at the difference between focus on the semantic and syntactic levels for EAI solutions. In order to illustrate more clearly why

Figure 8.8

An example of the syntactic/technical approach to EAI—moving data fields.

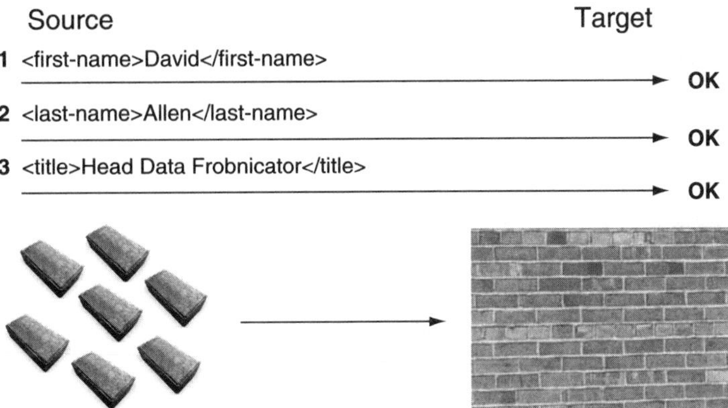
Moving Data Fields About an Employee
Source
Target
1 <first-name>David</first-name>
OK
2 <last-name>Allen</last-name>
OK
3 <title>Head Data Frobnicator</title>
OK

the semantic approach is important, we will use a very typical EAI example—an organization needs to move data from a personnel application to the payroll application.

In Figure 8.8, we see the syntactic and technical approach to EAI. A solution has been built that allows us to move data fields flawlessly from application to application. In this case, we are transmitting the information about a particular employee to the payroll application. The data moves through just fine, and once the individual fields arrive in the target system, they are reassembled into a complete picture of the employee including first name, last name, and title. This is like creating the idea of an employee in the other system by breaking it down into individual components like bricks, sending them through, and assembling those bricks into the complete brick wall or brick house on the other end. Certainly this approach will work, but the drawback is that effort and time must be spent on exactly how to construct the individual bricks, and how to put them together into a complete brick house on the other end. In addition, ach individual piece of data was properly transmitted and understood. The target system must also make sense of the actual items coming across the line, particularly in the common situation where its definition of employee may be different.

By contrast, in Figure 8.9, we see an example of a complete data structure being moved from the source system to the target system. Rather than sending individual snippets of data or XML, a complete XML document is sent that describes all that we want to communicate to the target system—an employee record. It is accomplished in one step,

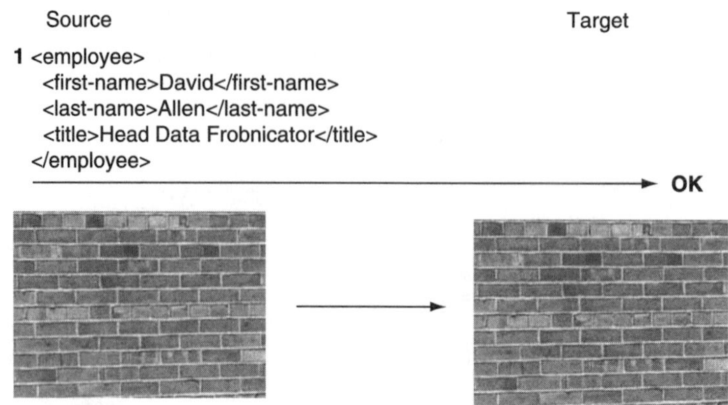
Moving an Employee Data Structure
Source
Target
1 <employee>
<first-name>David</first-name>
<last-name>Allen</last-name>
<title>Head Data Frobnicator</title>
</employee>
OK

Figure 8.9

An example of the semantic/meaning approach to EAI—moving data structures.

since the target system need only acknowledge the proper receipt of the data it was sent. There is no disassembly work done on the source side, and there is no reassembly work done on the target side. The associated errors that are possible as part of those processes are correspondingly eliminated.

The technical approach to EAI is focused on getting the bits and the bytes of EAI correct, at the expense of meaning and the purpose. After all, the point of this example is that the organization does not simply want to properly transmit first names, last names, titles, or strings of characters. It needs to transmit information properly about an entire employee. Using a data-structure perspective rather than a data field perspective allows the form of the solution to be dictated by what the organization is trying to accomplish, rather than the technical details of what types of strings a particular application can accept.

Generalized Approach to Integration

Each model (tightly coupled applications and loosely coupled applications) has costs and benefits when integrating with internal or external applications. Both types can include XML as a data format, but the tightly coupled model does not exploit all its advantages. Tightly coupled applications are designed to operate in tandem and to receive and send data while providing the highest performance and least latency when linking applications. Organizations that rely on tightly coupled applications must typically account for any future changes to application or data and create upfront agreements that applications use when communicating. Practically speaking, this means either purchasing the same application or codeveloping applications with partner enterprises. These inherent rigidities may not allow an enterprise to take advantage of the free flow of e-commerce.

Messaging technologies enable loosely coupled architectures. In loosely coupled architectures, applications are designed to accommodate XML and can make sense of "data on the fly." Of course, since the exact shape of the data cannot always be controlled, as the initial enforcement of business rules and validation of data might take place outside of an application's context, an application must include logic for accepting data that is perhaps not complete or contains too much information.

Resource Efficiencies

EAI should not be approached as something to be used because of industry trends, or even because this book told you that XML can help the process. It should be used because it will make an organization more efficient and nimble.

Do not approach EAI as "We need to do this." Just ask yourself, "What needs to be fixed?" Then make the business case, and go after the solution. What we are trying to achieve is resource efficiencies. If it takes 14 people to do maintenance, then we want to do the same job with fewer people, based on the EAI solution. This perspective should permeate data manager's thinking about EAI. Further, focusing on returns tends to make people less susceptible to the claim of the silver-bullet, solve-everything magic solution.

Engineering-Based Approach

Based on the lessons of the past and what data managers now know about EAI, tacking another letter onto the acronym—EAIE, or Enterprise Application Integration Engineering—refers to the new flavor of how these solutions are being created. The approach is to use the data-engineering principles that are discussed throughout this book as a core part of the development process, rather than an add-on at the end if budgeting allows. Within EAIE (sometimes pronounced "aieeeeeeee!" as a shrill cry of anguish at yet another acronym), the use of common metadata models is important.

Rather than viewing an EAI project as an island unto itself, work that was done on either of the systems being connected should be brought into the picture. The effort that was put into previous system projects should act as a solid foundation for the subsequent work of integrating those systems. Instead of looking at EAI as a simple connection between two things, it should be viewed within the context of the larger business systems network within an organization, and as such should be coordinated and planned like other organization-wide IT initiatives. This process requires involvement from data-management groups and architectural groups, in addition to the direct business users of the two systems being integrated, and the technical workers developing the solution.

One perceptual pitfall of EAIE to keep in mind is that since it is done at a high level, looking at a particular EAI solution as part of a larger architecture, people figure that this work will be accomplished in one big piece. The thought process is that if the scope is expanded, all of the organization's problems can be solved within one project. While it's tempting to think this, it is important to avoid anything that does not produce benefits within one calendar year. This effectively forces organizations to look only at the areas of biggest need, and to focus on addressing those issues while preparing for the solution. It is this prudence and occasional bit of restraint that prevents organizations from catching on to a new fad and implementing it everywhere. Too often in those situations, organizations find at a later point that technological developments have made their investment less valuable than previously expected, or that their grand unified solution might not have addressed requirements that a more step-wise process would have uncovered. Take the lesson from the Oracle CPG example (presented in the next sections), and slow down.

So how do effective EAI solutions get built? Figure 8.10 shows the typical process of developing successful EAI architectural components—or how to make sure that any particular EAI effort fits in with the overall architecture. There are two key things to note about this diagram. First, the main input of the entire process in the upper left-hand corner is the organizational strategy. Second, the output of the process is an architecture component. The characteristics of these components are that they are well understood, they are reusable, and they take into account the business requirements from the start.

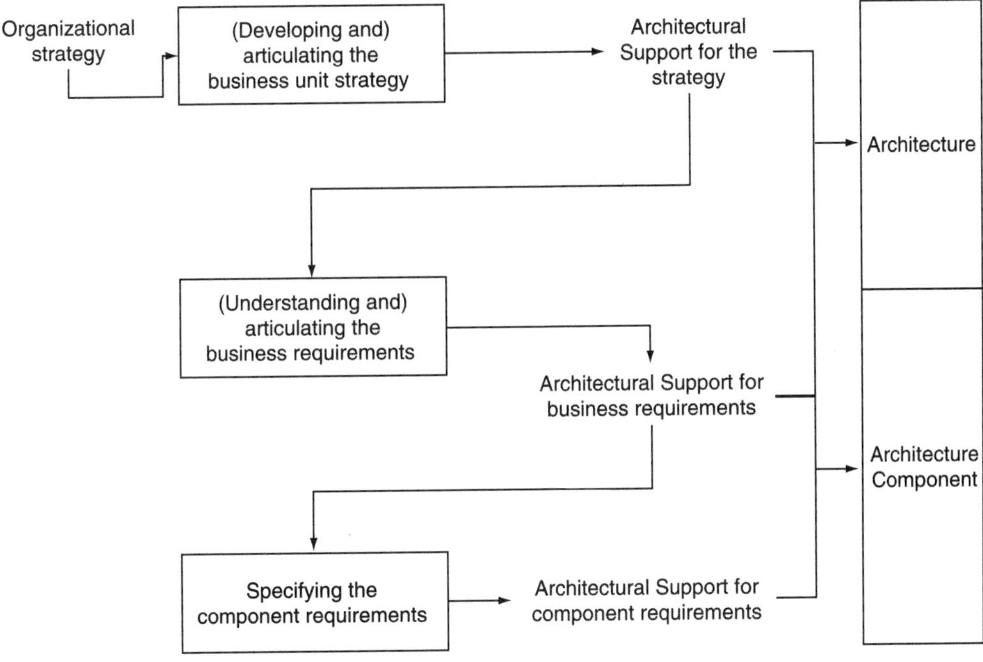

Figure 18.10

Steps in successful EAI development.

Using the EAIE approach, solutions may be built in a component manner like good software. EAI should not be like a freestanding house or edifice, but rather a solid brick wall, the construction of which can be easily duplicated in other places. The resulting components can then be appropriately assembled into larger system structures, while architects oversee the process, ensuring that everything falls into its proper place.

Key Factor: Scalability = EAI Success

One last very important concept that needs to be included in the discussion of EAI and XML is the technology's inherent scalability. While XML's scalability is useful in a number of different ways, its contributions to EAI—and in particular, EAI project and implementation scalability—are of particular note. EAI projects must prove themselves

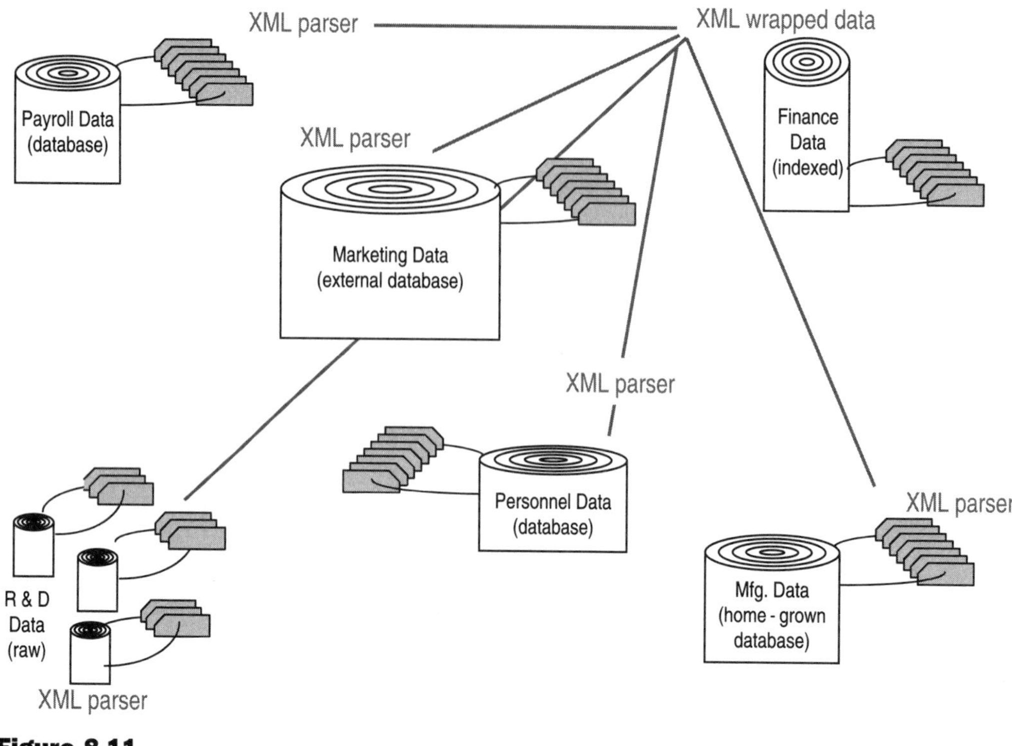

Figure 8.11

XML-izing applications and data can leverage two-way project scalability.

against negative perception. The ability to "XML-ize" applications and systems in small but meaningful ways is of critical importance to data managers.

Scalability can occur first in the project scope dimension—that is, how many data items and how much data are you going to try to cover with the XML vocabulary? Let us return to the example shown in Figure 8.11, presented earlier in this chapter, of wrapping the data in XML to facilitate interchange. The first part of the project might wrap only a portion of finance data and the payroll data to address a particularly thorny problem surrounding the management of cash flow around pay dates. The first XML components would be implemented to wrap just the targeted finance and payroll data. In the diagram below, when we mention "parser" we are referring to a software component that allows access to the data in the XML. The logic of what happens with that data of course depends on the application and system.

Once the organization has successfully implemented the first phase, it can then decide to scale the project in one of two ways: by adding more data items or by adding new parsers. Adding more data items—expanding the organization's XML vocabulary—can be done on a currently unwrapped set of data items without building new capabilities. Adding more parsers to the mix by, for example, enabling the personnel data, will increase the scope of the EAI effort to previously un-integrated data. Having this amount of flexibility gives integration specialists more feasible options when planning these complex tasks.

The key to successfully engineering XML-based EAI projects is to select the right-sized "chunks" to "XML-ize." If the chunk is too small, then results will be difficult to demonstrate. On the other hand, if the chunk is too large, you will have difficulty achieving those results. In some instances, it will be necessary to achieve data understanding at the third normal form level in order to implement a syntactically correct XML-based vocabulary and associated dialects. This is not to say that the XML data structures will be normalized in the way that relational structures are (which rarely happens), but simply that the data must be understood and well structured.

Somewhere in between the two extremes are a series of chunk-sized EAI projects that will complement existing integration efforts. The key for your effort to be successful is to define projects that are of the right size and scope, that are technically feasible, and that can be scaled up to build on success. The technological feasibility determination will require a good understanding of the tools and technologies described in the Data-Management Technologies chapter.

EAI Challenges

In order to understand what works about EAI, it is helpful to take a look at what has been difficult—the integration requirements. In this section, we will examine an example of a well-studied EAI failure, and learn its lessons of complexity and scope (Koch, 2001). By the way, our intention is not to pick on Oracle as used in this illustration. All big vendors have made similar miscalculations (recall IBM's AD/Cycle?), and we use the public Oracle example to avoid nondisclosure agreement–related issues. In

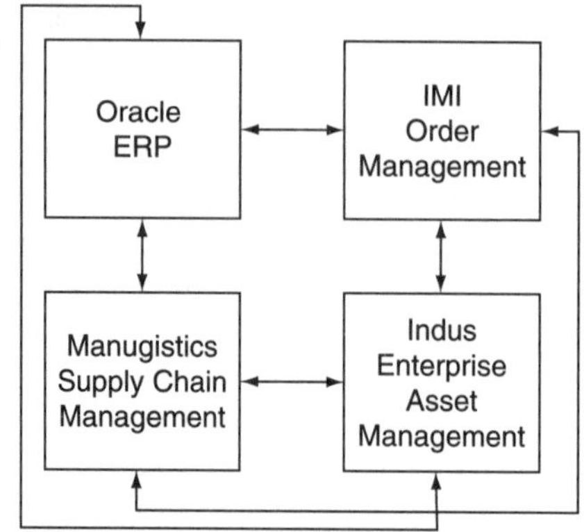

Figure 8.12

Oracle's attempt at using EAI to integrate four separate systems.

1996, part of Oracle's vision was their concept of Oracle CPG, or Consumer Packaged Goods.

This vision promised to integrate four completely different packages from different vendors into a seamless whole. The packages that were being dealt with were:

1. Oracle's own Enterprise Resource Planning (ERP) software
2. Indus's Enterprise Asset Management package
3. Manugistic's Supply Chain Management software
4. IMI's Order Management package

Consumer Packaged Goods companies manufacture and distribute just about anything that one might find on a grocery store shelf. The integration effort promised to run all aspects of CPG companies' businesses, handling everything from estimating future product demand to manufacturing scheduling and delivery of the product. In addition, Oracle pledged to take responsibility for the support and integration of the various software packages within the overall vision.

Kellogg was chosen to be the first customer and featured user, or "poster child," of the Oracle CPG effort, and stood to gain quite a bit if the system worked as promised. According to various sources, Kellogg spent over $10 million on the project, devoting more than 30 programmers and 3 years of time to Oracle to help them develop the CPG product. Assuming a cost of at least $60,000 per year for a full-time programmer, 30 programmers for 3 years comes out to $5.4 million in salary expenses alone. It is unclear whether that expense was figured into the $10 million price tag on the project. This also does not account for what Oracle spent on similar work as part of the venture. In return for this investment, Kellogg expected to be able to influence the CPG system's features in order to aid their specific objectives.

The results were mixed. Despite Oracle's statement to the contrary, some former customers claim that Oracle failed to finish CPG, and that failure cost the customers millions.

As part of this effort, Oracle had purchased Datalogix, and rewritten parts of this software to fit with Oracle's own technology and data model. Other pieces, however, were not integrated to become a single product. Instead, Oracle and CPG partners wrote software interfaces to translate information among the various CPG components. While this was cheaper and less complex than tight integration in the short term, the integration was very prone to error and ended up moving information more slowly than true integration would have. With more than 100 interfaces tied together with high levels of complexity, problems cropped up without end, and CPG release deadlines were missed.

What the CPG debacle demonstrates with frightening clarity is that the task of getting a host of different vendors to integrate complex software programs to the level that Oracle aspired to with CPG is more than difficult—it is impossible. "If you had to point a finger at the root of the problem, it was the integration," says Boulanger. "They could never get the different systems to talk to each other adequately. It was like trying to tie them together with bailing wire." "It's impossible to try to integrate four pieces like that from different vendors into a single product," agrees Barry Wilderman, a vice president for Stamford, Connecticut–based Meta Group (Koch 2001).

Now that we have seen some of the potential consequences of EAI integration challenges, as well as Oracle's particular approach to its situation, what lessons can we take from this failure to prevent the same from happening elsewhere?

Lesson One: All About Data Integration

Rather than focusing on tight integration and creating similarities between the different software packages that made integration natural, Oracle focused on creating a complicated set of communication links between the software. This is a typical approach taken in loose integration efforts, where communication between software packages is all that is desired, no matter how dissimilar they are. No common data model was developed, and there does not seem to be any evidence that effort was put in at the data structure level. The focus was simply on getting data from place to place between the applications.

The way this pitfall can be avoided is by planning out an integration effort thoroughly before beginning, and focusing on integrating applications as tightly as the time and budget will realistically allow. To determine whether loose or tight integration is more appropriate, try asking a simple question: Which is preferable, two systems that act as two arms of a unified approach to a problem, or two systems that do completely different things and that communicate from time to time for mutual convenience?

Lesson Two: Start Small

One of the most startling aspects of the Oracle CPG example is its sheer scope. When an organization is interested in integration work, it very much helps to start small and to focus on the area where there is the most pain, rather than attempting to take on the entire universe of problems and solutions simultaneously. Some people refer to the "phased approach" of implementation—putting various pieces in place as they are developed—and the "big bang" approach, which is to develop the entire system and put it into place all at once. Typically, the "big bang" approach lives up to its name—what organizations get is a really big explosion.

Integrating four totally different systems to create a unified system that runs an entire class of companies is biting off quite a lot. If a person were interested in mechanics and engineering, it might be wise not to attempt to build a toolshed instead of a whole house as a first project. Similarly, organizations that would like to improve their EAI could benefit by dividing the issues they have into different groups and conquering them individually, rather than all at once.

One of the sanity checks that are important to run on proposed ideas and projects is a simple examination of the complexity of the overall effort. If things have been constructed correctly, the chances are good that from an architectural perspective things will seem relatively straightforward. Those simple understandings may translate into quite a bit of underlying work, but all the same, the overall vision should have some simple, central idea. Looking at the Oracle CPG example, the simultaneous loose integration of four separate and massive systems does not seem very simple. It is possible that with more time for analysis, along with a more concerted effort to break down the whole project into smaller manageable components, the CPG project would have had a chance for success.

Another lesson that might have been learned is about data quality and EAI. The goal of the project is the formulation of technology that permits the automated data exchange of hundreds of data structures automatically. The old adage "garbage in—garbage out" becomes "garbage in—garbage throughout" when input data of insufficient quality is used to pollute other formerly decent-quality data. These situations are the impetus for data-quality initiatives, which are growing in organizational importance (for an example, see Allen, 2003).

Lesson Three: Core Technologies Lack EAI Support

This section leaves the Oracle example behind and will address technology and support for XML. We have discussed core XML technologies supporting EAI such as repositories, CASE tools, and translation technologies in previous chapters. However, a few observations are appropriate at this point to address the state of repository technology. Our surveys show that many organizations are not using best practices to manage their data sources (Aiken, 2002). Few organizations reported higher than a level three score on their data management maturity measurement (DM3).

- About half responded yes to the question, "Do you use any metadata catalog tools?"
- About 1 in 5 organizations are cataloging their metadata using any form of software tool support.
- Almost half the projects are proceeding ad hoc.
- The most popular repository technologies control only 16% of the market (see Figure 8.13).

The lesson here is that vendors are not yet providing us with the tools and technologies that we need. Much will have to be home grown and assembled from existing components and even (dare we say it) web services.

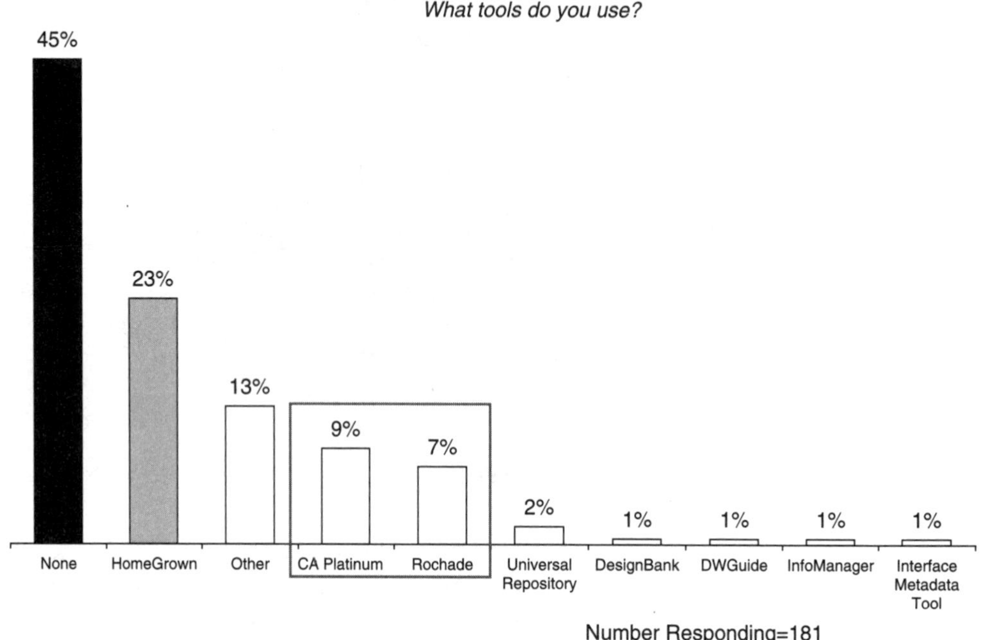

Figure 8.13

Repository technologies in use.

Conclusion

XML + DM = EAI makes a powerful motivation—XML provides the vocabulary and describes the content of messages, while EAI helps to define the business value. In order to take full advantage of the potential that XML offers, it is necessary that you examine your EAI-related business requirements and explore the alternatives presented in this chapter. You will likely discover how XML-based integration technologies will permit you to replace key system-problem areas with cleaner, more manageable data-integration management solutions.

References

Aiken, P. (2002). *Keynote address: Trends in Metadata.* Speech given at the 2002 DAMA International Conference, San Antonio, TX.

Koch, C. (2001, November 15). Why your integration efforts end up looking like this . . . *CIO.*[*]

Petrie, C. (1992). Forward to the conference proceedings. *Enterprise Integration Modeling: Proceedings of the First International Conference.* Cambridge, MA: MIT Press.

[*]The discussion of the controversy over the Oracle CPG project was taken from Christopher Koch's article.

9

XML, DM, and Reengineering

Introduction

So you might ask—and one reviewer did—why is an XML book talking about reengineering? Reengineering is another one of those love/hate topics for data managers and all kinds of IT professionals, similar to Enterprise Application Integration. On one hand, the possibilities for gains from reengineering as it has typically been described seem profound. On the other hand, for many organizations, none of these benefits have really panned out. The reasons for these disappointments are wide ranging, from excessively exuberant promises made on the part of those selling reengineering, to organizations simply choosing the wrong targets for their initial efforts. The purpose of this chapter is to show how XML can provide a different perspective on reengineering, to break it down into useful pieces, and to show how XML adds value to the entire process.

Before we move ahead with more information about XML and reengineering, it is important to first cover the two main types of reengineering, and discuss a bit of their similarities, differences, and most importantly, their interdependencies.

Two Types of Reengineering

In the early chapters of this book, we attempted to actually define such concepts as XML and metadata, since there is so much confusion surrounding these terms. When the term "XML" is used, it might actually refer to just about anything discussed in the component architecture chapter. The same situation applies to *reengineering*—a term that has typically been slapped onto just about anything as a convenient label to sell it to management (Hodgson & Aiken, 1998).

The Broad Definition of Reengineering

The involvement of upper management is key, and is a part of our functional definition of the overall concept of reengineering. Basically, reengineering is a popular approach used by management when reaching a particular solution requires a change that is more than incremental. In other words, when the required change is radical enough that a step-wise, incremental change just is not going to cut it, it may be time for management to consider a reengineering approach. Reengineering itself has risen in popularity to the point where lists of management tools typically include it.

As a broad concept, reengineering is not anything more than an approach or attempt to create significant change in an organization. Since a significant change is by definition quite a bit more radical than what incremental change might produce, it can be dangerous. Reengineering is a bit like a chainsaw: When wielded appropriately, it can perform very useful tasks and clear the way for real development. When used inappropriately or overzealously, well, it can create problems.

The process of reengineering is a broad area to discuss. The best way to talk about it is to split it down into components that have more to do with descriptions of the actual jobs that are involved. In terms of types of reengineering that are entailed, there are two broad categories: systems reengineering, and business process reengineering.

Systems Reengineering

The process of systems reengineering, or SR, is the attempt to radically improve information systems that support the business. From a technical perspective, these efforts are often undertaken to address any one of a number of challenges.

- **The addition of a new major feature to an existing application.** Sometimes, the architecture of an existing system creates sufficient barriers to adding a new needed feature that the system has to be "reengineered" in order to be able to do so. The alternative would be to create a brittle system where the new feature was forcibly shoehorned in. This type of approach typically causes problems down the line, and greatly increases maintenance costs.
- **The realignment of existing resources.** In other situations, systems get reengineered because the divisions between them start to morph or break down. For example, a "manufacturing" information system might be broken down into three logical areas as an organization grows: actual production, supply, and delivery of the product. As the functional boundaries change, the total number of logical systems may grow or shrink, and the existing systems must be reengineered to account for this realignment of resources.
- **Changing a system to reflect new technical requirements.** Occasionally, systems need to be reengineered because of a technical requirement that they run on a different platform, extend their capacity, change their native data format, or other considerations.
- **The phase-out of a system.** As some systems drop out of active service, other systems around them in some cases may need to pick up the slack. This might take the form of a major new feature described above, or a radical shift in the way data flows through the system.

When SR is done, it reflects an understanding that a simple patch to an existing system cannot solve the challenge confronted. Due to how radical the change can be, it tends to be more expensive and complicated than incremental modification. This is one of the many reasons that focus on overall architecture, particularly data engineering, is necessary at the outset of new-systems implementation. Ultimately, no matter how elegant or complete the architecture, business environments change, and it is inevitable that systems will run into situations that their architecture cannot accommodate. In those situations, SR is a decent alternative to simply throwing the existing system out the window and starting fresh.

Systems reengineering has become standardized in the IT community as a coordinated, reverse and forward, system engineering activity. (see Figure 9.1). Forward engineering benefits from information gained from reverse engineering activities. The five types of SR output are a documented understanding of:

1. Existing system design assets. How was the old system put together?
2. Existing system requirements. Why was it built that way?
3. New system requirements. What does the new thing have to do?
4. New system design. How is the new system going to do it?
5. The new system itself.

SR outputs 2 and 3 are optional—Figure 9.1 shows that it is possible to proceed directly from the existing design to a new design, bypassing the requirements processes when they are unnecessary.

The other steps are not optional. The typical pitfall in SR efforts is work that is focused too narrowly on exactly what the goal is. Of course, one needs to focus on the goal, but if it is an attempt to reengineer an existing system, careful thought should be put into exactly how the work is going to affect the ongoing operation of the system. Toward this end, data engineering principles need to be considered. Figure 9.2 shows the best path when reengineering the data structures within a system. One

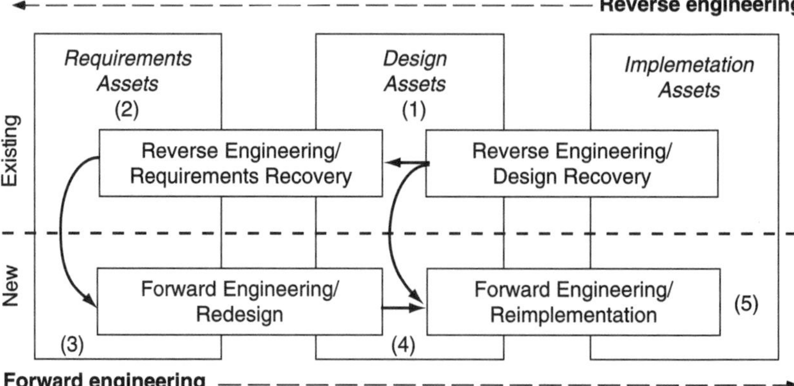

Figure 9.1

The Systems Reengineering Model. (Adapted from Chikofsky & Cross, 1990.)

starts with the physical "as-is" situation—how the data is currently stored. That is abstracted to the logical "as-is" level, giving insight into the business rules and processes that made the data the way it was to start. The requirements that go into the SR effort inform the logical "to-be" square in Figure 9.2, and those are in turn broken down into technical specifications for the specific data store, as the physical "to-be."

While Figure 9.2 shows how the process should be executed, Figure 9.3 shows the way that it is often done. This process skips directly from physical "as-is" to physical "to-be," jumping over the logical portions of the engineering effort. This is a problem for two reasons. First, since the logical components are where the business processes reside that the system is supposed to support, doing SR in this way misses the connection between SR and BPR. Second, since physical structures are often optimized for technical and platform reasons that have nothing to do with the system, moving straight from one physical specification to the next is simply hard for both business users and technical knowledge workers to understand because of the technical details that are not related to the system's real requirements.

SR is the technical component of overall reengineering efforts. The business and strategic component is what we will discuss next—business process reengineering.

Business Process Reengineering

The area of business process reengineering, or BPR, is a bit stickier than straight systems reengineering. Business processes are the procedures and methods that people within organizations follow in order to get a particular job done. For example, if a company acts as a distributor of a

Figure 9.2

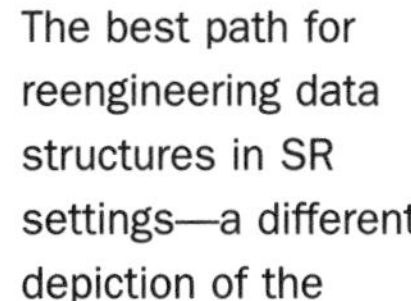

The best path for reengineering data structures in SR settings—a different depiction of the model shown previously in this book.

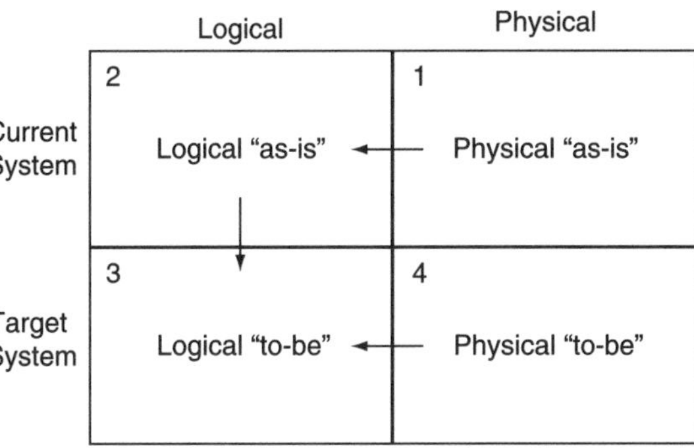

Figure 9.3

The incorrect way that some SR efforts reengineer data structures.

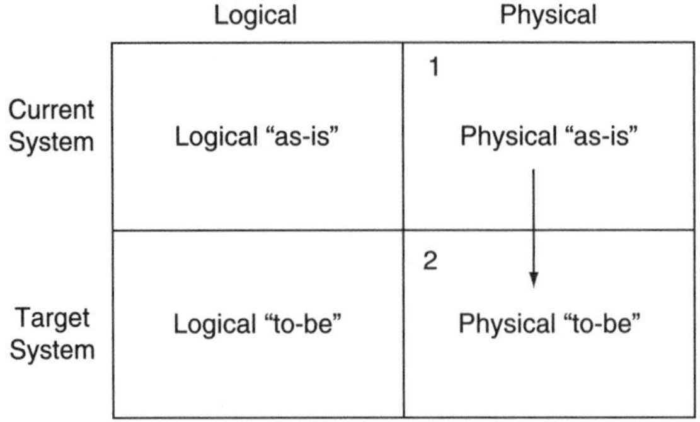

particular product, the process of selling the product might include numerous other processes, from gathering customer information, to packing the product into a crate and shipping it out, to making sure that invoices and returns are handled properly. The canonical definition for BPR is provided by Hammer and Champy (1993), who put it this way:

> Business process reengineering is the fundamental rethinking and radical redesign of business processes to achieve dramatic improvements in critical, contemporary measures of performance, such as cost, quality, service, and speed.

Business processes and their associated reengineering tasks are often difficult to get a handle on because they involve internal politics and social dynamics. These concerns arise as a result of the fact that ultimately a business process is something that will affect the daily jobs of many people, and support a specific and vital function of the organization.

Given these business processes, another definition for BPR would be the act of examining how information and other assets move through the organization, and optimizing that flow for a particular characteristic. Maybe that characteristic is overall delivery speed, total number of employees involved, cost of the entire process, or some other metric, as Hammer and Champy were alluding to in their definition. The core idea is that the organization is changing the way it does business in a particular area.

The four main phases of BPR are composed of specific tasks shown in Figure 9.4. These phases are described by associated process outcomes. BPR-related terms include activity modeling, business process improvement, industrial engineering, and reinvention.

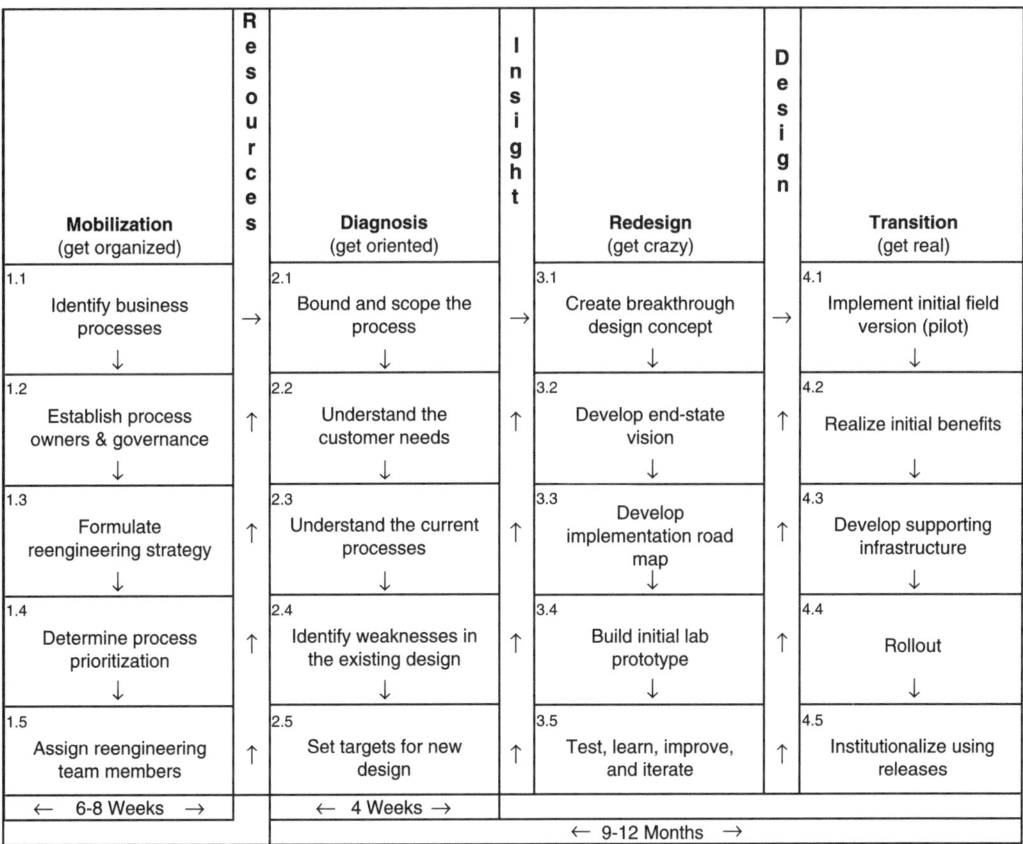

Figure 9.4

BPR as a process (Adapted from Hammer and Champy 1993.)

While BPR is a great conceptual idea, the way it has been implemented has in some cases been fraught with problems. Business process reengineering has all too often proceeded in a manner similar to the following:

1. A business process engineering team is put together for a purpose whose scope is not as specific as it should be.
2. The BPR team spends a lot of time thinking up the blue-sky scenario: complete integration, with perfectly functioning systems in coordinated support of newly created business processes.

3. The BPR team then goes to IT and requests the construction of the system that they envision. The IT department correctly tells them that the system requested is either impossible, or would take such exorbitant amounts of time and money that it is unrealistic.
4. The BPR effort comes to a grinding halt.

These problems tend to occur when a BPR effort is not grounded in what is technically feasible, and when there is not enough active interaction between SR and BPR efforts. Given active communication, SR experts can inform BPR workers of realistic options, as well as present new ideas that come as a result of system capabilities. What this hints at is the relationship between the two separate branches of reengineering, which is covered next.

The Relationship Between SR and BPR

SR and BPR are both part of the larger concept of reengineering because they are in many ways two sides of the same coin. Since information systems are primarily built for the purpose of supporting a particular business function, the systems within an organization are completely intertwined with the business processes. This means that when a BPR effort is undertaken, it will impact the systems that supported the old process. Likewise, when a systems reengineering project is started, it will have an effect on the business process that it supported.

There is a synergistic dependence between systems reengineering and BPR. What this means is that many reengineering efforts require situations where the overall effort is dependent on synergies resulting from successful BPR/SR integration. The noun *synergy* is defined as "the interaction of two or more agents or forces so that their combined effect is greater than the sum of their individual effects" in the *American Heritage English Dictionary*. The term *synergistic dependence* illustrates both the interdependency between BPR and SR efforts, as well as their mutual dependence on IT in order to successfully deliver change that is greater than what could be accomplished incrementally. Situations are defined as synergistically dependent if they require successful integration of both BPR and SR in order to be economically feasible.

The synergistic dependence of SR and BPR gives rise to an interesting point: efforts that cooperate may enjoy fruits that exceed the sum of the separate labors, but efforts that do *not* communicate may end up overlapping and canceling each other out, leading to a return that is less than the sum of the separate labors.

At this point, we have discussed the definition and background of reengineering. We will next take a look at exactly why reengineering has become so popular, and how business decision makers have embraced it financially.

How XML + DM Facilitates Reengineering Efforts

Fortunately, we have already presented much of the material required to tie XML technologies to reengineering efforts. Examine your reengineering projects with an eye for how XML-based technologies can play a role in developing solutions to your reengineering-related challenges. Reengineering is often based on working with disruptive technologies, such as in the classic example of businesses changing their processes to allow for the distribution of information to clients and suppliers via the world wide web, when it first came along. Disruptive technologies themselves are things that change the dynamic of a particular business so much that the original rules no longer apply. XML does just this in the realm of data understanding and management. Reengineering efforts frequently focus on helping a business adapt to a specific disruptive technology. These technologies cause large disruptions, and the radical change that reengineering provides is suited to helping a business to correspondingly change direction. XML has immediate involvement with reengineering in a number of ways, including the following:

- Since XML began to enjoy widespread use, it has found its way into many systems, giving the owners of those systems competitive advantages. Reengineering efforts going on within organizations are an attempt to respond to this disruption.
- An existing reengineering effort that addresses a specific business problem unrelated to XML may all the same choose to involve XML. Because XML is somewhat of a departure from the normal way of doing things, it piggybacks perfectly onto reengineering efforts, when substantive changes need to be made anyway.
- It allows connectivity that we have not had before; information appears in multiple places at once; it allows us to perform data-structure transformation based on semantic understanding

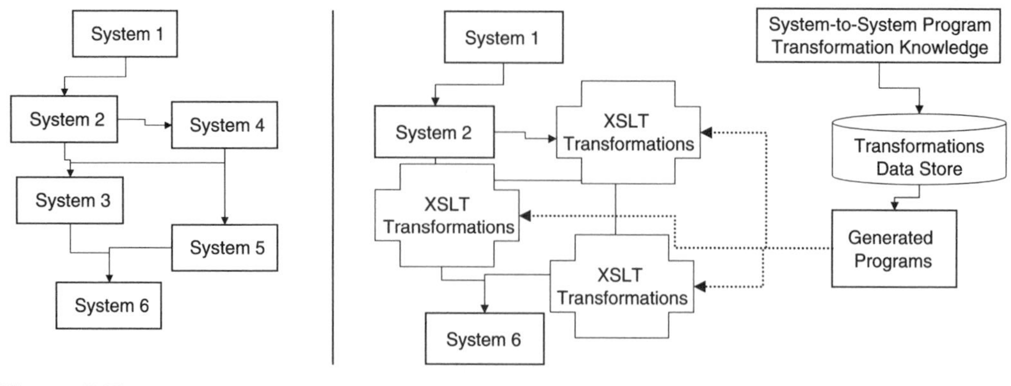

Figure 9.5

Left, system flow chart before reengineering; right, replacing three existing systems with XSLT "programs" generated from databases of XML transformations.

(different definitions for the same term), managing greater levels of complexity with data transformation.

- Reengineering is based on working with disruptive technologies. Data can be stored in a warehouse, etc. When doing warehousing, RF tags are now used to indicate where the item is instead of having to go find it. Reengineering takes advantage of new technologies like XML, not just at the technical systems level, but at the business level as well.
- If systems are changed to XML transformations, spaghetti code is replaced by XML. Systems can now talk to each other in ways that they could not before. This is working XML as a disruptive technology into the existing systems. We can now perform functions with the systems cooperating as a result of the integration, which we could not do before.

Business process engineering should go hand in hand with reengineering, and XML should be a component of all reengineering activities. XML should form the basis for part of the reengineering vocabulary—defining what facts can be obtained regarding the problem domain and the mapping between that and the business terminology used by the subject matter experts. To better understand the effect that XML can have on reengineering, consider the situation illustrated in Figure 9.5. The ability to develop a transformation

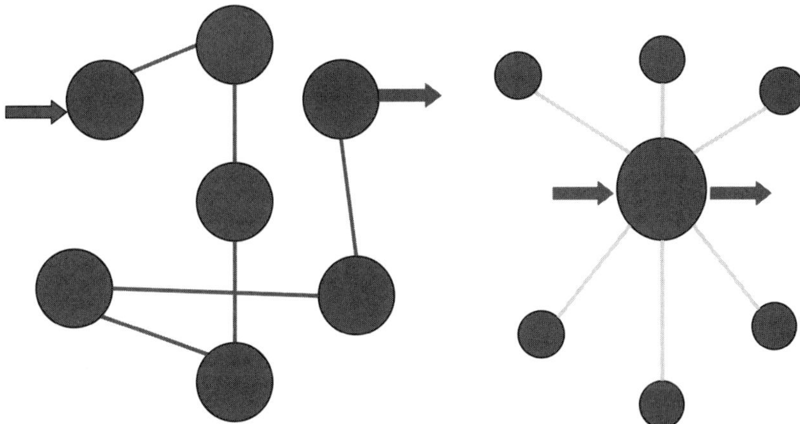

Figure 9.6

Business value of portals, transforming from surf-and-seek to focused, habitual, portal-based access. (Adapted from Lanham, 2001.)

replacement to Systems 3, 4, and 5 based in XML creates spillover into related business process areas. Consider how better control over information delivery might be used to support various business processes.

In some scenarios, the organization in question was able to use XML-based portals to support knowledge workers as they

- Increase business throughput by accomplishing more tasks in the same period of time, without the need for additional people or infrastructure
- Eliminate single points of failure by weeding out redundancies and inefficiencies by integrating people and getting everyone on the same page
- Anticipate business variances by delivering a heads-up display of leading indicators. This helps anticipate customer complaints, while regional and seasonal down trends can be identified and addressed immediately*

Figure 9.6 shows how the portal can dramatically affect the flow, and more importantly, the habit of information access within organizations. While project specifics may vary, hopefully you can see how good understanding of this material is key to exploiting potential reengineering opportunities.

*Adapted from Stephens, 2001.

Chapter Summary

Reengineering is needed because competition in the global marketplace is getting leaner, and meaner. Many situations have arisen where companies have gone out of business because they could not compete given their overhead due to poor systems and business processes. Systems need to be revamped according to changing market realities. For example, the business intelligence needed to create or sustain a competitive advantage may require a serious reengineering effort on a system that stores information about customers. If that reengineering work is not done, the business intelligence cannot be provided, resulting in serious business consequences.

On the other hand, processes also need to be remodeled to create a situation in which resources are being used as efficiently as possible, and the whole organization runs quickly and smoothly. Organizations like your local Division of Motor Vehicles might be able to get away with having poor business processes that cause 2-week delays in issuing driver's licenses; they have no competition. Slow or incorrect business processes can get many organizations shut down due to violations of new legal mandates, such as Health Insurance Portability and Accountability Act (HIPAA) in the health care field, or put out of business by competitors who are more than willing to pick up the slack.

Many types of organizations out there have seen this, and have started to invest heavily in reengineering. The averages here are astounding—more than $100 million is invested on average per company, with more than 22% of their IT budgets going to reengineering efforts. For these companies, reengineering is not a niche topic, but rather a core part of their yearly spending and organizational development.

Large portions of budgets have been and are being applied to the issue of reengineering, and organizations are changing rapidly as a result. Over the past few years, a number of industries have begun to consolidate, in part due to the increasing efficiency they are squeezing out of their business operations because of reengineering efforts. The result is that in some cases only the large and the expert can survive in a particular market.

XML-based portals represent a sort of pinnacle in XML-based data engineering. Knowledge workers coming into the workforce expect information systems will be based on the good ideas abounding on the World Wide Web. Knowledge workers already know what to do with the web. Why not allow them to do it with your legacy applications?

Using an XML-based portal to integrate disparate applications requires implementation of the hub and spoke integration architecture. Creating a portal for a single but expensive to maintain legacy application might pay for the portal purchase and implementation with the legacy application redesigned as a web service. The key is to choose a few of the most troublesome applications and a few of the most interconnected and useful applications. Adding these to the portal can make very exciting business process changes possible. Everyone involved in the reengineering effort should be aware of the potential to supply services and information via the portal as they consider redesign options.* The marginal cost of adding subsequent data collections will decrease as the collection reaches a critical mass.

References

Chikofsky, E., & Cross, J. II (1990). Reverse engineering and design recovery: A taxonomy. *IEEE Software 7*(1): 13–17.

Finkelstein, C., & Aiken, P. H. (1998). *Building corporate portals using XML.* New York: McGraw-Hill.

Hammer, M., & Champy, J. (1993). *Reengineering the corporation.* New York: Harper Business.

Hodgson, L., & Aiken, P. H. (1998). Synergistic Dependence Between Analysis Techniques." *Information Systems Management.* Fall 1998, pp. 55-67.

Lanham, T. (2001). *Designing innovative enterprise portals and implementing them into your content strategies: Lockheed Martin's compelling case study.* Proceedings from the Web Content II: Leveraging Best-of-Breed Content Strategies meeting, San Francisco.

Stephens, R. (2001). Equilon enterprises case study. Proceedings from the Web Content II: Leveraging Best-of-Breed Content Strategies meeting, San Francisco.

*Adapted in part from Finkelstein and Aiken, 1998.

10

Networks of Networks, Metadata, and the Future

Introduction

In this chapter we will take a look at some of the trends that have been going on in industry and government related to the application of metadata, and how those trends might be extrapolated. First, we will look at current systems in use today that take advantage of metadata within the larger marketplace, and then discuss some of the systems that may emerge over time. It is not our intention to forecast the future, but to provide information on how gains that have already been realized might be logically extended to offer benefit for individual organizations as well as their associated industries as a whole.

One of the themes that run throughout this book is the idea that effective application of metadata requires looking at data assets from a higher level. Rather than inspecting how a particular system module operates, we instead look at how the modules within the system communicate and collaborate to get a job done. Instead of looking at particular data items being sent from one system to another, we talk about the overall structure of moving data between arbitrary platforms or applications by using the metadata. In this chapter, we take those same ideas and apply them first to organizations, then to industries, and then between industries.

The concepts presented in this chapter run the gamut of XML technologies. We will discuss XML used as a translation facility, a metadata-representation technology, a communication enabler, and an e-business helper. We will view the automated electronic marketplace from a high level, taking into account what XML has to offer. To start, though, let us take a look at issues of data understanding to frame the discussion.

A Different Understanding of Data and Its Metadata

Human brains think of things and remember things based on ideas that are connected to other ideas. For example, when someone mentions the Internal Revenue Service, it is much more likely that a person's personal tax return will come to mind than, say, a favorite beach spot, or metadata. This is due to the close connection of those concepts within people's brains. Artificial-intelligence researchers have known this for some time, and they often use a structure called a "semantic network" to represent human knowledge. Semantic networks are essentially a bunch of nodes in a graph connected by edges that represent relationships. For example, the concept of "travel" might be connected with "airplane," the concept of "mortgage" connected with "house," and so on.

People also use these semantic networks as ways of remembering and understanding things. For some, new information can be learned by creating an association between two items that is similar to an association between two other things that they already knew about. As an example, if someone were to tell you that an XML element is only a small and detachable part of a larger document, it might be easier to conceptualize and remember if you understood it in terms of a leaf being only a small and detachable part of a larger tree.

The way people think about concepts and how they organize their understanding affects how they perceive things, and their perceptions of what they can do with them. Some scholars believe that the words available in the language a person speaks dictate in part what they are capable of even thinking about.* Figure 10.1 provides a simple example of how a short list of items can be understood in three completely different ways, according to which method of understanding is used: categorization, abstraction, or pattern recognition. These same conceptual patterns apply

---

*This is referred to as the Sapir-Whorf hypothesis. For more information, see http://en.wikipedia.org/wiki/Sapir-Whorf_hypothesis

Figure 10.1

Different ways of understanding the same information.

Given a list of items: Mangos, Mandarins, Melons, Mushrooms, and Mustard Greens	
Categorization	There are two classes: Fruits and Vegetables
Abstraction	All of the items are plants!
Pattern Recognition	All of the items start with the letter 'M'!

to understanding of data. Each perspective is correct, but they may have relative advantages given the situation.

This idea is important to the realm of data and its management because how we understand the practice in part determines how we actually perform it. This is one reason why earlier chapters took pains to define the various terms related to XML and data management, most notably defining metadata as a use of data rather than a type of data itself. In this section, we want to take a look at an alternate way of understanding plain vanilla relational data. This is certainly not the only or best way to understand the data, but it provides another option and perspective. Alternate ways of thinking of the vital concepts in data management are important, because new advancements in the field will come as a result of new understandings and organizations of data, not simply because of new data.

Figure 10.2 shows the most commonly adopted view of regular tabular data. When we understand data in this way, we tend to see it as a collection of records that have particular attributes. The attributes, or "columns," in this table are thought of as properties of particular records, and not the other way around, which would be to say that data items in rows "belong" to the columns. This is a hugely useful way of looking at and conceptualizing data, and it has the great side effect of allowing the

Figure 10.2

A record-oriented perspective of plain tabular data.

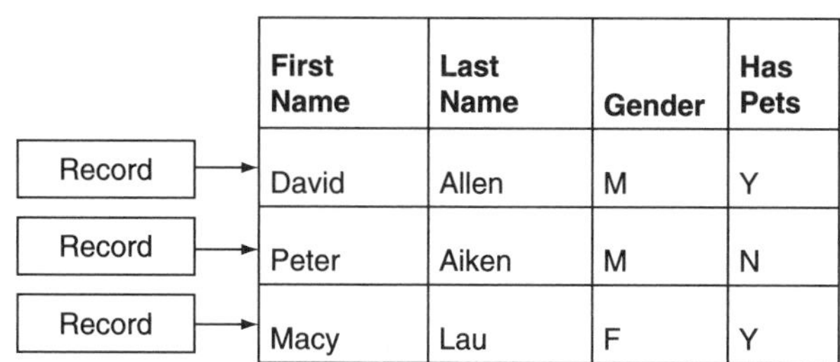

First Name	Last Name	Gender	Has Pets
David	Allen	M	Y
Peter	Aiken	M	N
Macy	Lau	F	Y

computer scientists of the world to write efficient applications that store, retrieve, and display data in this format. We are familiar with this understanding from our checkbook registers, paper account statements, and many other data-representation formats well outside the digital world.

Figure 10.3 provides a different viewpoint on the same data seen in Figure 10.2. Instead of viewing the data by rows, we look at it by the values contained in the various columns of the table, along with the relationships between those data items. The concept of the data "record" in Figure 10.3 simply serves to connect a collection of data items, paired with their metadata. For example, the fact "Peter" is paired with the context "First Name" to give it meaning, just as "Allen" is paired with the context "Last Name."

In the relational world, ideally a record would correspond to an instance of a particular entity. When entity-relationship diagrams are first created for the system, there are clearly defined entities such as "Customer." In practical implementations, however, logical entities are sometimes distributed among many tables and records for reasons of performance, accessibility, searchability, and a host of other technical considerations that have nothing to do with the way humans understand the data. The result is a situation where only someone who already knew something about the dataset would have a chance at interpreting what a particular row meant. In addition, it means that the cards are somewhat stacked against the human from the start, as the data is organized for the convenience of the machine, not the user. Logical models, complex CASE tools, and database-querying programs are just the tip of the iceberg of technologies that have been developed specifically to bridge this conceptual gap.

Figure 10.3

A different perspective on the same tabular data.

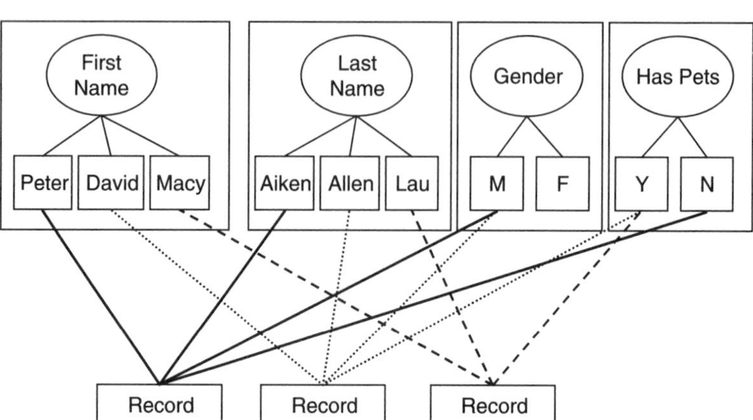

In Figure 10.3, the data is expressed in terms of its column definitions rather than its individual rows. This is not meant as an alternate suggestion for how to organize data inside of computers, but as a suggestion for how to understand what is already there. If the column definitions in Figure 10.2 were removed, one might not understand what was being expressed. On the other hand, if all of the data items in Figure 10.3 were removed, one might still be able to understand what the data structure was attempting to store. The difference between the two figures is simply a matter of perspective, and both perspectives have their pros and cons. Let us take a look at a few more positives to the representation seen in Figure 10.3.

- Since only unique values are represented, attached to their respective columns, just by glancing at a particular column definition (for example, "Gender"), we can see what the column's domain is—namely the values {"M," "F"} for "male" and "female." This alone is a tremendous advantage given the number of organizations that may not even know that their Boolean fields store "y," "1," and "t" to all mean "true," while using "n," "0," and "f" to mean "false."
- The data must be mentally organized and understood based on its context and metadata. By grouping the data and drawing the diagram as it is, we see that the metadata concepts take precedence over the individual data items. In many ways, this is as it should be, because data structures should have their own meaning, separate from the entity instances they hold. It usually is not advisable to generalize about the possible values of a particular entity based on its instances. For example, if all instances in a human resources database contain ages between 18 and 65, one cannot conclude that employees do not live past 65. On the other hand, some generalizations are possible if the metadata is understood. For example, age instances might range from 18 to 65, but if we understand that the column is storing age, we might generalize it to a wider range of possible values. Age acts as the metadata here because it provides context for our raw data, "18." If the field is understood to be an age, it might be generalized to allow values greater than 65, for instances where employees are older than 65.
- Like data is grouped with like data. From a record-oriented perspective, each record is a set of facts that must be properly associated with the context in order to get meaning. In Figure 10.3,

we see data as clusters of similar information, such as "Last Names," "Genders," and so on.

- Records are seen as relationships between facts. Some of the various facts share a common bond—they are all connected to a particular instance, which is different from saying that records share the common bond of all having the same column definitions. It makes further intuitive questions about the data possible, such as, "So if Macy Lau has a 'Has Pets' value of 'Y,' which other relationships have the same value?" Doesn't this seem more natural than telling a system to "Show me all records such that the 'Has Pets' field value is 'Y,' and then further restrict that set to the 'First Name' and 'Last Name' fields"?
- Updating data can be viewed as changing row relationships rather than actually modifying data. If Peter Aiken gets a dog, his record can be changed to point to "Y" in the "Has Pets" context rather than actually changing any data.

The drawback to the method of understanding data seen in Figure 10.3 is that computer systems are not built to quickly and efficiently dish out data in this manner. This is not to say that it is impossible; in fact, it is relatively straightforward. It just means that computers have been optimized to work with data in a particular way. When computing was young, it was done in this way because information could be quickly cataloged and retrieved in a time when computing resources were at an absolute premium. As prices have dropped and capacities skyrocketed, does it really make sense to understand data strictly in the same way as it was understood 30 years ago? With new computing capabilities comes the freedom to adopt new perspectives that are made possible only *because* of those new capabilities.

We have discussed at length the need for well-understood and well-architected data structures throughout the book. Since XML can so readily express metadata, the technology to represent data in different terms is already in the hands of data managers. Each data "understanding" and representation format will have its pros and cons, which must be carefully considered for the task at hand—hence the caveat that just because XML provides a method to represent data in alternate ways does not mean that it will do it for you, or that it is a good idea to represent data in that way to begin with.

The purpose here is to get the mental juices flowing and encourage new ways of thinking about challenges that are not new. This is the issue at the crux of human creativity and innovation. In the spirit of understanding new ideas in terms of concepts that we *already* understand, we will next present the Internet, its structure and growth model, as a metaphor for the understanding of systems communication within organizations.

The Internet Metaphor

The evolution of organizational data systems, and communication between them, is in many ways very similar to the development of the public Internet. There are differences between the two evolutionary paths, but where there are similarities, it is extremely helpful to look at the historical evolution of the Internet and to take lessons from it about what worked and what did not work. Doing this means that we may be able to avoid reinventing a solution to a problem that has already been solved within the context of the Internet. In technology, we should make a constant effort to reuse the experience and knowledge that others have created for us, rather than endlessly reinventing the wheel.

The Internet is often described as a "network of networks," and can be viewed at many different levels. Often, the average person does not understand just how many layers of complexity are transparently traversed each time a web page is fetched, or an email is successfully delivered. Within each organization, there is a computer network that shuttles information from PC to PC, and allows data to move in and out of the public Internet, usually through some type of firewall or other security provisioning system. Just looking at the organizational level, we can see that there is an entire network that may be either quite simple or enormously complex, depending on the size of the organization and the network topology.

But when information leaves the organizational network, it moves into the network of the organization's Internet service provider. That provider, too, has its network, which may encompass dozens or hundreds of clients. The purpose of the ISP, which acts as a network capacity provider, is to provide a stable uplink to the wider Internet. Once information moves out of the capacity provider's network, it may go through yet another larger provider's network, before moving onto what is referred to as a "backbone"—a high-speed connection that joins major providers with one another. Once across the backbone, information may be routed through a number of other providers' networks before finally being delivered to the network of the organization whose web page you requested.

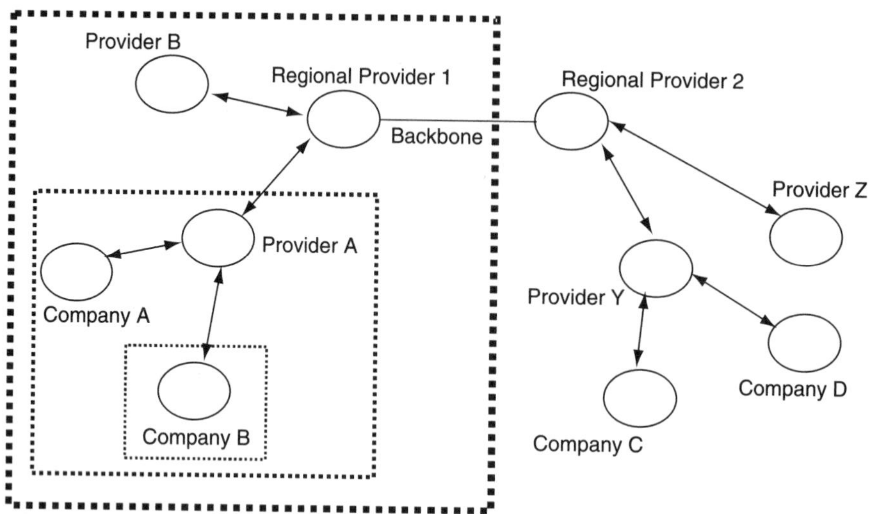

Figure 10.4

A simplified "network of networks" model of the Internet.

In this diagram, we see how the Internet is composed of a "network of networks." In order for Company B to communicate with Company D, it must send information through Provider A, Regional Provider 1, Regional Provider 2, Provider Y, and finally to Company D. The three dashed boxes in the diagram refer to three levels of networks. The innermost box shows the boundaries of Company B's network, which might consist of hundreds of PCs, along with a complement of servers and other equipment. Provider A has a larger network, consisting of Company A, Company B, and probably many other clients as well, each of whom has its own internal network. The Regional Provider in turn has a larger network that comprises a number of different providers, as well as all of the networks beneath them.

The point of illustrating this "network of networks" concept is to show the overall architecture of how things connect with one another. The actual public Internet is much larger; it would not be strange for information to jump through 16 different distinct points simply to make a one-way trip to another machine elsewhere. This Internet structure is already in place for organizations. It provides an easy network layer on top of which to build complex applications, and is so ubiquitous at this point that it is frequently taken for granted. The goal here is merely to illustrate how the architecture of the Internet applies to data and metadata interchange between companies and industries.

Internal Organizational Structure

Within organizations of any size, frequently the enterprise actually consists of a number of interrelated subsystems. For example, there might an HR department with a corresponding information system, a sales department, an accounting and finance department, and a manufacturing department.

Figure 10.5 takes a simple example to illustrate how a number of different departments with their own information systems might interoperate and share information critical to the enterprise. The way in which they do it, for the purposes of this discussion, is not very important. Whether the organization uses a hub and spoke model, or more of a point-to-point model (as illustrated in this diagram), the fact remains the same that information is being sent from system to system according to a set of business rules and processes. We can see that Company A clearly has to create and maintain this network within the organization in order to achieve certain goals.

Internal Organizational Data Interchange and the Internet Model

There are several elements of this diagram that relate nicely to the Internet model. Of course, each individual organization will have its own way of

Figure 10.5

A simplified view of an organization's data interchange needs.

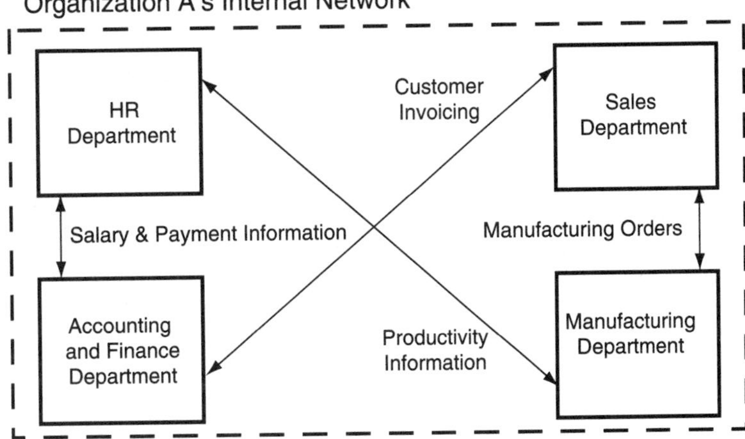

organizing its systems, networking them together, and sharing information. This is similar to the low-level networks out there on the public Internet. Some might use Ethernet; others might use token ring networks, or still other types of physical organization. In terms of the way machines on the network are named, there are also differences. Some organizations name each of their servers after cartoon characters, actual department names, or use some other naming convention. Information exchanged internally on the network is of no interest to parties outside of the network, and in fact should remain confidential. In these ways, the data interchange among information systems within organizations is very similar to the organization of local networks within the larger Internet.

These systems of internal data communication within organizations have of course been in place for years. Whether they were implemented as a messy collection of stovepipe interfaces from one system to another, or a more flexible XML-based hub model that utilizes metadata interchange, the need for these types of systems is so great that they have existed in a number of different forms for almost as long as organizations have found themselves dealing with multiple information systems. The technology to address this need is currently in existence, and widely deployed, although different organizations reap varying benefits depending on what type of architecture they have in place, and how well they use it.

The Use of XML-Based Metadata

Generally, when looking at communication between any two arbitrary entities, it makes more sense to inspect the language that the two speakers are using, and the concepts that are considered valid in a "conversation," rather than the actual specifics of what is being said. In human conversation, we are all aware of which concepts are understandable to the person we are speaking to, and we know what type of language we need to use when we address a particular person. Computer systems do not have the complexity or intelligence of human minds, but still share some common characteristics. If the language spoken among the systems is XML, then we know that most systems will either already be able to speak that language, or can be adapted to speak it. System metadata is roughly the same as a definition of what concepts are considered valid in the conversation. If System A wants to transfer data to System B, it may choose to send the data along with metadata that "explains" what the data means to System B. This is similar to when a human speaker is giving information to

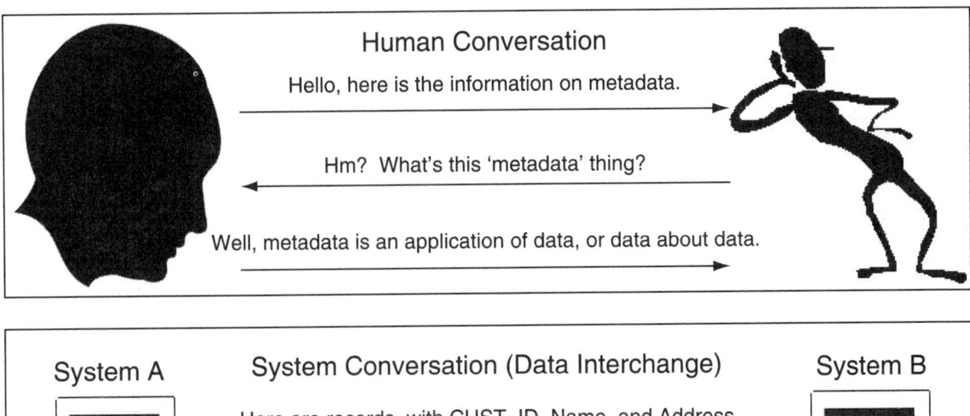

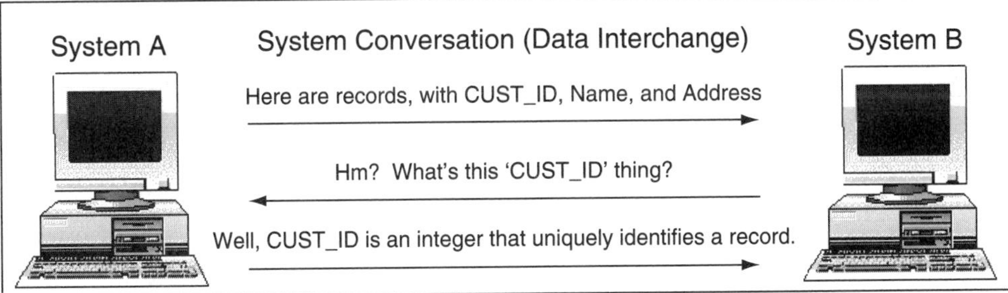

Figure 10.6

Comparing metadata conversations between systems and people.

another person. Occasionally, the person may stop to explain a particular word or concept used in the conversation, so that both parties understand what is being said. Just as this is done in human conversations, metadata can also be sent back and forth between systems that essentially explains the data being sent—in other words, what is "being said" in the conversation between the two parties.

One of the unique capabilities that humans have in conversation that systems have *not* had (at least until now) is this ability to explain concepts that are being discussed in the conversation. This means that at the beginning of the conversation, only one party understands the concept, but by the end of the conversation, both people understand the concept and can now use it. This exchange of information about the conversation is what makes humans capable of learning. Machines cannot currently learn in the way that humans do, but systems can be made "smarter" by exchanging metadata. This makes them able to discuss and explain concepts that are being discussed in their system conversations. In this diagram, we see that one person offers the other information about metadata, but needs to first explain what metadata really is. In the system conversation example, the same thing takes place. System A tries to send customer records to System B, but System B needs a bit of clarification as to what exactly System A means when it refers to "CUST_ID." Because System A is aware of the metadata related to the data it is working with, it can tell System B that "CUST_ID" uniquely identifies a record, or in other words, it acts as a key field for the data being sent.

Looking at system communication from a high level leaves out a lot of details. How exactly will these systems communicate when it gets down to the nitty gritty? The metadata is the answer to this question. Sending metadata along with the data allows the systems to reconcile each of their ideas about what different items are, and what they mean.

Industry Structure

Now that we have taken a look at the internal organizational structure of a particular organization, we will move up to the next level and inspect the interrelationships within a particular industry. For the purpose of this example, we will take a look at the chemical industry. Within industries, a lot of data interchange often takes place. Certainly plenty of competition exists within industries, but there is frequently quite a bit of collaboration as well, depending on the nature of the goods or services being offered.

Industry lines also may blur to include other organizations that may not strictly be considered a part of the industry, but nonetheless provide a given service to many organizations *within* the industry, and are thus very deeply involved in its functioning. For example, many credit card companies frequently consult the same credit reporting bureaus in order to pull credit reports for applicants, or to build lists of potential customers who will receive solicitations in the mail. In this case, the credit-reporting bureaus are not strictly in the credit card business, but provide a service that is used so frequently by the organizations within the industry that any map of the industry would be incomplete without including them.

Regardless of which organizations are considered a part of the industry, the fact remains that within any industry, there are a number of parties that constantly exchange data to the benefit of all of the parties involved. That type of architecture might look similar to Figure 10.7, which lays out a simplified model of the chemical industry.

Figure 10.7

Industry organization—relationships between organizations within the chemical industry.

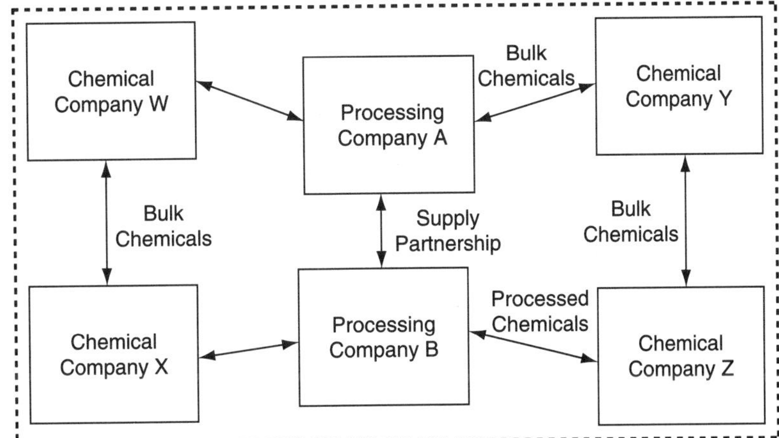

This is not meant to be an exhaustive list of the relationships that exist among companies in the chemical industry, but a few things are widely known about how companies interrelate:

1. Some companies sell raw chemicals to others in large amounts for processing.
2. Processed chemicals are bought and sold among companies, for subsequent sale.
3. Supply partnerships exist, both among larger and smaller firms, for filling specific orders from customers.
4. Given that chemicals are commodities, companies are interested in the pricing and volume structure of competitors.

Traditionally, the connections between organizations within an industry have almost always been point to point. The different standards and procedures used by each company have made it difficult to consider any other way, since often the only organization that would be able to standardize the interfaces between organizations within an industry would be one with a huge amount of market force and the ability to dictate standards and interfaces to others within the industry. As a result of the typically point to point interfaces that have existed, all of the pitfalls and maintenance burdens of the stovepipe interconnection model have been experienced by organizations that need to communicate with one another. Frequently, any problems that might arise in these communication systems require "out of band" communication—that is, manual human intervention by way of a telephone call, email, or fax from one organization to the other, attempting to iron out a problem due to failure of the automated system. This "out of band" communication causes delays, and costs extra resources.

XML and Intra-Industry Communication

With the advent of XML and a number of standards related to data interchange, the landscape changes quite a bit. Previously, it was difficult for one company within an industry to dictate the intercommunication technology, since a particular technology often implied a potentially huge investment in software and hardware for each of the organizations within the industry that wanted to participate. XML, on the other hand, is a platform-agnostic technology that is implemented by dozens of different software packages in many different arenas. For a company to initiate a policy of communicating externally with XML wherever possible no longer dictates to its communication partner what technology or investment the partner must make in order to participate. This is one of the core benefits of so-called "open standards": They can be implemented by anyone, anywhere, on any platform.

Since XML standards are publicly created and modified, organizations within industries also do not have to worry about one particular company seizing control of the standard and manipulating it to its own benefit. XML technology puts all organizations, small and large, on equal footing with regard to intercommunication.

As we've seen earlier, a communication hub for the chemical industry using XML is not a pipe dream; it is a reality, as are the sizeable benefits being derived by the member organizations. These systems are not in place for all industries, however. As with the early stages of the Internet, the investment for the first few industries that go down this road is potentially quite large. Consequently, the industries that have adopted this type of organization are typically those in which the amount of communication between organizations is quite large, or has traditionally been quite costly. Given the way these systems have been built, they also initially required large buy-ins from potential subscribers or members. This is similar to the beginnings of the Internet where the investment required to buy a data link was quite major.

The way that the Internet grew and evolved from this point is relevant to this discussion. When the Internet was quite small, data links were expensive and rare. As the Internet began to grow, two things happened to the investment that was required for organizations and individuals to connect. First, as the network grew, the price of data links dropped as more companies entered the market and began to compete to provide links to organizations. Second, the ISP, or "Internet Service Provider," arose—since individuals were requiring data links to their own homes, companies called ISPs would buy a data link themselves, and would sell their capacity to individual users over slower lines. At first, this was in the form of dial-up modem access; later it morphed and grew into the broadband industry. So the cost of connection to the Internet decreased over time because the mean cost of capacity decreased, and because of the creation and growth of companies who subdivided and resold Internet access.

Industry-wide communication mechanisms may likely evolve in a similar way. For example, right now the number of different options that organizations have for connecting to industry-wide networks is somewhat limited, but will probably grow dramatically as organizational interest and recognition of the benefits of these networks increase. This is analogous to the mean cost of access to the Internet decreasing with time. In addition, there have already been efforts made by providers of industry communication solutions (such as Envera mentioned earlier) to create web front-ends for smaller companies to communicate on the networks, when they may not have an entire back-office system dedicated to industry communication. This is analogous to the subdivision of network access—in this case, data interchange capabilities are increasingly being provided to the lower end of the market.

One of the interesting aspects of the Internet and industry communications is the relationship between growth and value of the network—the larger the number of participants on the network, the greater the value of the network for all parties involved. This fascinating point means that much to the luck of the early adopters, the value of their initial and ongoing investments increases with each subsequent addition to the network, since the number of potential clients and partners that they can communicate with in a standard way is enhanced with each new participant. Also, at some point, these industry networks may reach "critical mass," much as the public Internet has. Critical mass is the point at which the benefits of participation in the network are large enough that buying into the network becomes almost required in order to keep pace within the industry. Can you imagine what your organization would be like if it had no network connectivity internally or externally? The potential benefits of having an industry-wide automated system for data interchange are almost as large.

Inter-Industry Structure

We've inspected two different levels so far. First, we took a look at the intercommunication of data and metadata going on within organizations. Then we looked at how industries as a whole often communicate, how XML fits into that communication, and how hubs are currently being built and used that enable this communication. Finally, we will look at one more level of architecture—the exchange of data between industries. Internal organizational communication is like a network. Communication within an industry can be equated to a network of networks. Given this pattern, it is easy to look at inter-industry structure as yet another network of networks, namely, a network that connects all of the different networks comprising various industries. This is the last level that we will look at, and completes the analogy of organizational data interchange systems to the Internet architecture. Looking back at the original figure laying out the organization of the Internet, industry networks can be thought of as providers, while regional providers represent networks of industries.

It is easy to see the potential utility of interindustry data exchange networks. Just as organizations need to communicate with others in their industry, they must also be able to communicate with other industries. The financial department might like to set up an automated payment system that ultimately needs to communicate not only with the company's bank, but with a supplier in another industry as well. Maybe the sales department needs regular data extracts from a marketing company that creates targeted lists of customers for companies. The manufacturing division needs to communicate with shipping companies to ensure timely delivery of goods to the market. Organizations are not islands in a stream, but interdependent members of a larger economic network. More efficient communication within that network benefits everyone involved and allows enterprises to focus more resources on their mission and business.

In Figure 10.8, we can see that any company listed can communicate with any other company via the network connections that are in place. Chemical companies can fill their shipping needs by communicating automatically with shipping companies via metadata interchange, and at the same time negotiate and deliver payment for shipping through the financial services companies in yet another related industry network. Similarly,

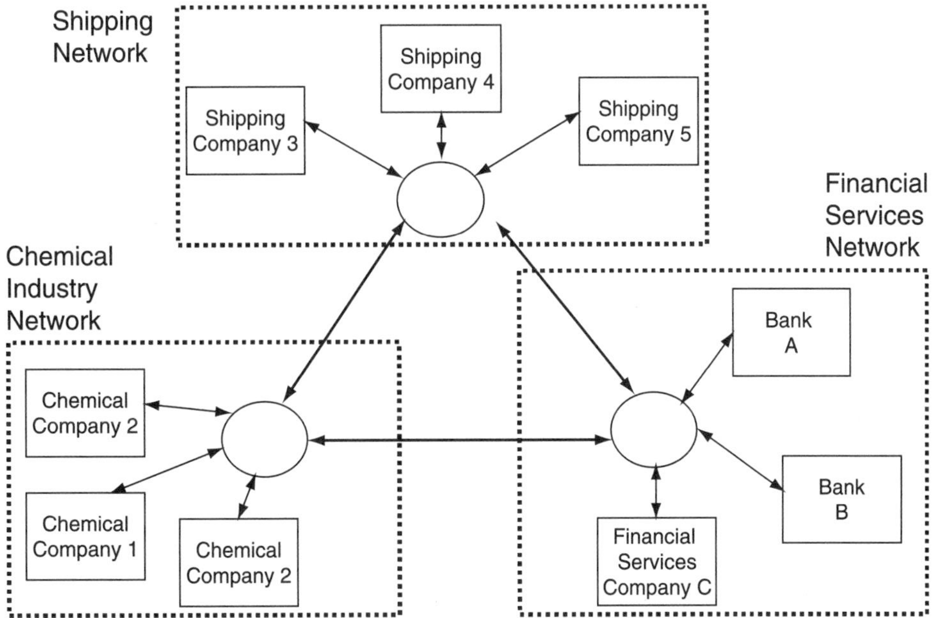

Figure 10.8

An illustration of inter-networked industries—a network of networks.

banks can attend to customer needs automatically, and shipping companies can work to get the right goods to the right place at the right time.

This discussion of connecting industries with automated systems is one interesting exception to the ongoing comparison of data interchange systems architecture to the Internet architecture. The Internet strangely grew from the inside out; in its early days, it was a research project sponsored by the government that connected a number of universities around the nation. As the Internet grew, networks were added on the outer edges of the system. It certainly is true that portions of the Internet were created by connecting local networks that had existed previously, but for the most part, the core of the Internet was created first and later grew outward. This happened as sites individually recognized the benefit of being part of the entire network. On the other hand, organizational networks have existed for some time, and industry networks are currently growing. This means that inter-industry connectivity is a process of networks growing from the outside in, which is the opposite of how the Internet grew.

Challenges Related to Connecting Industries

Of the three levels that we have looked at so far, two already have concrete implementations in the marketplace. Industry-wide networks exist, and though in their infancy, are growing. Automated communication facilities have existed within organizations for a long time. In contrast to these two levels, the level of automated inter-industry communication has not really been determined. There are some partial and limited examples of data-interchange facilities between industries, but generally they are just that—partial and limited. In practice, these are legacy communication systems not built around XML, but often constructed using arcane, binary-only representations of data that are only understandable with the aid of a 30-pound reference manual, and a few months of spare time. Here we will briefly address some of the challenges that stand in the way of creating inter-industry communication mechanisms, as well as potential solutions to these issues where possible.

Who Drives the Process?

When discussing the creation of industry-wide data interchange networks, we talked about the issue of deciding which organization will specify the data interchange standard. This problem can be best resolved by adopting XML as the core standard for interchange, rather than one organization's binary-only proprietary format. But the issue gets amplified between industries, because not only must an interchange standard be agreed upon, someone actually has to drive the process.

Industry trade groups exist that partially guide this process, to the extent that a trade group is able to delve into issues of data management on behalf of its constituents. Looking back, we know that networks generally are organized in either a point to point fashion, or in a hub and spoke architectural model. If industry communication were to be organized in a point to point fashion, there would have to be broad industry consensus on how exactly that industry would network with other industries. On the other hand, if a hub and spoke model is used (as illustrated in the earlier inter-industry communication figure), the hub operator is in a position of being able to come to an agreement with the operator of a different industry's hub about how data interchange will take place. Once those agreements are put into place, the hub operator need only notify its members of the required metadata and XML format to communicate with the foreign industry and its members; the hub manages the rest of the complexity. There certainly are architectural trade-offs associated with using a hub and spoke model as opposed to a point-to-point model, and these tradeoffs will inevitably be examined in detail by each industry as the need arises.

How Do Messages Move Between Industry Networks?

Different industries are separated by quite a bit of distance in terms of the way they do business, and how their practices differ. In order for them to communicate effectively, it is critical that effort be put in on the front end toward creating a flexible metadata model for information interchange. What types of metadata are required on either end of the connection?

Once the metadata requirements are determined, there is still the matter of actually converting XML messages flowing through the network into the appropriate format. Fortunately, the XML component architecture provides a number of tools for accomplishing this. Specifically, XSLT documents can be embedded inside of larger XML "exchange units" that outline methods by which one format of XML can be converted into another. This allows each industry hub to speak its own version of XML, while remaining interoperable with other hubs that prefer different "dialects" of XML. All that is required is that both hubs are aware of the message format, and how to apply XSLT documents to other XML documents. Hub operators then publish the descriptions of the required metadata elements to each of their network participants, and once implemented, each of the participants will then be able to communicate with anyone in the foreign industry (Figure 10.9).

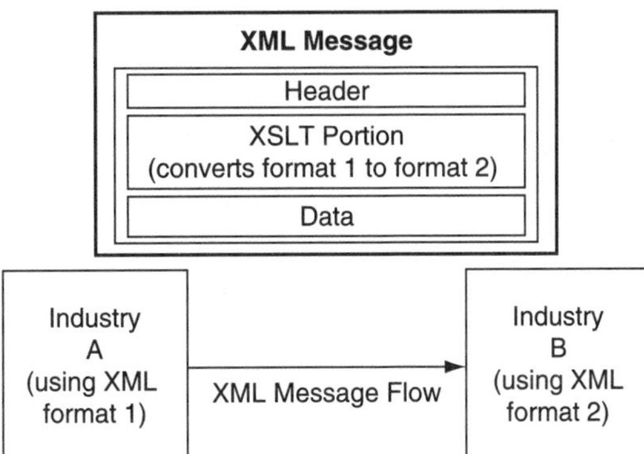

Figure 10.9

Converting XML messages between formats.

Bringing It Together: Observations About the Internet Metaphor

To recap several points that have been made at various levels in this chapter, there are a number of similarities between data interchange systems and the Internet.

1. At the local level, these systems are heterogeneous. On the Internet, the topology of your local network is irrelevant. As long as it is built on open protocols that are well understood, data interchange is possible.
2. Given XML architectural components (including, but not limited to, XSLT) it is possible to reconcile different XML formats to enable communication. Just like on the Internet, however, information cannot be added as it moves through the network, only modified. This necessitates prior agreement on metadata items that will be exchanged, just as Internet communication requires agreement on certain metadata parameters.
3. The Internet functions as a network of networks, and provides a pathway between systems. Organizational data interchange networks and industry networks do the same. As with the Internet, the complexity of the various steps from machine to machine—the "hops" that happen in the middle—should be hidden from the end-user systems.
4. The cost of entry into the Internet was high at first, and dropped as more participants came onto the network, and as the technology became more common. The initial cost of entry into industry networks was also high, and is currently decreasing for the same reasons.
5. The benefit to participants of both data exchange systems and the Internet is proportional to the number of participants in the network.

The primary difference between the Internet and the growth of these systems is that the Internet for the most part grew from the inside out, while current systems seem to be following the trend of growing from the outside in. The main architectural implication of this difference is that when things grow from the outside in, they often contain a number of different standards that must be reconciled before networks can be connected, while systems that grow from the inside out often standardize on one system (in the case of the Internet, TCP/IP) and require all new entrants to at least be conversant in that standard before they can initially connect.

Conclusion

There are certainly no guarantees in terms of how systems will evolve in the future. "Essentially everyone claiming to predict the future is lying (the honest ones write science fiction)."* This chapter is not meant to act as a roadmap for the way data interchange systems will grow and change. It does, however, offer a series of ideas that represent the underpinnings of how current systems work, and how new systems might grow around them in order to extend architectural ideas that are already implemented on smaller scales (such as within organizations or industries). The similarities between the architectural principles that go into the creation of automated data exchange networks and the public Internet should not be overlooked. Wherever possible, practitioners should look to other systems to extract knowledge and experience from the successes and failures of others.

Another point to take from this chapter is that the way in which a challenge is understood heavily affects how you will attack the problem. By comparing a new problem to one that is similar and has already been solved successfully, techniques and architectural ideas that worked once may be effectively recycled. As for these successful techniques, the saying goes, "If it ain't broke, then don't fix it." Why reinvent the wheel?

The investments that would be required to put admittedly elaborate systems such as these in place are substantial, but so are the potential benefits. All organizations, regardless of their industry or business, are constantly under pressure to streamline and to minimize the resources that are allocated to business processes that are not part of their core mission. Standardized, flexible, automated data interchange systems are a potential boon for any organizations that move toward implementing them for internal and external communication.

*Eric Allman, creator of the popular email server software 'Sendmail'.

11

Expanded Data-Management Scope

Introduction

Data management has been largely focused on the data at rest problem and not on the data movement problem so well articulated by Francis Hsu (2003). Only recently has anyone collected statistics on the movement of data and the associated costs (e.g., Zachman and IDC). It turns out that we may have been solving the wrong problem all along. If we consider DM to be only focused on management of data at rest as per our data modeling, we may be neglecting a far more important focus—how to manage data in motion, since the nature of the most important information is that it is constantly changing to reflect the business situation.

Now that we have seen the role XML plays as an enabling technology, it is easy to see that this is a most opportune time to work in information and data management. With the technologies at our command, we are able to create automated data management facilities to a greater degree than ever before. The previous chapters have indicated many of the existing technology directions that XML can significantly enhance (reengineering, EAI, metadata recovery, etc.). This last chapter will cover how XML actually expands the overall role of data management. While DM is a critical business support operation, we also find that it can have strategic implications for business.

Unfortunately, one significant aspect of the post-dot.com bust is that job security and the technology boom are things of the past. For many years, banks in New York City could lure experienced technical workers with the promise of more "causal dress" days. Those days are long gone and "lean" would be the appropriate adjective for the operations of the very same companies today. Inspired by the effectiveness argument advanced in "IT Doesn't Matter," by Nicholas Carr (2003) (see Figure 11.1), organizations are unwilling to support data management efforts that have solely a policy focus—instead, they want to see data management efforts that provide a strategic advantage, or solve newly arising business challenges.

For years, this has been the old joke:

Question: During cost cutting, how does a manager decide whether a report is used by anyone?

Answer: Stop generating the report and wait to see if anyone complains.

HBR
FROM THE HARVARD BUSINESS REVIEW
OnPoint
"The greatest IT risk is overspending — putting your company at a cost disadvantage. The lesson? Make IT management boring. Instead of aggressively seeking an edge through it, manage IT's costs and risks with a frugal hand and a pragmatic eye — despite any renewed hyper about its strategic value. Worrying about what might go wrong isn't glamorous, but it's smart business now."
ARTICLE
The smartest way to invest in IT today?
Less may be more.
IT Doesn't Matter
by Nicholas G. Carr
Harvard Business Review May 2003
Lessons
1) Spend less
2) Follow, don't lead
3) Focus on risks, not opportunities
22 - http://datablueprint.com
© Copyright9/3/03by Data Blueprint - all rights reserved!

Figure 11.1

Harvard Business Review article, "IT Doesn't Matter," by Nicholas Carr.

While elder information processing professionals laugh nervously, we acknowledge the wisdom of the tactic. Unfortunately, it is being used in a newer, more relevant sense.

Some managers cannot quite figure out what those folks in "the Data Department" do to contribute to the bottom line. It is easy to imagine the managers talking on the golf course, "So did you ever figure out what those data people are doing for you?" Finally, the manager had encountered someone who *did* like the reports, and laid off the data manager responsible for the report stoppage. The question naturally follows, "What happened? How did the company go on operating without them?" The answer is usually that they hadn't been missed—just like the reports!

More and more, employees who perform data job functions are being asked to demonstrate what they are doing directly to help organizations achieve strategic (much less tactical-level) objectives. It is becoming increasingly clear that the best way for the value of data management to be understood by upper management is by making the case that by investing X in data management, the organization will achieve a payback the original investment plus a premium. XML provides the means for data managers to take advantage of key strategic investments in data-management practices to reduce price, while increasing quality and speed.

As data managers, your goals include understanding and improving the management of information and data as key enterprise assets. Understanding how to manipulate data structures represents the next plateau in the use of data management technologies. Data managers will be taking on expanded roles. By this, we mean leading the reengineering of processes and systems, capacity planning advising, XBP development, and business-driven data integration, just to name a few future possibilities. Once mastered, organizations will possess very different abilities from the ones taught currently in business courses at all levels. The data management challenges listed below are explained in the remainder of the chapter.

1. Thought versus action
2. Understanding important data structures as XML
3. Resolving differing priorities
4. Expanding data management's mission: producing innovative XML-based IT savings
5. Expanding data management's mission: increasing scope and volume of data

6. Greater payoff for preparation
7. Understanding the growth patterns in your operational environment
8. (And let's not forget) standard data names, value representations, source analysis, increased data access and provisioning, and increased value of the organizational data assets.

There are differing perspectives on the role of data management within organizations. For the purpose of our seven data management challenges described in this chapter, we are looking at the practice of data management as a strategic as well as a support effort. The earliest efforts at data management were focused solely on technical issues surrounding getting the right information to the business to support operations and decision making. In this chapter, we focus on how XML will expand the traditional role of data management, which necessarily requires thinking about the practice outside of its normal roles.

Thought Versus Action

Data management challenge #1: thought versus action.

This can be summed up very quickly: Is data management a practice that requires thinking of things and coordinating policy, or actually doing things and producing results?

One of the authors of this book held the title "Reverse Engineering Program Manager" for the Department of Defense (DoD) and recalls the long debate over the role of data administration within the Department. Funding within most large bureaucracies has traditionally been competitive, and the program operated under constant threat of being cut or subsumed by another organization. Within the Center for Information Management, two schools of thought emerged about how DoD data management should operate.

One school reasonably argued that the US Department of Defense needed guidance and that the mission of our group, charged with "DoD data management," was to focus our entire effort on the development of policy that would be used by the rest of the DoD. From a policy perspective, they believed that the group was charged with developing and communicating DoD-wide guidance.

The school that the author was a part of insisted that a "policy only" focus would leave the program vulnerable to being labeled as unnecessary overhead. In order to keep the program alive, it had to demonstrate results that clearly illustrated progress, or the group would lose its funding. This second school of thought constantly attempted to demonstrate results that produced positive investments for the department by implementing data reengineering projects and producing real results. Perhaps the most notable was the development of a DoD-wide enterprise model (Aiken, Muntz, et al., 1994). In short, the real mission of a data administration group was to produce project results *and* to mentor other parts of the organization, as well as develop policy.

Eventually, the program mission was changed to "policy only." After a period of time, its effectiveness was questioned and the second school of thought appeared to have been right. Those remaining with the organization were perceived as a "think tank" that didn't impact daily operations. Directing all organizational efforts to policy only doomed the program to less effectiveness because the group lacked any enforcement mechanism for the policies they developed.

The DoD example is in some ways better and certainly no worse than the general population of data managers—take for example the data-administration work going on in the area of medical data administration. To provide a comparison, consider that 95% of all organizations are only at Level One—the initial level—of five possible levels on the Capability Maturity Model. As in most large organizations, effectiveness of data management or applications development is linked to an enforcement mechanism. Without it, software development groups do not understand the importance of data-centric development and thus are not motivated to develop the ability to correctly implement the policy. The results were less than had been hoped for from the effort (Aiken & Yoon, 1999). The moral of this little story is that the mission of policy development is a noble one, but leaves a working group open to attack in the future, and is of little value without the corresponding ability to enforce the policies that are developed.

Unfortunately, these types of stories are not widely known in the data-management community, and quite a number of organizations are going through similar thought-versus-action debates internally. With the arrival of XML, data management now has a set of technologies available that enable it to implement initiatives. These initiatives in turn can produce savings that exceed their cost. In short, now it is so much easier to implement projects and technologies resulting in savings; therefore there is no excuse not to do projects as well as implement policy. Should data management be involved in thought or action? The answer is both!

Incidentally, data management policy implementation is far easier now than it was in the past. As of fall 2003, most policy can be begged, bought, or borrowed in the form of templates. Relatively little effort is required to formulate data management policies for your organization. DAMA—the premiere organization for data professionals worldwide—is a great place to start the process of locating suitable resources.*

So at this point, the notion of a data management group providing advice and guidance to the remainder of the organization is pretty much history. Data management groups must produce results that demonstrate to the remainder of the organization that they more than pay for themselves. They must demonstrate this by producing their own type of products. This newer approach moves data managers from thought into action, and lessens the chance of unfortunate management discussions on golf courses, negatively impacting contributing data workers.

A very simple illustration of this concept would be a definable data-quality organization. Once an organization has committed to labeling one or more individuals as "focused on data quality" issues, or "improving data quality," those individuals must be able to demonstrate positive annual payback. Hypothetically speaking, consider a sizable data quality effort. The group consists of 10 persons paid $10,000 annually, including one-third overhead for taxes, and so on. The data quality group must demonstrate at least $100,000 of positive benefits realized in the first calendar year.

Before protesting, consider the alternate message sent by a data management group that costs an organization $100,000. And consider trying to pitch that amount of investment to management when it is not able to produce positive results. Perhaps management might hear that it will require more than $200,000 (for example, $100,000 for two years) before achieving positive results. This is typically unacceptable in this post-dot.com bust economy. Organizations have become leaner in part by rejecting these types of unacceptable proposals. Future data management operations will be bottom-up justified with real and visible results. The widespread knowledge of how XML can be used to finish projects rapidly makes it simple for data-administration groups to avoid confusion developing about their role. Future data management groups will be both thinkers and doers, and will show a positive return on investment in many situations.

---

*See the DAMA web site at: http://dama.org/.

This first item of thinking versus doing deals with the strategic placement of the data management operation within the larger organization. It also addresses how the data management operation is perceived, but does not go into how this magic will actually be accomplished. The first step of pulling off this transformation is covered next.

Understanding Important Data Structures as XML

Data management challenge #2: Understanding important data structures as XML.

Once a decision has been made to *do* something instead of just communicating how to do something, determining *what* to do becomes relatively easy. The first step is the process of understanding your important data structures in XML. Specifically, this means understanding the documented and articulated digital blueprint illustrating the commonalities and interconnections among the component metadata. "Understanding" is a shorthand reference for use of data-centric techniques to represent, manage, and develop system component models within a formally defined context. XML is not directly understood by applications in a human sense, but rather provides the ability to create rich taxonomies from which inference can be made. That inference represents real understanding.

The component models we are referring to are represented using the standardized CM2 notation (Common Metadata Model). The models are also sufficiently detailed to permit both business analysts and technical personnel to read the same model separately, and come away with a common understanding. These models must be developed in a cost-effective manner. Figure 11.2 shows the CM2 and how understood system components flow through to provide benefit to various business areas.

The first thing to "get" about understanding structures as XML is that your important data structures often include other nested data structures that are not within your stewardship. Sometimes these are external to your organization or even national boundaries. Some structures will come from systems belonging to partners, suppliers, service providers, and so on. This is typically the case for many companies that purchase data lists from other suppliers and partners, such as credit card companies that purchase lists from credit reporting bureaus. These data sources must be examined and ranked along with internal systems to determine which are important.

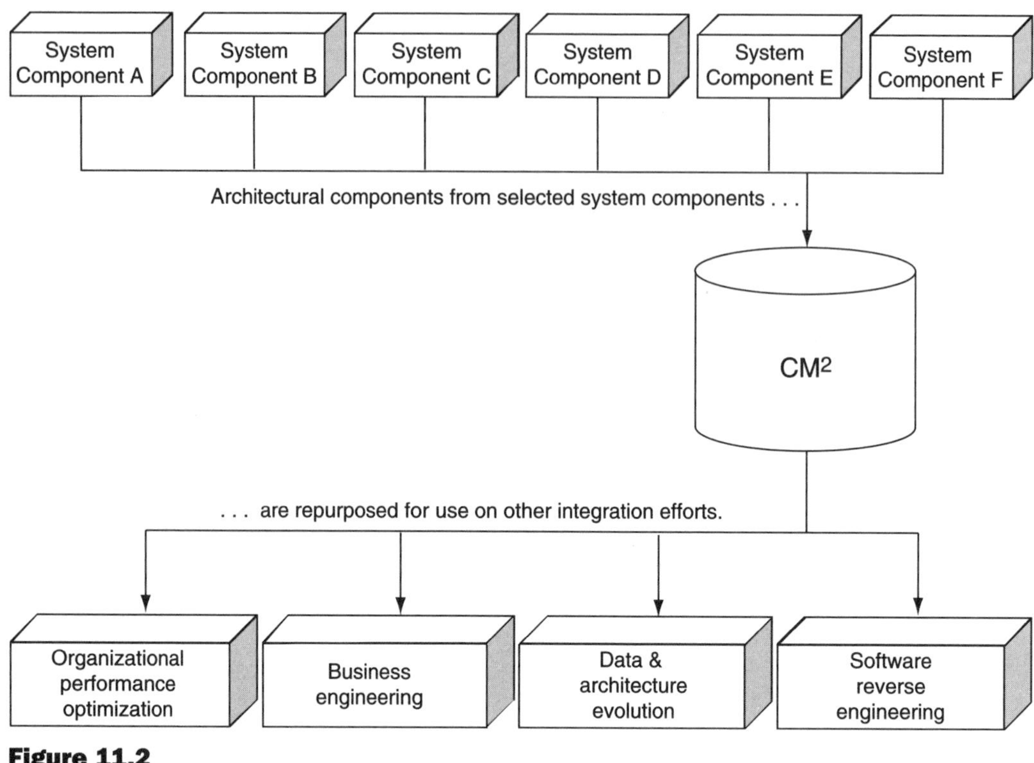

Figure 11.2

"Understood" data structures contributing to numerous business areas such as business engineering and performance optimization.

Keep in mind as well that the most typical use of XML is to wrap data items instead of data structures. Figure 11.3 illustrates how this lack of structure management results in organizations being able to apply just a fraction of the true power of XML. The result correlates with the low industry-wide maturity rankings.

XML lets data managers quickly implement systems that "understand" their important data structures. By maintaining even the most elementary of repository technologies, data managers can show organizations direct benefits in areas ranging from capacity management to legacy application maintenance to business engineering. While many other contributions are possible, we will take a look at specific examples of each of these three to illustrate the range of contributions, starting with capacity management.

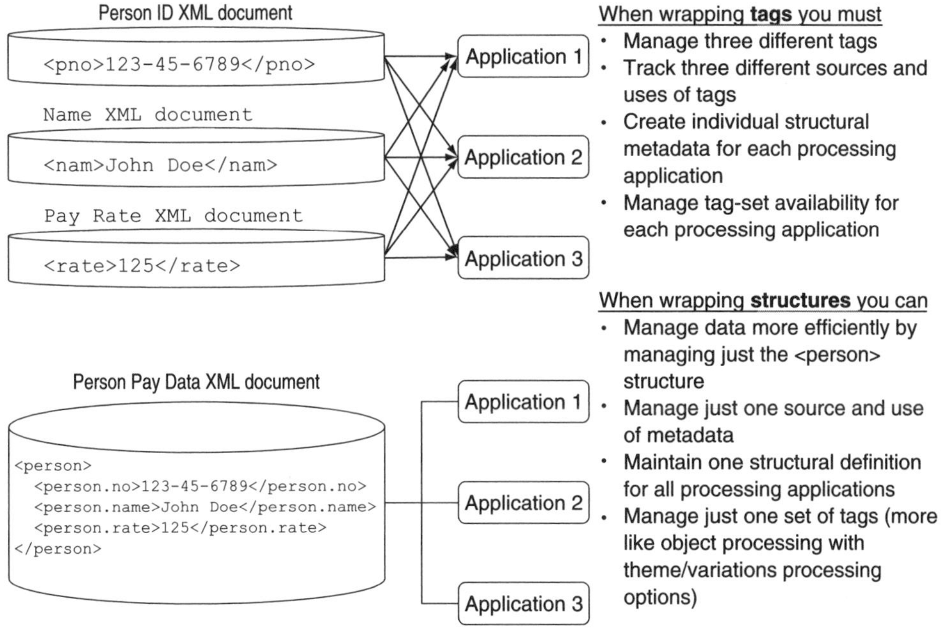

Figure 11.3

Wrapping data items requires more complexity to implement wrapping data structures.

Example: Capacity Management with XML

The particular data warehouse involved in this example already supported large volumes of data, and had quite a bit more waiting "in the wings" to be included. XML-based metadata management played a significant role in postponing capacity-related hardware upgrades. These were upgrades that everyone thought were necessary to increase the amount of data that could be held in the warehouse. Analysis of the data warehouse metadata revealed that some tables were not relationally normalized, and as a result, significant amounts of space were being wasted.

The XML-based metadata permitted data managers to model the effects of various normalization approaches and other data structure rearrangement schemes. The analysis identified more than 4.7 billion empty bytes in just three data warehouse tables, making a strong case for normalization and reducing the need to upgrade company infrastructure capacity (see Figure 11.4). Without understanding of the data structure,

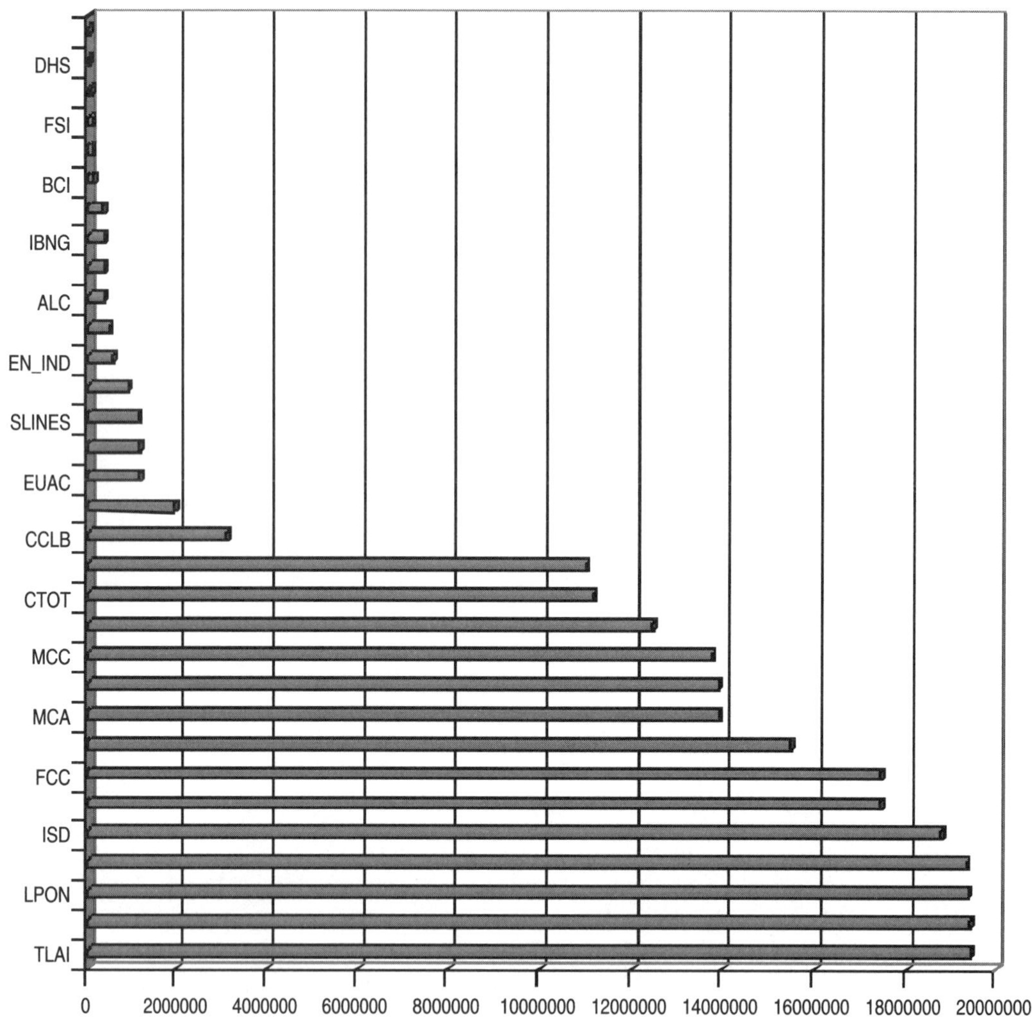

Figure 11.4

Population of data warehouse tables. (Note: Since one of the key foundations of data quality is having good data names, please note that the attribute names have been purposely butchered.)

these "empty bytes" that came from duplication of information that was not there in the first place could not have been identified. In this particular situation, of course a data manager could have let the situation continue without addressing it, since storage space is very inexpensive. However, minor inefficiencies like this, which come as a result of poor structure, tend to turn into major inefficiencies over the long haul. Those problems are never cheap, even if the stopgap solution of throwing more hardware at the problem might be.

The analysis yielded insight that led to further normalization of the data, permitting a huge hardware purchase to be postponed thanks to the use of software XML portals, not to mention more sound understanding of the data. This understanding using XML lets data managers implement automated means of measuring the cost of integration quickly so that they can apply XML more effectively.

The next example outlines a situation that every data manager deals with—the maintenance of legacy systems. It is sometimes said that any system that has been running for more than 5 minutes is a legacy system, and it is therefore important to see what XML can do in an area of common frustration.

Example: Legacy Application Maintenance Reduction

XML-based technologies, including WSDL, SOAP, and XML-based metadata, were used to transform an organization's legacy environment to the tune of more than $200 million in annual savings. Targeted legacy systems were systematically reduced to 20% of their original code size. The old systems that implemented the core business value consisted of a series of algorithms for implementing various production recipes. These functions were transformed into callable routines that are accessed through a portal. This granular approach allowed the knowledge worker to obtain required data, permitting various combinations of services to be developed, and supporting the individual needs of the knowledge worker as shown in Figure 11.5.

This example looks at XML from the perspective of technical systems, and reducing ongoing overhead associated with them, but what about how XML impacts business engineering efforts? The next example addresses how XML can aid this process by improving the nature and structure of the data provided to business processes.

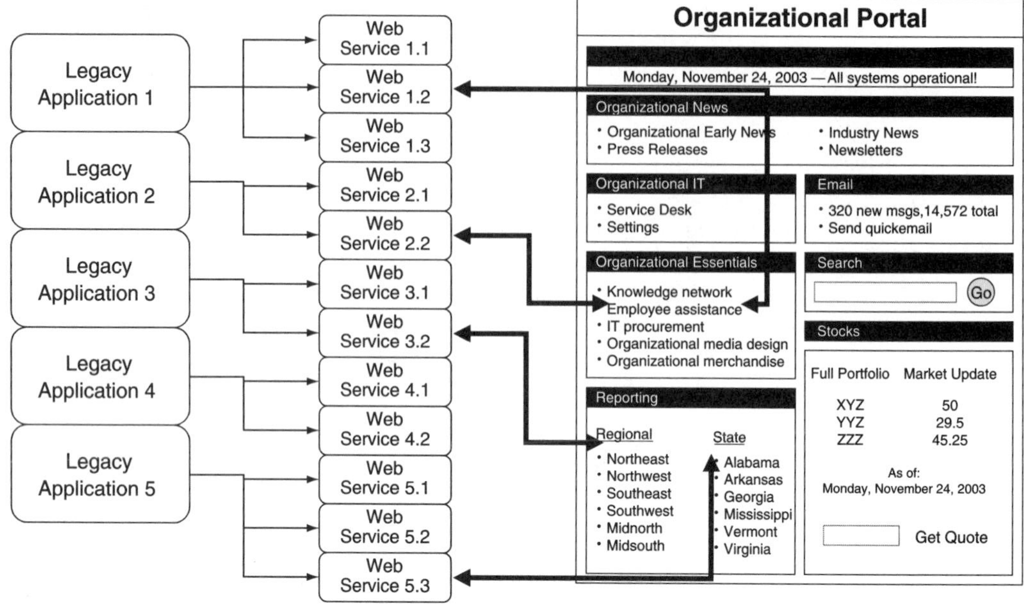

Figure 11.5

Legacy systems transformed into web services accessed through a portal.

Example: Business Engineering

In this example, understanding the relevant data structures facilitated the implementation of a business engineering project, replacing legacy pay and personnel systems. Figure 11.5 ahows how process, system, and data structure metadata were extracted before encoding them in XML and using them to support the project from a number of different perspectives.

One unexpected benefit resulted from the use of process metadata to estimate change propagation effects. Use of metadata in business-engineering projects helps accumulate a number of facts, such as exactly how much impact a proposed change would have, that are later used during the analysis.

Another example focuses solely on the replacement of legacy systems whose job was simple data transformation. This movement of data from one format to another format is a common process performed within organizations that has its own set of "gotchas" and drawbacks. As shown in Figure 9.5, once the transformation was understood, the legacy code

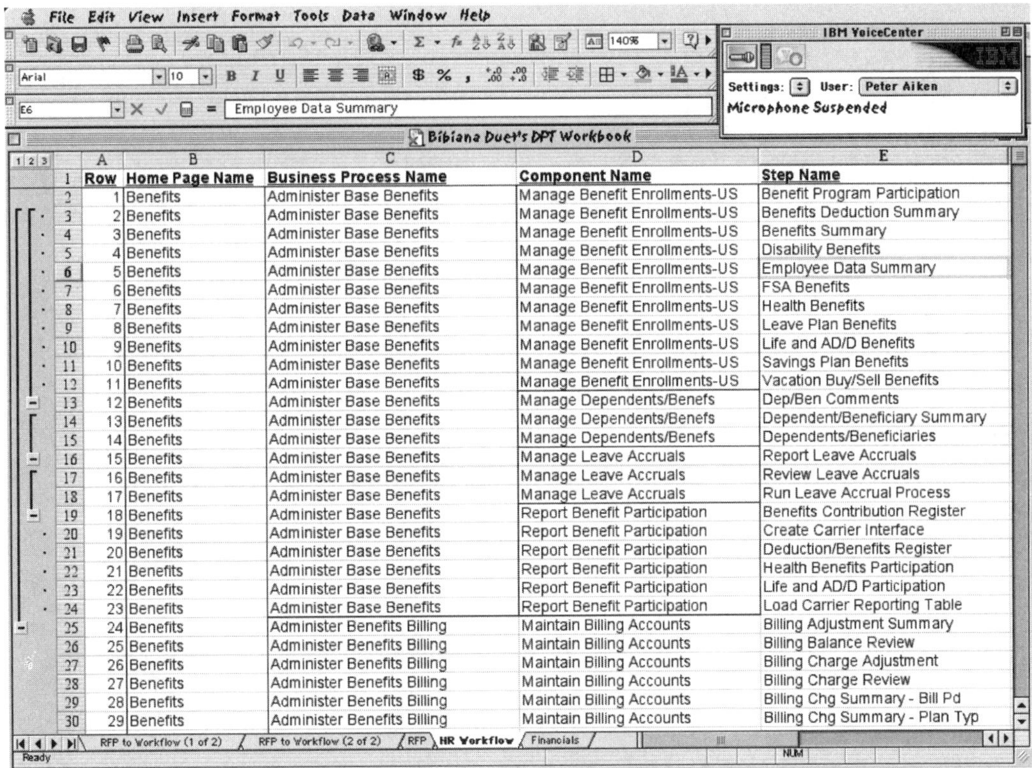

Row	Home Page Name	Business Process Name	Component Name	Step Name
1	Benefits	Administer Base Benefits	Manage Benefit Enrollments-US	Benefit Program Participation
2	Benefits	Administer Base Benefits	Manage Benefit Enrollments-US	Benefits Deduction Summary
3	Benefits	Administer Base Benefits	Manage Benefit Enrollments-US	Benefits Summary
4	Benefits	Administer Base Benefits	Manage Benefit Enrollments-US	Disability Benefits
5	Benefits	Administer Base Benefits	Manage Benefit Enrollments-US	Employee Data Summary
6	Benefits	Administer Base Benefits	Manage Benefit Enrollments-US	FSA Benefits
7	Benefits	Administer Base Benefits	Manage Benefit Enrollments-US	Health Benefits
8	Benefits	Administer Base Benefits	Manage Benefit Enrollments-US	Leave Plan Benefits
9	Benefits	Administer Base Benefits	Manage Benefit Enrollments-US	Life and AD/D Benefits
10	Benefits	Administer Base Benefits	Manage Benefit Enrollments-US	Savings Plan Benefits
11	Benefits	Administer Base Benefits	Manage Benefit Enrollments-US	Vacation Buy/Sell Benefits
12	Benefits	Administer Base Benefits	Manage Dependents/Benefs	Dep/Ben Comments
13	Benefits	Administer Base Benefits	Manage Dependents/Benefs	Dependent/Beneficiary Summary
14	Benefits	Administer Base Benefits	Manage Dependents/Benefs	Dependents/Beneficiaries
15	Benefits	Administer Base Benefits	Manage Leave Accruals	Report Leave Accruals
16	Benefits	Administer Base Benefits	Manage Leave Accruals	Review Leave Accruals
17	Benefits	Administer Base Benefits	Manage Leave Accruals	Run Leave Accrual Process
18	Benefits	Administer Base Benefits	Report Benefit Participation	Benefits Contribution Register
19	Benefits	Administer Base Benefits	Report Benefit Participation	Create Carrier Interface
20	Benefits	Administer Base Benefits	Report Benefit Participation	Deduction/Benefits Register
21	Benefits	Administer Base Benefits	Report Benefit Participation	Health Benefits Participation
22	Benefits	Administer Base Benefits	Report Benefit Participation	Life and AD/D Participation
23	Benefits	Administer Base Benefits	Report Benefit Participation	Load Carrier Reporting Table
24	Benefits	Administer Benefits Billing	Maintain Billing Accounts	Billing Adjustment Summary
25	Benefits	Administer Benefits Billing	Maintain Billing Accounts	Billing Balance Review
26	Benefits	Administer Benefits Billing	Maintain Billing Accounts	Billing Charge Adjustment
27	Benefits	Administer Benefits Billing	Maintain Billing Accounts	Billing Charge Review
28	Benefits	Administer Benefits Billing	Maintain Billing Accounts	Billing Chg Summary - Bill Pd
29	Benefits	Administer Benefits Billing	Maintain Billing Accounts	Billing Chg Summary - Plan Typ

Figure 11.6

PeopleSoft process metadata structure. Each business "process" was comprised of one or more "components," which were in turn comprised of one or more "steps."

was replaced with three sets of transformations that were maintained using XML in databases. It is important to note that each replacement must be examined for efficacy. Not all systems should be replaced with XML-based transformations simply for their own sake; like the other recommendations in this book, it should be followed only where it makes economic sense.

Understanding your important data structures, wrapping them in XML, and maintaining them in a simple repository or file system go a long way toward understanding the sources and uses of the data, organization-wide. Once everyone understands the easy accessibility of XML-based data, future development efforts will more frequently take advantage of XML capabilities. This is because it will end up being cheaper to implement

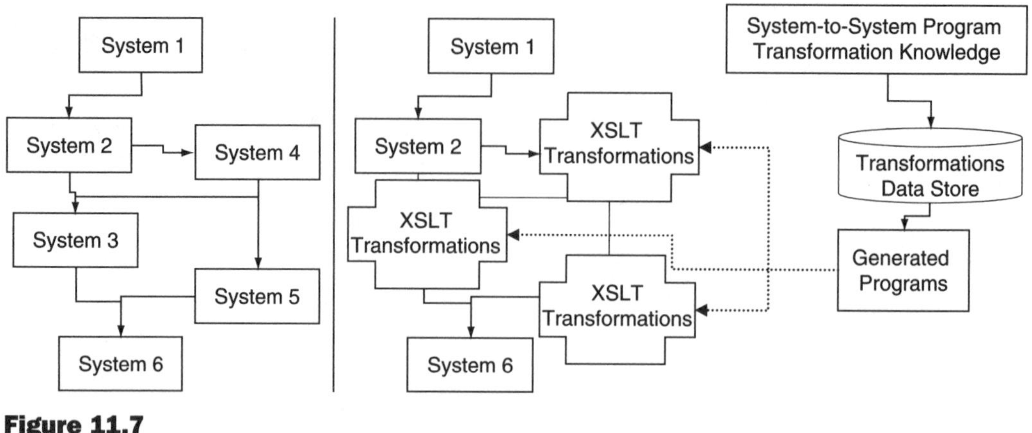

Figure 11.7

Left, system flow chart before reengineering; right, replacing three existing systems with XSLT "programs" generated from database of XML transformations.

interfaces and transformations using XML than without it. This will permit implementation of automated metadata management that greatly decreases maintenance costs. Through automated generation of metadata, such as data-structure sources and uses (CRUD matrices), business processes can obtain the maximum advantage from data.

Resolving Differing Priorities

Data-management challenge #3: Resolving differing priorities. Every organization has more priorities than they have time, people, and money. How do we determine which issues get attention?

Meta-analysis of CIO and data management practitioner surveys shows that each role possesses different views as to what the development priorities should be. In Figure 11.8, we can see just how divergent their respective priorities and expectations are.

According to surveys, CIOs are looking to XML to apply and to drive the program as a broadly focused effort. Items such as e-commerce, database-management systems, enterprise resource planning (ERP), and digital marketplaces require a longer-term payout than organizations are currently willing to stomach. Practitioners, on the other hand, are focused on provid-

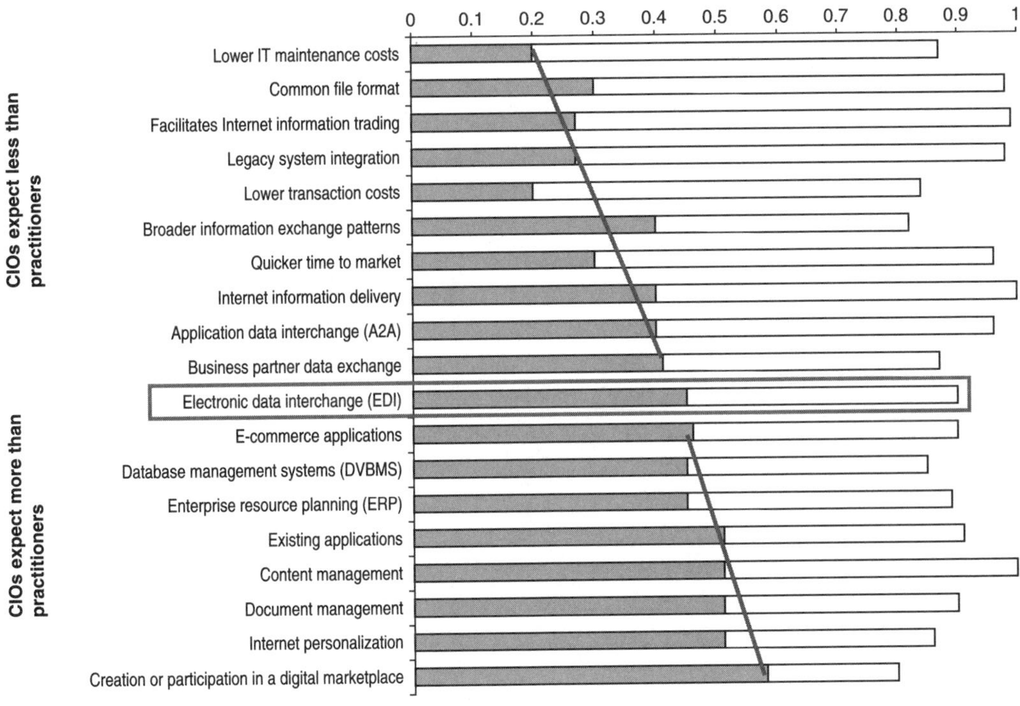

Figure 11.8

CIO versus practitioner XML-based expectations.

ing a more granular level of XML support. This more bottom-up approach permits implementation of results that are oriented toward direct benefits such as lower IT maintenance costs, reduced legacy system integration costs, and application data interchange. These goals appear as projects in very different ways. The key to achieving perceptible results is to obtain common understanding of the agreed-upon approach to XML implementation.

It is important to note that the newly acquired XML-based data-management capabilities and their related savings do not show up in the CIO management priorities as shown in Figure 11.9. This represents a vast untapped potential to demonstrate relevance early in the effort. Rapid results are likely obtainable in 95% of all organizations, and the benefits are greater if the data management maturity score is higher than the initial Level One. In short then, resolving differing developmental priorities will lead to clearer understanding of project objectives and approach.

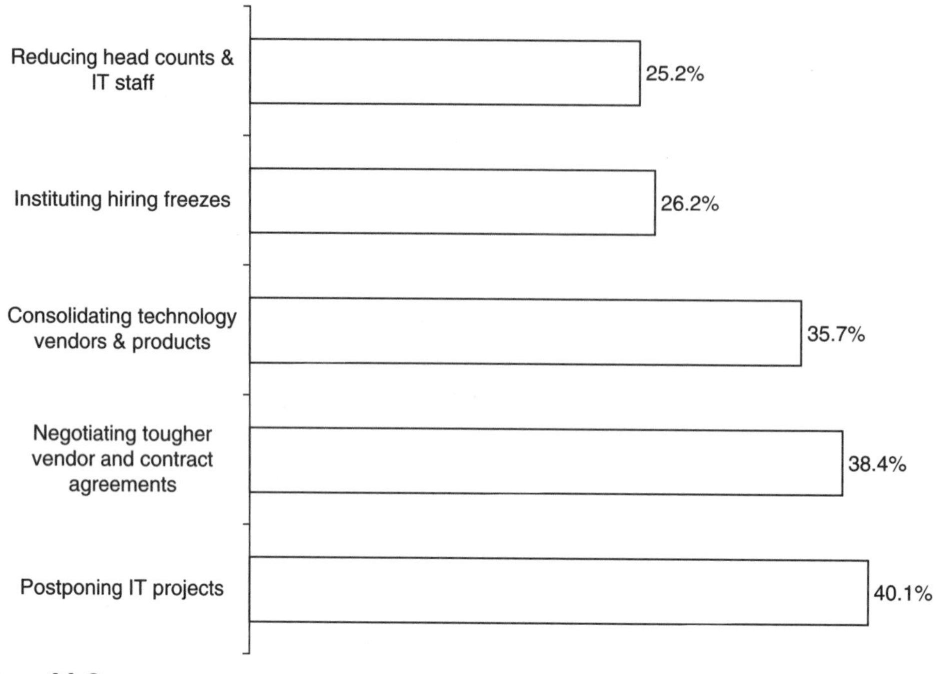

Figure 11.9

How do CIOs demonstrate reduction in IT expenses? (Taken from L. C. Ware & B. Worthen, CIO.com 8/1/01.)

Producing Innovative XML-Based IT Savings

Data management challenge #4: producing innovative XML-based IT savings.

The key to this area is to identify areas of "pain" experienced by the organization and address the data-management aspect of it using XML. Other chapters have contained descriptions of XML being used to increase the relative capacity of servers and other data storage technologies using technologies such as XLink. Many other types of IT savings can be gained by the application of XML-based technologies. The following are some examples from the PeopleSoft model.

- XML-based system metadata was used to determine the requirements that a software package could meet, and to document discrepancies between system capabilities and actual needs. XML-based data management capabilities were used to document discrepancies between capabilities and requirements. Panels were incorporated into the XML-based metadata to assist user visualization and recognition of the system functions.

- XML-based metadata types were used to assess the magnitude and range of proposed changes. For example, it is important to have facts such as the number of panels requiring modification if a given field length is changed. This information was used to analyze the costs of changing the system versus changing the organizational processes. It is only possible to do this type of impact analysis if the actual connections between components are known. Discovering that information and having it on hand in XML form opens up many new possibilities; this particular example is just one.
- Business practice analysis was conducted to identify gaps between the business requirements and the PeopleSoft software. XML-based metadata was used to map the appropriate process components to specific existing user activities and workgroup practices. The mapping helped users to focus their attention on relevant subsets of the metadata. For example, the payroll clerks accessed the metadata to determine which panels 'belonged' to them.
- Business practice realignment addressed gaps between system functionality and existing work practices. Once users understood the system's functionality and could navigate through their respective process component steps, they compared the system's inputs and outputs with their own information needs. If gaps existed, the XML-based metadata was used to assess the relative magnitude of proposed changes to add functionality. This information was then used to forecast system customization costs.
- User training specialists also used the metadata to obtain mappings between business practices and system functions to determine which combinations of mapped "panels," "menuitems," and "menubars" were relevant to user groups. A repository was used to display panels in the sequence expected by the system users. By reviewing panels as part of the system processes, users

> were able to swiftly become familiar with their areas. Additional capabilities for screen session recording and playback were integrated into the toolkit to permit development of system/user interaction "sequences."

The XML-based metadata helped the team to organize the analysis of the PeopleSoft physical database design systematically. Project documentation needs were simplified when a CASE tool was integrated to extract the database design information directly into XML from the physical database. The XML was also used to support the decomposition of the physical database into logical user views. Additional metadata was collected to document how user requirements were implemented by the system.

Statistical analysis was also useful for guiding metadata-based data integration from the legacy systems. For example, XML was used to map the legacy system data into target data structures. Statistical metadata summaries were also used to describe the system to users. For example, Figure 11.10 illustrates use of workflow metadata showing the number of processes in each home page and the Administer Workforce process com-

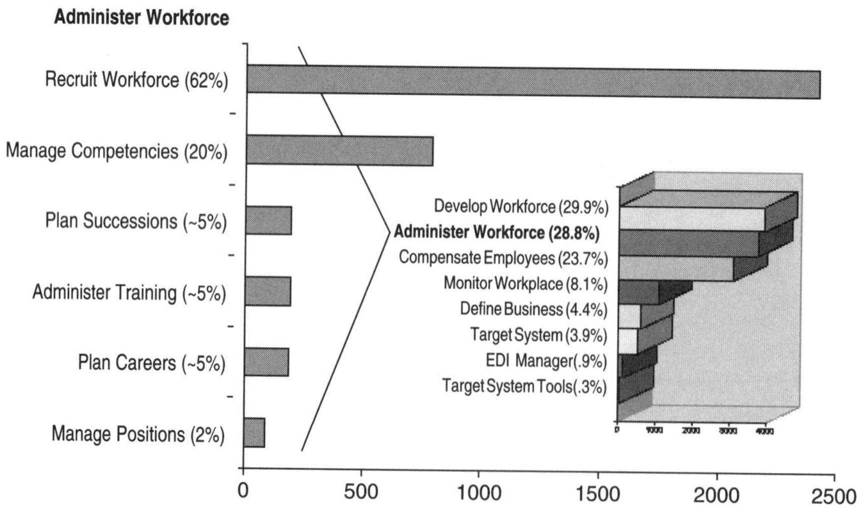

Figure 11.10

An example of a statistically derived introduction to the PeopleSoft Administer Workforce business process showing the relative complexity of the six components and how they fit into the home page structure.

ponents. It indicates the number of processes associated with each home page and that the two with the highest number are Develop Workforce, and Administer Workforce. The same chart was used to show users of the Administer Workforce why the recruiters were receiving separate training based on the relative complexity of the components comprising the Administer Workforce process.

These types of IT savings that can be produced through the use of XML address part of the financial case for XML, and how data management groups can show a positive return on investment. In the next example, we will take a look at how the scope and volume of data management can be increased, effectively expanding data management's reach and impact.

Increasing Scope and Volume of Data Management

Data management challenge #5: Increasing data management scope and volume.

Before illustrating how the scope and volume of data that data managers are expected to manage can be expanded, it will be useful to explain the distinction between structured and unstructured data.

Recall that structured data in many cases should really be referred to as tabular data, because it almost always occurs in rows and columns (see the spreadsheet shown in Figure 11.6). This is what data management has traditionally focused on in the past, because it seems that all of the software and theory is geared toward it. More recently, data managers are increasingly called on to manage increasing amounts of unstructured and semi-structured data. The volume of data requiring management by data managers is estimated to multiply perhaps as much as five times, as organizational support for management of unstructured data increases. Figure 7.17 illustrated the portion of Microsoft's implementation of unstructured document metadata. Accessing the "properties" selection under the "file" menu of any Office 2000+ document can preview this metadata—some default fields are provided, but others can be designed at the user's whim. This slightly increased degree of structuring permits queries to be developed for slide titles or other document structures. If these documents were to be centrally housed throughout an organization, imagine the benefit of being able to issue queries along the lines of "Show me all presentations created by Bob between these dates that contain the term 'System X Integration Project.'"

Unstructured and semi structured data will require understanding and development of new data management capabilities. As different as relational data is from hierarchical data, unstructured data differs even more from conventional formats, precisely because it is unstructured. New types of data management will help organizations use their existing data-management capabilities on new types of data, ranging from PowerPoint presentations to MPEG-based movies. While no complete toolset exists to simplify the problem, many vendors are providing the foundations of solutions—more development breakthroughs in this area are likely. Currently, claims of a total software solution to automatically translate unstructured formats into XML or some structured format should be viewed skeptically, but there are certainly packages that exist already that may aid the process, even if they cannot perform the process completely.

Greater Payoff for Preparation

Data management challenge #6: Greater payoff for preparation.

Preparation of organizational data, including data quality, permits rapid implementation of new EAI architectures and services. Because of XML's support for semantic understanding, the actual volume of data being maintained drops somewhat as well, as redundant data are identified and eliminated. This is one of the reasons why the semantic understanding that XML brings to the table is important, because misused data resources are frequently mis*understood* data resources. Increasing the reuse and relative velocity of data results in higher returns. This reduction of data being maintained due to the elimination of redundancies still cannot keep pace with the increasing scope of data management due to new data sources falling under the control of data management. While XML may help reduce the volume of existing managed data in some cases, the overall trend is clear: new types of data that require management for the first time will expand the global volume of data to be managed.

Understanding the Growth Patterns in Your Operational Environment

Data management challenge #7: identifying growth patterns.

It seems to us that a formal evaluation of how to incorporate XML most profitably into your mix will certainly uncover various important data growth patterns. These can be used to help determine the most effective upstream sources of data that can then be more effectively corrected. Understanding growth patterns can help to predict the effectiveness of alternative data correction strategies. After all, solutions that are built today should address today's problems, but should also at the very least attempt to look forward to what might be coming around the bend.

Chapter Summary

In addition to existing data management roles and responsibilities, the maturing of XML technologies means that you will have to gear up to face new data management challenges. These will occur as organizations spend proportionally less on IT, as they abandon the "bleeding edge" of technologies and choose to follow what has already worked for others, and as they finally settle on risk-averse postures with respect to technology support. Our savings will come about in the form of:

- XML-based tools that we build at first, but will later be able to purchase
- Our revised data engineering techniques
- Technologies already capable of noticeably contributing to our organizations' bottom line

Let's get started.

References

Aiken, P. H., Yoon, Y., et al. (1999). Requirements-driven data engineering. *Information & Management, 35*(3), 155–168.

Aiken, P. H., Muntz, A., et al. (1994). DoD legacy systems: Reverse engineering data requirements. *Communications of the ACM, 37*(5), 26–41.

Carr, N. G. (2003). IT doesn't matter. *Harvard Business Review,* pp. 1–11.

Hsu, F. (2003). Software Architecture Axiom 1: No Moving Parts. Washington, DC.

Glossary of Acronyms

The technology industry is full of acronyms, and the field of XML with its many acronym-named standards seems to have even more than average. Because of this phenomenon within XML and our own tendency to use acronyms from time to time rather than their often lengthy expansions, we provide a brief glossary of acronyms and their expanded names.

ADML Architecture Description Markup Language

API Application Programming Interface

CASE (As in CASE tools) Computer Aided Software Engineering

CM2 Common Metadata Model

CMM Capabilities Maturity Model

CSS Cascading Style Sheets

DBMS Database Management System

DM Data Management

DOM Document Object Model

DTD Document Type Definition

EAI	Enterprise Application Integration
EDI	Electronic Data Interchange
EJB	Enterprise Java Beans
ERD	Entity-Relationship Diagram
ERP	Enterprise Resource Planning (SAP, PeopleSoft, JDEdwards, etc.)
HTTP	Hypertext Transfer Protocol
IP	Internet Protocol
JAD	Joint Application Development (JAD sessions)
PIP	Partner Interface Process (RosettaNET term)
PKI	Public Key Infrastructure
RDF	Resource Description Framework
RNIF	RosettaNET Implementation Framework
RXMD	Repository-Based XML Metadata Documents
SAML	Security Assertions Markup Language
SAX	Simple API for XML
SGML	Standard Generalized Markup Language
SME	Subject Matter Expert
SOAP	Simple Object Access Protocol
SSL	Secure Socket Layer
TCP	Transport Control Protocol
TLS	Transport Layer Security
UDDI	Universal Description, Discovery, and Integration

WSDL Web Service Description Language

XBME XML-Based Metadata Engineering

XBP XML-Based Portal

XKMS XML Key Management Services/System

XML Extensible Markup Language

XSL Extensible Stylesheet Language

XSLT Extensible Stylesheet Language Transformations

Index

N